# PROCEEDS OF CRIME ACT 2002
## A PRACTICAL GUIDE

GW00569106

**Archer Heaney & Magee**
2nd Floor, Arthur Chambers,
10 Arthur Street,
BELFAST, BT1 4GD.
Tel: 028 90 330000
Fax: 028 90 331000

# PROCEEDS OF CRIME ACT 2002
## A PRACTICAL GUIDE

*Benjamin Gumpert*
MA (Cantab), Barrister at law,
Member of the Honourable Society
of the Inner Temple

*Jonathan Kirk*
LLB(Hons) (Lond), Barrister at law,
Member of the Honourable Society
of Lincoln's Inn

*Andrzej Bojarski*
LLB(Hons) (Lond), Barrister at law,
Member of the Honourable Society
of Gray's Inn

**JORDANS**

2003

Published by
Jordan Publishing Limited
21 St Thomas Street
Bristol BS1 6JS

**British Library Cataloguing-in-Publication Data**

A catalogue record for this book is available from the British Library.

ISBN  0  85308  806  3

Typeset by Mendip Communications Ltd, Frome
Printed in Great Britain by Bell & Bain Ltd, Glasgow

# CONTENTS

# TABLE OF CASES

References are to paragraph numbers.

# TABLE OF STATUTES

References are to paragraph numbers. References in *italic* are to
Appendix page numbers.

# TABLE OF STATUTORY INSTRUMENTS AND CODES OF PRACTICE

References are to paragraph numbers. References in *italic* are to
Appendix page numbers.

# TABLE OF EUROPEAN MATERIAL

References are to paragraph numbers.

# TABLE OF ABBREVIATIONS

| | |
|---|---|
| ARA | Assets Recovery Agency |
| CPR 1998 | Civil Procedure Rules 1998 |
| CPS | Crown Prosecution Service |
| PCA 2002 | Proceeds of Crime Act 2002 |
| PCC(S)A 2000 | Powers of Criminal Courts (Sentencing) Act 2000 |
| SOI | Statement of information |

# Chapter 1

# INTRODUCTION

## OVERVIEW

**1.1** The Proceeds of Crime Act 2002 (PCA 2002) provides the courts with a new set of powers to inquire into and restrain a person's assets and income where it is suspected that they are the proceeds of crime. A central distinction is drawn between confiscation or money laundering investigations, which now fall within the jurisdiction of the Crown Court, and the new civil recovery investigations, where jurisdiction is reserved to the High Court. A judge entitled to exercise the jurisdiction of the Crown Court will now be able to make intrusive and wide-ranging orders for the purpose of confiscation or money laundering investigations before convictions are obtained. However, orders in respect of the new civil recovery investigations are confined to High Court judges.[1] In addition to these new powers, the PCA 2002 brings together the powers of confiscation which have, until now, been exercised separately in respect of drug trafficking offences and all other offences. Confiscation of the proceeds of criminal activity, of whatever sort it may be, is now dealt with under the unified provisions of the PCA 2002. The confiscation powers and procedures themselves have been the subject of substantial overhaul, principally with the aim of making confiscation orders easier to obtain.

## ASSETS RECOVERY AGENCY

**1.2** The PCA 2002 creates an Assets Recovery Agency (ARA) which has three central functions:

(a) confiscation investigations;
(b) civil recovery investigations;
(c) the training, accreditation and monitoring of 'private' financial investigators.

**1.3** The PCA 2002 also stipulates that the ARA shall have a Director who must 'exercise his functions in the way which he considers is best calculated to contribute to the reduction of crime'. This is presumably to be achieved by facilitating and pursuing confiscation orders, although the Director must have regard to any guidance provided by the Secretary of State. The Director may delegate his responsibilities to any member of the ARA staff or agreed service provider.[2] Other organisations with functions relating to the investigation or prosecution of offences, for example the police, customs and the Crown Prosecution Service (CPS), have a statutory duty to co-operate with the Director in the exercise of his functions.[3]

---

1     Sections 343, 344. Unless otherwise stated, section numbers refer to sections of the PCA 2002.
2     Section 1(6).
3     Section 4.

## FINANCIAL INVESTIGATORS

**1.4** The Director has responsibility for the establishment of a system of accreditation for financial investigators. The system must include provision for monitoring of performance and withdrawing accreditation for a failure to comply with accreditation conditions. This opens the way for private financial investigators to become involved in the pursuit of confiscation orders. The Director must also make provision for training those involved in financial investigation and in the operation of the PCA 2002.

## APPROPRIATE OFFICERS

**1.5** Application for the orders provided by the new legislation must be made by 'appropriate officers' and, in some cases, 'senior appropriate officers'. These roles are defined by s 378. In so far as the police are concerned, a police constable is an 'appropriate officer' and a superintendent (or more senior officer) is a 'senior appropriate officer'.

## CODE OF PRACTICE

**1.6** The Secretary of State must prepare a code of practice for the ARA, police, customs and accredited financial investigators. The code will initially be published in draft form as a consultation exercise and, after amendment, will go before Parliament. There is a statutory duty to comply with the code of practice.[1] The code is admissible in proceedings, 'and a court may take account of any failure to comply with its provisions in determining any question in the proceedings'.[2] A failure to comply with the code does not, of itself, give rise to criminal or civil liability.[3] The draft code is set out in Appendix 3 to this book.

**1.7** The draft code makes it clear that it is only the draft code that is relevant to the exercise of the Part 8 confiscation powers, rather than the general Police and Criminal Evidence Act 1984 codes of practice.[4] The draft code suggests that 'minor deviations from [it] do not constitute a breach . . . provided there has been no significant prejudice to the investigation of persons connected with the investigation'.[5] The draft code recognises the intrusive nature of some of the confiscation powers. Any application must be clearly justified. In applying to exercise the powers, the appropriate officer has a duty to consider whether a less intrusive method could be used.[6] The appropriate officer must also consider the Human Rights Act 1998 and, in particular, whether a course of action is proportionate and sufficiently respects the right to privacy.[7]

---

1    Section 377(5).
2    Section 377(7).
3    Section 377(6).
4    Draft code of practice, para 8.
5    Ibid, para 2.
6    Ibid, para 10.
7    Ibid, paras 11 and 12.

**1.8**   There is a further duty upon an appropriate officer to take reasonable steps to check that information relied upon is accurate, recent and has not been provided maliciously.[1] When an application is based upon information from an anonymous source, there must be corroboration. The draft code recognises the need for ex parte applications, but creates a duty for the appropriate officer to consider the benefit of not holding proceedings inter partes.[2]

## EXCLUDED MATERIAL

**1.9**   The concept of 'excluded material' is imported into the PCA 2002[3] from the Police and Criminal Evidence Act 1984. Section 11 of that Act lists the following as 'excluded material':

(a)   confidential personal records created or acquired in the course of a profession, etc;
(b)   human tissue or tissue fluid held in confidence and taken for diagnostic or medical purposes;
(c)   journalistic material held in confidence.

## HUMAN RIGHTS

**1.10**   A determined challenge to the legitimacy of confiscation proceedings under the old regime was launched once the Human Rights Act 1988 came into force. The challenge rested on the assertion that confiscation proceedings often required the judge to decide whether or not the defendant was guilty of offences other than those on the indictment. For instance, where a defendant was caught with 20 grams of heroin in his pocket but was found to have £100,000 in cash under his mattress, he was likely to have been charged with possession with intent to supply the 20 grams. If convicted the judge had then to decide whether or not the £100,000 represented the proceeds of past dealing, as to which there had been no trial. He did so on the basis that the prosecution only had to prove their case on the balance of probabilities and the court was required to make certain assumptions about the money unless the defendant could prove they were invalid. It was asserted that the low standard of proof, and in particular the 'reverse onus' incorporated in the statutory assumptions, constituted a breach of Art 6(2) of the European Convention on Human Rights, since confiscation proceedings effectively involved the judge making a decision about a 'criminal charge'. Article 6(2) requires 'criminal charges' to be determined in accordance with the presumption of innocence.

**1.11**   The argument was first tackled by the higher courts in December 2000. In *R v Benjafield and Others* [2001] 3 WLR 75 the Court of Appeal found that, while Art 6(2) did apply to the legislation then in force (the Criminal Justice Act 1988 and the Drug

---

1     Draft code of practice, para 14.
2     Ibid, para 19. See also para **2.27**.
3     Section 379.

Trafficking Act 1994) the statutory provisions were not necessarily incompatible with it. The Court pointed out that Convention case-law established that the placing of a burden on the defendant, as here by virtue of the statutory assumptions, was legitimate in certain circumstances. The court regarded the following matters as of significance.

- Questions of confiscation only arose once the defendant stood convicted of an offence on the criminal standard.
- It would be relatively easy for the defendant to prove that an asset had no connection with criminal activity and relatively difficult for the prosecution to prove that it did.
- There was a discretion in the prosecution as to whether to begin proceedings.
- There was a responsibility on the court not to make the statutory assumptions where there was a serious risk of injustice.

The Court weighed up the substantial public interest in dealing effectively with the drug problem as against the impact of the assumptions on the defendant's rights and concluded that the legislation was a reasonable and proportionate response to the challenge faced by society. It was thus not a breach of Art 6(2).

**1.12**   The matter was next dealt with in February 2001 with reference to parallel legislation in Scotland. In *McIntosh v HM Advocate* [2001] 3 WLR 107 the Privy Council held that the relevant provisions did *not* involve the determination of a criminal charge and thus Art 6(2) was not engaged. Central to this decision was the finding that, while an assumption was being made that the accused had been involved in drug trafficking, there was no assumption that he had been guilty of drug trafficking offences as defined by the legislation. The court found that the confiscation process involved no inquiry into the commission of any offences at all. The court accepted that the defendant faced a financial penalty with custody in default, but found that this penalty was imposed for the offence of which he had been convicted in the original proceedings, and involved no accusation of any other offence. The court went on to consider what the position would have been if this line of reasoning was wrong, so that the presumption of innocence in Art 6(2) did apply. For much the same reasons as were given in *Benjafield*, it was held that, on balance, the statutory provisions were not incompatible with Art 6(2), since in this instance the general interest of the community outweighed the infringement of the rights of the individual.

**1.13**   The argument was considered by the European Court of Human Rights in July 2001. In *Phillips v UK* (2001) BHRC 280, the court held, by a majority of 5 to 2, that confiscation proceedings were analogous to the determination of the amount of a fine or the length of a sentence of imprisonment and thus part of the sentencing procedure, to which Art 6(2) did not apply. It is worth noting that one of the dissenting voices was Nicholas Bratza, the UK judge.

**1.14**   Somewhat surprisingly the European Court, having summarily disposed of the Art 6(2) point, found that Art 6(1) *was* applicable to the case in hand. The court found that a person's right in a criminal case to be presumed innocent, and for the prosecution to have to prove the allegations against him, applied throughout the proceedings, of which the determination of sentence (and thus confiscation proceedings) were a part. The rationale for this decision was that the right to be presumed innocent was to be taken as an integral part of the right to a fair trial established by Art 6(1), quite independently of Art 6(2).

**1.15** This finding appears to do away with the need for the separate protection of Art 6(2) and to undermine the distinction which has hitherto been drawn between sentencing proceedings and the determination of guilt or innocence: see *Welch v UK* (1995) 20 EHRR 247. Having let in what had, hitherto, been Art 6(2) considerations by this unconventional route, the Court went on to find that there was no breach.

**1.16** The Court emphasised that it was making no findings as to the compatibility of the legislation with the Convention, but rather dealing with the particular case before it. The Court found the following features of the confiscation proceedings in the *Phillips* case significant.

- There was no finding of guilt or innocence at stake.
- The procedure had safeguards in that the hearing was public, there was advance disclosure of the prosecution case, there was opportunity for the defendant to adduce evidence and the court could tailor the confiscation order to the established resources of the defendant.
- Most importantly, the judge had discretion not to apply the assumptions if he thought serious injustice might otherwise result, and the defendant had the opportunity to rebut the assumptions.
- On the particular facts of the case, every item or property taken into account by the judge was substantiated by the defendant's admissions or prosecution evidence.
- On the basis of the judge's findings there could have been no objection to the amount of the confiscation order even if the statutory assumptions had not been applied.
- If the defendant's account of matters were true, it would have been simple for him to demonstrate the true source of his assets.
- While the court would be concerned about the fairness of the proceedings where the amount of a confiscation order was based on the value of assumed hidden assets, this was not the instant case.

**1.17** Most recently, the Art 6 challenge was the subject of rulings by the House of Lords in *R v Rezvi and Others* [2002] UKHL 1, [2002] 1 All ER 801 and *R v Benjafield* [2002] UKHL 2, [2002] 2 WLR 235 (see **1.11** for the Court of Appeal's ruling in these matters which they heard under the lead name *Benjafield*). Their Lordships adopted the reasoning in *McIntosh* and referred to the decision in *Phillips* in finding that Art 6(2) did not apply to confiscation proceedings, since the confiscation scheme under the Criminal Justice Act 1988 and the Drug Trafficking Act 1994 were properly viewed as part of the sentencing procedure and did not involve the determination of a criminal charge. More generally, they ruled that the safeguards referred to in the foregoing paragraphs were sufficient to render the legislation compatible with Art 6 as a whole, providing the discretions given to the prosecutor and the court were properly exercised.

**1.18** It is suggested that in the light of the cases examined above, and given that the provisions of the PCA 2002 are wider than the old statutes, there is still considerable scope for challenge to confiscation proceedings on human rights grounds.

**1.19** First, it will be noted that there is a tension between the approach of the domestic courts and that of the European Court in *Phillips*. The domestic courts have attempted to deal with the problems presented by the legislation in principle, and have considered the overall compatibility of confiscation proceedings with the Convention. The European Court specifically disavowed this approach and its finding was made on the express basis that the statutory assumptions could not have affected the fairness of the proceedings, since the judge would have come to the same conclusions even if the assumption had not applied. The European Court thus made it clear that it gave no general seal of approval to the use of the statutory assumptions in confiscation proceedings and that there was scope under the legislation for the statutory assumptions to operate in a way which *would* constitute a breach of Art 6.

**1.20**    Secondly, the provisions of the PCA 2002 are wider than the legislation which gave rise to the case-law examined above. In particular, the 'criminal lifestyle' provisions, giving rise to the deployment of the statutory assumptions, now cover a very much larger range of offence (see Chapters 3 and 4 of this book). This may necessitate a revisiting of the 'balancing' which courts have performed between the threat posed to society by the activity at which the legislation is aimed and the interference with individual rights which the legislation permits.

**1.21**    A third potential challenge to the PCA 2002 may lie in the fact that it permits the court to confiscate property held as long as 6 years previously, and thus well before the enactment of the Act. If the imposition of a confiscation order is truly to be regarded as analogous to the imposition of a fine, and thus part of the sentencing process, some such orders may (at least in the early years of the Act) fall foul of Art 7, in that they will involve the imposition of a heavier penalty than was applicable at the time.

# PART 1
## CRIMINAL PROCEEDINGS

# Chapter 2

# RESTRAINT AND INVESTIGATION

## RESTRAINT ORDERS

**2.1**  A central feature of the new confiscation legislation is the power under s 41 of the PCA 2002 for Crown Courts to make restraint orders. This presents a common-sense development in the law of confiscation since few restraint orders were sought when the power was limited to the High Court. A restraint order allows the court, pending the final resolution of confiscation proceedings, to prohibit *any* specified person from dealing with *any* realisable property held by him, or transferred to him. When a restraint order is in force, there is also a power[1] to seize realisable property to prevent its removal from England and Wales. An application for the court to make a restraint order can only be made by the prosecutor, the Director of the Assets Recovery Agency (ARA), or an accredited financial investigator.[2]

## When can a restraint order be made?

**2.2**  Under s 40 of the PCA 2002 there are five separate circumstances in which a restraint order can be made. These reflect the various procedural stages of a confiscation investigation, starting when the criminal investigation begins. The five independent triggering conditions are as follows.

### *Criminal investigation into an offender who has benefited*
**2.3**  A restraint order may be made where a criminal investigation[3] has been started and there is reasonable cause to believe that the alleged offender has benefited from his criminal conduct. Unlike the other conditions, there is no requirement that the investigation was started without 'undue delay'.

### *Proceedings have been started against offender who has benefited*
**2.4**  A restraint order may also be made where proceedings for an offence have been started but not concluded and there is reasonable cause to believe that the alleged offender has benefited from his criminal conduct. Proceedings for an offence are started when a defendant is charged[4] and are generally concluded when the defendant is acquitted or the confiscation order is satisfied.[5] The PCA 2002 expressly states that this condition will not be met if 'there has been undue delay in continuing the proceedings, or the prosecutor does not intend to proceed'.[6] 'Undue delay' is not

---

1    Under s 45, exercisable by a constable or customs officer.
2    Section 42(1) and (2).
3    Under s 88(2), a criminal investigation is one 'which police officers or other persons have a duty to conduct with a view to it being ascertained whether a person should be charged with an offence'.
4    Or a summons is issued, or a bill of indictment is preferred (s 85(1)).
5    See ss 85(3) et seq. Detailed rules apply in relation to appeals.
6    Section 40(7).

defined in the legislation; however, it is likely to be a similar assessment to the due expedition test applied in custody time-limits cases.


## No confiscation order made

**2.5**   The PCA 2002 paves the way for confiscation orders to be made in cases where, for a variety of reasons, no order was made in the ordinary course of proceedings. This is supplemented by a power to make restraint orders in such circumstances. The four circumstances envisaged are:

(a)   when no order was originally made, but, within 6 years, fresh evidence is available to the prosecutor;[1]

(b)   when no order was made because it was found by the original court that the defendant did not have a criminal lifestyle or did not benefit from a criminal lifestyle, and, within 6 years, fresh evidence has become available that the defendant did benefit from general or particular criminal conduct;[2]

(c)   when no order was made because, although the defendant was convicted, he absconded and the prosecutor has asked the court to proceed in his absence;[3]

(d)   when no order was made because the defendant absconded before conviction and, after 2 years, the prosecutor has asked the court to proceed in his absence.[4]

**2.6**   If such an application has been, or will be, made and has not yet been concluded, a restraint order can be made if there is reasonable cause to believe that the defendant has benefited. No restraint order can be made if there has been 'undue delay' or the prosecutor has decided not to proceed.[5]


## Reconsideration of benefit after an order has been made

**2.7**   Where a prosecutor applies to recalculate the defendant's benefit (under s 21), a restraint order can be made before the application's conclusion if there is reasonable cause to believe that the recalculated benefit will be greater than that in the original order. No restraint order can be made, however, if there has been 'undue delay' or the prosecutor has decided not to proceed.[6]


## Reconsideration of the available amount after an order has been made

**2.8**   Where a prosecutor[7] applies to recalculate the defendant's available amount (under s 22) a restraint order can be made, before the application's conclusion, if there is reasonable cause to believe that the recalculated available amount will be greater than that in the original order. No restraint order can be made, however, if there has been 'undue delay' or the prosecutor has decided not to proceed.[8]

---

1    Section 19.
2    Section 20.
3    Section 27.
4    Section 28.
5    Section 40(8).
6    Ibid.
7    This includes the Director of the ARA and a receiver appointed under s 50 or s 52.
8    Section 40(8).

# Form of a restraint order

**2.9**  Under s 41, a restraint order can be made against 'any specified person', prohibiting him from 'dealing with any realisable property' held by him. It follows from the general wording of this section that a restraint order can be made against a person other than the alleged offender. The legislation does not require the person restrained to be the 'alleged offender', and a distinction is drawn by not using that expression. This reflects the position as it was under s 77 of the Criminal Justice Act 1988. The order may apply to all realisable property held, whether or not it is described in the order. It may also be applicable to any realisable property transferred to the specified person after the order is made.[1]

# Hearsay evidence

**2.10**  In restraint proceedings, the admissibility of hearsay evidence is governed by civil rules of evidence. As such, evidence will not be excluded on the ground that it is hearsay, and the procedural rules in ss 2, 3 and 4 of the Civil Evidence Act 1995 apply.[2] A hearsay notice in accordance with s 2 should be served if a party proposes to rely on hearsay evidence. Failure to serve a hearsay notice, however, does not render the evidence inadmissible; it is merely a factor to be taken account of when assessing its evidential weight and costs. Section 4 of the 1995 Act lists the considerations relevant to the weight that should be attached to such evidence.

# Exceptions

**2.11**  A restraint order can be made subject to exceptions for the provision of reasonable living and legal expenses. The PCA 2002 provides, in addition, an exception for the purpose of enabling any person to carry on any trade, business, profession or occupation.

## *Legal expenses for the triggering offence of benefit*

**2.12**  An exception cannot be made for legal expenses incurred[3] in relation to the particular offence of benefit that has triggered the restraint order. A defendant charged with offences of benefit in one indictment and, for example, an unrelated offence of violence in another indictment, may be entitled to legal expenses in relation to the latter but not the former.[4]

**2.13**  The PCA 2002 provides a general remedy for the prosecutor to ensure that a restraint order is effective.[5] After an order has been granted, the applicant can apply for the court to 'make such order as it believes is appropriate for the purpose of ensuring that the restraint order is effective'. It is not entirely clear what these provisions add to the general power of the prosecution to vary the order under s 42(3).

---

1  Section 41(2).
2  Section 46.
3  By the alleged offender or by a recipient of a tainted gift.
4  Section 41(4), (5).
5  Section 41(6), (7).

## Application for an order, discharge or variation

**2.14**    Section 42 of the PCA 2002, governs the procedure on applying for a restraint order, or applying to discharge or vary such an order. An application for a restraint order may be made ex parte to a Crown Court judge in chambers, but only by the prosecutor, Director of the ARA or an accredited financial investigator. Both the applicant and 'any person affected by the order' may apply for its discharge or variance. If proceedings for an offence or a reconsideration are brought, the restraint order must be discharged by the court on the conclusion of those proceedings. The question of discharge must ultimately be considered by the court, since only the court can discharge the order.[1] If the trigger to the restraint order was merely that an investigation had started, or that the prosecution intended to make a reconsideration application, the court must discharge the order 'within a reasonable time' to ensure that proceedings do not, or the application does not, take place.[2]

**2.15**    A restraint order can be registered against title under the Land Registration Acts in relation to any real property in which the restrained individual has an interest.[3]

## Management receivers

**2.16**    A restraint order essentially freezes an individual's assets until confiscation proceedings are resolved. In this interim period, the court has power to appoint a 'management receiver' who can commercially manage the property concerned. The court can provide the receiver with a wide variety of powers, including the power to sell and realise property, enter into contracts, sue and be sued, take possession of assets and realise property interests.[4] The court may also order somebody in possession of property, to which the restraint order applies, to hand it over to the receiver.[5]

**2.17**    The PCA 2002 sets out a number of principles that must be applied when the court or the receiver exercise their statutory powers.[6] The powers should be exercised:

(a)    with a view to the value for the time being of realisable property being made available (by its realisation) for satisfying any existing or future confiscation order;
(b)    with a view to securing that there is no diminution in the property's value;
(c)    without taking account of any obligation of the defendant or a recipient of a tainted gift, if the obligation conflicts with the object of satisfying any existing or future confiscation order;
(d)    with a view to allowing innocent parties to retain or recover the value of interest held by them;
(e)    with a view to recovering only the value of a tainted gift from its recipient.

**2.18**    Under s 69(4) property must not be sold if the court decides that it 'cannot be replaced' and so orders. This is of central importance to the management receiver's responsibilities, and is triggered only by an application by a defendant or recipient of a

1    Although in an agreed discharge the court is unlikely to require an oral hearing.
2    Section 42(7).
3    Section 47.
4    See s 49 for the complete list of powers.
5    Section 49(5).
6    Section 69(2) and (3).

tainted gift. It is therefore important that legal advisers are aware of s 69 so that representations can be made to the court about which assets could not be replaced. An order by the court may be revoked or varied.

**2.19** A court must give anybody holding an interest in property 'a reasonable opportunity to make representations' before it gives the management receiver power to manage property generally, or to realise property for the receiver's expenses. Such an opportunity should also be given before an order is made to separate the defendant's beneficial interest in property, by ordering another person with an interest to make a payment in respect of it.[1]

## Restrictions

**2.20** A number of restrictions apply by virtue of s 58 after a restraint order is made to protect the interests of the owner of the property. No distress can be levied against realisable property without leave being sought. If the order applies 'to a tenancy of any premises', leave must be sought by a landlord seeking to enforce a peaceable right of forfeiture because the tenant has failed to comply with the tenancy agreement. Furthermore, the PCA 2002 provides other courts with the power to stay proceedings in relation to property over which there is a restraint order in place.[2]

## Appeal against a restraint order

**2.21** The prosecution has a right of appeal to the Court of Appeal (Criminal Division) against the refusal of the Crown Court to make a restraint order,[3] although leave must be obtained from that court.[4] The prosecutor and any person affected by a restraint order have the right, subject to leave being granted, to appeal in relation to its discharge or variance.[5] A person affected must, however, have first applied to discharge or vary the order in the Crown Court. The capacity for either side to further appeal against or for a restraint order to the House of Lords is also preserved by the PCA 2002.[6]

## PRODUCTION ORDERS

**2.22** A production order may be made by a Crown Court judge in connection with any confiscation investigation.[7] A specific power is provided for investigating authorities to obtain relevant material held by third parties. An order may only be made for the purpose of a confiscation investigation, and any application must be made by an 'appropriate officer'. The order may compel a third party to produce material to a specified person or allow him access to it. The court should specify a period during

---

1    See s 45(8).
2    Although the applicant and receiver must be given an opportunity to make representations.
3    Section 43(1).
4    Section 89.
5    Sections 43(2) and 89.
6    Section 44.
7    Section 345. The power to make a production order is also available in a civil recovery
     investigation preceding an application for a recovery order.

which the order must be complied with. This will ordinarily be 7 days; however, there is a discretion to increase or reduce the period.[1]

**2.23**  If material is held on computer, the order may require the material to be produced in a visible and legible form.[2] Material held by government departments falls within the ambit of a production order. A duty is created for officers of government departments to bring the order to the attention of the relevant person within the department.[3]

## Order to grant entry

**2.24**  The court may also order that the investigating officers be given access to premises, 'to obtain access' to any material. This is extremely broad and is not limited to commercial premises.[4] It would appear that there is no additional hoop through which the prosecution must jump before this power could be attached.

## Requirements

**2.25**  Before a production order can be made in relation to a confiscation investigation,[5] three conditions must be satisfied:[6]

(a)  there must be reasonable grounds for suspecting that the investigated person has benefited from his criminal conduct;
(b)  there must be reasonable grounds for believing that the recipient of the order is in possession or control of the material;
(c)  there must be reasonable grounds for believing that the material will be of substantial value to the investigation;
(d)  there must be reasonable grounds for believing that its production is in the public interest, having regard to the likely benefit to the investigation.

**2.26**  A production order cannot require the production of 'privileged' material, except that a lawyer can be required to produce material containing only the name and address of a client.[7] Privileged material is defined as material that would be legally professionally privileged in High Court proceedings. Material held with the intention of furthering a criminal purpose is not privileged. The intention must be the intention of the person holding the material. A production order takes precedence over any other 'restriction', and therefore no data protection issues arise. An order cannot be made in relation to 'excluded material'.

---

1    Section 345(5).
2    Section 349.
3    Section 350.
4    Section 347.
5    Where the order is sought in the course of a civil recovery investigation, there must be reasonable grounds to suspect that the property specified is recoverable or associated property: s 346(2)(b). In addition, requirements (b) and (c) apply to a civil recovery investigation as they do to a confiscation investigation.
6    Section 346.
7    Section 348.

**2.27** Application for an order may be made ex parte in chambers.[1] There is no restriction on the timing of an application. Any person affected by the order can apply for its discharge or variance.[2] The draft code of practice suggests, however, that an application for a production order against a financial institution should normally be made on notice.[3] An appropriate officer also has a duty to make enquiries to establish what is known about the likely occupier of premises where material is held.[4]

## SEARCH AND SEIZURE WARRANTS

**2.28** The legislation provides new powers of search and seizure in relation to the making of confiscation orders.[5] A search and seizure warrant under the Act will provide a power for an 'appropriate person'[6] to enter and search premises, and to seize and retain material 'likely to be of substantial value' to the investigation.[7] Unnecessarily detailed requirements apply to the making of search and seizure orders. The drafting of this area of the legislation is cumbersome.

## When can a search and seizure warrant be obtained?

**2.29** Search and seizure orders may be made in the following situations:

(a) after a failure to comply with a production order; or
(b) when no production order has been sought, and
    (i) it is not practicable to make a production order; or
    (ii) it is not practicable to secure agreed entry to a premises.

The draft code of practice makes it clear that search and seizure warrants are the most invasive of the statutory powers. An appropriate officer has a duty to consider why he needs a search and seizure warrant, rather than a production order with an order to grant entry.[8]

## Failure to comply with a production order

**2.30** Under s 352(6) a search and seizure order may be made when a production order has not been complied with and there are 'reasonable grounds for believing that the material is on the premises'. It is important to note that orders under s 352 are not confined to premises occupied by those alleged to have benefited from criminal conduct or who are in possession of recoverable property.

---

1    Section 351(1).
2    Section 351(3).
3    Draft code of practice, para 9.
4    Ibid, para 50.
5    Sections 352–356. These powers also apply to civil recovery investigations.
6    A constable or customs officer, or an ARA staff member in civil recovery investigations (ss 352(5), 353(10)).
7    Section 352(4).
8    Draft code of practice, paras 73 and 74.

## No production order has been sought

**2.31**   When a production order has not been made, a search and seizure order can be made only if there is a reasonable suspicion[1] that:

(a)  (in a confiscation investigation) the person specified in the application for a warrant has benefited from criminal conduct;

(b)  (in a civil recovery investigation) the property specified in the application is recoverable or associated property;[2]

(c)  (in a money laundering investigation) the person specified has committed a money laundering offence.

**2.32**   If there are such reasonable grounds to suspect, an order will be made in two types of case: first, when it is not practicable to make a production order; and, secondly, when it is not practicable to secure agreed entry to a premises.

## Not practicable to make a production order

**2.33**   There are three requirements to be met under this category: first, that material on the premises is 'likely to be of substantial value' to the investigation;[3] secondly, that it is in the public interest for the material to be obtained having regard to the likely benefit to the investigation; and thirdly, that it would not be appropriate to make a production order for any one of the following three reasons:

(a)  it is not practicable to communicate with the person against whom the production order would be made; or

(b)  it is not practicable to communicate with the person who would be required to grant access to premises; or

(c)  the investigation might be seriously prejudiced unless immediate access to the material is secured.

## Not practicable to secure agreed entry to a premises

**2.34**   There are essentially four conditions that must be met before an application under this category will be granted. There must be reasonable grounds for believing that:

(a)  the material sought is on the specified premises; and

(b)  the material cannot be identified at the time of the application but:

    (i)   (in a confiscation investigation) it relates to the person specified in the application question of whether he has benefited from criminal conduct, or the extent or whereabouts of that benefit; or

    (ii)  (in a civil recovery investigation) it relates to the question of whether it is recoverable or associated property;

    (iii) (in a money laundering investigation) it relates to the person specified, or whether he has committed a money laundering offence;

---

1    Section 353.
2    See paras **10.10** and **10.34**.
3    Section 353(2)–(4).

(c) obtaining the material is in the public interest having regard to the likely benefit to the investigation.[1]

**2.35** In addition to these requirements, one of the following three conditions must be met:[2]

(a) it is not practicable to communicate with the person entitled to grant entry to the premises; or
(b) entry will not be granted unless a warrant is produced; or
(c) the investigation might be seriously prejudiced unless an appropriate person arriving at the premises is able to secure immediate entry

## Procedural requirements

**2.36** Application for a search and seizure warrant must be made by an 'appropriate officer' (see above) to a Crown Court judge. There is no requirement that an offender has been charged with an offence before the order is sought. The application must state:[3]

(a) that the person specified is subject to a confiscation investigation, money laundering investigation or civil recovery investigation;
(b) that the warrant is sought for the purposes of that investigation;
(c) the specified premises; and
(d) that the warrant is sought in relation to the material specified in the application, or to material that 'cannot be identified at the time' but which falls within s 353(6), (7) or (8) (when it is not practicable to secure agreed access to premises – see above).

**2.37** Search and seizure warrants cannot confer the right to seize privileged material[4] or excluded material.[5] The Secretary of State has the power to order that the search and seizure safeguard sections of the Police and Criminal Evidence Act 1984 apply to warrants in relation to confiscation and money laundering investigations.[6]

## Civil recovery investigation warrants

**2.38** Warrants for the purposes of civil recovery investigations can be made to continue only for a period of one month.[7] A warrant can be made ex parte to a judge in chambers and can be issued subject to conditions. The warrant can require the production of information held in a computer in a form that is visible, legible and can be taken away.[8]

---

1    Section 353(5)–(6).
2    Section 353(9).
3    Section 352(2)–(3).
4    Defined as material which a person would be entitled to refuse to produce in High Court proceedings (s 354(2)).
5    Section 354(3).
6    At the time of writing, no order had been made.
7    Section 356(4).
8    Section 356(5).

# CUSTOMER INFORMATION ORDERS

**2.39**   Sections 363–369 of the PCA 2002 provide for the making of customer information orders. The purpose of customer information orders is to identify bank accounts held by a person who is subject to a confiscation investigation. The information does not extend to the detailed records of balance, deposit or withdrawal, which can be obtained by a production order. Customer information orders can, however, be made against 'all financial institutions' to enable an investigator to discover the location of all bank accounts held by an investigated person. Such orders are also available in the course of a civil recovery investigation, where the person specified in the application appears to hold the property specified. The appropriate officer does, however, have a duty to consider existing information so as to limit the scope of the financial institutions.[1] Such orders should only be sought where there is an ongoing investigation of a 'relatively serious nature'.[2]

## Requirements

**2.40**   An application for a customer information order must be made by a 'senior appropriate officer', or an 'appropriate officer' authorised by a 'senior appropriate officer'.[3] The court cannot make an order unless:

(a)   there are reasonable grounds to believe that the customer information provided is likely to be of substantial value;[4]
(b)   there are reasonable grounds for suspecting that:
  (i)   (in a confiscation investigation) the specified person has benefited from criminal conduct[5]; or
  (ii)   (in a money laundering investigation) he has committed a money laundering offence; or
  (iii)   (in a civil recovery investigation) the property specified in the application is recoverable or associated property and the person specified holds all or some of it;
(c)   there are reasonable grounds to believe that providing the information is in the public interest, having regard to the likely benefit to the investigation.

**2.41**   By virtue of s 363(4), it is implicit that the order may specify that 'all financial institutions' provide the customer information required, or it can be limited to types of financial institution or particular financial institutions.

**2.42**   The information required by an order is principally whether a person (including a company) holds or has held an account at a particular financial institution.[6] In addition, information includes: the account name; account number; the person's date of birth; his addresses; the time period over which the account was held; the details of joint account holders; and information about other accounts to which the person is a

---

1   Draft code of practice, para 113.
2   Ibid, para 114.
3   Section 369(7). See s 378 for the definition of these terms.
4   Section 365(6).
5   Section 365(2).
6   Whether held jointly or solely – s 364(1).

signatory.[1] If the person is a company, other details need to be supplied, such as the business description, registered office and tax details.[2] It is important to note that a customer information order takes precedence over any restriction upon the disclosure of information,[3] such that data protection issues do not apply. The information must be produced to an 'appropriate officer' as and when required.[4]

## Criminal offences by financial institutions

**2.43** Section 366 of the PCA 2002 creates three criminal offences for financial institutions that fail to comply with customer information orders. First, a financial institution which fails, without reasonable excuse, to comply with an order commits a criminal offence that is punishable summarily by a fine. Two further offences are created by s 366(3), when a financial institution 'makes a statement which it knows to be false or misleading in a material particular' or recklessly makes such a statement. Both offences are triable either way, but are limited to a fine. The offences are modelled on s 14 of the Trade Descriptions Act 1968, the *mens rea* of which was considered by the House of Lords in *Wings v Ellis* [1985] AC 272.[5]

## Procedure

**2.44** Applications can be made ex parte to a judge in chambers.[6] Applications must state:[7]

(a) that the person specified in the application is subject to a confiscation or money laundering investigation, or the property is subject to a civil recovery investigation;
(b) that the order is sought for the purposes of the investigation; and
(c) the financial institutions that the order is sought against.

**2.45** The applicant[8] and any person affected by the order may apply to vary or discharge it. Where the applicant was an 'appropriate officer', any other 'appropriate officer', if suitably authorised, may make the application to vary or discharge.[9]

## ACCOUNT MONITORING ORDERS

**2.46** Sections 370–375 of the PCA 2002 provide for the making of account monitoring orders. An account monitoring order is an order that a financial institution

---

1    Any evidence of identity that was obtained by the bank for the purposes of the money laundering legislations – s 364(2)(f).
2    Section 364(3).
3    Section 368.
4    Section 363(6) (although it need not be the same individual – s 369(5)).
5    For a detailed discussion of s 14, see Gumpert and Kirk *Trading Standards Law and Practice* (Jordans, 2001).
6    Section 369(1).
7    Section 363.
8    Only a senior appropriate officer (or an appropriate officer with his authorisation) may apply to vary or discharge the order – s 369(7).
9    Section 369(5).

provide ongoing account information in relation to a bank account held by an investigated person. The value of such an order is that it can be made ex parte and there is no statutory requirement of disclosure to the alleged offender; indeed, such disclosure might frustrate its purpose.

**2.47**   An order can be made only for a period of 90 days beginning with the day on which it is made. An order cannot be made unless:[1]

(a)   there are reasonable grounds to believe that the account monitoring information provided is likely to be of substantial value;
(b)   there are reasonable grounds for suspecting that:
    (i)    (in a confiscation investigation) the specified person has benefited from criminal conduct; or
    (ii)   (in a money laundering investigation) he has committed a money laundering offence; or
    (iii)  (in a civil recovery investigation) the property specified in the application is recoverable or associated property and the person specified holds all or some of it;
(c)   there are reasonable grounds to believe that it is in the public interest for the account information to be provided, having regard to the benefit likely to accrue to the investigation.

## Procedure

**2.48**   Unlike a customer information order, an application for an account monitoring order can be made by an 'appropriate officer' rather than a 'senior appropriate officer'. The application can be made ex parte to a judge in chambers.[2] The written application must state:[3]

(a)   that the person specified in the application is subject to a confiscation or money laundering investigation, or the property is subject to a civil recovery investigation;
(b)   that the order is sought for the purposes of the investigation; and
(c)   the financial institutions the order is sought against.

**2.49**   The applicant[4] and any person affected by the order may apply to vary or discharge it. Where the applicant was an 'oppropriate officer', any other 'appropriate officer' may make the application to vary or discharge. Although the order can be made for up to 90 days, this should not be treated as the standard time-limit. 'Appropriate officers' ought to carefully consider and justify the time period requested.[5]

---

1    Section 371.
2    Section 373.
3    Section 370.
4    Only a senior appropriate officer (or an appropriate officer with his authorisation) may apply to vary or discharge the order – s 373(7).
5    Draft code of practice, para 128.

# Powers exercisable by the Director of the ARA

**2.50**   Two further powers are exercisable only by the Director of the Assets Recovery Agency in investigations undertaken by the ARA. The Director may apply to the court for a 'disclosure order' under which a person must answer questions, provide information or produce documents. The Director may also apply to the court for a 'letter of request for overseas evidence' under which an overseas court or tribunal may be ordered to provide information.

# Chapter 3

# CONFISCATION ORDERS IN THE CROWN COURT

**3.1** The PCA 2002 consolidates and broadens the existing statutory provisions in relation to criminal confiscation. There are now essentially two types of confiscation order available in the Crown Court:

(a) confiscation of the assets of a defendant with a 'criminal lifestyle'; and
(b) confiscation of the benefit obtained by a defendant's 'particular criminal conduct'.

**3.2** Any defendant with a 'criminal lifestyle' will be subject to the draconian assumptions that income, expenditure and assets are the benefit of crime. A defendant who falls outside the definition of 'criminal lifestyle' will not have the assumptions made against him. However, he may have the benefit from his <u>particular criminal conduct</u> confiscated.

## GUIDE TO MAKING CONFISCATION ORDERS

**3.3** What follows is a sequential step-by-step guide to the making of a confiscation order in the Crown Court. Words and phrases which are <u>underlined</u> are defined in the list of key words and phrases in Chapter 4.

### *Step 1*
**3.4** Has the defendant been:

(a) convicted in the Crown Court; or
(b) committed to the Crown Court for sentence; or
(c) committed to the Crown Court for consideration of confiscation in respect of a <u>s 70 matter?</u>[1]

If no, go to step 2.        If yes, go to step 3.

### *Step 2*
**3.5** No confiscation order can be made.

### *Step 3*
**3.6** Has the prosecution or the Director of the Assets Recovery Agency (ARA)[2] asked the court to begin confiscation proceedings, or does the court believe it is appropriate to do so?[3]

---

1    Section 6(2).
2    Section 1(2).
3    Section 6(3).

If no, go to step 2.          If yes, go to step 4.

## Criminal lifestyle

### *Step 4*

**3.7** Does the nature of any of the offences mean that the defendant has a criminal lifestyle?[1] Are any of the offences:

(a) a Schedule 2 offence;[2] or
(b) an offence which was committed over a period of at least 6 months and from which the defendant has obtained relevant benefit of not less than £5,000?[3]

If no, go to step 5.          If yes, go to step 6.

## Criminal lifestyle by four offences of benefit

### *Step 5*

**3.8** Has the defendant been proved, on the balance of probabilities, to have obtained relevant benefit of not less than £5,000 and has the offence been proved, by the same standard, to constitute conduct forming part of a course of criminal activity?[4]

If no, go to step 8.          If yes, go to step 6.

## Has the defendant benefited from his criminal lifestyle?

### *Step 6*

**3.9** The defendant has a criminal lifestyle. Has the defendant been proved on the balance of probabilities to have benefited from his general criminal conduct?[5] In answering this question, the court must make the statutory assumptions[6] unless:

(a) any such assumption is shown to be incorrect; or
(b) there would be a serious risk of injustice if the assumption were made.[7]

If no, go to step 8.          If yes, go to step 7.

---

1   Section 6(4)(a).
2   Section 75(2)(a).
3   Section 75(2)(c) and 75(4).
4   Section 75(2)(b), 75(3) and 75(4).
5   Section 6(4)(b).
6   Section 10.
7   Section 10(6). Where any statutory assumption is not made, the court must state its reasons – s 10(7).

# How much has the defendant benefited from his criminal lifestyle?

## *Step 7*

**3.10** The defendant has benefited from his general criminal conduct. What is the amount that can be proved, on the balance of probabilities, to be the 'benefit from the conduct concerned'?[1] In answering this question, the court must make the statutory assumptions unless:

(a)   any such assumption is shown to be incorrect;[2] or
(b)   there would be a serious risk of injustice if the assumption were made.[3]

Benefit is taken to be the value of property obtained by criminal conduct.[4] In deciding what the benefit from the conduct concerned is, the court must make certain deductions.[5] The benefit from the conduct concerned is called the 'recoverable amount'.[6] Once the recoverable amount has been decided, go to step 10.

# Benefit from particular criminal conduct

## *Step 8*

**3.11** Has the defendant been proven, on the balance of probabilities, to have benefited from his particular criminal conduct?[7]

If no, go to step 2.                    If yes, go to step 9.

# How much has the defendant benefited from his particular criminal conduct?

## *Step 9*

**3.12**   Given that the defendant has benefited from his particular criminal conduct, what is the amount which can be proved, on the balance of probabilities, to be the benefit from the conduct concerned?[8] (Benefit is taken to be the value of property obtained by criminal conduct.[9]) Once the recoverable amount has been decided, go to step 10.

---

1    Sections 6(5), 7(1). In answering this question the court must take account of conduct occurring and property obtained after conviction and up to the time it makes its decision – s 8(2).
2    Section 10(6)(a).
3    Where any statutory assumption is not made, the court must state its reasons – s 10(7).
4    Section 76(7).
5    The aggregate amount of any previous confiscation order made against the defendant, unless any such amount has already been deducted in previous confiscation proceedings under the Act and other enactments providing powers of confiscation – s 8(3), (4), (5), (6).
6    Section 7(1).
7    Section 6(4)(c). In answering this question, the court must take account of conduct occurring and property obtained up to the time it makes its decision – s 8(2).
8    Sections 6(5), 7(1). In answering this question the court must take account of conduct occurring and property obtained after conviction and up to the time it makes its decision – s 8(2).
9    Section 76(7).

## Deduction for alternative legal proceedings

### Step 10
3.13   Does the court believe that legal proceedings by a victim of the defendant's conduct have been started, or are intended? If so, the court may decide that the recoverable amount is a lesser sum than the benefit from the conduct concerned. The court may then fix the recoverable sum at an amount it believes is just.[1]

Having decided whether the court should adjust the recoverable amount in this way, go to step 11.

## 'Available amount'

### Step 11
3.14   What is the total value of all the defendant's free property and tainted gifts?[2]

Once the total has been decided, go to step 12.

### Step 12
3.15   From the total produced by step 11 must be deducted the total amount payable in pursuit of obligations.[3] The deduction required by this step produces the available amount. Now go to step 13.

## Amount to be paid under the confiscation order

### Step 13
3.16   Has the defendant shown, on the balance of probabilities, that the available amount is less than the recoverable amount?[4]

If no, go to step 14.                    If yes, go to step 15.

### Step 14
3.17   The court must make a 'confiscation order' requiring the defendant to pay the recoverable amount.[5]

### Step 15
3.18   In these circumstances, the court must make a confiscation order requiring the defendant to pay the available amount or, if the available amount is nil, a nominal amount.[6]

---

1     Sections 6(6), 7(3).
2     Section 9(1).
3     Section 9(2), (3).
4     Sections 6(7), 7(2).
5     Section 6(5).
6     Sections 6(5), 7(2).

# Chapter 4

# KEY WORDS AND PHRASES

## (in alphabetical order)

## BENEFITED

**4.1**  Section 76(4) of the PCA 2002 states that 'a person benefits from conduct if he obtains property as a result of or in connection with the conduct'. Where criminal conduct results in a pecuniary advantage (eg an offer of employment gained by the defendant lying about his criminal record), this is to be taken as obtaining property equal in value to the pecuniary advantage.[1] Where property is obtained only partly in connection with criminal conduct it is treated as if it were wholly so obtained.[2] Cases under the former enactments establish the following propositions, which are likely to remain good law:

(a)  where a defendant has taken part in a joint criminal enterprise from which he has received all of the proceeds before apportioning amounts to his accomplices, his benefit is to be treated as being the whole of the proceeds;[3]

(b)  where a fraud on the Inland Revenue causes the evasion of tax, the unpaid tax is to be treated as a pecuniary advantage;[4]

(c)  where the defendant has been involved in the evasion of duty on goods, but the goods have been seized immediately upon importation and thus before being sold or otherwise dealt with, he is to be treated as having obtained a pecuniary advantage valued at the amount of the duty evaded.[5]

## CONDUCT FORMING PART OF A COURSE OF CRIMINAL ACTIVITY

**4.2**  Section 75(3) of the PCA 2002 states that <u>conduct forming part of a course of criminal activity</u> is conduct from which the defendant has <u>benefited</u> and *either*:

(a)  there are three or more other offences from which he has benefited in the same proceedings;[6] *or*

(b)  he has been convicted of offences from which he has benefited on at least two separate occasions in the 6 years preceding the start of proceedings of the earliest of the instant offences.[7]

---

1    Section 76(5).
2    Section 76(6).
3    *R v Patel* [2000] 2 Cr App R(S) 10.
4    *R v Dimsey and Allen* [2000] 1 Cr App R(S) 497.
5    *R v Smith (David)* [2002] UKHL 68, [2002] 1 WLR 54, HL.
6    Section 75(3)(a).
7    Section 75(3)(b).

# FREE PROPERTY

**4.3**   Section 82 of the PCA 2002 defines free property as all property except that in respect of which the following orders are in force:

–   a forfeiture order under s 27 of the Misuse of Drugs Act 1971;
–   a deprivation order under art 11 of the Criminal Justice (Northern Ireland) Order 1994;
–   a forfeiture order under Part II of the Proceeds of Crime (Scotland) Act 1995;
–   a deprivation order under ss 23 or 111 of the Terrorism Act 2000;
–   an order under ss 255, 271, 298(2) or 301(2) of the Proceeds of Crime Act 2002.

# GENERAL CRIMINAL CONDUCT

**4.4**   Section 76(1) and (2) defines general criminal conduct as all the defendant's behaviour which would be an offence in England and Wales, whenever the conduct occurred and whenever the benefit from that conduct was obtained.

# PARTICULAR CRIMINAL CONDUCT

**4.5**   Section 76(3) of the PCA 2002 defines particular criminal conduct as the offence concerned, plus any other convictions or offences taken into consideration in the same proceedings.

# PREFERENTIAL DEBTS

**4.6**   Preferential debts are defined as having the meaning given by s 386 of the Insolvency Act 1986.[1] That section refers in turn to the debts listed in Sch 6 to the Insolvency Act 1986. Space does not permit the reproduction of Sch 6 in full. In short, the relevant debts are as follows:

–   money owed to the Inland Revenue for income tax deducted at source, VAT, car tax, betting and gaming duties;
–   social security and pension scheme contributions;
–   remuneration, etc of employees;
–   levies on coal and steel production.

# PROCEEDINGS

**4.7**   Proceedings are defined as having started when the defendant is charged or summonsed in respect of the offence or a voluntary bill of indictment is preferred.[2]

---

1   Section 9(3).
2   Section 86(1).

# RELEVANT BENEFIT

**4.8**   Relevant benefit is defined[1] as benefit from:

(a)   conduct which constitutes the offence;
(b)   conduct which constitutes an offence which has been or will be taken into consideration,

where the court is considering whether the defendant has a criminal lifestyle, because the offence concerned may constitute conduct forming part of a course of criminal activity, relevant benefit also includes benefit from conduct forming part of a course of criminal activity, providing it constitutes an offence of which the defendant has been convicted.

# RELEVANT DAY

**4.9**   Sections 10(8) (statutory assumptions) and 77(9) (tainted gifts) contain identical definitions of the relevant day. It is:

(a)   the first day of the period of 6 years ending with the day on which proceedings for the offence concerned were started against the defendant; or
(b)   if there are two or more offences, and proceedings for them were started on different days, the earliest of those days.

Proceedings are started by charge, summons or voluntary bill.[2]

**4.10**   The relevant day may be different for the purposes of making the statutory assumptions (but not in respect of tainted gifts) where a confiscation order has previously been made in the 6-year period described above. In that case, the relevant day will be the day on which the defendant's benefit was calculated for the purposes of the last such confiscation order.[3] Confiscation orders include not only those made under the PCA 2002, but also[4] those made under:

–   the Drug Trafficking Offences Act 1986;
–   Part I of the Criminal Justice (Scotland) Act 1987;
–   Part VI of the Criminal Justice Act 1988;
–   the Criminal Justice (Confiscation) (Northern Ireland) Order 1990;
–   Part I of the Drug Trafficking Act 1994;
–   Part I of the Proceeds of Crime (Scotland) Act 1995;
–   the Proceeds of Crime (Northern Ireland) Order 1996.

# SCHEDULE 2 OFFENCE

**4.11**   Schedule 2 to the PCA 2002 sets out the offences which automatically result in the defendant being found to have a criminal lifestyle. Offences of attempting,

---

1   Section 75(5) and (6).
2   Section 85(1).
3   Section 10(9)(a).
4   Section 7(7).

conspiracy or incitement to commit these offences, or of aiding, abetting, counselling or procuring their commission, will have the same result as the substantive offence. The offences are set out in Sch 2, para 10 under the following subject matter headings:

- *Drugs*
  - Unlawful production;[1]
  - Supply;[2]
  - Possession with intent to supply;[3]
  - Permitting certain activities relating to drugs;[4]
  - Assisting in or inducing the commission outside the United Kingdom of an offence punishable under a corresponding law;[5]
  - Importation;[6]
  - Exportation;[7]
  - Fraudulent evasion;[8]
  - Manufacture or supply of a substance specified in Sch 2 to the Criminal Justice (International Co-operation) Act 1990;[9]
  - Using a ship for illicit traffic in drugs.[10]

- *Money laundering*
  - Concealing, etc criminal property;[11]
  - Assisting another to retain criminal property.[12]

- *Directing terrorism*
  - Directing the activities of a terrorist organisation.[13]

- *People trafficking*
  - Assisting illegal entry.[14]

- *Arms trafficking*
  - Exportation;[15]
  - Fraudulent evasion;[16]
  - Dealing in firearms or ammunition.[17]

- *Counterfeiting*
  - Making counterfeit notes or coins;[18]

---

1 Misuse of Drugs Act 1971, s 4(2).
2 Ibid, s 4(3).
3 Ibid, s 5(3).
4 Ibid, s 8.
5 Ibid, s 20.
6 Customs and Excise Management Act 1971, s 50(2) or (3).
7 Ibid, s 68(2).
8 Ibid, s 170.
9 Criminal Justice (International Co-operation) Act 1990, s 12.
10 Ibid, s 19.
11 Proceeds of Crime Act 2002, s 372.
12 Ibid, s 328.
13 Terrorism Act 2000, s 56.
14 Immigration Act 1971, s 25(1).
15 Customs and Excise Management Act 1979, s 68(2).
16 Ibid, s 170.
17 Firearms Act 1968, s 3(1).
18 Forgery and Counterfeiting Act 1981, s 14.

- Passing counterfeit notes or coins;[1]
- Having counterfeit notes or coins;[2]
- Making or possessing materials or equipment for counterfeiting.[3]

● *Intellectual property*
- Making or dealing with an article which infringes copyright;[4]
- Making or possessing an article designed or adapted for making a copy of a copyright work;[5]
- Making or dealing in an illicit recording;[6]
- Making or dealing in unauthorised decoders;[7]
- Unauthorised use of trade mark.[8]

● *Pimps and brothels*
- Procuring women;[9]
- Detaining a woman in a brothel;[10]
- Causing or encouraging prostitution;[11]
- Man living on earnings of prostitution;[12]
- Woman exercising control over prostitute;[13]
- Keeping a brothel;[14]
- Letting premises for use as a brothel;[15]
- Living on earnings of male prostitute.[16]

● *Blackmail*
- Blackmail.[17]

# SECTION 70 MATTER

**4.12**   Section 70 of the PCA 2002 requires the magistrates' court, following a conviction in that court, to commit a defendant to the Crown Court, if it is asked to do so by the prosecutor with a view to a confiscation order being made by the Crown Court. Once they have been asked to commit in respect of a particular offence, the magistrates also have the power to commit a defendant in respect of any other offence of which the defendant has been convicted. The committal operates not just for

---

1    Forgery and Counterfeiting Act 1981, s 15.
2    Ibid, s 16.
3    Ibid, s 17.
4    Copyright Designs and Patents Act 1988, s 107(1).
5    Ibid, s 107(2).
6    Ibid, s 198(1).
7    Ibid, s 297A.
8    Trade Marks Act 1994, s 92(2), (3).
9    Sexual Offences Act 1956, ss 2, 3, 9, 22.
10    Ibid, s 24.
11    Ibid, ss 28, 29.
12    Ibid, s 30.
13    Ibid, s 31.
14    Ibid, s 33.
15    Ibid, s 34.
16    Sexual Offences Act 1967, s 5.
17    Theft Act 1968, s 21.

confiscation purposes but also for sentence, whether or not the Crown Court begins confiscation proceedings.[1]

**4.13** When the magistrates commit a defendant under s 70, they must state whether they would have committed the defendant for sentence in any event. Where the magistrates have done so, the Crown Court may deal with the defendant as if he had been convicted on indictment. In respect of other offences, the Crown Court's powers of sentence are limited to those of the magistrates' court.

## STATUTORY ASSUMPTIONS

**4.14** Section 10 contains four statutory assumptions:

(1) that property transferred to the defendant after the relevant day was obtained as a result of general criminal conduct and was obtained on the date on which the defendant first appears to have held it;[2]
(2) that property held after the day of conviction was obtained as a result of general criminal conduct and was obtained on the date on which the defendant first appears to have held it.[3] This assumption is not to be made in respect of any property held by the defendant on or before the day on which his benefit was calculated for the purposes of the last of any previous confiscation orders under the Act or any of the statutes set out in the paragraph dealing with the definition of the relevant day[4] (see **4.9**);
(3) that the defendant's expenditure after the relevant day was met from property obtained as a result of general criminal conduct;[5]
(4) that for the purpose of valuing it, any property obtained by the defendant was obtained free of any other interests in it.[6] This section is concerned only with the time that property was obtained. It does not preclude taking into account interests in property that have come about after it was obtained (see **4.22**).

## TAINTED GIFTS

**4.15** Gifts are defined as transfers of property by the defendant to another person for a consideration whose value is significantly less than the value of the property at the time the defendant obtained it.[7]

**4.16** Where a gift has been made in return for *some* consideration, albeit significantly less than the value of the property given, the gift is treated as a proportion of the property given. The proportion is ascertained by taking the difference between the

---

1      Section 71.
2      Section 10(2).
3      Section 10(3).
4      Section 10(9)(b).
5      Section 10(4). Where the defendant has been in possession of drugs, the court is entitled to find that he has incurred expenditure equal to the price of those drugs: *R v Satchell* [1996] 2 Cr App R(S) 258, *R v Dore* [1997] 2 Cr App R(S) 152.
6      Section 10(5).
7      Section 78(1).

consideration given and the value of the property at the time the defendant obtained as the numerator (top figure) of a fraction. The denominator (bottom figure) of the fraction is the value of the property at the time the defendant obtained it.

**4.17**   An illustration may be helpful:

*A defendant steals a car. At the time of the theft, it is worth £10,000. A month later, he gives it to his brother, in return for £5000. The difference between the two figures is £5000. This is the top figure in the fraction. The value of the car when the defendant obtained it is £10,000. This is the bottom figure in the fraction.*

*The fraction is:*

£5000
£10,000, *otherwise expressed as* ½

*Thus, the gift is to be treated as half of the value of the car.*[1]

**4.18**   Whether or not a gift is 'tainted' depends upon whether or not a court has made a decision that the defendant does *not* have a criminal lifestyle.[2] Where a court has not yet made such a decision, or has decided that the defendant *does* have a criminal lifestyle, any gift made at any time by the defendant after the relevant day is tainted.[3]

**4.19**   In addition, gifts of property obtained by the defendant as a result of or in connection with his general criminal conduct and gifts of property which represent in the defendant's hands, to any extent, property so obtained, are tainted.[4]

**4.20**   Where a court has decided that the defendant does not have a criminal lifestyle, any gift made at any time after the date on which the offence concerned was committed or, if his particular criminal conduct consists of two or more offences and they were committed on different dates, the earliest date, is tainted.[5] Continuing offences are considered to have been committed on the first occasion they were committed.[6]

## TOTAL AMOUNT PAYABLE IN PURSUIT OF OBLIGATIONS

**4.21**   The total amount payable in pursuit of obligations is simply the total amount of:

(a)   fines;
(b)   other financial orders made on conviction;
(c)   other obligations to pay sums that would be included among the preferential debts if the defendant's bankruptcy had commenced on the date of the confiscation order, or his winding-up had been ordered on that date.[7]

---

1   Section 78(2).
2   Section 77(1).
3   Section 77(2).
4   Section 77(3).
5   Section 77(5).
6   Section 77(6).
7   Section 9(1), (2).

# VALUE

**4.22**   Value is defined at ss 78, 79, 80 and 81 of the Act. Where, at the time of valuation, other people have an interest in property (eg a mortgagee), the value is the value of the defendant's interest. Charging orders under:

–   s 9 of the Drug Trafficking Offences Act 1986;
–   s 78 of the Criminal Justice Act 1988;
–   art 14 of the Criminal Justice (Northern Ireland) Order 1994;
–   s 27 of the Drug Trafficking Act 1994;
–   art 32 of the Proceeds of Crime (Northern Ireland) Order 1996,

are to be ignored at this stage.[1]

**4.23**   Generally, property is to be given its market value at the time of valuation.[2] However, property obtained by criminal conduct is to be given a value which is the greater of *either*:

(a)   its value at the time the defendant obtained it, adjusted for inflation; *or*
(b)   its value at the time the court makes its decision.[3]

**4.24**   Where the defendant no longer holds property obtained by criminal conduct, the property to be valued is any property which directly or indirectly represents it in his hands.[4] Where the defendant has disposed of part of the property obtained by criminal conduct, the property to be valued is the part he still holds, plus any property that directly or indirectly represents, in his hands, any part of it he has disposed of.[5]

**4.25**   Before ascertaining the value of a tainted gift it is necessary to establish what the recipient of the gift has done with it.[6]

(1)   If it remains in his hands, the value of the tainted gift is either its value at the time of the gift, adjusted for inflation, or its current value, whichever is the greater.
(2)   If the recipient has wholly disposed of it, the value of the tainted gift is either its value at the time of the gift, adjusted for inflation, or the current value of any property that directly or indirectly represents it in the recipient's hands, whichever is the greater.
(3)   If the recipient retains part and has disposed of part of the gift, the value is either its value at the time of the gift, adjusted for inflation, or the current value of the retained part plus the current value of any property that directly or indirectly represents the part disposed of in the recipient's hands, whichever is the greater.

---

1   Section 79(3).
2   Section 79(2).
3   Section 80(1), (2).
4   Section 80(3)(b).
5   Section 80(3)(c).
6   Section 81.

# Chapter 5

# PROCEDURE FOR OBTAINING CONFISCATION ORDERS IN THE CROWN COURT

## COMMENCEMENT

**5.1**　By virtue of s 6(3) of the PCA 2002, the process of making a confiscation order may be commenced in one of two ways: either the prosecutor (or the Director of the Assets Recovery Agency (ARA)) may ask the court to proceed; or the court may believe that it is appropriate to do so. In either case, the court is obliged to commence confiscation proceedings.

**5.2**　The cases of *R v Ross* [2001] Cr App R(S) 484, *R v Woodhead* [2002] EWCA Crim 45, [2002] Crim LR 323 and *R v Davis* [2002] Crim LR 224 are authority for the proposition that, under the old law,[1] where the court had passed sentence for an offence without making a confiscation order in respect of that offence, it could not make a confiscation order thereafter unless, prior to passing sentence, it had exercised its statutory power to postpone the confiscation proceedings.

**5.3**　Further, under the old law, a decision to postpone had to be an express decision, and the postponement had to be for a specified period; the court should have applied its mind to the relevant statutory provisions, although no particular form of words was required. The PCA 2002 was originally drafted, in respect of the commencement and postponement of proceedings, in identical terms to the Criminal Justice Act 1988 and the Drug Trafficking Act 1994. In the course of its passage through Parliament a substantial change was made so as to remove the mandatory provision whereby confiscation orders (unless made in duly postponed proceedings) had to be made before sentence.

**5.4**　Furthermore, changes were made to the statutory expression of the court's power of postponement so that proceeding to confiscation before sentence or postponing confiscation until after sentence are now expressed as the only two alternatives available to the court.[2] It remains to be seen whether this will affect the views of appellate courts on the propriety of instigating confiscation proceedings after sentence, when no mention of that possibility has been made at the time of sentence.

## POSTPONEMENT

**5.5**　Under s 14 of the PCA 2002, once confiscation proceedings have been commenced, the court may, of its own motion or on the application of either party, postpone the proceedings for any specified period provided the postponement does not end after the 'permitted period'.

---

1　Criminal Justice Act 1988, s 72A(1); Drug Trafficking Act 1994, s 3; see also *R v Phillips* [2001] EWCA Crim 2790, [2002] Crim LR 232, CA.

2　Section 14(1).

**5.6**   Any period of postponement may be extended in the same manner and with the same limitation as to time. Applications for extension must be made within the period of postponement, but may be granted after what would have been its expiry. Normally, the permitted period is a period of 2 years after the date of conviction, but it may be longer where the defendant appeals against his conviction. In that case, the permitted period is 2 years after conviction, or that period of time which expires on the last day of a period of 3 months from the day the appeal was determined, whichever is the longer.[1] Unlike the old legislation, it is not necessary for the applicant to make out any particular grounds for a postponement.

**5.7**   The cases on the old legislation[2] make it clear that, in addition to the statutory power of postponement, the court possesses a common-law power to adjourn any proceedings. *R v Shevki and Steele* [2001] 2 Cr App R(S) 178 is authority for the proposition that such an adjournment may be to a date beyond the statutory time-limit, but that such adjournments should be ordered only where the circumstances are compelling (eg one of the parties is ill or the judge is unavailable).

## Postponement for longer than the permitted period

**5.8**   A specified period of postponement may end after the end of the permitted period only where there are 'exceptional circumstances'.[3]

**5.9**   *R v Chuni* [2002] EWCA Crim 453, [2002] 2 Cr App R(S) 371 is authority, under the old law,[4] for the proposition that failure to use the words 'exceptional circumstances' in postponing a case beyond the time-limit does not invalidate such a postponement where the inference was that the court had the appropriate test in mind and where the grounds did justify the postponement. These principles are likely to continue to be applied by the courts.

**5.10**   In *R v Gadsby* [2002] Cr App R(S) 423, a case under s 3(3) of the Drugs Trafficking Act 1994, it was held that the existence of 'exceptional circumstances' was a matter on which judges might properly disagree. In that case, the judge found exceptional circumstances where the defence solicitor had refused to accept service of the prosecutor's statement 21 days before the hearing and, consequently, the hearing could not be concluded within the statutory period. The Court of Appeal ruled that the judge's decision was not unreasonable.

## Effect of postponement

**5.11**   Where confiscation proceedings are postponed the court may proceed to sentence the defendant, but the sentence must not include a fine, compensation order, forfeiture order or deprivation order. Any sentence passed during the period of

---

1    Section 14(5) and (6).
2    *R v Zelzele* [2001] EWCA Crim 1763, [2001] Cr App R(S) 261, [2001] Crim LR 830; *R v Shevki and Steele* [2001] Cr App R(S) 178; *R v Lingham* [2001] 1 Cr App R(S) 158.
3    Section 14(3), (4).
4    Criminal Justice Act 1988, s 72A(3).

postponement may be varied by the imposition of the forgoing orders within 28 days of the expiry of the postponement period.[1]

## STATEMENT OF INFORMATION

**5.12**   Where the prosecutor (or the Director of the ARA) asks the court to commence confiscation proceedings, he must give the court a statement of information (SOI). Where the proceedings are commenced because the court believes it appropriate to do so, it may order the prosecutor to provide an SOI. In either case, the court may fix a time-limit for the service of the SOI.[2]

**5.13**   There is no statutory obligation on the prosecutor (or the Director of the ARA) to provide the defendant with a copy of the SOI, but the ordinary rules of disclosure would require him to do so. In any event, it is only when he is served with the SOI that the court can order the defendant to respond.

**5.14**   If the prosecutor (or the Director) contends that the defendant has a criminal lifestyle the SOI must state all matters relevant to:

(a)   whether the defendant has a criminal lifestyle;[3]
(b)   whether the defendant has benefited from his general criminal conduct;[4]
(c)   the amount of the defendant's benefit from his conduct;[5]
(d)   making the statutory assumptions;[6]
(e)   the possible decision that the statutory assumptions should not be made.[7]

**5.15**   If the prosecutor does not contend that the defendant has a criminal lifestyle the SOI must state all matters relevant to:

(a)   whether the defendant has benefited from his particular criminal conduct;[8]
(b)   what the defendant's benefit from his conduct is.[9]

The prosecution may, at any time, voluntarily give the court a further SOI or the court may order the prosecutor to do so within a specified period.[10]

## Defendant's response to an SOI

**5.16**   Once the defendant has been served with an SOI the court may order him,[11] within a specified period and in a specified manner:

(a)   to indicate the extent to which each allegation in the SOI is accepted;

---

1    Section 15.
2    Section 16(1), (2).
3    Section 16(3)(a).
4    Section 16(3)(b).
5    Section 16(3)(c).
6    Section 16(4)(a).
7    Section 16(4)(b).
8    Section 16(5)(a).
9    Section 16(5)(b).
10   Section 16(6).
11   Section 17(1).

(b)   so far as an allegation is not accepted, to give particulars of any matters upon which he proposes to rely.

**5.17**   If the defendant fails to comply with the court's order he may be treated as accepting any unanswered allegations in the SOI, except any allegation that he has benefited from general or particular criminal conduct.[1] If the defendant accepts any allegation in the SOI this may be treated as being conclusive of the matters to which it relates.[2] If the defendant's response does accept that he has benefited from criminal conduct, this is *not* admissible in proceedings for an offence (ie a prosecution rather than confiscation proceedings).[3]

## COURT'S POWER TO ORDER DEFENDANT TO PROVIDE INFORMATION

**5.18**   Where the court is conducting confiscation proceedings or considering whether to do so, it may, but only for the purpose of obtaining information to help it in carrying out its functions, order the defendant to give specified information.[4] The order may also specify the manner in which, and the time by which, such information must be given.[5]

**5.19**   Failure to comply with the order entitles the court to draw such inference as it believes is appropriate.[6] If, in providing information in response to such an order, the defendant accepts that he has benefited from criminal conduct, this is not admissible in proceedings for an offence (ie a prosecution rather than confiscation proceedings).[7]

**5.20**   *R (on the application of Dechert) v Southwark Crown Court* (2001) *The Independent*, 1 October is authority for the proposition that, under the old law,[8] the power to order the defendant to provide information was restricted to the defendant and did not include third parties, including his solicitor. There are no substantive differences between the old law and the equivalent new provision[9] and thus the same limitation on the court's power is likely to continue to apply.

## PROSECUTOR'S ACCEPTANCE OF DEFENCE ALLEGATION

**5.21**   The prosecutor may accept an allegation made by the defendant in any statement to the court, and the court may treat such acceptance as conclusive of the matters to which it relates.[10]

---

1    Section 17(3).
2    Section 17(2).
3    Section 17(6).
4    Section 18(1), (2).
5    Section 18(3).
6    Section 18(4).
7    Section 18(9).
8    Criminal Justice Act 1988, s 73A.
9    Section 18.
10   Section 18(6).

# DEFENDANT ABSCONDING AFTER CONVICTION

**5.22**  If the defendant absconds after his conviction, or after his committal to the Crown Court for sentence, or in respect of a s 70 matter, and the prosecutor asks the court to proceed or the court believes that it is appropriate to do so, the court must commence confiscation proceedings.[1]

**5.23**  Where the court proceeds in the above circumstances:

(a)  any person the court believes likely to be affected by the order may appear and make representations;[2]
(b)  the court may not make a confiscation order unless the prosecution has taken reasonable steps to contact the defendant;[3]
(c)  the statutory assumptions do not apply.[4]

# DEFENDANT ABSCONDING BEFORE CONVICTION OR ACQUITTAL

**5.24**  Where the defendant absconds after criminal proceedings have been started against him, and 2 years have elapsed since he absconded, the prosecutor may apply to the court to commence confiscation proceedings. If the prosecutor does so, or the court believes that it is appropriate, the court must commence such proceedings.[5] Where the court proceeds in the above circumstances:

(a)  any person the court believes likely to be affected by the order may appear and make representations;[6]
(b)  the court may not make a confiscation order unless the prosecution has taken reasonable steps to contact the defendant.[7]

# TIME FOR PAYMENT

**5.25**  Confiscation orders must be paid when they are made, unless the defendant shows that he needs time to pay, in which case the court may allow payment to be made in a specified period not exceeding 6 months from the date of the order. The defendant may apply to the court for an extension of the specified period, which the court may grant if there are exceptional circumstances. The total period, if extended, must not exceed 12 months. An application for an extension may be made after the expiry of 6 months but not after the expiry of 12 months from the date of the confiscation order.[8]

---

1   Section 27.
2   Section 27(5)(a).
3   Section 27(5)(b).
4   Section 27(5)(d), (e).
5   Section 28(2), (3).
6   Section 28(5)(a).
7   Section 28(5)(b).
8   Section 11.

## EFFECT ON OTHER ORDERS

**5.26**    Where the court has made a confiscation order, it must take account of the order before imposing a fine, compensation order, forfeiture order or deprivation order. Save in respect of these disposals, the confiscation order must be ignored in sentencing the defendant. Where both a confiscation order and a compensation order are made, the court must specify the amount of compensation to be paid out of the sums recovered under the confiscation order: this amount must be the amount the court believes would otherwise not be paid because of the defendant's lack of means.[1]

## UNPAID SUMS

**5.27**    Interest must be paid on confiscation orders unpaid by the due date at the rate specified in s 17 of the Judgements Act 1838 (currently 7 per cent). The interest is treated as part of the amount to be paid under the order.[2] Interest may cause the period of imprisonment fixed in default of payment to be increased.[3]

---

1    Section 13.
2    Section 12.
3    Section 39(5), (6).

# Chapter 6

# ENFORCEMENT

**6.1**   The PCA 2002 does not alter the basic method of enforcing confiscation orders which is by ordering a period of imprisonment in default. The periods of imprisonment remain those applicable for default of fine payments. However, the PCA 2002 introduces detailed rules for the recovery of assets using 'enforcement receivers'.

## ENFORCEMENT AUTHORITIES

**6.2**   In any confiscation order where the court is asked by the Director of the Assets Recovery Agency (ARA) to proceed or reconsider, the court must appoint the Director as the enforcement authority.[1] In all other cases, the confiscation order is treated as a fine under s 139 of the Powers of Criminal Courts (Sentencing) Act 2000 (PCC(S)A 2000), with some modifications. A term of imprisonment in default of payment must be served at the conclusion of any sentence of imprisonment for the triggering offence or offences.[1]

> 'The periods set out in the second column of the following Table shall be the maximum periods of imprisonment *or detention* under subsection (2) above applicable respectively to the amounts set out opposite them.

TABLE

| | |
|---|---|
| An amount not exceeding £200 | 7 days |
| An amount exceeding £200 but not exceeding £500 | 14 days |
| An amount exceeding £500 but not exceeding £1,000 | 28 days |
| An amount exceeding £1,000 but not exceeding £2,500 | 45 days |
| An amount exceeding £2,500 but not exceeding £5,000 | 3 months |
| An amount exceeding £5,000 but not exceeding £10,000 | 6 months |
| An amount exceeding £10,000 but not exceeding £20,000 | 12 months |
| An amount exceeding £20,000 but not exceeding £50,000 | 18 months |
| An amount exceeding £50,000 but not exceeding £100,000 | 2 years |
| An amount exceeding £100,000 but not exceeding £250,000 | 3 years |
| An amount exceeding £250,000 but not exceeding £1 million | 5 years |
| An amount exceeding £1 million | 10 years'[2] |

## ENFORCEMENT WHEN DIRECTOR IS NOT APPOINTED

**6.3**   Under s 35 of the PCA 2002, when making a confiscation order the Crown Court *must* fix a term of imprisonment in default of payment of all or part of the amount

---

1   Section 34.
2   Section 139(4) of the PCC(S)A 2000.

ordered to be paid. The maximum period of imprisonment depends upon the amount of the confiscation order, and is set out in the table at s 139(4) of the PCC(S)A 2000. The period over which the confiscation order can be paid is determined *only* by s 11 of the PCA 2002. Where the Director is not involved, the question of default will be determined by the magistrates' court, as if the confiscation order were a fine. However:

(a)  there is no power for the magistrates to dispense with immediate payment, by allowing time for payment or payment by instalments, under s 75 of the Magistrates' Courts Act 1980;[1]

(b)  s 81 of the 1980 Act, which modifies the enforcement of fines for young offenders, does not apply;[2]

(c)  there is no power to remit a fine because of a change in circumstances, under s 85 of the 1980 Act;[3]

(d)  there is no requirement to consider a defendant's means under s 87 of the 1980 Act.[4]

## PART PAYMENT

**6.4**  Section 79(2) of the Magistrates' Courts Act 1980 allows magistrates to make a proportionate reduction in the period of imprisonment in default if, after a period of imprisonment has been imposed, the defendant pays[5] part of the sum. This provision applies to sentences of imprisonment in default of confiscation order payments.[6] Section 79(2) reads:

> 'Where, after a period of imprisonment ... has been imposed in default of payment ... payment is made ... of part of the sum, the period of detention shall be reduced.'

## ENFORCEMENT BY THE DIRECTOR

**6.5**  If the Director is appointed as the enforcement authority, enforcement of the confiscation order by way of imprisonment for default takes place in the Crown Court. If a confiscation order has not been satisfied because of the defendant's 'wilful refusal or culpable neglect' and the Director has done 'all that is practicable' to enforce the order, the defendant can be brought back to the Crown Court and imprisoned in default of payment.[7] The term of imprisonment must be reduced proportionately for any amounts already paid. After a defendant has been committed to prison, he can secure his release or a reduction of the period (in relation to the default imprisonment) by paying the amount remaining or a portion of it.

---

1    Section 38.
2    Section 35(3)(a).
3    Section 35(3)(b).
4    Section 35(3)(c).
5    In accordance with r 55 of the Magistrates' Courts Rules 1981, SI 1981/552.
6    Section 140(3) of the PCC(S)A 2000.
7    Section 37.

# ENFORCEMENT WHERE A CONFISCATION ORDER IS VARIED

**6.6**  A confiscation order can be reconsidered and varied[1] such that the maximum period of imprisonment in default is reduced or increased because the amount falls within a different band in the table of maximum sentences. If the effect is to reduce the maximum below the default period of imprisonment originally set, the court *must* reduce that period of imprisonment accordingly.[2] Alternatively, if the effect is to increase the maximum period, the court *may*, on the application of the prosecutor or Director, increase the default period accordingly.[3]

# ENFORCEMENT RECEIVERS

**6.7**  A central purpose behind the PCA 2002 is the effective enforcement of confiscation orders by the appointment of a receiver with substantial powers ultimately to sell the defendant's realisable property. This was available under pre-existing legislation, but the process was complicated and used infrequently. The appointment of receivers will now take place in the Crown Court, which will have wide-ranging powers to authorise the receiver to deal with the defendant's assets and ultimately realise them. This is a substantial development, and both Crown Court judges and practitioners will need to familiarise themselves with concepts usually encountered in the county court and High Court.

**6.8**  A fundamental proposition of the Act is that a defendant who serves a period of imprisonment in default does not extinguish the confiscation order. The order continues 'to have effect so far as any other method of enforcement is concerned'.[4] Continued enforcement of a confiscation order will ordinarily take place by the appointment of an enforcement receiver. If a confiscation order is not satisfied, the court *may* appoint a receiver on an application by the prosecutor.[5] If, however, the Director is the enforcement authority, the Crown Court *must* appoint a receiver, on the Director's application, unless the confiscation order is satisfied.[6]

**6.9**  The powers that can, when ordered, be exercised by the receiver are the same whether he is appointed on application by the prosecutor or the Director.[7] They are wide-ranging and broadly the same as the powers available to a management receiver appointed in relation to a restraint order (see para **2.16**). The powers must be exercised, however:[8]

(a)  with a view to the value for the time being of realisable property being made available (by the property's realisation) for satisfying any confiscation order; and

---

1  Under ss 21, 22, 23, 29, 30, 32 or 33.
2  Section 39(1) and (2).
3  Section 39(5).
4  Section 38(5).
5  Section 50.
6  Section 52.
7  Sections 51, 53.
8  Section 69.

(b)   without taking account of any obligation of the defendant or a recipient of a tainted gift, if the obligation conflicts with the object of satisfying the confiscation order; and

(c)   with a view to securing that there is no diminution in the property's value; and

(d)   with a view to allowing innocent parties to retain or recover the value of interest held by them; and

(e)   with a view to recovering only the value of a tainted gift from its recipient.

**6.10**   The PCA 2002 provides rules about the order in which payments are to be made out of the proceeds of property which has been realised. Sums held by enforcement receivers are dealt with at s 54, while sums held by Director's receivers are dealt with at s 56. The rules are essentially the same. Payments must be made in the following order:

(a)   payment of the expenses incurred by the receiver;

(b)   payments which the Crown Court has directed must be made (eg compensation orders);

(c)   payments to satisfy the confiscation order;

(d)   if there is anything left, the receiver must return to the Crown Court for directions on making payments to such persons who held interests in the property concerned. There is no guidance about the principles that should be applied when the Court gives such directions other than that any person with such an interest must be given an opportunity to be heard.

## RESTRICTIONS

**6.11**   A number of restrictions apply after an enforcement receiver has been appointed in order to protect the interests of the owners of the property. No distress can be levied against realisable property without leave being sought. If the order applies 'to a tenancy of any premises', leave must be sought by a landlord seeking to enforce a peaceable right of forfeiture because the tenant has failed to comply with the tenancy agreement. Furthermore, the Act provides other courts with the power to stay other proceedings in relation to property over which an enforcement receiver has been appointed.[1]

## APPLICATION OF SEIZED MONEY WHERE NO RECEIVER APPOINTED

**6.12**   After a confiscation order has been made, money may be seized by the prosecutor and then placed in a bank account, or frozen in a bank account under a restraint order. In simple cases, a receiver may not have been appointed by the Crown Court. Where this is the case, it is the magistrates' court that must distribute the money-making payments in the order set out in s 55 of the PCA 2002. The PCA 2002 gives the enforcing magistrates' court the power to order the relevant bank or building

---

1   Sections 55 and 60 (although the applicant and receiver must be given an opportunity to make representations).

society to pay the money over to satisfy the confiscation order.[1] Before the magistrates can make such an order, the following conditions must have been met:

(a) money held in an account has been frozen by a restraint order, or seized and held in an account maintained by police or customs; and

(b) a restraint order applies; and

(c) a confiscation order has been made but not satisfied (and the period for doing so has expired); and

(d) neither the Director nor a receiver has been appointed to enforce the confiscation order.[2]

The failure of a bank or building society to comply with such an order is a summary criminal offence, punishable summarily by a fine.[3]

## ENFORCEMENT ABROAD; REQUESTS FOR ASSISTANCE

6.13 The PCA 2002 makes provision to both prevent the disposal of assets held abroad and secure their realisation.[4] Before any steps can be taken, there must either be a confiscation order in place, or the existence of the s 40 conditions for making a restraint order. If the prosecutor believes that realisable property is situated outside the United Kingdom, he may send a request for assistance to the Secretary of State who, if appropriate, will forward the request to the government of the relevant country. The effect of such a request will depend upon the co-operation of that government. The request may be that any person is prohibited from dealing with realisable property, or that such property is realised and the proceeds applied in accordance with the country's domestic laws. A certificate from that country, detailing the realisation of such assets, is admissible in evidence of the facts stated in confiscation proceedings.

---

1    Section 67(5).
2    Section 67(2)–(4).
3    Section 68(6).
4    Section 74.

# Chapter 7

# RECONSIDERATION, VARIATION, DISCHARGE AND APPEAL

## THE PROSECUTION'S OPTIONS

### No confiscation proceedings

**7.1**   If, within 6 years of the date of a defendant's conviction in respect of which there could have been confiscation proceedings in the Crown Court, new evidence emerges which was not available to the prosecutor on 'the relevant date', he or the Director of the Asset Recovery Agency (ARA) may ask the court to consider whether, after examining the new evidence, it is appropriate to conduct confiscation proceedings after all. Where the court does consider this to be appropriate, confiscation proceedings must be started.[1] Reference should be made to Chapters 3 and 4 with the following modifications.

**7.2**   The relevant date is either the date on which a decision was made not to conduct confiscation proceedings, or, if no such decision was made, the date of conviction.[2]

**7.3**   Such 'after the event' proceedings are conducted in the same way as they would have been shortly after conviction, except that:

(a)   in deciding whether the defendant has benefited, the court must take account not only of conduct occurring and property obtained before the relevant date, but also any property obtained on or after the relevant date if it was obtained as a result of, or in connection with, conduct occurring before that date;[3]

(b)   the first and second statutory assumptions do not apply to property first held by the defendant on or after the relevant date;[4]

(c)   the third statutory assumption does not apply to expenditure incurred by the defendant on or after the relevant date;[5]

(d)   the fourth statutory assumption does not apply to property assumed to have been obtained on or after the relevant date;[6]

(e)   the 'recoverable amount' cannot exceed the amount which would have been arrived at in proceedings shortly after conviction, but may be such lesser sum as the court believes is just. This 'just amount' must take into account the 'benefit from the conduct concerned', any fine imposed in respect of the offence and any order for compensation, forfeiture or deprivation.[7]

---

1   Section 19(1), (2).
2   Section 19(9).
3   Section 19(4).
4   Section 19(5)(a).
5   Section 19(5)(b).
6   Section 19(5)(c).
7   Section 19(6), (7).

**7.4**   Where (as will almost invariably be the case) the defendant has been sentenced in respect of the relevant conviction then the defendant must be treated as if his particular criminal conduct included any offences taken into consideration when his original sentence was decided.[1]

## Confiscation proceedings but no order made

**7.5**   Where the court has decided in the course of confiscation proceedings that the defendant has not benefited from general criminal conduct or particular criminal conduct, that decision may be reconsidered.[2] If the original confiscation proceedings took place at the request of the Director, the conditions for such a reconsideration are that:

(a)   the Director now has evidence which was not available to him at the time of the court's decision;

(b)   the Director has applied for a reconsideration within 6 years of the date of conviction;

(c)   the court concludes that the original decision would have been different in the light of the new evidence.[3]

**7.6**   If the original confiscation proceedings took place at the request of the prosecutor, the conditions for such a reconsideration are that:

(a)   there is now evidence which was not available to the prosecutor at the time of the court's decision;

(b)   the prosecutor or Director has applied for a reconsideration within 6 years of the date of conviction;

(c)   the court concludes that the original decision would have been different in the light of the new evidence.[4]

**7.7**   The reconsideration proceedings are conducted in the same way as the original decision,[5] except that:

(a)   in deciding whether the defendant has benefited, the court must take account not only of conduct occurring and property obtained before the date of the original decision, but also any property obtained on or after the date of the original decision if it was obtained as a result of, or in connection with, conduct occurring before that date.[6]

(b)   the first and second statutory assumptions do not apply to property first held by the defendant on or after the date of the original decision;

(c)   the third statutory assumption does not apply to expenditure incurred by the defendant on or after the date of the original decision;

(d)   the fourth statutory assumption does not apply to property assumed to have been obtained on or after the date of the original decision;[7]

---

1    Sections 19(3), 76(3).
2    Section 20(2), (5).
3    Section 20(3).
4    Section 20(4).
5    See Chapters 3 and 4.
6    Section 20(8).
7    Section 20(9).

(e)  the recoverable amount cannot exceed the amount which would have been arrived at in proceedings shortly after conviction, but may be such lesser sum as the court believes is just. This just amount must take into account the 'benefit from the conduct concerned', any fine imposed in respect of the offence and any order for compensation, forfeiture or deprivation.[1]

**7.8**  Where (as will almost invariably be the case) the defendant has been sentenced in respect of the relevant conviction, the defendant must be treated as if his particular criminal conduct included any offences taken into consideration when his original sentence was decided.[2]

## Order made fixed too low

**7.9**  Where, after a confiscation order has been made, the Director or the prosecutor comes into possession of information which was not available to either of them when the defendant's benefit was calculated, and which would have affected that calculation, either the prosecutor or the Director may apply to the court to consider the evidence. If the evidence persuades the court that it is appropriate, it must make a new calculation. Applications must be made by the Director or prosecutor within 6 years of the date of conviction. The new calculation is conducted in the same way as the original calculation,[3] except that:

(a)  in making the new calculation, the court must take account not only of conduct occurring and property obtained before the date of the original calculation, but also any property obtained on or after the date of the original calculation if it was obtained as a result of, or in connection with, conduct occurring before that date;[4]

(b)  the original confiscation order must be ignored;[5]

(c)  the first and second statutory assumptions do not apply to property first held by the defendant on or after the date of the original calculation;

(d)  the third statutory assumption does not apply to expenditure incurred by the defendant on or after the date of the original calculation;

(e)  the fourth statutory assumption does not apply to property assumed to have been obtained on or after the date of the original calculation;[6]

(f)  if the amount produced by the new calculation exceeds the amount previously found as the defendant's benefit the court may vary the amount required to be paid and substitute such amount as it believes to be just. This 'just amount' must take into account any fine imposed in respect of the offence and any order for compensation, forfeiture or deprivation.[7]

**7.10**  Where (as will almost invariably be the case) the defendant has been sentenced in respect of the relevant conviction, the defendant must be treated as if his particular

---

1    Section 20(10).
2    Section 20(7).
3    See Chapters 3 and 4.
4    Section 21(4).
5    Section 21(5).
6    Section 21(6).
7    Section 21(7), (8), (9).

criminal conduct included any offences taken into consideration when his original sentence was decided.[1]

## Appeal to the Court of Appeal by the prosecutor or Director

**7.11**   The prosecutor or Director can appeal against the court's refusal to make a confiscation order. They can also appeal in respect of any order the court does make. Appeals are to the Court of Appeal, which may confirm, quash or vary any order made. Where the Court of Appeal upholds an appeal against the Crown Court's refusal to make an order, it may either hold confiscation proceedings itself or direct the Crown Court to do so.[2] Procedure on appeal to the Court of Appeal is dealt with at s 89 of the PCA 2002.

**7.12**   Where the Court of Appeal varies a confiscation order, or holds confiscation proceedings itself, or where the Crown Court does so on the direction of the Court of Appeal, regard must be had to any fine imposed in respect of the offence, and any order for compensation, forfeiture or deprivation.[3]

**7.13**   In holding the proceedings, the court must take account not only of conduct occurring and property obtained before the date on which the Crown Court originally decided not to make a confiscation order, but also any property obtained on or after that date if it was obtained as a result of, or in connection with, conduct occurring before that date.[4]

**7.14**   The first and second statutory assumptions do not apply to property first held by the defendant on or after the date of the original decision. The third statutory assumption does not apply to expenditure incurred by the defendant on or after the date of the original decision. The fourth statutory assumption does not apply to property assumed to have been obtained on or after the date of the original decision.[5]

## Appeal to the House of Lords

**7.15**   Parties may appeal against the decision of the Court of Appeal to the House of Lords.[6] The House of Lords may confirm, quash or vary any order which results from the Court of Appeal's decision.[7] Procedure on appeal to the House of Lords is dealt with at s 90 of the PCA 2002.

**7.16**   Where the House of Lords finds that the Crown Court's refusal to make a confiscation order was wrong, or that Court of Appeal was wrong to quash such an order, it may direct the Crown Court to hold confiscation proceedings. Where the House of Lords varies a confiscation order or where the Crown Court holds confiscation proceedings on the direction of the Court of Appeal, regard must be had to

1    Sections 21(3), 76(3).
2    Sections 31, 32.
3    Section 32(4), (7).
4    Section 32(8).
5    Section 32(9).
6    Section 33(1), (2).
7    Section 33(3).

any fine imposed in respect of the offence and any order for compensation, forfeiture or deprivation.[1]

**7.17** In holding the proceedings, the court must take account not only of conduct occurring and property obtained before the date on which the Crown Court originally made the order (or decided not to make a confiscation order, as the case may be), but also any property obtained on or after that date if it was obtained as a result of, or in connection with, conduct occurring before that date.[2]

**7.18** The first and second statutory assumptions do not apply to property first held by the defendant on or after the date of the original decision. The third statutory assumption does not apply to expenditure incurred by the defendant on or after the date of the original decision. The fourth statutory assumption does not apply to property assumed to have been obtained on or after the date of the original decision.[3]

# THE DEFENCE'S OPTIONS

## Insufficient funds to pay the confiscation order

**7.19** Where the defendant (or an enforcement receiver appointed by the court) believes that the currently 'available amount' (ie the value of the defendant's free property and tainted goods) is inadequate for the payment of any amount remaining under the confiscation order, an application may be made to vary the order.[4]

**7.20** Where an application is made, the court must calculate the currently available amount and, where it finds that it is inadequate, may vary the order by substituting for the amount remaining to be paid any smaller sum which it believes is just.[5]

**7.21** The court may disregard any inadequacy which it believes is wholly or partly attributable to anything done by the defendant to preserve property held by the recipient of a tainted gift from realisation under the confiscation order.[6] Where the amount remaining under the confiscation order is less than £1000 and the available amount is inadequate because of a fluctuation in the exchange rate (or any other reason specified in a statutory instrument), the magistrates' court clerk may apply to the Crown Court for the order to be discharged.[7]

## Small amounts outstanding

**7.22** Where the amount remaining under the confiscation order is £50 or less the magistrates' court clerk may apply to the Crown Court for the order to be discharged.[8]

---

1   Section 33(6)–(9).
2   Section 33(10).
3   Section 33(11).
4   Section 23(1).
5   Section 23(2), (3).
6   Section 23(5).
7   Section 24.
8   Section 25.

## Variation of order made while defendant was an absconder

**7.23** A confiscation order can be made in the defendant's absence if he has absconded from the proceedings before his conviction or acquittal.[1] Where this has happened, and the defendant later ceases to be an absconder, the court has power to reconsider or even discharge the order.[2]

**7.24** Where the defendant, after ceasing to be an absconder, is tried and acquitted on all counts then, on his application, the court must discharge the order.[3]

**7.25** Where, after the defendant has ceased to be an absconder, the prosecutor does not intend to proceed, or there is an undue delay in continuing the proceedings, the defendant can apply for the order to be discharged and the court may discharge the order.[4]

**7.26** Where the defendant, after ceasing to be an absconder, is convicted, he may apply, within 28 days of the date of conviction, for a reconsideration of the confiscation order if he believes it was too large an amount.[5]

**7.27** The court must consider the evidence put forward by the defendant in support of the application and, if it concludes that the defendant's belief is well founded, must decide what amount should have been required to be paid under the confiscation order, and substitute for the amount in the order such amount as it believes is just.[6]

**7.28** No order is to be made under s 29 while it is possible that proceedings might still be taken in respect of any other offence from which the defendant has absconded.[7]

## Appeal to the Court of Appeal

**7.29** The legislation does not provide the defendant with any new statutory right of appeal against a confiscation order made by the Crown Court. Equally, it does not remove or detract from the defendant's existing right of appeal under ss 9 and 50 of the Criminal Appeal Act 1968, the combined effect of which is to create a right of appeal against any Crown Court sentence and to include a confiscation order within the definition of a 'sentence'. Section 50 is amended appropriately by virtue of para 4 of Sch 11 to the PCA 2002. Defendants will continue to be able to appeal to the Court of Appeal in this way. Procedure on appeal to the Court of Appeal is dealt with at s 89 of the PCA 2002.

## Appeal to the House of Lords

**7.30** By s 33 of the PCA 2002, parties to an appeal to the Court of Appeal may appeal against the decision of that court to the House of Lords. The considerations for such an appeal are set out at **7.15**. Procedure on appeal to the House of Lords is dealt with at s 90 of the PCA 2002.

---

1  Section 28.
2  Section 28(1).
3  Section 30(1), (2).
4  Section 30(3), (4).
5  Section 29(1), (3).
6  Section 29(2).
7  Section 29(4).

## Compensation

**7.31** Section 72 of the PCA 2002 gives the Crown Court a limited discretion to pay compensation to those who have suffered unjust loss because of 'serious default' by the prosecutor. Compensation is payable by the body responsible for the default. The conditions that must be met before the discretion arises are as follows:[1]

(a) a criminal investigation has been started with regard to an offence; and
(b) that investigation does not end in a conviction because:
    (i) proceedings are not started, or
    (ii) it does not result in a conviction, or
    (iii) a conviction is later quashed or the offender pardoned;
(c) there has been 'serious default' on the part of the police, the Crown Prosecution Service, the Serious Fraud Office, Customs or the Commissioners of Inland Revenue;
(d) the proceedings would not have been started or continued if the default had not occurred;
(e) the claimant has suffered loss in consequence of anything done in relation to it by or in pursuance of an order under the confiscation part of the PCA 2002.

**7.32** Compensation is then payable only if the court considers it 'just' to do so. The PCA 2002 provides no guidance on the circumstances in which it will be 'just' to refuse to make a compensation payment. The discretion provided by such a general test is obviously intended to be very broad. The courts may adopt a similar approach to the awarding of defence costs, and refuse to do so when the applicant has brought the prosecution on himself.[2]

**7.33** There is no definition of 'serious default'; however, reference to the code of practice may provide some assistance in determining the question. The use of the adjective 'serious' suggests that the courts will construe the test narrowly. It is likely to be more difficult to satisfy than merely showing that the prosecution has not acted with due expedition. The PCA 2002 does not expressly state that the burden of proof is upon the applicant; however, it is likely that the courts will construe the section in that way. The application is compensatory in its nature and the assertor must prove his case. The standard of proof, in the absence of express provision to the contrary, will be on the balance of probabilities.

**7.34** A court may vary[3] or discharge[4] a confiscation order originally made in the defendant's absence. The court may pay compensation, as it believes just, to any person who held realisable property and has suffered loss in consequence of the original order. In such circumstances, compensation is payable by the Lord Chancellor.[5]

---

1    Section 72(2)–(8).
2    See *R v Lord Spens (No 2)* (1992) 142 NLJ 528; *Mooney v Cardiff Magistrates' Court* (2000) 164 JP 220; and *Leutscher v Netherlands* 24 EHRR 181.
3    Section 29.
4    Section 30.
5    Section 73.

# Chapter 8

# MONEY LAUNDERING OFFENCES

## CRIMINAL PROPERTY

**8.1**   The concept of 'criminal property' is central to the way in which the money laundering offences created by ss 327–330 of the PCA 2002 have been expressed. The term 'criminal property' carries within itself the mental element of the offences, so that the sections creating the offences are expressed in very simple terms. In arriving at a definition of criminal property, certain other terms have also to be defined. Reference should be made to s 340 which deals with interpretation. The most important terms are analysed below.

### Property

**8.2**   By virtue of s 340(9), property includes personal property, real property, things in action, other intangible property and, obviously, money.

### Criminal conduct

**8.3**   By virtue of s 340(2), criminal conduct is conduct that is an offence in the UK. Such conduct is still criminal even if it is carried out abroad.

### Benefit

**8.4**   By virtue of s 340(5), (6) and (7), a person benefits from conduct if he obtains property, or a pecuniary advantage, either wholly or partly as a result of or in connection with that conduct.

### Criminal property

**8.5**   By virtue of s 340(3), criminal property is property which:

(a)   either constitutes a person's benefit from criminal conduct, or represents (in whole or part and whether directly or indirectly) a person's benefit from criminal conduct; and

(b)   is known or suspected by the alleged offender to constitute or represent such a benefit.

**8.6**   By virtue of s 340(4), questions of who carried out the conduct or who benefited from it are immaterial to the determination of whether or not property is criminal property. Similarly irrelevant is the question of whether the PCA 2002 was in force at the time the conduct was carried out.

# CONCEALING, DISGUISING, CONVERTING, TRANSFERRING AND REMOVING

**8.7**   Section 327(1) of the PCA 2002 makes it an offence to conceal, disguise, convert or transfer criminal property, or to remove such property from England and Wales. Concealing and disguising include concealing or disguising the nature, source, location, disposition, movement or ownership of any property or any rights with respect to it.[1]

**8.8**   'Converting' is not defined in the PCA 2002. The authors suggest that it must be given its conventional legal meaning, that is to say that the 'convertor' has dealt with the property in a manner inconsistent with the rights of the true owner. It is worth noting that the broad drafting of s 327 (which follows its statutory predecessors) means that almost every case of handling stolen goods and theft will also constitute an offence under this section. This may have important consequences, since a conviction for a single such offence will mean that the defendant is liable to be found to have a 'criminal lifestyle' under s 6(4)(a), and thus to have the statutory assumptions under s 10 made against him.

## *Draft indictment*

### STATEMENT OF OFFENCE

Concealing criminal property, contrary to section 327(1)(a) of the Proceeds of Crime Act 2002.

### PARTICULARS OF OFFENCE

Andrea Burton, between the first day of January 2003 and the thirty-first day of March 2003, concealed £250,000 in cash, which was criminal property in that, as she knew or suspected, it constituted the benefit of her husband, Colin Burton, from criminal conduct, namely the supply of controlled drugs, by causing it to be used for the purchase of a property known as The Farm, Little Snoring, in the county of Shropshire, which property was conveyed into her sole name.

# ACQUISITION USE AND POSSESSION

**8.9**   Section 329(1) makes it an offence to acquire, use or have possession of criminal property.

## *Draft indictment*

### STATEMENT OF OFFENCE

Acquiring criminal property, contrary to section 329(1)(a) of the Proceeds of Crime Act 2002.

---

1   Section 327(3).

PARTICULARS OF OFFENCE

Andrea Burton, between the first day of January 2003 and the thirty-first day of March 2003, acquired a property known as The Farm, Little Snoring, in the county of Shropshire, which was criminal property in that, as she knew or suspected, it represented the benefit of her husband, Colin Burton, from criminal conduct, namely the supply of controlled drugs, by causing it to be conveyed into her sole name.

# ARRANGEMENTS

**8.10**   Section 328(1) makes it an offence to enter into or become concerned in an arrangement which the alleged offender knows or suspects facilitates, in any way, another person acquiring, retaining, using or controlling criminal property. This is a fuller list of activities than that contained in s 327(1), but the section is aimed at those who assist persons who are directly committing s 327 offences. Under the legislation which is replaced by this section,[1] it has been held that converting money into another currency could constitute this offence if it had the necessary 'facilitating' effect, even if this was not the immediate reason for the conversion.[2]

## *Draft indictment*

STATEMENT OF OFFENCE

Becoming concerned in an arrangement, contrary to section 328(1) of the Proceeds of Crime Act 2002.

PARTICULARS OF OFFENCE

David Evans, between the first day of January 2003 and the thirty-first day of March 2003, in the course of his work as a conveyancing solicitor, knowing or suspecting that the arrangement facilitated the acquisition of criminal property by another person, became concerned in an arrangement for the acquisition by Andrea Burton of a property known as The Farm, Little Snoring, in the county of Shropshire, which was criminal property in that it constituted the benefit of Colin Burton from criminal conduct, namely the supply of controlled drugs.

# DEFENCES

## Authorised disclosures

**8.11**   It is a defence to the offences created by ss 327–329[3] for a person to show that he made an authorised disclosure under s 338. That section defines 'authorised disclosures' as disclosures which:

---

1   Drug Trafficking Act 1994, s 59.
2   *R v MacMaster* [1999] 1 Cr App R 402, in which the purpose of the conversion was to purchase drugs rather than to 'launder' money.
3   Under subs (2)(a) of each section.

(a) reveal[1] to a constable, customs officer or a person nominated by the discloser's employer to receive such disclosures;[2]
(b) that property is criminal property; and
(c) are made either:
  (i) before the alleged offender does the prohibited act, or
  (ii) after the prohibited act, providing there is good reason for failing to make disclosure before the act, the disclosure is made on the alleged offender's own initiative and made as soon as is practicable.

**8.12**   Where an authorised disclosure has been made before doing the prohibited act, the alleged offender may still commit the offence if, having made the disclosure, he fails to obtain the appropriate consent.[3] In essence, a person making an authorised disclosure will be treated as having the appropriate consent if he has not heard to the contrary from the person to whom he made it within 7 days. Even if the appropriate consent is refused within this period, the alleged offender may still avail himself of the defence. Refusal to grant consent is not final; it merely imposes a 31-day 'moratorium' on the prohibited acts from the day notice of refusal was received.[4] Once that moratorium period has expired, a person making an authorised disclosure will be treated as having the appropriate consent and able to avail himself of the defence.

## Protected disclosures

**8.13**   In addition to the category of authorised disclosures defined above, s 337 of the Act creates a category of disclosures which are described as 'protected'. These are disclosures made not by a person about to do an act which would otherwise be criminal (as with authorised disclosures), but instead by a person who has come by information, in the course of his work, which causes him to suspect that money laundering is occurring. Where such information is disclosed to an appropriate person[5] as soon as is practicable after its receipt, the disclosure is 'protected', ie it is not to be taken as breaching any restriction, however imposed, on the disclosure of information. It is worth noting that authorised disclosures under s 338 are similarly protected.[6]

## Reasonable excuse

**8.14**   It will be observed that the making of an authorised disclosure can take place after the prohibited act has been performed. This possibility caters for the person who goes to the authorities before he falls under suspicion or is arrested. There remains a defence for an alleged offender who falls under suspicion or is arrested before making

---

1   Section 338(1).
2   Section 338(5). *NB*: nominated officers, who will not be police or customs men, have a further duty of disclosure to the appropriate authorities. Furthermore, nominated officers cannot give appropriate consent unless they, in turn, have received it from the appropriate authorities – s 336. They commit an offence under s 336(5) if they do so.
3   Section 335.
4   Section 335(6).
5   Section 337(4).
6   Section 338(4).

an authorised disclosure, if he can show that he intended to make an authorised disclosure, but has a reasonable excuse for not doing so.[1]

## Law enforcement

**8.15** A person (such as a police officer) who has a law-enforcement 'function' in relation to criminal conduct[2] will have a defence to a charge of money laundering if what he has done is done in the course of carrying out that function.[3]

## Adequate consideration

**8.16** It is a defence for a person accused under s 329 of acquiring, using or possessing criminal property to show that he did so for adequate consideration.[4] Adequate consideration is consideration which is not significantly less than the value of the property or the use or possession of it which is proved against the alleged offender.[5] Where the alleged offender has provided goods or services, knowing or suspecting that this may help another person to carry out criminal conduct, this does not constitute consideration.[6]

## Burden of proof

**8.17** Cases[7] under the legislation which was replaced by ss 331–333 established that where the defendant wishes to raise one of the statutory defences, the onus is on him to do so on the balance of probabilities.

# DISCLOSURE OFFENCES

## Regulated sector

**8.18** Schedule 9 to the PCA 2002 defines those businesses which are in the 'regulated sector'. Detailed reference to Sch 9 may be necessary to establish whether or not a particular business is in the regulated sector. In essence, the regulated sector comprises banking, money lending and investment businesses.

**8.19** Under s 330 of the PCA 2002, an offence is committed by a person who:

(a) knows, suspects or has reasonable grounds for knowing or suspecting that another person is engaged in money laundering; and
(b) came by that knowledge, suspicion or the reasonable grounds in the course of a business in the regulated sector; and

---

1    Sections 327(2)(b), 328(2)(b), 329(2)(b).
2    Defined at s 340(2).
3    Sections 327(2)(c), 328(2)(c), 329(2)(d).
4    Section 329(2)(c).
5    Section 329(3)(a), (b).
6    Section 329(3)(c).
7    See *R v Colle* (1992) 95 Cr App R 67; *R v Butt* [1999] Crim LR 414; *R v Gibson* [2000] Crim LR 479.

(c)  does not disclose, in the approved fashion,[1] his knowledge, suspicion or the reasonable grounds to a nominated officer,[2] as soon as is practicable.

## Draft indictment

### STATEMENT OF OFFENCE

Failing to make a required disclosure, contrary to section 330(1) of the Proceeds of Crime Act 2002.

### PARTICULARS OF OFFENCE

Frederick Graham, between the first day of January 2003 and the thirty-first day of March 2003, in the course of his work as the manager of the Little Snoring branch of Shropshire Bank plc, a business in the regulated sector, had reasonable grounds for knowing or suspecting that Andrea Burton was engaged in money laundering, in that she made unexplained deposits to a total of £50,000 in cash at the said branch during the said period, but failed to disclose the said grounds to a nominated officer or other authorised person.

**8.20**  Under s 331 of the PCA 2002, an offence is committed by a s 330-nominated officer who:

(a)  knows, suspects or has reasonable grounds for knowing or suspecting that another person is engaged in money laundering; and
(b)  came by that knowledge, suspicion or the reasonable grounds in consequence of a s 330 disclosure; and
(c)  does not disclose, in the approved fashion,[3] the knowledge, suspicion or the reasonable grounds to an authorised person,[4] as soon as is practicable.

## Draft indictment

### STATEMENT OF OFFENCE

Failing to make a required disclosure, contrary to section 331(1) of the Proceeds of Crime Act 2002.

### PARTICULARS OF OFFENCE

Harold Ingram, between the first day of January 2003 and the thirty-first day of March 2003, in the course of his work as an officer of Shropshire Bank plc, a business in the regulated sector, received a disclosure from Frederick Graham under section 330 of the Proceeds of Crime Act 2002 which caused him to have reasonable grounds for knowing or suspecting that Andrea Burton was engaged in money laundering, but failed to disclose the said grounds to an authorised person.

---

1    See s 330(9)(b).
2    Defined by s 330(9) as a person nominated by the alleged offender's employer to receive such disclosures.
3    See s 331(5)(b).
4    Section 331(5)(a).

## Relevant guidance

**8.21** In deciding whether an offence has been committed under ss 330 and 331 the court must consider whether the alleged offender has followed any relevant and approved guidance which has been published in a manner so as to bring it to the attention of people likely to be affected by it.[1]

## Non-regulated sector

**8.22** Employers outside the regulated sector of banking, money lending and investment may also appoint nominated officers to receive authorised disclosures, as defined above. These persons will also commit an offence if they fail to pass on disclosures made to them in this capacity. Under s 332 they will commit an offence if they:

(a) know or suspect that another person is engaged in money laundering; and

(b) the information or other matter on which the knowledge or suspicion is based was received in consequence of a disclosure made under ss 337 or 338; and

(c) they do not disclose, in the approved fashion,[2] the knowledge, suspicion or the reasonable grounds to an authorised person,[3] as soon as is practicable.

### *Draft indictment*

#### STATEMENT OF OFFENCE

Failing to make a required disclosure, contrary to section 332(1) of the Proceeds of Crime Act 2002.

#### PARTICULARS OF OFFENCE

Jack King, between the first day of January 2003 and the thirty-first day of March 2003, in the course of his work as a partner in the solicitors firm King and King and being a person nominated to receive disclosures under sections 337 and 338 of the Proceeds of Crime Act 2002, received a disclosure from David Evans under section 338 of the Act which caused him to know or suspect that Andrea Burton was engaged in money laundering, but failed to disclose the said knowledge or suspicion to an authorised person.

## Tipping off

**8.23** Under s 333, any person, whether or not he is a nominated officer, commits the offence of tipping off if:

(a) he knows or suspects that a disclosure falling within ss 337 or 338 has been made; and

---

1   Section 330(8).
2   See s 332(5)(b).
3   Section 332(5)(a).

(b) he makes a disclosure which is likely to prejudice any investigation which might be conducted following such a disclosure.

## *Draft indictment*

### STATEMENT OF OFFENCE

Tipping off, contrary to section 333(1) of the Proceeds of Crime Act 2002.

### PARTICULARS OF OFFENCE

Lorraine Mather, between the first day of January 2003 and the thirty-first day of March 2003, in the course of her work as a secretary at the solicitors firm King and King, came to know or suspect that a disclosure falling within section 338 had been made by David Evans to Jack King and, by informing Andrea Burton of her knowledge or suspicion, made a disclosure likely to prejudice an investigation which might have been conducted.

## DEFENCES

**8.24** It is a defence for a person alleged to have committed an offence under ss 330–332 of the PCA 2002 to show that he had a reasonable excuse for his non-disclosure.[1]

**8.25** In addition, it is a defence for a person alleged to have committed an offence under s 330 to show that either:

(a) he is a professional legal adviser and the information or other matter came to him in privileged circumstances;[2] or

(b) he has not been provided with such training as is specified by the Secretary of State *and* does not know or suspect that that the other person is engaged in money laundering.[3]

**8.26** In relation to an allegation that a person has committed a 'tipping off' offence under s 333, it is a defence[4] for such a person to show that:

(a) he did not know or suspect that the disclosure was likely to be prejudicial to any investigation; or

(b) the disclosure was made in the course of his law-enforcement 'function' in relation to criminal conduct; or

---

1   Sections 330(6)(a), 331(6), 332(6).
2   Information coming to a person in privileged circumstances is defined by s 330(10) as information received either:
    (a) from a client and in connection with giving advice to that client; or
    (b) from a person seeking legal advice; or
    (c) from a person in connection with legal proceedings or contemplated legal proceedings.
    By s 330(11), information is not privileged where it is communicated with the intention of furthering a criminal purpose.
3   Section 330(7).
4   Section 333(2).

(c)  he is a professional legal adviser and the disclosure was to a client in connection with the giving of legal advice, or to any person in connection with legal proceedings or contemplated legal proceedings.

**8.27**  No defence will be available if the disclosure is made with the intention of furthering a criminal purpose.[1]

## PENALTIES

**8.28**  Money laundering offences under ss 327–329 carry a maximum term of imprisonment, on indictment, of 14 years.[2]

**8.29**  Disclosure offences under ss 330–333 carry a maximum term of imprisonment, on indictment, of 5 years.

---

1    Section 337(4).
2    Section 338(1).

# Chapter 9

# INSOLVENCY AND THE
# PROCEEDS OF CRIME ACT 2002

**9.1**  It will not be uncommon to find that confiscation proceedings under the PCA 2002 take place against a background of insolvency proceedings either already under way or in contemplation in relation to the individual or company concerned. Part 9 of the PCA 2002 deals with the relationship between confiscation proceedings and insolvency proceedings.

**9.2**  The relationship between civil proceedings for a recovery order and insolvency proceedings are dealt with in s 311 of the Act. That relationship is considered in Chapters 10 and 11 of this book dealing with civil recovery orders. The only part of this chapter which is relevant to civil recovery proceedings as well as confiscation proceedings is the section concerned with insolvency practitioners (see **9.25**).

## BANKRUPTCY AND CONFISCATION PROCEEDINGS

**9.3**  Property subject to a s 41 restraint order made prior to a bankruptcy order in respect of the owner of the property does not form part of the bankrupt's estate.[1] Once a bankruptcy order is made, however, the court may not make a restraint order in respect of that property.[2]

**9.4**  Where an enforcement receiver is appointed under the Act, the property subject to the receivership is also excluded from the bankrupt's estate but, whereas a restraint order excludes property from the bankrupt's estate only where the restraint order was made prior to the bankruptcy order, an order appointing a receiver under either s 50 or 52 appears to exclude the property from the bankruptcy even if that order is made after the bankruptcy order.[3] This apparent freedom to make such an appointment of a receiver is qualified by s 418 which prevents the court using its powers under ss 41–67 of the Act in respect of property which is comprised in the bankrupt's estate. There is circularity here, which is discussed further below (see **9.7–9.9**).

**9.5**  Where an interim receiver has been appointed under s 286 of the Insolvency Act 1986 in respect of the assets of a debtor, and any of the debtor's property is made subject to a restraint order, the interim receiver under the Insolvency Act 1986 loses his powers over that property so long as the restraint order applies.[4]

**9.6**  In the event of a bankruptcy order being made in respect of a person, the Crown Court may not subsequently use the powers contained in ss 41–67 of the PCA 2002,

---

1   Section 417(2)(a).
2   Section 418.
3   Section 417(2)(b).
4   Section 417(4).

and a receiver appointed under ss 48, 50 or 52 may not use any of his powers in respect of any of the following:[1]

(a) property comprised in the bankrupt's estate for the purposes of Part 9 of the Insolvency Act 1986 (which excludes property made subject to a receiving order made pursuant to ss 50 or 52 of the PCA 2002[2]);

(b) after-acquired property in respect of which the trustee in bankruptcy may, without leave of the court, serve a notice under ss 307, 308 or 308A of the Insolvency Act 1986;

(c) property to be applied for the benefit of creditors of the bankrupt by virtue of a condition imposed under s 280(2)(c) of the Insolvency Act 1986;

(d) any sums remaining in the hands of the receiver following the making and full satisfaction of a confiscation order.

**9.7** The effect of this provision is that once a bankruptcy order is made, the court's ability to use its powers under ss 41–67 is excluded from the property categorised as part of the bankruptcy process. The powers of a receiver appointed in confiscation proceedings are similarly limited: he may not deal with the property subject to the bankruptcy. It is important to note, however, that where a receiver is appointed under ss 50 or 52 of the PCA 2002 (but not where a receiver is appointed under s 48, ie to give effect to a restraint order) the property subject to his receivership is excluded from the bankrupt's estate, even though the receiver may have been appointed after the bankruptcy order, and so the court's and receiver's powers are not limited in respect of that property.

**9.8** These provisions create a confusing circularity in that although s 417(2)(b) excludes property subject to a receiving order made under ss 50 or 52 from the bankrupt's estate whenever the receiving order was made, s 418 prohibits the court from using its power to appoint a receiver under ss 50 or 52 where a bankruptcy order has already been made. By reason of the bankruptcy order the court may not make one of the receiving orders which would cause the property to cease to be comprised in the bankrupt's estate. The property, therefore, remains comprised in the bankrupt's estate and, therefore, prevents the court making a receiving order. This circularity means that despite the appearance given by s 417(2) that restraint orders take priority over a bankruptcy order only where the former is made before the latter, while receiving orders made under ss 50 or 52 take priority over the bankruptcy whenever made, this is not the true effect of the PCA 2002.

**9.9** The effect of the provisions as drafted appears to be that where a bankruptcy order is made first, it takes priority over all the confiscation powers, whereas where a restraint or receiving order is made first, it will take priority over the bankruptcy. It is not clear whether this was the draftsman's intention. If it was his intention, the provisions have been drafted in a particularly cumbersome fashion. If there was some other intention, it is not clearly apparent from the sections. The general policy of the PCA 2002 is that an individual should not be allowed to use the fruits of criminal conduct to meet his liabilities. On that basis, one would expect the enforcement of confiscation orders to take priority over bankruptcy. The PCA 2002 only goes so far as

---

1    Section 418.
2    Section 417(2)(b) and **9.4**.

to give the confiscation powers priority where they are used first. Where a bankruptcy order is made first, the bankruptcy regime will have priority.

**9.10** There is a general requirement that the Insolvency Act 1986 may not be used to restrict the use of the powers conferred on the court and receiver by ss 41–67 of the PCA 2002, other than in so far as these provisions restrict the use of those powers.[1]

**9.11** Special provisions are made for cases where a bankruptcy order or receiving order was made on a petition presented before 29 December 1986, when the Insolvency Act 1986 came into force.[2]

**9.12** These provisions have no effect where an interim receiving order is made pursuant to s 246 in High Court civil recovery proceedings. The relationship between such orders dealing with recoverable property and insolvency are dealt with by s 311 of the PCA 2002.[3]

## TAINTED GIFTS AND BANKRUPTCY

**9.13** The court's powers under ss 339, 340 and 423 of the Insolvency Act 1986 to set aside certain transactions in insolvency proceedings are limited where the property concerned is a tainted gift made by the bankrupt.[4] Tainted gifts bear the meaning used in Part 2 of the PCA 2002.[5] The court may not make an order avoiding a transaction using the powers under the Insolvency Act 1986 where:[6]

(a) any property of the recipient of the tainted gift is subject to a restraint order under s 41; or

(b) there is in force in respect of such property a receiving order under ss 50 or 52.

**9.14** The principle is plainly that tainted gifts, being the proceeds of criminal conduct, should, where possible, be dealt with within the confiscation procedure. Where, after the discharge of a restraint order or receiving order under ss 50 or 52, the court is asked to make an avoidance order under the Insolvency Act 1986, it must take into account the extent to which any property has already been realised against the recipient of the tainted gift.[7] It would plainly be unfair to recover the sum from the recipient twice over, once in confiscation proceedings and again in insolvency proceedings.

---

1 Section 418(4).
2 Section 418(5).
3 See Chapter 11 at **11.139–11.141**.
4 Section 419. These rules also apply to the equivalent powers in the Bankruptcy Act 1914, which preceded the Insolvency Act 1986 – s 419(5).
5 Section 77. See **4.15** *et seq.*
6 Section 419(2).
7 Section 419(3).

# WINDING-UP OF COMPANIES AND CONFISCATION PROCEEDINGS

**9.15**   The provisions concerned with the winding-up of companies and confiscation proceedings are similar, but not identical, to the provisions concerned with bankruptcy. If a company passes a resolution for its voluntary winding-up, or the court makes a winding-up order, the liquidator may not exercise his functions in respect of:[1]

(a)   any property for the time being subject to a restraint order made under s 41 before the 'relevant time'; or

(b)   any property in respect of which a receiving order under ss 50 or 52 is in force.

**9.16**   The 'relevant time' for this purpose means:

(a)   where no order for winding-up has been made but the company has passed a resolution for voluntary winding-up, the time of the passing of the resolution;

(b)   where an order for winding-up has been made but it was based on a resolution for voluntary winding-up, the time of the passing of the resolution;

(c)   if an order has been made, but there has been no resolution for a voluntary winding-up, the time of the making of the order.

**9.17**   Where a resolution for voluntary winding-up or an order for winding-up has already been made, the powers of the court under ss 41–67 and of any receiver appointed under ss 48, 50 or 52 are restricted. Whereas in the context of bankruptcy there is an absolute prohibition on the use of those powers, the restriction in the context of winding-up is limited to not exercising the powers:[2]

(a)   so as to inhibit the liquidator from exercising his functions for the purpose of distributing property to the company's creditors; or

(b)   so as to prevent the payment out of any property or expenses (including the liquidator's expenses) properly incurred in respect of the property.

**9.18**   The provisions are adapted to deal with cases where the winding-up commenced prior to the commencement of the Insolvency Act 1986.[3]

# TAINTED GIFTS AND WINDING-UP

**9.19**   As with bankruptcy orders, where a company is the subject of a winding-up order or a resolution for voluntary winding-up and it has made a tainted gift, the court may not make an avoidance order under ss 238, 239 or 423 of the Insolvency Act 1986 or a decree under ss 242 or 243 of that Act in respect of the gift at any time when:

(a)   any property of the recipient of the tainted gift is subject to a restraint order under s 41; or

(b)   there is in force in respect of such property a receiving order under ss 50 or 52.

---

1     Section 426(1).
2     Section 426(6).
3     Section 426(9).

**9.20**   The principle is to ensure that tainted gifts, which, by definition, represent the proceeds of crime, are dealt with within the confiscation regime rather than the insolvency regime. Once the restraint or receiving order is discharged the court may make an avoidance order in the insolvency proceedings but, in doing so, it must take into account any realisation under a confiscation order of property held by the recipient of the tainted gift so as to prevent double recovery.[1]

## FLOATING CHARGES

**9.21**   Where a creditor holds a floating charge over a company's assets he will usually have the power to appoint a receiver out of court to take control of the assets subject to the charge. The receiver's powers are not exercisable in respect of property which is subject to a restraint order under s 41 prior to the appointment of the receiver, or where a receiver has been appointed in respect of the property under ss 50 or 52.[2]

**9.22**   Where a receiver has been appointed by a creditor pursuant to a floating charge the court's powers to make orders under ss 41–67 and the receiver's powers under ss 48, 50 or 52 are not to be exercised:[3]

(a)   so as to inhibit the receiver from exercising his functions for the purpose of distributing property to the company's creditors; or

(b)   so as to prevent the payment out of any property or expenses (including the receiver's remuneration) properly incurred in the exercise of his functions in respect of the property.

**9.23**   Apart from these provisions, however, the provisions in the Insolvency Act 1986 may not be used to restrict the powers under ss 41–67.

## LIMITED LIABILITY PARTNERSHIPS

**9.24**   The provisions as to the winding-up of companies, tainted gifts and winding-up, and floating charges, also apply to limited liability partnerships capable of being wound-up under the Insolvency Act 1986 as if they were companies for the purposes of the PCA 2002.[4]

## INSOLVENCY PRACTITIONERS

**9.25**   It is likely that cases will arise where an insolvency practitioner[5] involved in taking control of the property of an individual during bankruptcy proceedings, or of a company during winding-up proceedings, may deal inadvertently with property already subject to a restraint order in confiscation proceedings, or an interim receiving

---

1   Section 427(4).
2   Section 430(2).
3   Section 430(6).
4   Section 431.
5   Defined at s 433.

order in civil proceedings for a recovery order. The PCA 2002 provides insolvency practitioners with a defence to any proceedings brought against them for 'meddling' with assets subject to such order so long as the practitioner has reasonable grounds to believe that he is entitled to seize or dispose of the property[1] and has not been negligent.[2]

**9.26** Further provisions also provide for the insolvency practitioner's remuneration from the property he dealt with inadvertently, which include his right to a lien over the property.[3]

# AMENDMENTS TO THE INSOLVENCY ACT 1986

**9.27** Amendments are made to the Insolvency Act 1986 under Sch 11 to the PCA 2002. The most significant amendment is the introduction of new ss 306A, 306B and 306C to the 1986 Act. Between them, these sections ensure that where property which has been excluded from a bankrupt's estate by the provisions of the PCA 2002 ceases to be subject to confiscation proceedings,[4] it vests in the trustee in bankruptcy as part of the bankrupt's estate. Without these provisions, the property would return to the bankrupt because the existing provisions under the Insolvency Act 1986 only automatically vest property in the trustee in bankruptcy upon the making of the bankruptcy order.

---

1     Section 432(1).
2     Section 432(2).
3     Section 432(3)–(10).
4     Either because a restraint order or receivership is discharged, a surplus remains after a confiscation order is satisfied in full, or a confiscation order is discharged or quashed.

# PART 2
# CIVIL PROCEEDINGS

# Chapter 10

# CIVIL RECOVERY OF THE PROCEEDS OF UNLAWFUL CONDUCT AND OF CASH INTENDED FOR USE IN UNLAWFUL CONDUCT

## OVERVIEW

**10.1** Part 5 of the PCA 2002 contains innovative provisions for the recovery of proceeds of crime, regardless of whether a conviction for any offence has been obtained or intends to be obtained. The powers created by Part 5 are intended to be draconian, and that aim appears to have been achieved by the draftsman of the PCA 2002. The new powers are intended to be flexible enough to allow the recovery of proceeds of crime, and of property which represents such proceeds, even where sophisticated attempts have been made to put the assets beyond the reach of the authorities.

**10.2** There are two distinct civil recovery regimes created by Part 5 of the PCA 2002, although both use common terminology and principles. The two regimes are:

(a) civil recovery in the High Court of property which is, or which represents, property obtained through unlawful conduct; and
(b) forfeiture within civil proceedings in a magistrates' court of cash which is, or which represents, property obtained through unlawful conduct, or which is intended to be used in unlawful conduct.

**10.3** The procedure for forfeiture of cash is not entirely new. It is largely based on the powers to seize and forfeit cash representing the proceeds of, or intended for use in, drug trafficking, which are set out in ss 42–48 of the Drug Trafficking Act 1994. These proceedings are to be brought by police constables or customs officers. The Director of the Asset Recovery Agency (ARA) is given no power to bring these proceedings in the magistrates' courts. The new powers are wider than the existing powers and permit searches for cash and its seizure. Such searches are to be without warrant, but will in most cases require the 'prior approval' of a justice of the peace or a senior police or customs officer.

**10.4** The Act also provides entirely new powers for the Director of the ARA to apply to the High Court for an order to recover property which was obtained as a result of criminal activity. The Director is known as the 'enforcement authority' for the purposes of these provisions. These powers will be exercisable whether or not criminal proceedings have been brought in respect of the same criminal activity, and regardless of the outcome of any such proceedings.[1] Indeed, these powers can be used even if a confiscation order has already been made against the criminal, although there are rules to avoid double recovery of the proceeds of the same criminal conduct. Where the property which is sought to be recovered is solely in the form of cash, as defined by the

---

1    Section 240(2).

PCA 2002,[1] the High Court procedure may not be used and magistrates' court proceedings must be brought by the police or customs officers, as appropriate.

**10.5**    The definitions of 'recoverable property' and 'unlawful conduct' are the same for both the High Court and summary procedures contained within Part 5. This chapter deals with those terms before their application within the two different procedures considered in Chapters 11 and 12.


# UNLAWFUL CONDUCT

**10.6**    For property to be recoverable property within the meaning of Part 5 of the PCA 2002 it must have been obtained through unlawful conduct. Unlawful conduct is defined by reference to criminal law. Unlawful conduct is, in reality, criminal conduct. Conduct is unlawful if:

(a)    it occurs in any part of the United Kingdom and is unlawful under the criminal law of that part; or

(b)    it occurs in a country outside the United Kingdom and is unlawful under the criminal law of that country and it would be unlawful under the criminal law of any part of the United Kingdom if it occurred in that part.[2]

**10.7**    Determining the criminal law of England and Wales should not be difficult for the High Court. Determining the criminal law in another country or in another part of the United Kingdom will be more difficult. It is clear that the law of a foreign country falls to be determined as a matter of fact to be determined by the judge on the basis of evidence.[3] Save in limited circumstances where the court may take judicial notice of foreign law, rely on earlier determinations as to that law by an English court,[4] accept in evidence the Acts, ordinances or statutes of any British possession,[5] or refer the question to a foreign court within the Commonwealth,[6] its findings will be based on evidence of experts in the law of that jurisdiction. Such evidence is unlikely to be contested in many cases, although there may be situations where there is doubt as to the applicable law. It would appear that the law of Scotland and Northern Ireland for these purposes should also be regarded as foreign law outside the knowledge of the court save in so far as it is proved by evidence. It is likely that in most cases in the High Court, the court will direct that expert evidence on questions of foreign law be given by a single joint expert.[7] Although the Civil Procedure Rules 1998 (CPR 1998), SI 1998/3132 do not apply in the magistrates' court, where questions of foreign law arise there it seems likely that the court will also urge the use of a single joint expert, although it is unclear to what extent the court will be able to compel the parties to use a joint expert.

---

1    Section 289(6).
2    Section 241.
3    Administration of Justice Act 1920, s 15.
4    See *Cross & Tapper on Evidence* (Butterworths), Ch XIX, s 1.
5    Pursuant to the Evidence (Colonial Statutes) Act 1907 and the Colonial Laws Validity Act 1865, s 6. See also the Evidence (Foreign, Dominion and Colonial Documents) Act 1933.
6    Pursuant to the British Law Ascertainment Act 1859.
7    See CPR 1998, r 35.7.

**10.8**    The drafting of s 241 is in the present tense: 'conduct . . . *is* unlawful conduct if it *is* unlawful under the criminal law' (emphasis added). It does not make it clear whether the conduct needs to have been unlawful under the criminal law as it stood at the time the alleged act was committed, or whether it suffices that the conduct is unlawful under the criminal law at the time the matter comes to be considered by the court. The latter construction carries a clear retrospective effect and is unlikely to be accepted by the courts. The ambiguity is likely to be resolved in favour of a construction of the section as if it reads 'conduct . . . is unlawful conduct if at the time it occurred it was unlawful under the criminal law . . .'.

**10.9**    Any previous criminal conviction can be relied upon to prove unlawful conduct by production of a memorandum of conviction as evidence.[1] Convictions in a foreign jurisdiction could be proved in a similar fashion, although formal evidence of the conviction would be required in the form of a statement from an official able to confirm the contents of the court records as an accurate record of the outcome of court proceedings.

## RECOVERABLE PROPERTY

**10.10**    Recoverable property is a key term in Part 5 of the PCA 2002 and is broadly defined. The basic definition is 'property obtained through unlawful conduct',[2] although this simple definition is subject to very significant expansion, and is also subject to important exceptions, by subsequent sections contained in Chapter 4 of Part 5 of the Act. Those various provisions are considered below once the general definition is explained.

**10.11**    A person obtains property through unlawful conduct if he obtains the property by or in return for the unlawful conduct. The conduct need not be that of the person who actually obtained the property but may be the conduct of another person.[3] By this definition, recoverable property will include, for example, the proceeds of sale of illicit drugs, as well as money obtained by a hit man as payment for assassinating another person. A payment to a person which is obtained by an act of criminal deception or forgery by a third party would also be recoverable even though the recipient of the payment had done nothing unlawful. The recovery provisions cannot, therefore, be avoided by a criminal's ensuring that the proceeds of his criminal activity are always paid to third parties, such as members of his family, rather than to him.

**10.12**    Further, in deciding whether any property was obtained by unlawful conduct, the court is to ignore any sums 'invested' in the unlawful conduct (eg for the purchase of drugs or equipment which allowed the conduct to take place), and the court need not show a direct link between the property being obtained and a particular kind of conduct provided it is shown that it was obtained by unlawful conduct of one or a number of

---

1    Civil Evidence Act 1968, s 11.
2    Section 304(1). 'Unlawful conduct' is defined at s 241 and is dealt with below at **10.15**.
3    Section 242(1). For example, if A deceives B into paying money to C and C is unaware of the fraud, despite C being innocent of any unlawful conduct he will have obtained property through unlawful conduct for the purposes of this Act.

kinds.[1] This latter provision means that if it is proved that the property was obtained by a person involved in a number of criminal enterprises, for example drug trafficking, money laundering, smuggling contraband, etc, provided it is proved on a balance of probabilities that the property was obtained by one or more of the types of unlawful conduct, the enforcement authority need not attribute each part of the property to some specific enterprise. This attempts to address some of the difficulty that the authority will have in proving that property was obtained by unlawful conduct without the assumptions which can be made in confiscation proceedings following criminal conviction. Ultimately, however, the authority will still have to prove that particular property was obtained by unlawful conduct. In cases where a person has a combination of legitimate and illegitimate income, this may be no easy task.

## PROPERTY

**10.13** Property includes all property wherever situated and in whatever form it may be, including things in action and intangible property.[2] It includes profits accrued from property.[3] Interests granted in recoverable property are also treated as a disposal of recoverable property.[4] For example, if a person has a house which is or represents recoverable property and grants a lease of that house, the grant of the lease will be a disposal of the property within the meaning of the Act and the lease will become recoverable property, even though it is an entirely new form of property. Any disposal is subject to the possibility that it can be brought within the categories of property excluded from being recoverable (see **10.26** *et seq*). Being the creation of a new right of property which did not formerly exist, the tracing and following provisions (see **10.20** *et seq*) would not apply to such a grant but for this provision.

## FOLLOWING AND TRACING RECOVERABLE PROPERTY

**10.14** To limit recoverable property to the actual property originally obtained by unlawful conduct would give the civil recovery provisions very limited scope. The PCA 2002 expands the categories of recoverable property dramatically by introducing new statutory mechanisms by which the property can be followed into the hands of other persons, traced into new assets acquired in place of the original property and traced into mixed funds or assets acquired with the property. These provisions give the court power to follow and trace the recoverable property as if the party bringing the proceedings had some proprietary interest in it, which it clearly does not have at any time before a recovery order is made.[5] The provisions are complex and may result in the recoverable property which is subject to an application for a recovery order being many

---

1    Section 242(2).
2    Section 316(4).
3    Section 307. For example, interest on cash in a bank account, dividends from shares, shares granted in lieu of a dividend, etc.
4    Section 310.
5    In the absence of a proprietary interest in the recoverable property, the enforcement authority (in the case of High Court proceedings) or the police or Customs and Excise officials (in the case of proceedings in the magistrates' courts) have no basis for seeking any form of common-law or

times greater than the value of the property originally obtained by the unlawful conduct, and held by a large number of people, as explained at **10.20** *et seq.*

## Following property into the hands of another

**10.15**   In order to ensure that the recovery powers can operate *in rem* and seize the actual property obtained by the unlawful conduct, the PCA 2002 creates a power to follow the recoverable property into the hands of persons who subsequently obtained it on a disposal by the initial holder of the property.[1] Property can be followed in this way along a chain of disposals. Provided the property can be followed into the hands of another, it remains recoverable property.

**10.16**   In order to be followed, the property must first be recoverable property: it must have been obtained by unlawful conduct. If the person who first obtained the property by the unlawful conduct (even if he did not commit the unlawful conduct) disposes of it to another, the property is followed into the hands of the person obtaining it on that disposal. If the person obtaining the property then makes a further disposal of the property, it is yet again followed into the hands of that person and so on into infinity, unless the chain is broken at some point by the property ceasing to be recoverable on one of the grounds set out in the PCA 2002 (as to which, see **10.26** *et seq*).

**10.17**   For this purpose, 'disposal' is very broadly defined as including:[2]

–   disposal of part of the property;
–   granting an interest in it (eg a tenancy in a property);
–   making a payment with it (eg using proceeds of drug trafficking to carry out a legitimate transaction such as purchasing a car or a house);
–   allowing it to pass to another on death, either by will or by intestacy.

**10.18**   On this basis, even payment under a court order would be a disposal. The authority's claims will not necessarily be frustrated by means of a settlement of court proceedings or by way of a financial ancillary relief order in divorce proceedings unless the person obtaining the property on the disposal can show that the property has ceased to be recoverable by the time it passed into his hands.[3]

**10.19**   The grant of a new interest in recoverable property (eg a lease in a freehold property) is not ordinarily a disposal of property. In law, it is the creation of a new type of property. Property created by such a grant is treated within the PCA 2002 as a disposal and also gives rise to recoverable property subject to the rules for following and tracing property.[4] Therefore, where a long lease is granted in a property where the freehold is recoverable property, the lease will be recoverable unless the leaseholder can show that he obtained it in circumstances where the lease was not recoverable property within the meaning of the PCA 2002.

---

equitable tracing of the property or its proceeds. The Act therefore creates a new statutory scheme of tracing for the purposes of Part 5.
1   Section 304(2), (3).
2   Section 314.
3   For example, by reason of his having obtained the property in good faith and for value in accordance with s 308(1) (see **10.26**).
4   Section 310.

## Tracing property

**10.20**  Where property obtained through unlawful conduct ('the original property') is exchanged for other property, the new property is also recoverable.[1] Where a person disposes of recoverable property and obtains other property in its place the other property represents the original property. So, for example, if a person uses the proceeds of drug trafficking to purchase a car, the car represents the original recoverable property and itself becomes recoverable. This is in addition to the cash being followed into the hands of the vendor of the car[2] and remaining recoverable, subject to any defence he can show as to why the property ceases to be recoverable in his hands.

**10.21**  This process of tracing will continue through subsequent disposals of property. On each disposal, the property obtained in place of the property disposed of becomes property which represents the original property. Further, on each disposal the property disposed of (being recoverable property representing the original property) is capable of being followed into the hands of the person who obtains it. To return to the example of the car purchased with the proceeds of drug trafficking, if that car is sold to another person for cash, the cash produced on the sale represents the original property and becomes recoverable property, and the car remains recoverable property which is capable of being followed into the hands of the purchaser, unless he demonstrates that one of the provisions which cause it to cease to be recoverable property applies (see **10.26** *et seq*).

**10.22**  The combination of following and tracing property in this way gives the enforcement authority considerable scope to decide how best to recover the proceeds of crime. In each case, the authority will ultimately have to decide which property it should pursue. There is nothing preventing the authority from naming, in its application for a High Court recovery order, all the property which has been traced or followed into the hands of others, although in practice it will presumably apply realistic limits to which property it pursues. As will be seen below, the court must ensure that the value of the original property obtained by unlawful conduct is recovered only once, and so despite the possible proliferation over time of recoverable property which stems from the original property, it seems unlikely that all that property will need to be specified in an application for a recovery order.

## Mixing property

**10.23**  To complement the statutory following and tracing powers, the Act also provides for situations where the recoverable property is mixed with other property which is not recoverable (whether that property belongs to the same person as the recoverable property or to another). Mixing property includes increasing funds in a bank account, using property in part payment for the acquisition of an asset, using it for the restoration or improvement of land, or using it to purchase a freehold in land held under a lease.[3] Where property is mixed in such a way, the portion of the mixed

---

1     Section 305.
2     By virtue of s 304.
3     Section 306(3).

property acquired with the recoverable property represents the property obtained through unlawful conduct.[1]

**10.24**   In a simple case it is easy to see how this provision works. To continue to use the example of the car purchased with the proceeds of drug trafficking: if, instead of selling the car to another purchaser for cash it is applied in part-exchange, amounting to, say, £10,000, for another car costing £20,000, with the balance being made up by legitimately obtained cash, half the value of the new car would represent the original recoverable property. The other half would be 'associated property', which is explained at **10.34** and **11.90**.

**10.25**   It is more difficult to see how the mixing and tracing provisions will operate in more complex cases. For example, if £10,000 of recoverable property is paid into a joint bank account to clear a £10,000 overdraft on that account (ie discharging a joint and several debt), and then £5000 is withdrawn against the overdraft by the joint account holder (who is not guilty of any unlawful conduct at any time) and used to purchase a car, is the car recoverable property in part or at all? It is difficult to see within the statutory powers how the money can be followed or traced into the hands of the joint account holder in such circumstances. The recoverable property can, it seems, only be followed into the hands of the bank which obtained the cash on the disposal.[2] As there is no fiduciary relationship between the enforcement authority and any of the persons holding the property at any time, it is difficult to see how any of the flexible and far-reaching equitable tracing powers available to the court in trust proceedings could be used in these circumstances. It remains to be seen whether the courts are willing to attempt to use the statutory following and tracing powers in the Act in a flexible and far-reaching fashion so that they mirror the equitable tracing powers.

## WHAT IS EXCLUDED FROM BEING RECOVERABLE PROPERTY?

### Property obtained in good faith for value

**10.26**   The concept of 'equity's darling' is introduced into the PCA 2002 and is the main protection for persons dealing with anyone holding recoverable property. If recoverable property is disposed of to a person who obtains it (a) in good faith, (b) for value, and (c) without notice that it was recoverable property, it may not be followed into his hands and ceases to be recoverable.[3] This breaks the chain along which that property may be followed. Property is obtained for value only once the consideration has become executed.[4] The recovery regime cannot be frustrated, therefore, by a transfer of recoverable property on the promise of payment which is never made or pursued.

---

1   Section 306(2).
2   The bank will certainly raise the good-faith defence under s 310(1) to prevent the cash being recovered from it.
3   Section 308(1).
4   Section 314(4).

**10.27**    Although on such a disposal the property disposed of ceases to be recoverable, the property obtained in its place on the disposal remains recoverable.[1]

## Property subject to a civil recovery or forfeiture order

**10.28**    Once property is made subject to a recovery or forfeiture order pursuant to the PCA 2002 which vests or forfeits the property, or if it is disposed of during the interim receivership, it ceases to be recoverable.[2] Anyone dealing with the interim receiver or the trustee for civil recovery in respect of property which has been subject to a recovery order will not acquire property which might remain subject to recovery.

## Damages for unlawful conduct obtained from recoverable property

**10.29**    Where a defendant to civil proceedings pays damages to a claimant for a claim based on his unlawful conduct, those damages are not recoverable even if they are paid out of what would otherwise be recoverable property.[3] This is in marked contrast to the position where damages are paid in respect of a civil claim which does not arise from unlawful conduct. In those cases, the payment of damages would be a disposal subject to following into the hands of the successful claimant. The claimant would have to show that the good-faith defence is made out to avoid recovery of the damages being made against him. The distinction made between those claiming damages for unlawful conduct within the meaning of the PCA 2002 (ie criminal conduct) and those claiming for other civil wrongs is because the rationale behind the Act is that the proceeds of crime should only be used to compensate the victims of crime. The principle is that general civil liabilities should be met out of a person's legitimate property and not from the proceeds of crime.

## Payments under criminal compensation or restitution orders

**10.30**    Where a compensation order[4] or a restitution order[5] is made against a person in criminal proceedings and is paid out of recoverable property, the payment ceases to be recoverable.[6] The rationale appears to be that the victims of crime should not be deprived of their compensation, even if that compensation is met from the proceeds of crime.

---

1    Section 308(10).
2    Section 308(2).
3    Section 308(3).
4    Pursuant to s 130 of the Powers of Criminal Courts (Sentencing) Act 2000.
5    Pursuant to ibid, s 148(2).
6    Section 308(4), (5).

## Payments following financial services offences

**10.31**   Restitution payments made from recoverable property following orders of the court or of the Financial Services Authority pursuant to the Financial Services and Markets Act 2000[1] are not recoverable.[2]

## Property subject to a restraint order

**10.32**   Property is not recoverable while a restraint order under s 41 of the PCA 2002, or under the other types of criminal confiscation proceedings, applies to it.[3] Confiscation proceedings take priority over civil recovery proceedings. If the confiscation proceedings end without an order in respect of the property and the restraint order is discharged, the property becomes recoverable again.

## Property taken into account in confiscation proceedings

**10.33**   Where property is taken into account in deciding a person's benefit from criminal conduct in confiscation proceedings (either under the PCA 2002 or the related legislation listed at s 8(7)(a)–(g)) it is not recoverable.[4] This prevents double recovery of the same proceeds of crime.

## Associated property

**10.34**   The concept of 'associated property' is introduced into the PCA 2002 to deal with non-recoverable property that is formally tied up with recoverable property in a way which makes it impossible to deal with the recoverable property without interfering with the associated property. Associated property is only likely to be an issue in High Court recovery proceedings and so it is dealt with in Chapter 11. Problems of associated property, or more likely the related concept of an 'excepted joint owner', may arise in the magistrates' court where proceedings concern 'cash' which is not in the form of readily separable currency, but in the form of a cheque or bond held in joint names. Nevertheless, the fact that such instruments can be readily converted into cash suggests that the magistrates' court is unlikely to be faced with many complicated decisions on this issue. Cash which is not recoverable property can easily be separated from the recoverable cash and returned to its owner.

---

1   Sections 383(5) and 384(5), respectively.
2   Section 308(6), (7).
3   Section 308(8).
4   Section 310(9).

# Chapter 11

# CIVIL RECOVERY IN THE HIGH COURT

## OVERVIEW

**11.1**  The new statutory powers given to the High Court are wide ranging and complex. The Director of the Assets Recovery Agency (ARA) is to become the 'enforcement authority' with sole power to bring civil recovery proceedings in the High Court.[1] He will be able to seek a 'recovery order' in respect of any 'recoverable property' by bringing a civil action in the High Court. Such proceedings are to be subject to ordinary civil procedures and civil rules of evidence.

**11.2**  'Recoverable property' is property obtained through unlawful conduct, and also other property which represents such property. Special powers for following and tracing such property into other property are provided by the PCA 2002. 'Unlawful conduct' means conduct which is unlawful under the criminal law of any part of the United Kingdom or which is unlawful under the criminal law of a foreign country and would also be unlawful under the criminal law of any part of the United Kingdom if it occurred there. 'Unlawful conduct' within the meaning of the Act is, therefore, to all intents and purposes 'criminal conduct'. These terms are explained in more detail in Chapter 10.[2]

**11.3**  The draftsman of the PCA 2002 has used the term 'unlawful conduct' rather than 'criminal conduct' in an attempt to avoid proceedings under Part 5 being categorised as criminal proceedings for the purposes of ss 6 and 7 of the Human Rights Act 1998. The burden of proving 'unlawful conduct' will lie on the Director as enforcement authority, but the standard of proof will be the balance of probabilities.

**11.4**  The provisions also deal with the legitimate interests of persons in property which is associated with recoverable property but which is not itself recoverable. There is power to divest persons of such interests in return for compensation if that is necessary for the effective recovery of recoverable property.

**11.5**  The new civil recovery powers are not, unlike the confiscation powers in Part 2 of the PCA 2002, aimed directly at the criminal but at the property which has been obtained by unlawful conduct. The purpose of the PCA 2002 appears to be to give the Director power to bring actions *in rem* rather than *in personam*. This emphasis towards the property rather than the individual is to enable proceeds of crime to be traced into other property and to follow such property into the hands of other persons who subsequently obtain it. It also appears that the Government hopes that creating a procedure which operates *in rem* against property rather than *in personam* against individuals may defeat some of the expected challenges to the new powers pursuant to the Human Rights Act 1998.[3]

---

1    Section 316(1).
2    See **10.6–10.9**.
3    See **10.26**.

**11.6**    The effect of the focus on property rather than individuals is that many of the respondents to applications for recovery orders will not be accused of any unlawful conduct at all but may be innocently holding property which some other person obtained through unlawful conduct. The unlawful conduct may have occurred a long time prior to the property passing into the hands of the person who becomes the respondent to the proceedings for a recovery order. Indeed, there will be cases where the person who is said to have originally obtained the property by unlawful conduct is not a party to the proceedings, and may not even be alive or identifiable.[1] Innocent purchasers of property in good faith and for value will have available to them a defence against a recovery order being made in respect of the property.[2] Many innocent holders or owners of property subject to recovery proceedings will not have this defence,[3] and will be deprived of property which was otherwise lawfully their own. By including within the definition of recoverable property not only the property originally obtained by unlawful conduct but also all property which represents that property in the hands of the person who originally obtained it and in the hands of every person who subsequently held all or part of the original property, or property representing the original property, the scope of the recovery powers are breathtakingly wide.[4] There will be cases where the court will have the discretion to make a recovery order against a wide range of property held by a large number of individuals, most, if not all, of whom have no direct involvement with any form of criminal activity.

**11.7**    The enforcement authority will also have power to apply for interim receivership orders, without notice prior to the issue of proceedings where justified, to appoint an interim receiver to investigate and control the property at issue in the proceedings. The court will be able to bestow extensive powers on the interim receiver. A trustee for civil recovery has been created, whose duty will be to deal with property recovered under a recovery order. His powers are modelled on the powers of a trustee in bankruptcy.

**11.8**    The recovery provisions are designed to have retrospective effect. Although there is to be a new limitation period created for such proceedings, it will allow recovery of property obtained as a result of unlawful conduct provided the original property was obtained no more than 12 years prior to the commencement of recovery proceedings, and the relevant provisions of the Act must be read as though they were in force at the time the property was obtained. There is no limitation as to how long ago the unlawful conduct relied upon to found the proceedings might have occurred. The retrospective nature of the procedure is likely to result in a challenge under the Human Rights Act 1998, but will succeed only if the proceedings are categorised under the European Convention on Human Rights (the Convention) as being criminal in nature.[5]

**11.9**    In practice, it is not envisaged that the civil recovery powers will be used as routinely or frequently as the confiscation powers under the PCA 2002. The intention appears to be to reserve the civil recovery powers for serious cases, and in particular to

---

1    For example where property was stolen, but the thief was never identified, that property may come to light at a later time in the hands of some person; however, it may be possible to show that it was obtained through unlawful conduct even though the thief cannot be identified.

2    See s 308(1) and **10.26**.

3    For example if they obtained the property not for value, eg as a gift or by bequest through a will.

4    See **10.15–10.25** for detailed consideration of the tracing and following provisions.

5    See **11.139–11.147**.

tackle individuals characterised by the Government as the 'Mr Bigs', against whom criminal convictions are difficult to obtain but who accumulate wealth by reason of criminal activity. The Agency anticipates dealing with 15 such applications in its first year of operation, rising to 20 cases per year thereafter.[1] The Government has, it seems, grossly underestimated the costs likely to be involved in bringing civil recovery proceedings, bearing in mind that such cases are likely to be of considerable complexity, dealing with extensive assets tied up in various forms of property and perhaps involving dozens of interested parties.[2]

## JURISDICTION TO APPLY FOR A RECOVERY ORDER

**11.10**   Only the Director, as the enforcement authority for the purposes of Part 5 of the Act, may bring recovery proceedings in the High Court.[3] The discretion to bring proceedings is broad. Section 243(1) allows the enforcement authority to bring recovery proceedings against 'any person who the authority thinks holds recoverable property'. This use of the word 'thinks' is unusual in a statute. Use of the word 'believes' might have been more conventional. The draftsman appears to seek to make the power as open-ended as possible, and the use of subjective terminology is perhaps to avoid challenge by way of judicial review of decisions to bring such proceedings.

**11.11**   A financial threshold for bringing recovery proceedings may be set by the Secretary of State.[4] The Government has indicated that this is likely to be set at 'not less than £10,000'.[5] The enforcement authority may not initiate proceedings unless it reasonably believes that the aggregate property subject to recovery proceedings is worth not less than the threshold limit.[6] Provided reasonable grounds exist for that belief at the time proceedings are commenced the proceedings may continue even if it appears subsequently that the property subject to the recovery proceedings is worth less than the threshold limit.[7]

**11.12**   Where the recoverable property consists only of cash[8] found in the United Kingdom, no proceedings for a recovery order in the High Court may be brought.[9] The cash forfeiture procedure in the magistrates' court should be used instead. Only if the cash is located outside the United Kingdom, or the proceedings are brought in respect of other (non-cash) property held by the same person who holds the cash, may the High Court recovery procedure be used. This may lead to separate proceedings being brought in the High Court and the magistrates' court in respect of the same unlawful conduct where one person holds property other than cash obtained by the criminal conduct, while another person holds only cash obtained by that conduct.

---

1   Home Office Explanatory Notes to the Bill (HL Bill 57 – EN), para 677.
2   Ibid. The Government's expectation appears to be that legal costs to the public purse (ie on both sides of the case) will average less than £20,000 per case.
3   Sections 243(1), 316(1).
4   Section 287(2).
5   Lord Rooker speaking in House of Lords, HL Deb, vol 633, col 16 (25 March 2002).
6   Section 287(1). The same requirement applies to the authority before it applies for an interim receiving order prior to commencement of proceedings – s 287(3).
7   Section 287(4).
8   See the extended definition of 'cash' contained in s 289(6).
9   Section 282(2).

## LIMITATION OF CLAIMS AND RETROSPECTIVE EFFECT

**11.13**　The PCA 2002 introduces a new s 27A into the Limitation Act 1980.[1] The limitation period is 12 years from the date on which the cause of action accrues. Time ceases to run when either a claim form is issued or the Director applies for an interim receiving order.[2] The Director's cause of action under the civil recovery provisions of the PCA 2002 accrues at the time the property was obtained through unlawful conduct.[3] Where the proceedings are in respect of recoverable property which represents the property originally obtained through unlawful conduct, rather than the original property itself, the cause of action also accrues at the time the original property was obtained through criminal conduct. There is no limitation as to the time when the unlawful conduct through which the property was obtained might have occurred. An unlawful act could have been committed much more than 12 years ago but, provided property was originally obtained within the 12-year period, the action will not be time-barred.[4]

**11.14**　The 12-year limitation period will not, of itself, provide retrospective effect. Retrospective effect is, however, provided by s 316(3), which directs the court considering whether property was recoverable at any time (including times before commencement of the PCA 2002) to assume that Part 5 of the Act was in force at that and any other relevant time. Any property obtained through unlawful conduct prior to the commencement of the PCA 2002 will, therefore, be recoverable provided the 12-year limitation period is observed (but subject to any successful challenge pursuant to the Human Rights Act 1998).[5]

## DIRECTOR'S INVESTIGATORY POWERS

**11.15**　The Agency is able to apply its full investigatory powers prior to bringing civil recovery proceedings.[6] Any information gained in the course of the Director exercising one of his other functions, for example in investigating and pursuing a confiscation order, may be used by him for the purposes of bringing civil recovery proceedings.[7] This power is important for the effective operation of the Act because it provides the Director with several different routes to get at the proceeds of crime, and those routes are not mutually exclusive in the sense that each of them can be used in respect of the same criminal activity.

**11.16**　The commencement of civil recovery proceedings under Part 5, or the prior making of an interim receiving order, brings to an end the civil recovery investigation in respect of the property that is the subject of the proceedings or the interim receiving order.[8] This provision is presumably to ensure that once civil recovery proceedings are

---

1　Section 288.
2　Limitation Act 1980, s 27A(3) (as inserted by s 288 of the PCA 2002).
3　Ibid, s 27A(4) (as inserted by s 288 of the PCA 2002).
4　An example might be the fraudulent preparation of some form of instrument (eg a will) but under which property was obtained only many years later when the instrument became effective.
5　See **11.134**.
6　See Part 8 of the Act and **2.22–2.50**.
7　Section 435.
8　Section 341(3).

under way, there is no flavour of criminal proceedings given to them by reason of extensive evidence-gathering powers being held by one party which are not available to the respondents to the application. The Government wishes to present the recovery proceedings as straightforward civil proceedings between litigants of equal standing, rather than give any impression of the full machinery of the State bearing down upon an individual.

**11.17** Although the issue of proceedings brings to an end any civil recovery investigation in respect of the property to be recovered within those proceedings, the ARA may continue to investigate the respondent in respect of other property which is not subject to the proceedings or receiving order, and there appears to be no bar upon any information incidentally obtained in such further investigations being used in the existing proceedings. It remains to be seen whether this happens in practice and what approach the courts will take to admitting such evidence within the civil proceedings, or to granting the investigatory orders available under Part 8 of the PCA 2002 once separate recovery proceedings in respect of the respondent are under way.

## INTERIM RECEIVING ORDERS

**11.18** An important mechanism for the effective pursuit of recoverable property is the interim receiving order.[1] The enforcement authority may apply for such an order either before or after bringing the application for a recovery order.[2] In practice, an interim receiving order will usually be applied for prior to proceedings being commenced. The application may be made without notice, if it is shown that giving notice of the application for the order would prejudice the right of the enforcement authority to obtain a recovery order in respect of any property.[3] Where an order is made without notice it will presumably contain the normal liberty for any person affected by it to apply to the court for its discharge or variation.[4] As with any without-notice application to the court, the enforcement authority will be under an obligation to make full and frank disclosure to the court on its without-notice application. Failure to do so may justify an order which was obtained subsequently being set aside. The enforcement authority will also be obliged to make available to the respondents to the proceedings the evidence upon which the interim receiving order was obtained. The authority will not be able to use a without-notice hearing to put before the court evidence it does not wish the respondents to see.

**11.19** An interim receiving order has dual effect:[5]

–    it provides for the detention, custody or preservation of property (ie it has the effect of a freezing order[6]); and

---

1    In Scotland, the equivalent provision will create an 'interim administration order' appointing an 'interim administrator'.
2    Section 246(1).
3    Section 246(3).
4    But even where it does not do so it will be open to anyone affected by the order to apply for its variation or discharge pursuant to s 251(3).
5    Section 246(2).
6    Formerly known as a *Mareva* order.

– it provides for the appointment of an interim receiver.

Each of these effects will be considered in more detail below.

**11.20** The application for an interim receiving order is an application for an order either prior to the commencement of proceedings, or in the course of proceedings. In either case, Part 23 of the CPR 1998 will have effect. Evidence will be required to be served with the application setting out the grounds upon which the relief is sought. Such evidence will need to be verified by a statement of truth. If the application is made without notice, the grounds for why such a course of action is necessary will need to be stated in the application. Given the serious effect and scope of an interim receiving order it is likely that the application will be dealt with by a High Court judge rather than by a master or district judge.

**11.21** The application form must nominate a suitably qualified person who is to be appointed as interim receiver. He may not be a member of staff of the ARA.[1] The interim receiver is an officer of the court and owes duties to the court which might conflict with an employee's duties to his employer. Interim receivers are likely to be appointed from the pool of insolvency practitioners who are normally appointed as receivers either by the court or by the holders of debentures or charges which permit such appointments out of court. A group of practitioners with particular experience of recovery orders is likely to form, and the ARA is likely to make its appointments from a relatively small number of appropriately experienced individuals.

**11.22** Two conditions must be satisfied before the court makes an interim receiving order:[2]

(1) it must be established that there is a good, arguable case that the property to which the application relates is, at least in part, recoverable property and, if only part of it is recoverable, that the rest of the property is associated property; and

(2) where the property subject to the application includes associated property but the identity of any person who holds the associated property has not been established, the enforcement authority must have taken all reasonable steps to identify him.

## Content of the interim receiving order

**11.23** The enforcement authority is likely to produce its own form for an interim receiving order, unless the CPR 1998 direct a particular form to be used. In many respects, the order will be modelled on the ordinary civil freezing order.[3] The order must:

---

1   Section 246(7).

2   Section 246(4), (5), (6).

3   The form for which is annexed to the practice direction to CPR 1998 Part 25. There is no provision within the Act for the enforcement authority to give any form of undertaking in damages as a condition of obtaining the order. In view of the fact that the Act provides expressly for compensation of innocent persons caused damage by an interim receiving order which freezes property not ultimately subject to a recovery order (as to which, see **11.119** _et seq_), it seems unlikely that an undertaking as to damages can justifiably be required of the enforcement authority.

- specify the property to which it relates;[1]
- grant powers to the interim receiver and define the steps he must take during the interim receivership;[2]
- require the interim receiver to report to the court and to the enforcement authority on any material change of circumstances, and especially as to whether he has found that any property subject to the order is not recoverable or associated property, that he has discovered any further recoverable or associated property which is not already subject to the order, or that any property subject to the order is held by someone different from the person who was alleged to hold it in the claim form or application;[3] and
- prohibit any person to whose property the order applies from dealing with the property save to any extent permitted by the order.[4]

**11.24**   The order may also make provision for any person to whose property the order applies to produce the property or any documents relating to the property to the receiver or to deliver it to a specified place, or to do anything which the receiver reasonably requires of him to preserve the property.[5]

**11.25**   It seems clear that an interim receiving order, even in a relatively straightforward case, will be a lengthy document.

**11.26**   Where an interim receiving order is made prior to the commencement of proceedings for a recovery order the court may also make it a term of the order that the enforcement authority should issue such proceedings within a certain time, or extract an undertaking from the authority to like effect. It seems likely that the court will wish to do so to ensure that interim receiving orders last no longer than required to determine whether a recovery order should be made.

**11.27**   The prohibition against dealing with property can apply to property which is specified or generally described in the order.[6] The order may make exclusions to any such prohibition to allow any person to meet his reasonable living expenses or to carry on any trade, business, profession, or occupation, and conditions may be attached to any such exclusion.[7] Such exclusions are common in freezing orders and may be imposed when the order is first made or on an application to vary the order.[8] The court must ensure that any such exclusion does not unduly prejudice the enforcement authority's right to recover recoverable property.[9] No such exclusion may be made to enable a person to meet legal expenses in respect of the proceedings for a recovery order or cash forfeiture proceedings.[10] This follows the general policy of the PCA 2002 that a

---

1    Which will include the property identified in the claim form, or which will be identified in the claim form when issued, but which may be much broader in scope where the application is brought prior to the issue of proceedings when the exact nature of the assets to be recovered may not yet have been clearly established.
2    Section 247(1), (2).
3    Section 255(1).
4    Section 252(1).
5    Section 250.
6    Section 252(5). A general description might refer to, eg, 'all monies held in bank accounts in the name of X, wherever held'.
7    Section 252(3).
8    Section 252(2).
9    Section 252(6).
10   Section 252(4).

person's expenses should be met out of his legitimately obtained property and not out of property which is the fruit of criminal activity. Public funding will be available for proceedings in the High Court for recovery orders subject to the normal means and merits tests.

## Incidental effects of an interim receiving order

**11.28**   The making of an interim receiving order brings to an end any civil recovery investigation, so that the Director may no longer use the investigatory powers contained in Part 8 of the PCA 2002 in respect of the property subject to the order.[1]

**11.29**   The High Court may stay any other proceedings in respect of the property to which the interim receiving order applies.[2] If proceedings are pending in respect of any property in any court in England and Wales and that court is satisfied that an interim receiving order has been made in respect of that property, the court may either stay the proceedings or set terms as to the continuation of those proceedings.[3] Before a court makes any such order it must give the enforcement authority, the interim receiver (if appointed) and any other affected party (eg the other litigants in the other proceedings) the opportunity to be heard.[4]

**11.30**   Unless leave of the court is first obtained, an interim receiving order also prevents distress being levied against any property to which the order applies[5] or a landlord of property exercising any right of forfeiture in respect of a tenancy subject to the interim receiving order.[6] If the court grants leave for distress to be levied or forfeiture obtained it may attach conditions as to the exercise of any such right.

## Interim receiver

### *Powers*
**11.31**   The interim receiver's powers are to be specified in the interim receiving order. It appears that the interim receiver will have no powers arising automatically by his appointment.[7] The interim receiving order must, therefore, be carefully drafted to ensure that the receiver obtains the powers necessary for the effective performance of his duties within the specific circumstances of each case.

**11.32**   A 'menu' of powers the court may confer on the interim receiver is set out in Sch 6 to the PCA 2002.[8] These are broad in scope and have a potentially draconian effect. When making the interim receiving order the court should ensure that the powers are proportionate to the aim of the order, otherwise challenges to interim receiving orders under the Human Rights Act 1998 will be successfully mounted. The powers of an interim receiver listed in Sch 6 include:

---

1   Section 341(3)(b).
2   Section 253(1)(a).
3   Section 253(2).
4   Section 253(4).
5   Section 253(1)(b).
6   Section 253(3).
7   Section 247(1) requires the court to authorise the interim receiver to use any powers listed in the Act or otherwise. If his appointment automatically gave rise to any such powers, the court's authorisation would be unnecessary.
8   Section 247(1).

–   power to seize property to which the order applies;
–   power to obtain information or to require a person[1] to answer any question. Such a
    requirement must be obeyed regardless of any other restriction on the disclosure
    of the information (unless it is subject to legal professional privilege). Any answer
    given to such a requirement to provide information cannot be used as evidence
    against him in criminal proceedings (except proceedings for perjury based on the
    answer, or where the answer is inconsistent with evidence given by that person in
    subsequent criminal proceedings). This power may be conferred upon the interim
    receiver either as a general power to be used at his discretion, or as a limited power
    to be used only in specified circumstances, or in relation to specified matters;
–   power to enter any premises to which the interim order applies and search for or
    inspect anything described in the order, take copies, photographs or other records
    of any such item and to remove anything which may be required as evidence in the
    proceedings. The order may identify specific items to be subject to this power or
    merely provide a general description of items or a class of items;
–   power to manage any property to which the order applies (which includes a power
    to sell any perishable goods or goods of diminishing value), carrying on a business,
    or incurring capital expenditure in respect of the property.

**11.33**   In addition to the requirement which might be included in an order to require a
person to answer questions put by the interim receiver, the order may place an
obligation upon any person[2] to assist the interim receiver by giving him access to
premises which he has been given authority to enter and search, or to give the interim
receiver any assistance he may require for the taking of steps to search premises and
copy, photograph, record or remove anything therein.[3] An order made under this
provision may oblige a person, for example, to open a safety deposit box, or to assist the
receiver in accessing information securely stored in a computer.

**11.34**   The wide scope of these powers suggests that it will be inappropriate for a court
to make an order granting to an interim receiver all the powers available under Sch 6.
The scope to involve third parties in the inquiries should be carefully circumscribed by
any order to ensure that the interim receiver's powers do not extend beyond those
reasonably necessary for the effective performance of his duties.

**11.35**   The court's authority to give the receiver powers and to place obligations upon
him does not appear to be limited to those expressly provided by the PCA 2002.[4] It
would appear to be intended to permit the court to use its broad inherent powers to
make whatever orders are required to assist or restrict the interim receiver in carrying
out his duties.

**11.36**   The provisions of the Land Registration Acts 1925 and 2002 and the Land
Charges Act 1972 apply to interim receiving orders, thereby giving the interim receiver
the power to protect any real property subject to an interim receiving order against
third-party dealings by making appropriate entries on the land registers.[5]

---

1    Meaning in effect 'any person', even if not a party to the proceedings.
2    Ie not merely a person who is party to the proceedings.
3    Sch 6, para 4(2).
4    Section 246(8).
5    Section 248.

## Duties

**11.37**    An interim receiver under Part 5 of the PCA 2002, like any receiver appointed by the court, is an officer of the court and must not act in a partisan manner. It is not clear whether he will bear any fiduciary duties towards owners of the property subject to his receivership, or towards the enforcement authority seeking recovery of those assets. There is no guidance on this in the Act and it would appear that the normal rules as to receivers' duties will apply, adapted as necessary to fit the circumstances created by the Act.

**11.38**    The court may specify in the interim receiving order what specific tasks the interim receiver is to undertake.[1] The receiver's general function is to achieve the aims of the interim receiving order, namely to identify, secure and preserve property subject to the order. Any specific directions as to his duties which the court includes in an interim receiving order must go to one of those aims. His duties extend to investigating matters and bringing to the court's and the enforcement authority's attentions any further property which appears to be recoverable and which ought to be included in the proceedings. He must also promptly inform the court and the enforcement authority if property subject to the order is not recoverable property or associated property, thus enabling the court to vary the order to exclude such property. He is also obliged to identify any other persons who ought to be parties to the proceedings, either in addition to or in substitution for the existing respondents.[2]

**11.39**    As well as informing the court as soon as he learns of any material changes of circumstances or any important new information, the interim receiving order must require the interim receiver to report his findings in relation to the matters with which he has been ordered to deal.[3] He must be required by the court to serve his report on the parties and on any person affected by the report. Although the PCA 2002 does not require a time-limit to be imposed on the preparation of such a report, it is likely that the court will set a timetable in the interests of efficient case management.

**11.40**    The PCA 2002 makes no specific provision for challenging the interim receiver's findings, but it must be presumed that the parties will be able to do so at any interim hearing where discharge or variation of an interim receiving order is being considered, or at the final hearing of the application for the recovery order. The interim receiver will be subject to cross-examination by the parties at that stage.

## Court supervision

**11.41**    As with all court-appointed receivers the court retains a supervisory role as to the performance of the interim receiver's duties. This means that the interim receiver, any respondent to the proceedings or any person affected by any action taken or proposed to be taken by the interim receiver may apply to the court for directions as to the exercise of the interim receiver's functions.[4] On any such application, the court must afford to anyone else affected by the decision an opportunity to be heard.[5] The court's use of this power will largely determine whether the powers given to interim

---

1    Section 247(1).
2    Section 255(1).
3    Section 255(2).
4    Section 251(1).
5    Section 251(2).

receivers infringe a person's rights under the European Convention on Human Rights. The right to apply to the court for such directions should meet the requirement for access to a court and for an effective remedy as required by Art 6 of the Convention.

**11.42** Either on such an application for directions or at any other time, the court may vary or set aside an interim receiving order,[1] although it may not do so of its own motion or on the application of any one party without first giving all other parties affected by the decision the right to be heard.[2] Such an application may be brought by a person who claims that property is not recoverable, following a report by the interim receiver that property is not recoverable, or because there is further recoverable or associated property which should be included in the interim receiving order.

**11.43** The court must vary an interim receiving order so as to exclude from it any property which it decides is neither recoverable property nor associated property.[3] The court may also vary an interim receiving order to exclude any associated property the removal of which will not prejudice the enforcement authority's right to obtain recoverable property.[4] Such property may be excluded subject to conditions or terms.[5] For example, it may be a condition of the exclusion of associated property from the receiving order that the owner of that property does not dispose of it, or deal with it in a particular way.

## *Remuneration*

**11.44** The Act makes no provision for the remuneration of the interim receiver. It has been held that statutory receivers appointed under the criminal confiscation provisions of the Criminal Justice Act 1988 and the Drug Trafficking Act 1994 should be treated in the same way as their common-law counterparts unless the statute expressly provides otherwise.[6] The same principle appears to apply to the PCA 2002. The interim receiver will, therefore, be entitled to look to the assets in his receivership for his remuneration, unless he comes to some other agreement with the parties.

**11.45** The court will retain overall control in respect of the receiver's remuneration, either by fixing it by reference to a specified scale, or by subjecting it to assessment by a master or costs judge.[7] It may be that the practice that has grown up in relation to receivers in confiscation proceedings, whereby a receiver has an agreement with the prosecuting authority to provide an indemnity in respect of such costs which are not recovered from the assets in his control, may be adopted between the enforcement authority and interim receiver appointed under Part 5 of the PCA 2002. Although there is no provision for such agreements in the PCA 2002, individuals will be reluctant to accept appointment as interim receivers without some assurance that their costs will be met.

---

1   Section 251(3).
2   Section 251(4).
3   Section 254(1).
4   Section 254(2).
5   Section 254(3).
6   *Hughes and Others v HM Customs & Excise* [2002] EWCA Civ 670, [2002] 4 All ER 633. Petitions for leave to appeal to the House of Lords have been presented.
7   See RSC 1965, Ord 30, r 3, annexed to the CPR 1998; and see also *Hughes*, above.

**11.46**   Payment of the interim receiver's costs from the property subject to the interim receiving order does not mean that the property should be depleted to the prejudice of innocent individuals. If, at the end of the proceedings, it is decided that the property was not recoverable property after all, the sum returned to the holder of the property may be less than the property was worth prior to the interim receiving order being made. This may also occur in respect of associated property, even though such property was innocently mixed with recoverable property. In such circumstances, the affected individual may be able to claim compensation from the enforcement authority.[1] Although the enforcement authority need not give undertakings to reimburse loss caused by the interim receiving order (as an applicant for an ordinary civil freezing order would), the authority should be deterred from making speculative applications for interim receiving orders by the potential for a significant liability for compensation arising if subsequent recovery proceedings are unsuccessful.

### *Partial immunity from suit*

**11.47**   The interim receiving order may refer to property only by general description or as a class. There may be some doubt, therefore, as to what property actually falls within the scope of the order. If in doubt, the interim receiver must apply to the court for directions. It may, nevertheless, be the case that an interim receiver innocently deals with property which is not included in the order. Strictly, such dealing would amount to a trespass or conversion in respect of the property and would be actionable against him. To prevent interim receivers from acting with such caution that the effect of an order is substantially weakened, the PCA 2002 provides a receiver with a defence to actions brought against him. Provided he can show that he dealt with the property, believing, on reasonable grounds, that he was entitled to do so in pursuance of the order, he will be exempt from liability.[2] He will not, however, be able to avail himself of this defence if he acted negligently.[3]

**11.48**   This creates no new right of action for individuals affected by the interim receiver's actions. It merely provides the interim receiver with a partial defence to actions brought against him by the owners of property. Although the PCA 2002 expressly excludes from the defence only negligent conduct, it is presumed that parties affected by any fraud or misfeasance by an interim receiver will retain their right to sue him. The PCA 2002 is silent as to this, but in the absence of any clear bar to such an action in the PCA 2002 it is difficult to see why any such action could not be brought.[4]

## Breach of the interim receiving order

**11.49**   The PCA 2002 does not provide any special procedures or penalties in the event of a breach of the order by any person. Being a civil order of the court such breaches will amount to a contempt of court punishable by way of committal proceedings.

---

1    See **11.119** *et seq.*
2    Section 247(3).
3    This provision largely mirrors the similar protection for a receiver or a trustee in bankruptcy within insolvency proceedings under the Insolvency Act 1986, ss 284(4), 304(4).
4    Such an action could be brought in the analogous circumstances of a receiver or trustee in bankruptcy within insolvency proceedings.

## BRINGING THE APPLICATION

**11.50**   Proceedings pursuant to Part 5 are civil proceedings, and the CPR 1998 apply. Proceedings must be commenced by the service of a claim form. It is not clear whether any special practice direction supplementing the CPR 1998 is intended to be issued in respect of civil recovery proceedings. The Act does not specify whether the CPR 1998, Part 7 or Part 8 procedure should be followed, although reference to 'particulars of claim' at s 243(4) suggests that the Part 7 procedure is envisaged as being appropriate. Given the nature of recovery proceedings and the likelihood of considerable factual disagreements, it seems that the Part 7 procedure will be most appropriate.

**11.51**   It is likely that a practice direction will specify which division of the High Court will deal with civil recovery proceedings. The Queen's Bench Division will probably be specified, although there will be cases where the financial arrangements that the court will have to attempt to unravel would fall to be dealt with more appropriately with the particular expertise of judges of the Chancery Division.

## PLEADINGS

**11.52**   The claim form and particulars of claim must define the property that the enforcement authority wishes to be subject to the proceedings, and whether the property is alleged to be recoverable property or associated property.[1] The normal requirements for the contents of a claim form will apply,[2] and the unlawful conduct relied upon will need to be explicitly pleaded, since this is fundamental to the cause of action existing. A respondent will be able to seek further information or clarification if of the view that the particulars of claim are not sufficiently clear.[3]

**11.53**   The respondents will have to serve any defence in accordance with the CPR 1998, Part 15. Failure to do so will risk judgment in default being obtained by the enforcement authority.

**11.54**   Summary judgment will be available as a remedy for any party to the proceedings, although the nature of the proceedings suggests that it will be in only very clear cases that circumstances will justify the court making an order against a respondent without a trial.

## PARTIES TO THE ACTION

**11.55**   It would appear that recovery orders may be made against a person wherever he may be domiciled, resident or present, and it would also appear that the property concerned may be situated anywhere in the world. The respondent to the application will be the person or persons who holds the recoverable property.[4] The proceedings

---

1   Section 243(3), (4).
2   CPR 1998, r 16.2.
3   CPR 1998, Part 18.
4   Section 243(1), (2). Such a person may or may not be a person who is accused of unlawful conduct, depending on how they came to hold the property.

must also be served on any person who holds 'associated property'. Although holders of associated property are not referred to in the PCA 2002 as 'respondents', it seems likely that they will be joined as parties to the proceedings even if not named as respondents in the claim form.[1] The enforcement authority will wish to join to the proceedings any holder of associated property to ensure that the court has full jurisdiction to make orders binding such a person.

**11.56**    Any person who seeks to assert an interest in property subject to the proceedings, or who has some other issue to raise with one of the parties which it would be convenient to deal with at the same time as the application for the recovery order, will be able to apply to be joined as a party in the normal way.[2]

## TRIAL

**11.57**    The hearing of the recovery order application will follow ordinary civil procedure for trial in the High Court. Directions will be given at an early case-management conference to prepare the matter for trial. The court may, at an early stage of the case-management process, decide that there are issues which should be tried separately from others. In many cases, the question of whether there has been unlawful conduct will be a readily identifiable discrete issue which can be tried prior to the more complex questions of identifying recoverable property.

**11.58**    Trial will be in open court unless the court orders otherwise.[3] When the court comes to consider details of an individual's personal financial affairs it may be persuaded to conduct part of the hearing in private to protect confidentiality.[4]

**11.59**    Ordinary rules of civil evidence will apply. Unlike criminal proceedings, there is no limit as to admission of hearsay evidence,[5] although bearing in mind the need for particularly cogent evidence to prove serious wrongdoing,[6] it is unlikely that the enforcement agency will be able to prove unlawful conduct purely on the basis of hearsay evidence. Where criminal convictions have previously been obtained, the authority will be able to rely upon those as evidence of unlawful conduct.[7] Similarly, where there have been findings as to criminal conduct in earlier recovery proceedings, those might be relied upon in subsequent proceedings on the basis of issue estoppel, if the conditions for such an estoppel are satisfied.

---

1    CPR 1998, r 19.2.
2    Ibid, r 19.4.
3    Ibid, r 39.2.
4    Ibid, r 39.2(c), (g).
5    Subject to the notice provisions of the Civil Evidence Act 1995 and CPR 1998, Part 33.
6    See the burden of proof at **11.64–11.65**.
7    Civil Evidence Act 1968, s 11.

# CONDITIONS FOR MAKING A RECOVERY ORDER

**11.60**   The court must make a recovery order where it is satisfied that any property is recoverable.[1] The definition of recoverable property is complex and is dealt with in Chapter 10.

**11.61**   Despite the mandatory requirement to make a recovery order where there is any recoverable property, there are two exceptions. First, the court may not make any provision in the order in respect of any recoverable property if each of four specified conditions is met, and it would not be just or equitable to make the provision.[2] The four conditions are that:[3]

(a)   the respondent obtained the recoverable property in good faith;

(b)   he took steps after obtaining the property which he would not have taken if he had not obtained it or he took steps before obtaining the property which he would not have taken if he had not believed he was going to obtain it;

(c)   when he took the steps, he had no notice that the property was recoverable;

(d)   if a recovery order were made in respect of the property, it would, by reason of the steps, be detrimental to him.

**11.62**   This imports into the PCA 2002 a principle similar to equitable estoppel, providing the court with a discretion to avoid injustice which the mandatory regime might otherwise impose on someone who had acted to his detriment in ignorance of the property being recoverable. In deciding whether it would be just and equitable to include the provision in the recovery order, notwithstanding the four conditions being met, the court must balance the degree of detriment suffered by the respondent against the public interest in the enforcement authority obtaining its interest in the property.[4] This provision ensures that the court considers the proportionality of making the order.

**11.63**   The second exception is that the court may not include in a recovery order any provision which is incompatible with any Convention right within the meaning of the Human Rights Act 1998.[5] This broad exception to the otherwise mandatory regime is intended to ensure that the provisions of Part 5 of the PCA 2002 do not infringe the Convention by empowering the court to make orders only if they comply with the Convention.

# STANDARD AND BURDEN OF PROOF

**11.64**   The burden of proof is firmly on the enforcement authority throughout the proceedings. The authority must prove all the matters required to obtain a recovery order.

---

1   Section 266(1).
2   Section 266(3). The second 'any' in this provision appears to refer to specific property to which the four conditions apply, rather than imposing a bar against the court including in the order any recoverable property at all.
3   Section 266(4).
4   Section 266(6).
5   Section 266(3)(b).

**11.65**   For the avoidance of any doubt, it is made clear that proof of the facts alleged to constitute unlawful conduct is on a balance of probabilities.[1] Although this leaves no doubt as to the appropriate standard of proof, the court will have in mind 'that the more serious the allegation the less likely it is that the event occurred and, hence, the stronger should be the evidence before the court concludes that the allegation is established on the balance of probability'.[2] The allegation of unlawful conduct must be based upon proof that acts amounting to criminal conduct were committed. The allegation is therefore a serious one and requires a particular cogency of evidence to be satisfied. The same cogency of evidence may not be required when the issue of whether particular property was obtained through the unlawful act comes to be considered. That does not appear to involve any further allegation of criminality.

## CONSENT ORDERS

**11.66**   Consent orders may be made in proceedings for recovery orders. The court has discretion whether to stay proceedings on the terms agreed by the parties.[3] This seems to envisage a *Tomlin* order with the terms of agreement annexed to it, rather than a detailed recovery order. The consent order may make provision for recoverable property to cease to be recoverable, and may also make any further provision that the court thinks appropriate.[4] What level of scrutiny of settlements the court will perform before agreeing to stay proceedings remains to be seen. The fact that such a 'consent order' is not, within the terminology of the PCA 2002, a 'recovery order' means that the court is not constrained by the terms of s 266 in deciding whether to make the consent order.

**11.67**   For the court to be able to make a consent order, each person (to whose property the proceedings or the agreement relates) must be a party both to the agreement and to the proceedings.[5] This includes not only those who hold recoverable property, but also any holder of associated property, any excepted joint owner of property and the holder of any other property which was subject to the proceedings even if such property is not subject to the recovery order. If proceedings have reached an advanced stage by the time an agreement is reached, most, if not all, of these individuals are likely to be parties to the proceedings. If, however, agreement is achieved very early in the process, it may be necessary to add further parties purely for the purpose of staying the proceedings on the basis of the agreement.

**11.68**   A consent order staying the proceedings need not vest property in the trustee for civil recovery because it is not a recovery order.[6] Where property is vested in the trustee for civil recovery by an agreement between the parties, the trustee is obliged to deal with it as if it had been vested in him by a recovery order.[7] Where the agreement vests the property in someone other than the trustee for civil recovery, that person appears to be free to deal with it as he sees fit, unconstrained by the terms of the PCA 2002.

---

1   Section 241(3).
2   *Re H (Minors) (Sexual Abuse: Standard of Proof)* [1996] AC 563, at p 586, per Lord Nicholls of Birkenhead.
3   Section 276(1).
4   Section 276(2).
5   Section 276(1).
6   Therefore, s 266(2) does not apply.
7   Section 276(3).

# RECOVERY ORDERS

## Terms and effects

**11.69**    The recovery order must vest the recoverable property in the trustee for civil recovery.[1] The court may impose conditions as to the manner in which the trustee for civil recovery deals with property for the purpose of realising it.[2] Such conditions may, for example, protect the interests of the owner of associated property by postponing a sale of property.

**11.70**    The recovery order may also provide for joint property to be severed so as to permit recovery of, for example, part of the proceeds in a jointly owned property or part of the funds held in a joint bank account.[3]

**11.71**    A recovery order has priority over any rights of pre-emption, etc which may exist in relation to the property. Section 269, which deals with such rights, is a complex provision whose meaning is, on first reading, somewhat opaque. A recovery order is to have effect in relation to any property notwithstanding any provision which prevents, penalises or restricts the vesting of the property. The order also renders inoperable any clause which seeks to pre-empt it or to provide for return to a third party of the property. Thus, if any person has an enforceable option to purchase property on a disposal of that property, his option will not be exercisable upon the making of a recovery order which vests the property in the trustee for civil recovery, even though the making of the order would otherwise be a disposal triggering the exercise of the option. The recovery order cannot be defeated by an agreement which ensures that ownership in property reverts to some third party upon the making of the order. Analogous clauses exist in many leases to prevent the lease falling into the bankrupt's estate upon insolvency.[4] Where rights of pre-emption, irritancy, return or similar do exist in favour of some third party, they are preserved for the benefit of that person following the making of the recovery order as if the vesting of the property as a result of the recovery order had not occurred.[5] The trustee for civil recovery or other person in whom the property is vested following the recovery order[6] effectively stands in the place of the prior holder of the property so far as the pre-emption rights are concerned.

**11.72**    The effect of these provisions appears to be as follows. Where, for example, the recovery order concerns a property which some third party has a first option to purchase in the event of any disposal of that property by the holder (ie the respondent to the application for a recovery order), that option will not be capable of being exercised when the disposal order vests the property in the trustee for civil recovery, but the option will then be exercisable by the third party against the trustee when he subsequently attempts to realise the property by sale.

**11.73**    Associated property and jointly owned property is subject to special treatment within a recovery order. The provisions relating to this are dealt with separately below.[7]

---

1    Section 266(2).
2    Section 266(8).
3    Section 266(7).
4    See also *Romalpa* clauses in contracts for the sale of goods.
5    Section 269(3).
6    For example, a joint owner of the property or an owner of associated property following an agreement between that person and the enforcement authority. See s 274 and **11.86** *et seq.*
7    See **11.86** *et seq.*

## Limits on scope

**11.74**   As already noted, the expansive definition of 'recoverable property' created by
the provisions for following and tracing such property over a period of up to 12 years
results in the original recoverable property spawning a potentially massive range of
recoverable property, all stemming from the original recoverable item of property. To
prevent double recovery of the same proceeds of crime, limits are imposed on the
recoverable property which may be specified in a recovery order.

**11.75**   These limitations are tortuously drafted.[1] They apply in two possible
situations:

(1)   where the enforcement authority seeks a recovery order in respect of both (a) the
      property originally obtained through unlawful conduct ('the original property') or
      property which represents such original property *and* (b) any 'related property'
      (which means any items of property which represent the original property);
(2)   where the enforcement authority seeks a recovery order in respect of property
      which is or represents the original property, and a previous recovery order has
      been made in respect of other property related to that property.

**11.76**   The main limitation is that the court may not make a recovery order if it thinks
that the authority's right to recover the original property has already been satisfied by a
previous recovery order.[2] The intention of this provision appears to be that if, for
example, the whole proceeds of drug trafficking are used to purchase a car from a
person who knows that the money is recoverable property (and so cannot avail himself
of the good-faith defence), and a recovery order is made in respect of the cash, the court
will not be able to make a subsequent recovery order in respect of the car.[3] Where only
part of the proceeds are used to buy the car, the recovery order may specify the car and
the remainder of the proceeds, or the cash paid to the seller of the car and the remainder
of the proceeds retained by the buyer.[4] What if all the cash is used to buy the car, the car
is first subject to a recovery order and, subsequently, the cash used for its purchase is
followed into a deposit account. It is not clear in those circumstances whether the court
may make a recovery order in relation to part of the cash in addition to recovery of the
car if the value of the recovered car is insufficient, as a result of depreciation, to satisfy
the authority's right to recover the full extent of the original proceeds of drug
trafficking.

**11.77**   For the purposes of the above provision, certain other types of order are
deemed to be recovery orders. The court must regard as a recovery order any of the
following types of order made in respect of property related to the property subject to
the recovery proceedings:

–     an order for forfeiture of cash which is recoverable property under s 298, but not
      forfeiture of cash which is intended for use in unlawful conduct;[5]

---

1     Section 278(1), (2).
2     Section 278(3).
3     Section 279(2).
4     See s 279(3).
5     Section 278(7), but not a civil judgment based on conduct which is not 'unlawful conduct' within
      the meaning of the Act.

- a civil judgment in a claim based on a defendant's unlawful conduct;[1]
- a confiscation order under the PCA 2002 or the provisions listed at s 8(7)(a)–(g) made after taking the property into account in assessing the person's benefit from criminal conduct.[2]

**11.78**    In circumstances where no previous recovery order has been made in respect of any of the property related to the original property, and the authority seeks recovery orders in respect of two or more related items of recoverable property, the court has a discretion as to which of the two items of property it subjects to a recovery order to satisfy the authority's claim.[3] It may make the recovery order in relation to only some of the items of property, or to only part of any of the related property. In the earlier example of the cash and the car, therefore, if the application were for recovery of both the car and the cash in the deposit account, the court could decide to make a recovery order only in respect of the cash, or in respect of the car, or in respect of the car and only part of the cash.

**11.79**    The above limitations do not prevent the court making a recovery order in respect of any of the profits which have accrued in respect of recoverable property, even if no recovery order is made in respect of the property itself.[4]

## TRUSTEE FOR CIVIL RECOVERY

**11.80**    The trustee for civil recovery is appointed by the court to give effect to the recovery order.[5] He is an individual nominated by the enforcement authority and may be a member of its staff. His task is similar to that of a trustee in bankruptcy and, in practice, is likely to have the skills and experience of an insolvency practitioner. The trustee acts on behalf of the enforcement authority and must comply with any directions given to him by it,[6] but he must also conform to any conditions as to the exercise of his function which are imposed by the court in the recovery order. Unlike an interim receiver, the trustee is not an officer of the court.

**11.81**    The trustee's duty is to realise the property vested in him by the recovery order, so far as practicable, in the manner best calculated to maximise the amount payable to the enforcement authority.[7] His functions are to secure the detention, custody or preservation of any property vested in him by the recovery order, to realise the value of property other than money for the benefit of the enforcement agency, and to perform any other functions conferred upon him.

**11.82**    The trustee's powers are listed in Sch 7 to the PCA 2002. He obtains those powers automatically upon appointment by the recovery order. The recovery order does not need to grant him the powers in the way they must be granted to an interim receiver. In summary, the powers are:

---

1    Section 278(8).
2    Section 278(9), (10).
3    Section 278(4), (5).
4    Section 278(6), although the profits must accumulate from property which is proved to be recoverable property.
5    Section 267(1).
6    Section 267(4).
7    Section 267(5).

– to sell property or any part or interest in it;
– to incur expenditure to acquire any property not vested in him, or to discharge liabilities or extinguish any rights to which property vested in him is subject;
– to manage property in the same way as a receiver of property under the PCA 2002 could manage;
– to conduct legal proceedings in respect of the property;
– to compromise or make arrangements in connection with any claim relating to the property;
– to exercise any of his powers by using his own name to hold property, enter contracts, sue and be sued, employ agents and execute any documents;
– to do anything which is necessary or expedient for the exercise of his powers.

**11.83**  The sums realised from recoverable property vested in the trustee must be applied: first, to make any payment of compensation to an owner of associated property required by the order pursuant to s 272; and, secondly, to pay the expenses of any insolvency practitioner who has accidentally and innocently incurred expenditure in respect of any recoverable property. The balance remaining after those payments must then be paid to the enforcement agency.[1]

**11.84**  It is not clear how the trustee for civil recovery is to be remunerated for his services. If he is an employee of the enforcement authority, he will be salaried. If he is not such an employee, presumably the enforcement authority will enter into an agreement with the individual concerned prior to nominating him to the court.

**11.85**  Schedule 10 to the PCA 2002 makes various special provisions as to the taxation of dealings with property by the trustee when exercising his functions pursuant to a recovery order.

# JOINT PROPERTY AND ASSOCIATED PROPERTY

## Joint property

**11.86**  Recoverable property will often be mixed with, or incorporated within, property which is not recoverable. The part of the property which is not recoverable is called 'associated property' for the purposes of the PCA 2002. The associated property may be held by the same person who holds the recoverable property or it may be held by another person.

**11.87**  Property owned jointly by two or more persons (as opposed to property held by those persons in common, in which case the other tenants in common would be owners of associated property) does not involve associated property until the joint interest is severed. This is because there is only one undivided interest in jointly owned property, which is held by each of the parties jointly rather than in separate parts. In law, apart from these provisions of the PCA 2002, if recoverable property were only used in part to acquire the joint property, that part would not be an identifiable separate interest in the property, with the result that the whole property would appear to be recoverable under the definition of 'recoverable property'. To avoid injustice to a joint owner of property who acquired his interest in that property without the use of recoverable

---

1     Section 280.

property (such a person is termed 'an excepted joint owner') the court treats his interest as if it had been severed from the part of the joint property which is referable to recoverable property, but without actually severing it before a recovery order is made.

**11.88**   To leave associated property and excepted joint owners of property entirely beyond the powers of the PCA 2002 would have the twofold effect of, first, depriving the court of the ability to ensure that injustice is not caused to owners of such legitimate property, and, secondly, making it difficult for the enforcement authority to recover the full value of property which it obtains pursuant to a recovery order.[1] The PCA 2002 provides that when making a recovery order the court may, either by virtue of an agreement between the parties or by its own order, make an order in respect of the associated property as well as the recoverable property, but the owner of the associated property or the excepted joint owner may be paid compensation for the loss or reduction of his interest.

**11.89**   These provisions are of enormous importance since they determine how the court deals with the interests of persons whose legitimately obtained property has become enmeshed with recoverable property. As well as spouses and dependants of persons involved in unlawful conduct, individuals who have entered into investments or into business with persons who hold recoverable property will be drawn into proceedings for recovery orders by reason of these provisions. They merit detailed consideration.

## Associated property

**11.90**   Associated property is defined as property (including property held by the respondent to the recovery proceedings) which is not itself recoverable property and which falls within one of the following descriptions:[2]

–   any interest in the recoverable property: examples are a tenancy which exists in a recoverable freehold property, or a charge obtained in respect of a property;
–   any other interest in the property in which the recoverable property subsists. Thus, if the recoverable property involves the lease of a flat in a block, the other leases in the same freehold block would be associated. The freehold interest of the block in which the lease which is recoverable property is held would also be associated property;
–   where the recoverable property is a tenancy in common, the tenancy of the other tenants;
–   where the recoverable property is part of a larger property, but not a separate part, the remainder of the property. The example given in parliamentary debates was that if a painting was recoverable property, but the frame in which it was mounted was not recoverable, the frame would be associated property.

**11.91**   A degree of incorporation of the recoverable property in the other property appears to be required for the other property to be associated property. If the

---

1   For example, if the recoverable property is the freehold of a property subject to a very long lease, the value of the freehold to the enforcement agency is likely to be very small, or realisable at full value only far in the future. Only by having the power to deal with the interest of the leaseholder by way of the recovery order will effective recovery be possible.

2   Section 245(1).

recoverable property can be removed without altering the remaining property it would appear not to be associated. In that respect, the painting and frame example may not be apt unless the two are intrinsically related in a way which is more than transient. A better example might be a replacement engine in a car. If the engine was recoverable property, once it was fitted to the car the rest of the car clearly becomes associated with the engine.[1] Cash paid into a bank account where it becomes mixed with other cash would also appear to fall within this definition.

**11.92**   Pension schemes are treated differently to avoid the interests of the other beneficiaries of the pension scheme becoming associated property, with the possibility of the enforcement agency having to name thousands of beneficiaries as respondents to the application.[2]

## Excepted joint owner

**11.93**   An excepted joint owner is a joint tenant who obtained the property in circumstances in which it would not be recoverable as against him.[3] If, therefore, two people buy a property, one using recoverable property and the other using property which is not recoverable, the latter will be an excepted joint owner. The same would appear to apply if a couple buy a property using a deposit which came from recoverable property and the balance of the purchase price was made up by a mortgage in joint names which was repaid using solely legitimate income (ie not recoverable property).

**11.94**   It is clear that determining the excepted owner's share will, in many cases, be a difficult and complicated task. The court will have to approach the matter as if it were dealing with contributions amounting to a resulting or constructive trust. The definition of the excepted joint owner's share as 'so much of the recoverable property as would have been his if the joint tenancy had been severed' appears to import ordinary principles of property and trusts law into this exercise. This is qualified by the requirement that an excepted joint owner's 'share' of the property is limited to his obtaining the property in 'circumstances in which it would not be recoverable as against him'. Where one person buys a property using only recoverable property but places that property in the joint names of himself and his cohabitee with an express declaration of trust that it is held beneficially for the two of them, the cohabitee will not become an excepted joint owner because his interest arises from a disposal of recoverable property and is, therefore, also recoverable. Where the property is bought using solely recoverable property in one person's name without any express written declaration of trust, and that person's cohabitee seeks to assert a beneficial interest in the property under a constructive trust,[4] or by way of proprietary estoppel, it may be open to the cohabitee to argue that he has become an excepted joint owner by reason of having acted in good faith, for value and without notice that it was recoverable property.[5]

---

1   The case-law on incorporation into other property of goods supplied subject to a retention of title
    clause in a contract for the sale of goods may offer some assistance in the application of this term.
2   Section 245(3). Pensions are dealt with at **11.107** *et seq.*
3   Section 270(3), (4).
4   In line with the test set out in *Lloyds Bank plc v Rosset* [1991] 1 AC 107, HL.
5   Section 308(1).

**11.95** A problem which is common in the bankruptcy regime will arise in many of these cases. Spouses and cohabitees who are not legal owners of property subject to proceedings will assert a beneficial interest acquired by reason of their detrimental reliance upon some agreement or understanding reached with the legal owner of the property (their spouse or cohabitee). In many such cases, only the married couple or the cohabitees know what may have been agreed between them or what either of them may have done or contributed towards the property. If both present a united front to the court when it is establishing what interest either has obtained and the manner in which that interest was obtained, the enforcement authority may have great difficulty in attempting to go behind their evidence. This is readily identifiable as providing what is likely to be one of the most commonly visited battlegrounds created by Part 5, and one where battles are likely to be very hotly contested.

## Agreements about associated and joint property

**11.96** Where certain conditions are met, the court may order that, instead of the recoverable property vesting in the trustee for civil recovery, the owner of the associated property or the excepted joint owner must make a payment to the trustee for civil recovery.[1] In return for the payment, the recovery order may vest, create or extinguish any interest in property.[2] A recovery order in respect of recoverable property following such an agreement must state that the recoverable property ceases to be recoverable. The chain along which recoverable property may be followed is broken by such an agreement and order.

**11.97** The conditions for such an agreement are that:

– the associated property must be specified or described in the claim form;[3]
– if the associated property belongs to someone other than the holder of the recoverable property the claim form must have been served on that person;[4] and
– the enforcement authority (on the one hand) and the person who holds the associated property or the excepted owner (on the other hand) have agreed to the making of the order.[5]

**11.98** The amount of the payment to be made by the owner of associated property or the excepted owner is not set by the court but must be agreed by the parties as being:

– in the case of an order concerning associated property, the value of the recoverable property which is effectively being purchased from the trustee for civil recovery by the owner of associated property;
– in the case of an excepted owner, the value of the recoverable property less the value of the excepted owner's share (ie applying the fiction that the joint tenancy has been severed for the purposes of identifying the recoverable property and the excepted owner's interest).[6]

---

1   Section 271(1).
2   Section 271(2).
3   Section 270(2)(a).
4   Section 270(2)(b). A joint owner of recoverable property would already have been served because he will be a respondent to the application as a person who holds recoverable property.
5   Section 271(1).
6   'Value' means the market value – s 316(1).

**11.99**    The payment to the trustee can be reduced by an agreed reasonable amount to take into account any loss suffered by the owner of the associated property or the excepted joint owner as a result of an interim receiving order.[1]

**11.100**    Where there is more than one item of associated property or more than one excepted joint owner, all the holders of such property and excepted joint owners must agree between each other and the enforcement authority how much each of them is to pay.[2]

## Orders in respect of associated and joint property in default of agreement

**11.101**    The court may not compel an owner of associated property or an excepted joint owner to 'buy out' the interest which the enforcement authority would otherwise have in recoverable property if there is no agreement to make such a payment and its amount. The court may, however, make an order in relation to the associated property or the excepted joint owner's interest in recoverable property even if they do not agree. Such an order may be necessary to ensure that the enforcement authority is able to obtain effective recovery of the proceeds of crime. Where interests in associated property or joint property are affected in this way the court must ensure that the affected person is compensated.

**11.102**    The court may, in the absence of agreement and if it considers it just and equitable to do so,[3] provide in a recovery order that:[4]

–    the associated property is to vest in the trustee for civil recovery;
–    in the case of joint property, the excepted joint owner's interest is extinguished or severed.

**11.103**    If the recovery order makes any such provision it may also provide for any or all of the following:[5]

–    a payment by the trustee to the holder of the associated property or the excepted joint owner;
–    an interest in the property in favour of that person;
–    impose liabilities or conditions in relation to the property vested in the trustee.

**11.104**    In making any of these orders the court must balance, on the one hand, the rights of any holder of the associated property or excepted joint owner and the value of the property to him, which includes any value that cannot be assessed in terms of money and, on the other hand, the enforcement authority's interest in receiving the realised proceeds of the recoverable property.[6] This obliges the court not merely to look at the financial value of property but also any practical value or sentimental attachment

---

1     Section 271(4); and see, more generally, **11.119** *et seq.*
2     Section 271(5).
3     Section 272(1).
4     Section 272(2).
5     Section 272(3).
6     Section 272(4).

it may have, and, most importantly, to any particular rights which may arise under Art 8, or Art 1 of the First Protocol of the Convention. The need to balance those rights against the public interest in recovering the proceeds of criminal activity should ensure that these draconian powers to divest individuals of otherwise legitimately obtained and held property are not in contravention of the Convention. Of course, the application of the powers by the court must also, in practice, respect the Convention.

**11.105** These are very broad powers capable of flexible application as the court sees fit. There is no set formula for how the value of any payment is to be set by the court, save that it must carry out the balancing exercise noted above. It is impossible to set out the full extent of the types of orders which could be made, but the following certainly appear to be available:

–  vesting of associated property in the trustee in exchange for a payment to the holder of that property and/or the grant of some other interest in the property (eg a lease, a life interest, etc) with or without further conditions (eg the payment of an occupation rent or some other charge for use of an asset);

–  extinguishing an excepted joint owner's interest in a joint property in return for a payment and/or the grant of some other interest in the property (eg a lease, life interest, etc) with or without further conditions (eg the payment of an occupation rent or some other charge for use of an asset);

–  severance of a joint tenancy with or without a payment to an excepted joint owner to compensate him for the loss of possibly acquiring the whole property upon the death of the joint owner;

–  vesting of associated property in the trustee, or the extinguishment of a joint interest with conditions as to use or sale of that property by the trustee either with or without a further payment;

–  severance of a joint tenancy with conditions and restrictions as to the trustee's use and/or realisation of his tenancy in common, either with or without a further payment to the excepted joint owner (conditions might be postponement of sale until the death of the excepted joint owner or limitations upon the trustee's right to enter into possession of the property).

**11.106** At the same time as the court makes any order, it may require the enforcement authority to pay compensation to the holder of associated property or the excepted joint owner for any loss suffered by that person as a result of an interim receiving order in respect of the property.[1] The amount of such compensation is at the discretion of the court, taking into account all relevant circumstances.[2]

# PENSIONS

**11.107** Property obtained by unlawful conduct which takes the form of pensions, or pensions acquired by the use of recoverable property, is recoverable under the PCA 2002.[3] Special rules deal with pensions because of their complex nature (being a combination of contract, trusts and revenue law) and because a person's pension rights are

---

1    Section 272(5).
2    Ibid.
3    Pensions are defined at s 275(4), (6) and include a retirement annuity contract.

usually held in a pension fund together with the pension rights of thousands of other individuals. It is expressly provided that any rights under a pension scheme are not to be treated as associated property.[1]

**11.108** Recoverable property which is followed or traced into a pension scheme is not recovered by vesting of the property in the trustee.[2] The enforcement agency will not want to obtain pension rights which would not be paid until the beneficiary claimed the pension; it seeks to recover cash sums as quickly as possible. Recovery of rights under a pension scheme takes place by way of a payment to the trustee by the trustees or managers of the pension scheme of a cash sum equivalent to the value of the recoverable pension rights.

**11.109** Regulations are likely to be made as to the calculation of the cash value of the rights,[3] and these are virtually certain to adopt the 'cash equivalent transfer value' of pension rights, which has already become the standard basis for calculating the value of pensions in respect both of the pensions legislation generally and of pension-sharing orders within matrimonial proceedings.[4] It will be for the pension managers or trustees to carry out the appropriate calculations in accordance with any regulations made for this purpose.

**11.110** A recovery order made in respect of pension rights overrides any rules in the pension scheme which conflict with the recovery order.[5] Particular statutory provisions which place restrictions upon the assignment of pension rights are also disapplied from recovery orders.[6] The recovery order cannot, therefore, be restricted or frustrated by any pension scheme rules which prevent or penalise transfers out of the scheme, or by statutory provisions which prevent payment of pension rights directly as cash to a person. Recoverable property cannot be put beyond the reach of the enforcement authority by placing it in a private pension scheme which has tight restrictions on transfers from it.

**11.111** A recovery order dealing with pensions must provide for the pension scheme's liabilities to be reduced in accordance with the payment out under the recovery order.[7] The order must give the pension-scheme managers or trustees power to do this. This may reduce or completely extinguish a person's rights to a pension under the scheme. It would plainly frustrate the purpose of the legislation if the person whose pension rights have been recovered by way of a payment to the trustee by the pension-scheme managers or trustee could still seek payment of his pension from the scheme at some point in the future.

**11.112** The recovery order may also make provision for how the costs incurred by the pension-scheme managers or trustees in providing information to the court, and subsequently complying with the order, will be met.[8] In all likelihood, this will be by way of a deduction from the sum that they are ordered to pay to the trustee.

---

1    Section 245(3).
2    Section 273(2).
3    Section 275(1), (2).
4    See the Divorce etc (Pensions) Regulations 1996, SI 1996/1676, reg 3; the Welfare Reform and Pensions Act 1999; the Matrimonial Causes Act 1973.
5    Section 273(3).
6    Section 273(5).
7    Section 273(4).
8    Section 276(5).

**11.113**   Where the application for a recovery order is compromised, the court will not make a recovery order but will instead stay the proceedings.[1] The pension trustees or managers may compromise the part of the claim relating to pensions by adding themselves as parties to the agreement. In order to do so effectively they will require their release from any terms of the pension scheme preventing them from making payments out from the scheme in this way. The court, in making the order staying the proceedings, may make provision for the managers or trustees to make the payment in accordance with the agreement and to give effect to any other provision made in respect of the scheme (such as recovery of their costs).[2] The order also grants them power to enter into the agreement regardless of the scheme rules, and overrides the provisions of the scheme so far as they conflict with its terms. The powers to reduce the scheme's liabilities to the person whose rights in the scheme are being removed are also implied by the making of such an order.

## VICTIMS OF THEFT ETC – CLAIMS BY THE OWNER OF THE PROPERTY

**11.114**   Property which is subject to recovery proceedings may not lawfully belong to the holder of that property. It may have been stolen or obtained by fraud. Any person who claims that the property alleged to be recoverable property, or any part of it, belongs to him may apply to the court within the recovery proceedings for a declaration to that effect.[3] Once the declaration is made, the property ceases to be recoverable property. If the applicant for the declaration also applies for an order for return of the property,[4] the court may order its return to him.

**11.115**   The court may make the declaration if a three-part condition is met. The condition is that:[5]

–   the person was deprived of the property, or of the property which it represents, by unlawful conduct;
–   the property was not recoverable property immediately before he was deprived of it; and
–   the property belongs to him.

**11.116**   Persons claiming ownership of property subject to proceedings for a recovery order also benefit from an extended limitation period. Ordinarily, any action for conversion must be brought within 6 years of the original conversion.[6] At the end of the 6-year period the original owner's title to the goods is extinguished.[7] By the new s 27A(5) and (6), introduced into the Limitation Act 1980 by the PCA 2002,[8] the original owner's claim to the property is revived by an application for a recovery order being made in respect of it. The original owner may apply for the declaration

---

1   Section 276(1); and see **11.66** *et seq.*
2   Section 277.
3   Section 281(1).
4   Pursuant to the Torts (Interference with Goods) Act 1977.
5   Section 281(3).
6   Limitation Act 1980, s 3(1).
7   Ibid, s 3(2).
8   Section 288.

notwithstanding the fact that he would not have a cause of action for recovery of the asset because of the effluxion of a limitation period. If the declaration is granted, his title to the property is restored and there appears to be no new limitation period imposed for bringing a claim for recovery of the property. This is probably because it is envisaged that upon making the declaration the court will order the return of the property to the rightful owner, failing which the interim receiver will do so by applying to vary any interim receiving order or restraining order in respect of the property.

## EXEMPTIONS

**11.117**   The Secretary of State may, by order, exempt from the operation of the recovery provisions specified persons or classes of persons, or classes of property.[1] The following classes of property are automatically exempt from recovery proceedings:

–   recoverable property held by the Financial Services Authority;[2]
–   property subject to specified charges imposed within regulation of the financial services sector;[3]
–   recoverable property held by a person by reason of his acting, or having acted, as an insolvency practitioner.[4]

**11.118**   Property may also not be recoverable if it is either prescribed property, or is disposed of in pursuance of a prescribed enactment or an enactment of a prescribed description.[5] Such property or enactments are to be prescribed by orders made by the Secretary of State. It is not clear how or when these powers are to be used.

## COMPENSATION

**11.119**   There are several different provisions in Part 5 of the PCA 2002 dealing with compensation for individuals affected by interim receiving orders and proceedings for recovery orders. The drafting of the Act means that these various provisions are somewhat scattered around Part 5. They are all set out below.

### Where property is found not to be recoverable property or associated property

**11.120**   Where the enforcement authority obtains an interim receiving order in respect of property but does not ultimately succeed in proving within the recovery order proceedings that the property is recoverable property or associated property, the owner of the property may apply to the court for compensation.[6] Such an application cannot be made if the court has made a declaration that the property belongs to a person who has been deprived of it by unlawful conduct,[7] because otherwise the holder of the

---

1    Section 282(1).
2    Section 282(3).
3    Section 282(4).
4    Section 282(5).
5    Section 309(1).
6    Section 283(1).
7    Ie an application pursuant to s 284 – s 283(2)(a).

property would be compensated for holding the proceeds of unlawful conduct. Such an application may not be made if a recovery order was made by consent,[1] the rationale appearing to be that if a consent order is made, all matters must be agreed, including the question of any compensation.

**11.121**    Any such application for compensation must be brought within 3 months of either the court's making a decision by reason of which no recovery order could be made in respect of the property,[2] or the discontinuance of the proceedings in respect of the property.[3] There is no provision in the PCA 2002 for extension of the limitation period for making such an application. It would appear that once the 3-month limitation period has elapsed any claim for compensation is absolutely barred. There is no power to extend the period.

**11.122**    Where the property is found not to be recoverable or associated property, and it is not subject to a declaration that it belongs to someone who was deprived of it by unlawful conduct, it will be returned to the holder. The compensation which may be ordered by the court in such a case is, therefore, limited to the loss caused as a result of the interim receiving order: an interim receiving order may have tied up a person's property for a considerable time, effectively depriving him of its enjoyment or use; its value may have depreciated over that time; a potential sale at a profit may have been missed; a business may have missed lucrative opportunities to expand its trade. Where loss can be shown to have been caused as a result of the interim receiving order, the court may make an order for compensation.[4]

**11.123**    The court may make an order for compensation to be paid by the enforcement authority. The amount of compensation is at the discretion of the court, being what it considers to be reasonable having regard to the loss suffered and any other relevant circumstances.[5]

**11.124**    Where an interim receiving order has been in force in respect of property associated with other property, or in respect of joint property, the owner of the associated property or the excepted joint owner may have suffered loss as a result of the interim receiving order, as discussed above. The court may make an order in respect of joint property and associated property with or without the parties' agreement,[6] and provision for the payment of compensation for such losses can be made within the order.

**11.125**    Where such an order is made by agreement, the parties may agree compensation due to the owner of associated property or the excepted joint owner and deduct it from any payment made by that person to 'buy out' the enforcement

---

1    Section 283(2)(b).
2    Section 283(3). For example, a decision that: there was no unlawful conduct; the property in question was not obtained by such property; the original property cannot be traced or followed into the property subject to the proceedings; some exception applies to the property by reason of which it cannot be recovered.
3    Section 283(4). Note that the effective date is the date of discontinuance of proceedings in respect of the property for which compensation is claimed. The same set of proceedings may continue in relation to other property but the limitation period for the compensation claim will already be running.
4    Section 283(5).
5    Section 283(9).
6    Sections 271, 272; and see **11.96** *et seq.*

authority's interest in the recoverable property.[1] This is not an application for compensation since it does not involve the court and is based on agreement between the parties.

**11.126** In default of any such agreement between the owner of associated property or an excepted joint owner and the authority, the court may, when making the recovery order in respect of the joint property, or the property with which property is associated, order the payment of compensation for any loss caused by the interim receiving order to the associated owner or the excepted joint owner.[2] The order can be only made if it is 'just and equitable' to do so.[3] The amount of compensation is at the court's discretion, having regard to the person's loss and to any other relevant circumstance.[4]

## Where a person has lost rights of pre-emption, etc by the making of a recovery order

**11.127** A recovery order has the effect of suspending or excluding the operation of pre-emption rights, etc.[5] Where the effect of the recovery order vesting the property in the trustee for civil recovery is that the rights can no longer be exercised by the person who held them prior to the making of the recovery order, the court may require the enforcement authority to pay compensation to that person.[6] This provision deals with a situation where a person, prior to the making of a recovery order, may have obtained an option to buy property at a specific date but that date passed during the currency of the recovery order so that he could not exercise it and, therefore, lost the benefit of it. If he paid for the right to have the option that person will be able to apply to the court for compensation in a like amount. If the option was to buy the property at an advantageous price, he may also be able to obtain compensation for the loss of profit on the transaction he might have obtained. The amount of compensation lies in the discretion of the court, being what it considers to be reasonable having regard to the loss suffered and any other relevant circumstances.[7]

**11.128** An application for compensation must be made within 3 months of the vesting of the property pursuant to the recovery order,[8] which is likely to be the same time as the recovery order is made. There is no scope to extend the limitation period for making the claim.

## Where the interim receiver dealt with property outside the scope of an interim receiving order

**11.129** Circumstances in which an interim receiver has dealt with property which was not within the scope of an interim receiving order were considered above.[9] Persons

---

1    Section 271(4).
2    Section 272(5).
3    Section 272(1).
4    Section 272(6).
5    Section 269. See also **11.71–11.72**.
6    Section 283(6), (8).
7    Section 283(9).
8    Section 283(7).
9    See **11.47**.

affected by such action must bring an ordinary civil claim for the torts or other wrongs committed by the interim receiver. There is no special remedy within the Act, although the interim receiver may be able to avail himself of the partial defence provided by the PCA 2002.[1]

## INSOLVENCY

**11.130** If specified insolvency proceedings have commenced in relation to property, no proceedings for a recovery order may be taken or continued unless the court responsible for the insolvency proceedings[2] gives leave.[3] Leave may be given subject to conditions. The application for leave may be made without notice to any person, but notice must be given to an insolvency practitioner or the official receiver if the Insolvency Rules require it. The insolvency courts have powers to give leave under this provision.[4]

**11.131** The property subject to this restriction is any property which is:[5]

–  an asset of a company being wound-up in pursuance to a voluntary winding-up resolution;
–  an asset of a company which is the subject of a voluntary arrangement under Part 1 of the Insolvency Act 1986 (or the equivalent provisions in Northern Ireland and Scotland);
–  subject to the appointment of an interim receiver under s 286 of the Insolvency Act 1986 (or the equivalent provisions in Northern Ireland and Scotland);
–  comprised in the estate of a bankrupt (or the Scottish equivalent);
–  an asset of a person subject to an individual voluntary arrangement under Part 8 of the Insolvency Act 1986 (or the equivalent in Northern Ireland and Scotland).

## COSTS AND PUBLIC FUNDING

**11.132** Applications for recovery orders are ordinary civil proceedings and the normal civil rules as to costs will apply.[6] The rules on Part 36 payments and offers will also apply so that both the enforcement authority and the respondents to proceedings will be able to make offers to settle all or any part of the proceedings without prejudice.[7]

---

1    Section 247(3).
2    Section 311(8)(b).
3    Section 311(1). Since it is a prerequisite of an application for an interim receiving order that an application for a recovery order may be brought (s 246(1)), it follows that an application for an interim receiving order cannot succeed unless such leave to bring the main application has first been obtained.
4    Section 311(6).
5    Section 311(3).
6    CPR 1998, Parts 43–48.
7    CPR 1998, Part 36.

**11.133**   Public funding will be available to respondents and interested parties seeking to join High Court proceedings, subject to the normal rules as to means and merits. The Legal Services Commission statutory charge will also apply to any property a respondent successfully recovers or preserves within the proceedings.


# COMPATIBILITY OF THE CIVIL RECOVERY PROVISIONS WITH THE HUMAN RIGHTS ACT 1998


**11.134**   Although there is no express statement to this effect in the PCA 2002 itself, it is implicit within the legislation that the civil recovery provisions will be used in cases where a criminal prosecution cannot successfully be brought against an individual in order to invoke the confiscation procedure and the reverse burden of proof therein. The lower standard of proof and less restrictive evidential rules available within civil litigation should allow the recovery of the assets of those who are beyond the reach of the criminal law, either because the evidence to convict them of criminal conduct is lacking or because they are enjoying the proceeds although not themselves guilty of crime. The legislation is, without doubt, tough. The Government has specifically promoted it as such. Part 5 of the PCA 2002 will inevitably generate a significant body of reported case-law, much of which will either be based upon, or involve, questions of the legislation's compatibility with the European Convention on Human Rights.

**11.135**   The Convention rights most likely to be raised in civil recovery proceedings are:

–    Art 6: right to a fair trial – in particular, the question of whether the extended protections afforded to those charged with a 'criminal offence' apply to proceedings under Part 5 of the PCA 2002;
–    Art 7: no punishment without law – the retrospective effect of the legislation would offend this right if the proceedings under Part 5 are categorised as 'criminal' in nature;
–    Art 8: right to respect for private and family life – likely to be invoked in particular where a family home is the subject of civil recovery proceedings;
–    Art 1 of the First Protocol: protection of property – likely to be engaged in every set of proceedings because the whole purpose of Part 5 is the frustration of a person's peaceful enjoyment of property obtained through unlawful conduct, and the recovery of such property.

**11.136**   Convention rights will not arise in the same way in every case. Although it is clear that Art 1 of the First Protocol will be engaged (but not necessarily infringed) in every case under Part 5, Art 8 will not be engaged with the same frequency. There is also a possible distinction between cases where the respondent of the property in question is himself accused of unlawful conduct and cases where the respondent merely holds property which is or represents property obtained by unlawful conduct, but conduct in which he has no involvement. In the former case, the respondent will be defending himself against an allegation of conduct which is by definition criminal, while in the latter case the issue may simply be whether or not the property is recoverable without any accusation of wrongdoing against the respondent at all, although such an accusation will be made in respect of some, possibly unidentified, individual who is not a party to the proceedings. Such a distinction, if followed by different classification of the proceedings for Convention purposes, has the potential for inconsistent treatment of cases under Part 5 of the PCA 2002 depending on whether or not the alleged wrongdoer is a party to the proceedings.

**11.137**   Each relevant article of the Convention will now be discussed in turn.

# ARTICLE 6: RIGHT TO A FAIR TRIAL

**11.138**   Part 5 of the PCA 2002 does not create any new procedural code. It merely grants new substantive powers to the High Court which are to be exercised in the course of ordinary civil litigation. It is unlikely that many successful challenges to the CPR 1998 can be mounted,[1] although the application of those Rules by the court must always have the Convention rights in mind.

**11.139**   The real issue is likely to be whether the proceedings are properly categorised as 'civil' or 'criminal' in nature. The Government has stated very firmly its view that this part of the legislation creates a civil remedy only. The draftsman of the Act has taken great care to use terminology which avoids giving the impression that it creates some sort of criminal procedure.[2] The Government has placed reliance upon the decision of the European Court of Human Rights in *Phillips v United Kingdom* [2001] Crim LR 817 and of the House of Lords in *R v Rezvi and Others* [2002] UKHL 1, [2002] 1 All ER 801 and *R v Benjafield* [2002] UKHL 2, [2002] 2 WLR 235 as support for that argument. Those cases all concerned the confiscation regime pursuant to the Drug Trafficking Act 1994 and the Criminal Justice Act 1988 and were based on a finding that the confiscation schemes were part of the sentencing exercise following a criminal conviction. They decided that the legislation created no new criminal proceedings and laid no new charges. The new civil recovery scheme created by Part 5 is different. It stands independently from any criminal proceedings. It is plainly not part of the sentencing process but a freestanding civil process. The existing authority on the criminal confiscation regime is not apposite to the civil recovery regime.[3] The question of whether proceedings for civil recovery are criminal or civil must be looked at afresh.

**11.140**   The Government view is that this new regime is civil. It does not focus on individuals but on property obtained through unlawful conduct. Whether the person who holds the property was responsible for the unlawful conduct is largely immaterial to the result of the case because the remedy is sought to be *in rem* and not *in personam*. Reliance appears to be placed upon decisions by the European Court of Human Rights

---

1   The 'over-riding' objective at CPR 1998, r 1.1 effectively places the court under an obligation to consider the basic Art 6 rights. CPR 1998, r 39.2 largely replicates the 'public hearing' requirements of Art 6(1).

2   For example, references to 'unlawful conduct' rather than 'criminal conduct', although the meaning is clearly the same; 'recovery' rather than 'confiscation'.

3   Although the general *dicta* in those cases as to the infringement of the Art 1 of the First Protocol right to property being justified and proportionate in the 'general interest' might be of relevance to the new Part 5.

that such rights of forfeiture in favour of the Government which operated *in rem* would not raise criminal proceedings.[1] This approach has recently met with further support by the European Court's admissibility decision in *Butler v United Kingdom* (unreported) 27 June 2002.

**11.141** Such an argument is likely to succeed in cases where the holder of the property is not alleged to have been involved in any form of criminal conduct but merely holds recoverable property. The same analysis does not work as well where that person has taken part in conduct which is criminal in nature, since the court will be determining not only whether the property itself is recoverable but whether the party to proceedings has been guilty of unlawful conduct. There appears to be no good reason why a person who holds property that he himself obtained by unlawful conduct should have greater rights concerning that property, solely by reason of being the person accused of criminal activity, than the person who has committed no crime but innocently holds property which is alleged to be recoverable by reason of the wrongdoing of someone else. The argument for the civil recovery powers being concerned only with the property and its source, and not with the need to find wrongdoers, has the merit of ensuring that the recovery scheme is applied consistently. It avoids a situation where a case in which a holder of property is alleged to be a wrongdoer is dealt with differently from a case where the wrongdoer has long since divested himself of the property and any property representing it so that he is no longer a party to the proceedings. The respondent in the former case would have greater procedural protections if he showed that he was subject to a 'criminal charge' than the respondent in the latter case who was not accused of any wrongdoing whatsoever, but merely happened to hold recoverable property.

**11.142** Whatever the convenience of dealing with all holders of recoverable property equally, the central question remains whether an allegation against a respondent to an application for a recovery order amounts to a criminal charge. It is well established that the notion of 'criminal charge' in the Convention has an autonomous meaning and classification of the proceedings as 'civil' in domestic law does not mean that they will be so classified in Convention law.[2] In the case of *Raimondo v Italy*[3] (1994) 18 EHRR 237 the European Court of Human Rights held that anti-mafia confiscation powers granted by Italian law were not criminal in nature, although the precise reasoning leading to this result is not apparent in the Court's judgment.[4] In many respects, the regime created in Italy was comparable to that created by the PCA 2002 and, if anything, the Italian model was more draconian.[5]

**11.143** There are problems in categorising the civil recovery powers as purely civil. First, the allegation of unlawful conduct amounts to an allegation of criminal conduct.

---

1    *Air Canada v United Kingdom* (1995) 20 EHRR 150, at para 52, a case concerning threatened
     forfeiture of an aircraft pursuant to s 141 of the Customs and Excise Management Act 1972. See
     also *AGOSI v United Kingdom* (1987) 9 EHRR 1.
2    See *Engel and Others v Netherlands* (1979–80) 1 EHRR 706.
3    It is perhaps notable that on appeal in Italy, Mr Raimondo managed to have the orders seizing his
     property set aside, so that by the time his application came before the Court he had recovered his
     property.
4    The description in domestic law of the measures as 'preventative' of crime, rather than 'punitive'
     appears to have figured as an important factor.
5    It appears to have placed the onus on the respondent to show that the assets had been lawfully
     acquired, rather than obliging the State to prove otherwise.

Whether this allegation in the claim form or particulars of claim amounts to a 'criminal charge' remains to be seen. On the one hand, there will be no entry on a person's criminal record following a finding under these provisions. On the other hand, he will have a public finding of a court declaring him to have indulged in conduct which was criminal, and that finding will be capable of being used against him in subsequent proceedings for recovery orders. Further, once the finding has been made he will be deprived of property which he has obtained through that conduct, or which represents such conduct.

**11.144**    Secondly, the new powers differ from situations where a victim of crime sues for loss caused during the commission of a crime, such as a victim of rape who sues her attacker for trespass to the person, because there is: (a) no element of compensation for a wronged person in the civil recovery regime; and (b) a finding of unlawful conduct depends entirely on a full breach of the criminal law (by contrast, a person may commit a tortious trespass to the person but not be guilty of the offence of rape). There may be an argument to say that the provisions are designed to compensate society for the wrong done to it by criminal conduct, but this argument does not appear to stand up to any rigorous analysis, particularly considering the extensive criminal compensation powers made available within the PCA 2002. A stronger argument is that the recovery order is limited to the property obtained by unlawful activity. The effect of the powers is limited by the amount of property obtained. There is no element of fixing the recovery order in proportion to the seriousness of the crime or the extent of any injury or damage caused by it.

**11.145**    Thirdly, the recovery provisions are clearly meant to have a deterrent effect. Their purpose is to make it plain that those who think they can provide a comfortable life for themselves and their families by way of criminal conduct are mistaken. The extensive powers to obtain information during an interim receiving order and to follow and trace property through all manner of complex financial devices, when combined with the absence of any obvious compensatory object to the legislation, gives the regime the flavour of criminal proceedings. In *Bendenoun v France* (1994) 18 EHRR 54, heavy tax surcharges were held to be deterrent in effect rather than compensatory, and therefore had a criminal character.

**11.146**    Fourthly, unlike most civil litigation between individuals, proceedings for a recovery order will follow a civil recovery investigation (or possibly a criminal investigation) by the ARA on behalf of the Director (who, for the purpose of Part 5, is the 'enforcement agency') during which very extensive and intrusive investigatory powers will have been available. Although this does not appear to raise any 'equality of arms' issues once proceedings have been commenced,[1] the statutory regime seen as a whole has close parallels with a criminal prosecution. With that said, there are similarities with the investigation of matters relating to the tax or customs systems which are not generally considered to be criminal.

**11.147**    In *Butler v United Kingdom* (above) the European Court of Human Rights considered similar arguments in respect to the provisions in ss 42 and 43 of the Drug Trafficking Act 1994 relating to the forfeiture of cash representing the proceeds of drug trafficking, or intended for use in drug trafficking. These are powers which are largely

---

1    Normal civil procedures will operate ensuring a fair hearing for both sides, and public funding should be available for a respondent unable to pay for his own legal representation.

replicated in the summary cash forfeiture powers of the PCA 2002. The European
Court rejected the arguments that the provisions were criminal in nature. The Court's
reasoning was not developed at length, but weight was placed on the earlier decisions in
*Raimondo v Italy* (1994) 18 EHRR 237, *Arcuri v Italy* Application No 54024/99, *Riella
v Italy* Application No 52439/99, *AGOSI v United Kingdom* (1987) 9 EHRR 1 and *Air
Canada v United Kingdom* (1995) 20 EHRR 150. The Court regarded the procedure as a
'preventive measure' rather than a criminal sanction. It was designed to take out of
circulation money which was bound up with the international trade in illicit drugs. The
analogy with the new civil recovery powers is clear, but not entirely identical. In view of
the European Court's decision in *Butler*, there appears to be every prospect of the new
civil recovery procedures being found by the courts to be civil proceedings within the
meaning of the Convention, but arguments remain that they are in fact properly
categorised as criminal in nature. These arguments are likely to arise for decision very
soon after the provisions first come into operation.[1]

**11.148**   If the recovery provisions are found to be criminal in nature, it is difficult to
foresee how the High Court will deal with cases where the respondent is a person
accused of unlawful conduct. The general civil procedures will go a considerable way
towards meeting the fair trial guarantees required by Art 6. The Act already places the
burden of proof on the enforcement authority and makes no assumptions as to the guilt
of the 'accused'. It is difficult to foresee how the court would attempt to reconcile the
disparities between the trial of a 'criminal charge' under the PCA 2002 with the
different procedures which would be used in the criminal courts. A trial could proceed
in the High Court under the CPR 1998 without infringing the Convention, even if it
concerned a criminal charge, but the standard of proof would be different from true
criminal proceedings in England and Wales and there would be other significant
differences, for example there would be no automatic right to a jury, hearsay evidence
would be permissible, a merits test would apply to the grant of public funding, etc.

**11.149**   One area of difficulty if the proceedings are to be considered criminal is the
powers which can be granted to an interim receiver to require persons to answer
questions and provide him with information. Use of information gained in that way
may infringe the Convention rights in criminal proceedings: (a) to remain silent and
not contribute to incriminating oneself;[2] and (b) to receive a caution prior to
questioning.[3] The receiver's powers are already subject to restrictions as to the use in
criminal proceedings of information obtained in this manner.[4]

**11.150**   A problem which has already been mentioned is the possible disparity in
rights between those accused of wrongdoing and those who merely hold the proceeds of
such wrongdoing. If the former is able to say that he faces a 'criminal charge' he will
have the benefit of the extended Art 6 protections, and the protections of Art 7, while
the latter will have to rely on the basic Art 6 rights and have no right to invoke Art 7 at
all. So, for example, a drug dealer who faces proceedings for the recovery of a car
purchased from the proceeds of his drug dealing might be able to invoke the Art 6

---

1    See also *Clingham v Kensington and Chelsea Royal London Borough Council* [2002] UKHL 39,
     [2002] 4 All ER 593.
2    *Funke v France* (1993) 16 EHRR 297.
3    *Saunders v United Kingdom* (1997) 23 EHRR 313.
4    Sch 6, para 2.

extended rights, making the obtaining of a recovery order against him more difficult than it would be against the person who sold him the car legitimately, but knowing that he was a drug dealer who was funding the purchase from the proceeds. The enforcement agency, in such circumstances, would be likely to find it easier to leave the person accused of unlawful conduct out of the proceedings and pursue only those who have obtained property on disposals from him. In the absence of the alleged wrongdoer before the court the issue of determination of a criminal charge may not arise at all.

# ARTICLE 7: NO PUNISHMENT WITHOUT LAW

**11.151**    Article 7 will be engaged only if the proceedings are properly classified as criminal in nature.[1] There is again scope here for a distinction to be drawn between those cases where a respondent is alleged to have been the perpetrator of the unlawful conduct (where a 'criminal charge' may have arisen and Art 7 will have been engaged) and those where the respondent is a holder of the property but innocent of any wrongdoing (where there is nothing in the nature of a criminal charge faced by any party to the proceedings and Art 7 will not apply).

**11.152**    What follows applies only if the allegation of unlawful conduct against a person amounts to a criminal charge against him. Although the Act does not appear to create 'offences' retrospectively, relying as it does on the criminal law at the time of the conduct relied upon for the definition of 'unlawful conduct', it does potentially retrospectively change the penalty for an offence. There are clear parallels in this context with the criminal confiscation powers. In *Welch v United Kingdom* (1995) 20 EHRR 247, the European Court of Human Rights concluded that the powers under the Drug Trafficking Offences Act 1986 amounted to a penalty which had retrospective effect. The new civil recovery powers are likely to be considered a penalty if the allegation of unlawful conduct upon which the recovery order is based is found to amount to a criminal charge against the holder of that property.

**11.153**    The recovery powers may have retrospective effect. There appears to be some scope for use of an argument successfully used in *Taylor v United Kingdom* [1998] EHRLR 90.[2] There the defendant faced a confiscation order arising from a conviction for drug offences committed between 1990 and 1993. The confiscation order, however, assessed his benefit from drug trafficking as far back as 1974, based on earlier convictions after guilty pleas in 1986 for drug dealing in the period between 1974 and 1979. He complained that this retrospectively increased the penalty for those offences. The European Court disagreed. It found that the penalty arose for the offences in 1990 to 1993. When the defendant committed those offences, the confiscation regime already existed and it was known that the penalty for drug trafficking would include confiscation for the proceeds of such activity extending even beyond the introduction of the Drug Trafficking Offences Act 1986. In cases under Part 5 of the PCA 2002 a similar argument might be used but may be less likely to succeed. The 1986 Act provided for specific penalties against the offender for drug trafficking offences. Part 5

---

1    See **11.139–11.147**.
2    Admissibility decision.

creates a wholly new procedure which is not tied to any particular offender but to the proceeds of his offences. It is directed not only at that offender but also at individuals who have, possibly innocently and in ignorance of its provenance, acquired the property. At the time any of those people obtained the property prior to the commencement of the Act they could not have known that there was a risk of it being recovered in this way.

## ARTICLE 8: RIGHT TO RESPECT FOR FAMILY AND PRIVATE LIFE

**11.154**    There are likely to be many cases where the property sought to be recovered comprises a family home or its contents. In each such case, the effect of a recovery order is likely to interfere in the enjoyment of that home. Either all or some of those who live in the home may be entirely innocent of any wrongdoing. The principle of the PCA 2002 is that no one should be able to enjoy property which was originally obtained by way of criminal activity, even if they themselves had no part in that activity. A person who is deprived of property due to his own unlawful conduct is unlikely to be able to complain of an unjustified infringement of his Art 8 rights. However, the position of an innocent party who is likely to be affected by a recovery order is different.

**11.155**    The civil recovery regime has been structured in such a way as to ensure that the court must always consider the interests and rights of any affected party. The court has an overriding discretion not to make a recovery order where to do so would infringe a person's rights under the Convention.[1] It has broad powers to apply conditions to the exercise of the trustee for civil recovery's powers in relation to property vested in him. There are also extensive powers to protect the interests of owners of associated property and excepted joint owners, ensuring that any rights they have are protected whilst still achieving the proportionate aims of the PCA 2002. The PCA 2002 specifically requires the court to balance the legitimate rights of those affected by an order against the public interest in recovering the proceeds of crime, thus ensuring that proportionality must be expressly considered by the court in respect of most decisions which may infringe a person's rights. There is, accordingly, nothing within the Act itself which is plainly contrary to Art 8. Nevertheless, Art 8 is likely to be raised in persuading a court as to what orders it should make.

## ARTICLE 1 OF THE FIRST PROTOCOL: PROTECTION OF PROPERTY

**11.156**    It seems likely that the Government will be able successfully to contend that the interferences with a person's property created by the PCA 2002 are justified on the basis of previous decisions on the confiscation and forfeiture powers contained in the Drug Trafficking Act 1994.[2] It is to be noted, however, that those cases concerned the

---

1     Section 266(3).
2     See, eg, *Phillips v United Kingdom* [2001] Crim LR 817, ECHR; *R v Rezvi and Others* [2002] UKHL 1, [2002] 1 All ER 801, HL; most recently, *Butler v United Kingdom* (unreported) 27 June 2002.

particular evils caused to society by illegal drugs. The new civil recovery powers relate to all criminal conduct, including so-called 'victimless crime'. There remains scope to argue in some cases that the powers may be disproportionate to the evils they have been designed to combat.

**11.157** The problems with compatibility with Art 1 of the First Protocol to the Convention seem lessened where the person who faces the recovery order holds the goods as a result of his own unlawful conduct. More problematic situations will arise where property is followed into the hands of persons far removed from the original wrongdoer, and where the rights of owners of associated property and excepted joint owners are involved. As with Art 8 above, the PCA 2002 appears to contain sufficient checks and balances on the use of the court's powers to ensure that it accords with the Convention requirements.[1] In each case, the court will have to ensure that its order is proportionate to the legitimate purposes of the PCA 2002, and that each affected person's rights are properly respected. The breadth of discretion and the width of the powers provided by the PCA 2002 should make this possible in each case, but challenges to decisions under Art 1 of the First Protocol remain likely.

---

1    Especially the good-faith defence under s 308(1), the reliance provisions of s 266(4), the limits on recovery in s 278, the provisions of s 272 and the compensation provisions in s 283.

# Chapter 12

# FORFEITURE OF CASH IN SUMMARY PROCEEDINGS

## OVERVIEW

**12.1**   Chapter 3 of Part 5 of the PCA 2002 creates a new procedure for the recovery of cash in summary proceedings in a magistrates' court. These provisions are closely based on the existing cash forfeiture provisions contained in Part II of the Drug Trafficking Act 1994. The existing provisions are to be repealed by the PCA 2002 and replaced by new powers applying to all criminal conduct, not merely drug offences.

**12.2**   The cash recovery procedure complements the High Court civil recovery procedure created by the PCA 2002. Although it is limited to the recovery of cash, its scope is wider than the recovery of the proceeds of crime. The powers allow the seizure and forfeiture of both 'recoverable property' and any cash which is intended by any person for use in unlawful conduct. The definitions of 'recoverable property' and 'unlawful conduct' are the same as those used for the High Court civil recovery proceedings (but limited to property in the form of 'cash' which is broadly defined by the PCA 2002 (see below)), and reference should be made to Chapter 10 which deals with those definitions.[1]

**12.3**   The PCA 2002 intends to create a relatively straightforward procedure for the seizure, retention and forfeiture of cash which is either recoverable or intended to be used for unlawful conduct. Although the procedures may be straightforward, the issues that may arise in cases, especially where cash is said to be recoverable property which is either traced back to property obtained by unlawful conduct or followed into the hands of the respondent, could present formidable difficulties. Where cash is sought to be recovered along with other non-cash assets, and the case is one of complexity, it is likely that that the Assets Recovery Agency (ARA) will deal with the matter within the High Court civil recovery procedure. Where, however, the only asset sought to be recovered is cash found in the United Kingdom, the High Court civil recovery procedure will not be available for use[2] and the matter will have to proceed in the magistrates' court. It is possible that the magistrates will have to deal with complex arguments concerning property and trusts law in such cases in order to determine what part of the cash can be traced or followed back to recoverable property.

---

1   The summary forfeiture procedure is not subject to any limitation period: Limitation Act 1980, s 27A(1), as inserted by s 288 of the PCA 2002. Accordingly, cash which is recoverable property can be forfeited regardless of when it, or the recoverable property that it represents, was obtained as a result of criminal conduct.

2   Section 282(2).

## MEANING OF 'CASH'

**12.4**   'Cash' is given an extended meaning so that it includes:[1]

- notes and coins in any currency;
- postal orders;
- cheques of any kind, including travellers' cheques;
- bankers' drafts;
- bearer bonds and bearer shares.

**12.5**   The Secretary of State may by order specify types of monetary instrument, which will then also be included within the definition of 'cash'.

**12.6**   To be subject to the seizure and forfeiture powers, the cash must have been found in the United Kingdom.


## MINIMUM AMOUNT

**12.7**   For the seizure, retention and confiscation powers to arise, the cash must be worth at least the minimum amount to be specified by the Secretary of State by order.[2] The Government has indicated that the minimum amount is likely to be set at £10,000, which is the current minimum amount for the cash forfeiture procedure pursuant to the Drug Trafficking Act 1994. Foreign currency is to be converted into an equivalent sterling value by applying the prevailing rate of foreign exchange.[3] It is presumed that the exchange rate to be adopted is that prevailing at the date on which the property was found rather than any other date, although the PCA 2002 does not make this clear.


## SEARCH POWERS

**12.8**   The summary cash recovery powers are to be exercised by the police and/or customs officers. Search powers are conferred to assist officers in seizing cash. Customs officers are entitled to exercise the powers only if they have reasonable grounds for suspecting that the unlawful conduct in question relates to the matter assigned to Customs and Excise investigation by the Customs and Excise Management Act 1979.[4] Police and customs officers are permitted to use the search powers only so far as reasonably required for the purpose of finding cash.[5] The Government considers these procedures to be civil in nature and therefore wishes to limit the powers to those absolutely necessary for seizing cash. The intention is plainly to avoid any suggestion that the width of the search powers provided by the Act is such that they amount to part of a criminal procedure.

**12.9**   The search powers do not require a warrant for their exercise. They do, however, require prior approval unless, in the circumstances, it is not practicable to

---

1    Section 289(6).
2    Section 303(1).
3    Section 303(2).
4    Section 289(5)(a).
5    Ibid.

obtain that approval before exercising the power.[1] The appropriate approval may be given by a justice of the peace or, if that is not practicable in any case, a senior officer.[2] A senior officer in relation to the police means an officer of at least the rank of inspector.[3] A senior officer in respect of a customs officer means a customs officer of rank designated as equivalent to that of a police inspector.[4]

**12.10** When a customs officer or police constable is lawfully on any premises he may search for cash provided he has reasonable grounds for suspecting that:

– there is on the premises cash which is recoverable property or is intended for use in unlawful conduct by any person;[5] and
– the amount is not less than the minimum amount.[6]

**12.11** There is also a power to search a person or any article he has with him so far as the officer or constable thinks it 'necessary or expedient'.[7] The grounds for such a search are the same as for a search of premises, save that the reference to cash being on the premises is replaced by a requirement that the officer or constable has reasonable grounds for suspecting that the person is carrying such cash.[8] The suspect may be detained for as long as necessary to carry out the search of his person.[9] No person can be submitted to an intimate search or strip search in the exercise of these powers.[10] There is no power to detain a person in order to search any article he has with him.

**12.12** The Secretary of State is to appoint an individual (the 'appointed person'[11]) to monitor the use of the search powers, who must be independent of government. Whenever a search takes place without prior approval of a justice of the peace (ie with only the approval of a senior officer, or with no approval at all) and the search does not result in seizure of cash, or cash seized is detained for 48 hours or less before being returned, the constable or officer who made the seizure must report in writing to the appointed person, explaining the circumstances of the search and why the prior approval of a justice of the peace was not considered practicable.[12] The appointed person is to report to the Secretary of State each year on the use of the search powers, with any recommendations he may have.[13]

**12.13** The Secretary of State must issue a code of practice relating to the search powers and, as under the Police and Criminal Evidence Act 1984, the codes will be admissible in evidence in any criminal or civil proceedings.[14] Breach of the codes does not render any constable or customs officer liable to any criminal or civil proceedings,[15]

---

1    Section 290(1).
2    Section 290(2).
3    Section 290 (4)(b), (5).
4    Section 290(4)(a).
5    Ie the unlawful conduct need not be intended by the person who holds the cash at the time of search or seizure.
6    Section 289(1).
7    Section 289(3).
8    Section 289(2).
9    Section 289(4).
10   Section 289(8).
11   Section 290(8).
12   Section 290(6), (7).
13   Section 291.
14   Section 292.
15   Section 292(6).

although any search which does not comply with the requirements of s 289 may be actionable as a trespass.

## SEIZURE OF CASH

**12.14**   If a customs officer or constable has reasonable grounds for believing that cash is recoverable property or intended by any person for use in unlawful conduct, he may seize that cash.[1] He may also seize any other cash mixed with the cash which is recoverable property or intended for use in unlawful conduct if it is not reasonably practicable to seize only that part which is recoverable or intended for use in unlawful conduct.[2] That part of the cash about which the reasonable suspicion exists must not be less than the minimum amount. Thus, if £12,000 is found at a person's home, but reasonable grounds exist for believing that only £5000 is recoverable property or intended for use in unlawful conduct, no seizure may be made.

## DETENTION OF CASH

**12.15**   Once seized, cash may be detained for 48 hours without the need for a court order, but the reasonable grounds for suspicion must remain throughout that time.[3] Detention beyond the 48 hours may take place only with an order of a magistrates' court extending the period of detention.[4] The first extension may be made by a justice of the peace, but subsequent extension applications must go before a magistrates' court.[5] Each extension may only be for a period of 3 months, and no extensions may be made beyond the period of 2 years of the initial order. This provides the police or customs officers with a maximum period of 2 years either to fully investigate the source of, or intended use for, the cash, or to await the outcome of any criminal proceedings relating to the cash. It is expected that court rules will be issued dealing with the conduct of such applications, and special court forms may also be produced.[6]

**12.16**   The application for an order extending the detention period is made by a constable or the Commissioners of Customs and Excise. The court or justice of the peace, as appropriate, may only make the order if either:[7]

(a)   there are reasonable grounds for suspecting that the cash is recoverable property and that either (i) its continued detention is justified while its derivation is investigated or consideration is given to bringing proceedings against any person for an offence with which the cash is connected, or (ii) proceedings against any

---

1   Section 294(1).
2   Section 294(2).
3   Section 295(1).
4   Section 295(2).
5   Section 295(3).
6   The procedure under the Drug Trafficking Act 1994 is set out in the Magistrates' Courts (Detention and Forfeiture of Drug Trafficking Cash) Rules 1991, SI 1991/1923, and the new procedure is likely to be based on these Rules.
7   Section 295(4).

person for an offence with which the cash is connected have been started but not concluded; or[1]

(b) there are reasonable grounds for suspecting that the cash is intended to be used in unlawful conduct and that either (i) its continued detention is justified while its intended use is investigated or consideration is given to bringing proceedings against any person for an offence with which the cash is connected, or (ii) proceedings against any person for an offence with which the cash is connected have been started but not concluded.[2]

**12.17** The requirement of 'mere suspicion' that the cash falls into one of the two definitions makes the threshold for the making of an order for continued detention relatively low.

**12.18** The court or justice of the peace may also permit continued detention of any cash which was seized but which is not recoverable property or cash intended to be used in unlawful conduct, but only if satisfied that the conditions for detention of the rest of the cash are met and it is not reasonably practicable to detain only that part,[3] for example because findings need to be made as to the full extent of the recoverable property.

**12.19** It does not appear that the application for an order is intended to be heard on notice, although notice of the order, once made, must be given to persons affected by it.[4] Once any such person has notice of the order he may apply to the court for the release of the whole or part of the cash.[5] The court may only accede to such an application if the conditions for continued detention are no longer met in relation to the cash to be released. If a constable or customs officer decides that detention of the cash is no longer justified, he may release it without any need for an order of the court, although he must notify the court that he is doing so.[6]

**12.20** If cash is to be detained for more than 48 hours, it must be paid into an interest-bearing account at the first opportunity, unless it is required as evidence of an offence or evidence within the summary recovery proceedings.[7] Any interest earned is added to the cash upon its forfeiture or release at the conclusion of the proceedings.[8] When the cash is paid into the account, the constable or officer must release any part of the cash to which suspicion does not relate.[9]

## FORFEITURE

**12.21** At any time while cash is detained pursuant to these powers, the constable or the Commissioners of Customs and Excise may apply to a magistrates' court for an

---

1  Section 295(5).
2  Section 295(6).
3  Section 295(7).
4  Section 295(8).
5  Section 297(2), (3).
6  Section 297(4).
7  Section 296(3).
8  Section 296(1).
9  Section 296(2).

order for forfeiture of the whole or part of the cash.[1] Provided the application is made within the 2-year and 2-day maximum period of detention, there is no obligation upon the police or customs officers to bring the application sooner. Once the application is made, the cash is to be detained until the proceedings are concluded.[2] There is no need at that stage for further orders extending the period of detention, and the 2-year maximum period for detention no longer applies.

**12.22**    The court may order the forfeiture of the cash or any part thereof if it is shown that all or part of the cash is either:

(a)    recoverable property; or
(b)    intended by any person for use in unlawful conduct.

**12.23**    There appears to be no restriction on the court making a forfeiture order where the amount found to be subject to forfeiture is less than the minimum amount capable of seizure and detention. It seems, therefore, that provided the reasonable suspicion giving grounds for detention exists up to the making of the application for the forfeiture order, the court may make the forfeiture order even if it ultimately finds that only a small part of the cash is recoverable property or intended for use in unlawful conduct.

**12.24**    The burden of proving that unlawful conduct has occurred for the purpose of showing that the cash is recoverable property or that a person intends to use the cash in unlawful conduct falls upon the constable or Commissioners bringing the application for forfeiture. The standard of proof is the balance of probabilities.[3] Where an allegation of unlawful conduct is made, it amounts to an assertion that a person either has committed, or intends to commit, a criminal act. The more serious the allegation, the more cogent the evidence to prove that allegation must be.[4] This means that a straightforward 51 per cent to 49 per cent test is not necessarily apt where allegations of conduct amounting to serious criminality arise. The question of the standard of proof of unlawful conduct is dealt with in more detail at **11.64–11.65**.

**12.25**    'Recoverable property' bears the same meaning in relation to summary forfeiture proceedings as it does in High Court recovery proceedings. This means that cash will be recoverable if it can be followed into the hands of a person holding it after a disposal by another person in whose hands the cash was recoverable,[5] and any cash which can be traced back to recoverable property will represent that property and also be recoverable.[6] The effect of these provisions can be complex and reference should be made to their detailed consideration in Chapter 10.

**12.26**    Where cash has been seized which belongs to joint tenants[7] and one of them is an excepted joint owner,[8] the court may not make a forfeiture order in respect of that

---

1    Section 298(1).
2    Section 298(4).
3    Section 241(3).
4    *Re H (Minors) (Sexual Abuse: Standard of Proof)* [1996] AC 563.
5    Section 304.
6    Section 305.
7    For example, a cheque payable to two individuals jointly or cash withdrawn from a joint bank account.
8    Part of the property was obtained by one joint owner in circumstances where it was not recoverable as against him – s 270(4) (and see **11.93** et seq). An example would be where A paid £15,000 of proceeds of unlawful conduct into a joint bank account where the other joint account holder, B, had deposited £3000 of legitimately earned income. If all £18,000 was subject to

part of the jointly owned cash which is attributable to the excepted joint owner's share.[1] This provision is likely to be required relatively rarely in cash recovery cases, and is only likely to arise in cases where forfeiture is being sought in respect of cash which represents recoverable property, for example where the cash represents the proceeds of sale of jointly owned property, part of which was acquired with property obtained by unlawful conduct and part of which was acquired with a contribution of non-recoverable property by the joint owner.

**12.27**   Proof of intention to use the cash for unlawful conduct will not be simple. The police or customs officers will need to present evidence which shows that in all probability the cash was to be used for a criminal purpose and not for a legitimate one. The legal burden of proof lies with the party applying for forfeiture, although an evidential burden continues to lie on the respondent once a case is made against him and the court may be able to rely on a respondent's failure adequately to explain the origin or purpose of cash to support a finding that the cash is subject to forfeiture. Where a person with whom the cash can be associated has a record of a particular type of offending, that is likely to be used in evidence against him.[2] Since summary forfeiture proceedings are civil proceedings, it appears that hearsay evidence will be admissible,[3] although it seems unlikely that serious allegations of unlawful conduct will be satisfactorily capable of proof by hearsay evidence alone. The Civil Procedure Rules 1998 (CPR 1998) will not apply in the magistrates' court and the court will have to give directions for the service of evidence and disclosure during the proceedings as it sees fit.

## APPEALS

**12.28**   Appeal from a magistrates' court's making a forfeiture order lies to the Crown Court.[4] The appeal must be made within 30 days of the making of the order.[5] The Crown Court will deal with the matter by way of rehearing and may make whatever order it thinks appropriate.[6] It appears from the wording of the Act that the Crown Court is not limited to the making of a simple forfeiture order or an order allowing the appeal, but may make any order that it considers right in the circumstances. On its face, this seems to give the Crown Court an unlimited power to make any order it deems fit rather than one of the orders provided by the forfeiture procedure. It remains to be seen whether this provision is interpreted as broadly as it seems to be drafted.

**12.29**   If the magistrates' court refuses to make a forfeiture order it does not appear that an appeal to the Crown Court is available to the constable or Commissioners who made the application. Appeals to the Crown Court are limited to cases 'in which an

---

forfeiture proceedings, but B showed that he was an excepted joint owner of the £3000 which was not recoverable property when he paid it into the account, that sum may not be subject to a forfeiture order.

1   Section 298(3).
2   Previous convictions can be used as evidence in accordance with s 11 of the Civil Evidence Act 1968. As to the use of such evidence in forfeiture proceedings, and the inferences which can be drawn from a course of previous offending, see *Ali v Best* (unreported) 23 May 1995, CA.
3   See Civil Evidence Act 1995, s 1(1).
4   Section 299(1).
5   Section 299(2).
6   Section 299(4).

order is made under section 298 for the forfeiture of cash'.[1] Where no forfeiture order is made, it would appear that the aggrieved applicant must seek to challenge the decision by way of an application to the High Court for case stated or judicial review.

**12.30**    There is no provision within the Act for appealing a decision of a justice of the peace or a magistrates' court extending the period for detention of cash. Any party aggrieved by such a decision must presumably apply to the High Court by way of case stated or judicial review.

## APPLICATION OF FORFEITED CASH

**12.31**    Cash forfeited under the provisions of the Act is dealt with as if it were a fine paid to the court and must be paid into the Consolidated Fund,[2] but it may not be paid into the Fund before the time for bringing an appeal against the order passes[3] or, if an appeal has been made against the order, until the conclusion of the appeal process.

## APPLICATIONS BY OWNERS OF THE CASH

**12.32**    Any person who claims that cash detained under the provisions of the PCA 2002 belongs to him may apply to the magistrates' court at any stage for an order that it be released to him.[4] The court may release the cash to the applicant where the applicant shows that:

(a)    the cash belongs to him;
(b)    he was deprived of the cash, or of property which it represents,[5] by unlawful conduct; and
(c)    immediately before he was deprived of the cash, or property it represents, it was not recoverable property.[6]

Thus, a victim of a theft or deception can apply for the return of the cash to him. Similarly, where a victim had an item of property stolen which was later sold in return for the cash which is detained, he may seek release of that cash to him by reason of it being traceable to his property. The court retains discretion as to whether it will release the cash. Where the victim has recovered the original property, it would be wrong to allow him also to recover the cash representing that property following a disposal. The Act offers no guidance as to how such a situation should be approached by the court; thus, it will lie with the court to apply common sense to ensure that no double recovery of unlawfully obtained property occurs.

**12.33**    Where the owner of cash was not deprived of it by unlawful conduct, he may only have it returned to him if it is not subject to further detention or forfeiture pursuant to these provisions.[7] If the owner of the cash was not the same person as the

---

1      Section 299(1).
2      Section 300(1).
3      Thirty days – s 299(1).
4      Section 301(1), (2).
5      Ie which can be traced back to the property by s 305.
6      Section 301(3).
7      Section 301(4).

person from whom it was seized,[1] he may apply to the court for its return. The court may order its return to either the applicant or the person who held it when it was seized only if:

– it is shown that the cash belongs to him;
– the conditions for continued detention of the cash no longer apply, or forfeiture proceedings result in the court declining to make a forfeiture order in respect of the cash; and
– no objection to return of the cash to the applicant is made by the person from whom it was seized.

**12.34** The effect of this provision as drafted appears to be that if the person who held the cash when it was seized does not agree to the court deciding to whom it should be released, the court will not be able to make an order releasing it to the person claiming to be the owner. None of the provisions explains to whom release of the cash should be made in those circumstances, but it must be presumed that it should be released to the person from whom it was seized. In the event of a dispute between that person and someone else who owns the cash (but who cannot show that he has been deprived of it by unlawful conduct), the magistrates will not be able to resolve the dispute unless the person from whom the cash was seized agrees. If he does not agree, the dispute will have to be resolved by separate proceedings in the county court or the High Court. This seems a somewhat strange result, and leaves one to wonder whether there has been an error of drafting in respect of this provision, although the intention may be to avoid the magistrates' court becoming a forum for civil disputes which would be better resolved in the county court or the High Court.

## COMPENSATION

**12.35** The primary protection for any person whose cash is detained but then released without a forfeiture order being made is the requirement to pay the cash into an interest-bearing account.[2] On its release, interest will be paid out with the cash. Where the cash is not paid into an interest-bearing account in breach of the provisions, the owner of the cash, or the person from whom it was seized, may apply to the magistrates' court for compensation[3] and the court may order an amount of compensation to be paid, equivalent to the interest which would have been earned if the cash had been paid into an interest-bearing account.[4]

**12.36** Where the applicant for compensation can show other loss beyond that compensated by way of interest, the court may order further compensation to be paid, but may only make such an order where the circumstances are exceptional.[5] The amount of compensation is to be such as the court considers reasonable having regard to the loss suffered and all the other relevant circumstances.[6] It seems that only cases of particular hardship, or where there have been particularly grave failings on the part of

---

1    The former may not be a respondent to the proceedings, while the latter will.
2    Section 296(1).
3    Section 302(2).
4    Section 302(3).
5    Section 302(4).
6    Section 302(5).

the constable or customs officers who initiated the seizure of the cash, that further compensation will be paid, and even then it may not cover the full extent of the person's loss.

**12.37**   Compensation must be paid from the local police fund for the force whose constable seized the cash,[1] or by the Commissioners for Customs and Excise if a customs officer made the seizure.[2]


## PUBLIC FUNDING

**12.38**   The Access to Justice Act 1999 is amended to ensure that civil public funding is available to persons affected by cash forfeiture proceedings, subject to the ordinary means and merits tests.[3]


## COMPATIBILITY WITH THE HUMAN RIGHTS ACT 1998

**12.39**   The European Convention on Human Rights issues which arise in respect of the summary recovery provisions are similar to those under the High Court recovery procedure.[4] The principal issue is whether the procedure is one in the nature of the determination of a criminal charge, or merely a civil procedure. So far as the forfeiture of cash which is recoverable property is concerned, the issues are exactly the same as for the High Court procedure[5] and the reader is referred to the discussion of the compatibility of the recovery powers with the Convention in Chapter 11. This section deals with the forfeiture of cash which is intended for use in unlawful conduct.

**12.40**   To prove that cash may be forfeited (if it is not recoverable property) it must be shown that either the person from whom the cash was seized, or some other person, intends to use it for unlawful conduct. The definition of 'unlawful conduct'[6] means that the allegation will be that the cash will be used to commit a criminal offence. In some cases it may be that the evidence will show that plans are sufficiently developed or advanced to prove that a conspiracy to commit a criminal offence exists. There may be cases where the cash is seized at the virtual point of committing an offence, and the evidence would be sufficient to prove an attempted offence.[7] At the other end of the scale there may be cases where the person holding the cash has no personal involvement with crime, but it can be shown that the money is held for someone who is a known criminal and who is likely to use it for criminal activity. It is clear that in some applications for forfeiture of cash, the court will be asked to find that a person has committed all the necessary ingredients to be guilty of an attempted offence or conspiracy. In other cases, there will be no clear allegation of planned wrongdoing

---

1    Section 306(7).
2    Section 302(6).
3    See amendments to Sch 2 to the 1999 Act in Sch 11 to the 2002 Act.
4    See Chapter 11.
5    Whether the procedure is criminal in nature, retrospectivity, infringement of rights to family life and to property, etc.
6    Section 241.
7    For example, where cash is seized at the point where a person attempts to purchase drugs with it.

against any party to the proceedings, and it may even be that the person from whom the money was seized chooses to play no part in the proceedings so that the application is effectively unopposed.

**12.41**   It is difficult to predict how the courts will deal with these matters when Convention points are raised. On the one hand, there are powerful arguments to say that the allegation that cash is held with the intention of committing a criminal offence amounts to an allegation of criminality which, if proven, will result in the forfeiture of the cash. The provisions are, it is assumed, intended to have a deterrent effect. This all points to the proceedings being criminal in nature. On the other hand, where the person holding the cash is not the person who it is alleged intends to use it for criminal purposes, he will find it difficult to argue that he faces a criminal charge, unless it is argued that he will knowingly permit its use in that way, in which case he is likely to be an accessory to the crime in any event and is effectively being accused of an intention to commit a criminal offence.

**12.42**   The Government will contend that this forfeiture provision is not criminal in effect. It will no doubt rely upon the European Court of Human Right's decisions in cases such as *Raimondo v Italy* (1994) 18 EHRR 237 (where confiscation proceedings which were part of the Italian Government's anti-mafia laws were assumed by all involved in the case to involve no charges of a criminal nature), *AGOSI v United Kingdom* (1987) 9 EHRR 1, and *Air Canada v United Kingdom* (1995) 20 EHRR 150 (cases concerning customs and exercise forfeiture powers) to support that contention. Particular support for the Government's position comes from the fact that the existing forfeiture powers under the Drug Trafficking Act 1994 have been considered by the European Court of Human Rights and found not to be criminal in nature.[1] This view is supported by the absence of an entry upon a person's criminal record by reason of any finding in forfeiture proceedings, and the absence of a criminal penalty against a person involved in the proceedings. Cases where a significant financial penalty was imposed for breach of tax laws have been categorised as criminal in nature.[2] It is not clear whether those cases were expressly considered by the European Court of Human Rights in *Butler v United Kingdom* (unreported) 27 June 2002. In any event, in that case the Court took the view that the forfeiture powers were preventive in effect rather than punitive or deterrent, and therefore not criminal in nature. Forfeiture proceedings are likely to concern sums of cash in excess of £10,000,[3] so the penalty involved in the making of a forfeiture order will be significant. The forfeiture provisions also include powers of search and seizure which are criminal in character, and which may go to categorising the whole process as the determination of a criminal charge where the ground for forfeiture relied upon is intention to use the cash for unlawful conduct. Despite these arguments, the *Butler* case presents a significant hurdle to any argument that the new provisions are criminal in nature.

**12.43**   If the forfeiture proceedings are categorised as civil in nature, they are likely to be found to comply with the requirements of Art 6 of the Convention by virtue of the

---

1   *Butler v United Kingdom* (unreported) 27 June 2002.
2   See *Perin v France* Application No 18656/91, 1 December 1992 and *Bendenoun v France* (1994) 18 EHRR 54; but see also *Smith v United Kingdom* (1996) 21 EHRR CD 74 where a smaller financial penalty was held not to give rise to a criminal penalty.
3   The likely amount to be set as the minimum amount under s 303.

fact that a public hearing is available in the magistrates' court, and public funding is available. Even if they are criminal in scope, it is difficult to point to any obvious breaches of Arts 6 or 7 of the Convention by the legislation itself, bearing in mind that the burden of proof lies on the applicant for the forfeiture order and there is no retrospectivity involved in an allegation that cash is intended to be used for unlawful conduct. There is, however, a clear possibility of retrospective effect where the cash subject to proceedings is recoverable property relating to unlawful conduct that occurred prior to the commencement of the Act.[1] If the English courts do decide that the process is criminal in nature according to the Convention jurisprudence, it may be that a higher standard of proof[2] and a more restrictive approach to hearsay evidence will be adopted. Although these are not necessarily requirements of Art 6, the courts may feel that justice requires that all proceedings with a criminal character should have similarity of procedures and rules. There will also need to be sensitivity to the use of evidence acquired against a person either by compulsion[3] or without the benefit of a caution.[4] Similarly, the merits test attached to public funding may be considered inappropriate if the proceedings are deemed to be criminal in scope.

**12.44**　　The forfeiture powers appear to be justified as a means of preventing crime[5] and are, therefore, in the general interest.[6] They are, on their face, likely to be justified infringements of the Convention rights raised against them.[7] In so far as the forfeiture procedures deal with recoverable property, they need to be exercised with a view to proportionality between the rights of affected individuals and the aims they seek to achieve. The court has the discretion to ensure that it only makes orders which can be so justified. Unlike the civil recovery powers, which the Act expressly states may only be made if there is no infringement of the Human Rights Act 1998,[8] there is no such reference within the forfeiture powers, but the court has a discretion as to whether or not to make a forfeiture order. If it considers that such an order would unjustifiably interfere with a person's Convention rights, or there is any other good reason why the making of a forfeiture order would be unjust, it may decline to so order. Where the ground relied upon for forfeiture is an intention to use the cash for unlawful conduct, the balance is more likely justifiably to fall in favour of forfeiture, but the court has a discretion whether to make the order. Where to order forfeiture would infringe a person's rights under the Convention without appropriate justification, it should decline to so order. The compensation provisions must also be read with a view to ensuring that Convention rights are respected.

---

1　　See Chapter 11.

2　　Although the Act specifically refers to the standard of proof being the balance of probabilities (s 241), making it difficult for a court to read the Act in a way which allows the standard to rise to beyond reasonable doubt.

3　　*Funke v France* (1993) 16 EHRR 297.

4　　*Saunders v United Kingdom* (1997) 23 EHRR 313.

5　　See Art 8 of the Convention.

6　　See Art 1 of the First Protocol to the Convention.

7　　See *Raimondo v Italy* (1994) 18 EHRR 237; *Phillips v United Kingdom* [2001] Crim LR 817; *R v Rezvi and Others* [2002] UKHL 1, [2002] 1 All ER 801; *Butler v United Kingdom* (unreported) 27 June 2002. All those cases concerned the particular evils of either mafia activity or dealing in illicit drugs. It remains to be seen whether, in cases of more minor, and less socially damaging, criminality, the measures contained in the forfeiture provisions are proportionate to the aim.

8　　Section 266(3).

# Chapter 13

# DIRECTOR'S GENERAL REVENUE FUNCTIONS

**13.1**  The general purpose of the PCA 2002 is to provide as many powers for the recovery of the proceeds of criminal conduct as possible. The confiscation, recovery and forfeiture powers are clearly the most direct means of achieving that purpose. The granting of revenue powers to the Director of the Assets Recovery Agency (ARA) is an acknowledgement that there will be cases where he may be unable to meet the evidential thresholds required to use any of those powers, but his investigations may have uncovered extensive income for an individual which has not been declared for tax purposes. Part 6 of the PCA 2002 permits the Director to take over the functions normally exercised by the Commissioners of Inland Revenue in respect of that person's tax affairs over a specified period.

**13.2**  The exercise of the revenue powers under the PCA 2002 will require the Director to apply the ordinary principles of revenue law, adapted slightly by the provisions of the PCA 2002. Detailed consideration of revenue law lies beyond the scope of this book. What follows is a brief summary of the Director's revenue powers. Specialist works on revenue law should be consulted for the full scope of the Director's revenue powers conferred by the PCA 2002.

## ADOPTION OF REVENUE FUNCTIONS BY THE DIRECTOR

**13.3**  The Director has access to the wide investigatory powers contained within Part 8 of the PCA 2002. Where he discovers information during an investigation for confiscation or civil recovery proceedings he is not restricted to using the information within those proceedings.[1] If, in the course of the investigation, he discovers income for an individual or a company which has not been declared for tax purposes, he need not simply report the matter to the Inland Revenue. The Director may, if he wishes and if the conditions set by the PCA 2002 are met, adopt the Inland Revenue's powers for himself in respect of that person or company. The functions he may assume are in relation to the following matters:[2]

- income tax;
- capital gains tax;
- corporation tax;
- National Insurance contributions;
- statutory sick pay;
- statutory maternity pay;
- statutory paternity pay;
- statutory adoption pay;

---

1    Section 435.
2    Section 323.

–  student loans;
–  inheritance tax (so far as the Commissioners or Inland Revenue deal with this).

**13.4**  The qualifying condition for the Director to acquire revenue-collecting powers is that either:[1]

(a)  a person has earned income, or made a chargeable capital gain, which is chargeable for tax from the criminal conduct[2] of himself or another person; or
(b)  a company is chargeable for corporation tax on profits which have arisen from criminal conduct.

**13.5**  The qualifying condition is drafted in broad terms so that the person or company chargeable to tax need not have been responsible for the criminal conduct. Further, the income, capital gain or profit need only have arisen partly and indirectly from criminal conduct.

**13.6**  Similar provisions deal with inheritance tax for transfers of property whose value is attributable to criminal property[3] and for settlements of criminal property.[4] Criminal property, for these purposes, means property which constitutes a person's benefit from criminal conduct (whether his own conduct or someone else's) or represents such a benefit (in whole or in part and whether directly or indirectly).[5]

**13.7**  Criminal conduct means conduct which constitutes an offence in any part of the United Kingdom[6] but does not include revenue offences normally dealt with by the Commissioners of Inland Revenue.[7] The criminal conduct may have occurred prior to the commencement of the PCA 2002 for these purposes.[8]

**13.8**  When the qualifying condition is met, the Director may serve a notice on the Commissioners of Inland Revenue, specifying:

(a)  the person or company concerned;
(b)  the chargeable period within which the income, gain or profit arose, and stating that the Director intends to carry out in relation to that person or company for that period such of the general Revenue functions as are set out in the notice.[9] The notice may be in respect of more than one chargeable period if necessary.[10] The chargeable period may be before the commencement of the PCA 2002.[11]

**13.9**  Service of the notice automatically vests in the Director the Revenue functions he has specified within the notice for the period concerned,[12] but the Director's powers for dealing with the PAYE and National Insurance requirements of a company which is an employer, or the National Insurance obligations of a self-employed person, are

---

1    Section 317(1).
2    Note that the term 'unlawful conduct' used in Part 5 of the Act is not adopted here.
3    Section 321.
4    Section 322.
5    Section 326(4).
6    Section 326(1).
7    Section 326(2).
8    Section 326(3).
9    Section 317(2).
10   Section 317(5).
11   Section 317(9).
12   Section 317(3).

limited.[1] The Revenue is not divested of those powers; as such, there are, for the currency of the notice, two bodies with revenue powers.[2] At any time, the Director may serve a further notice on the Revenue, withdrawing the previous notice,[3] provided the notice is served as soon as the qualifying condition ceases to be satisfied. Service of a withdrawal notice divests the Director of the revenue functions specified within it.[4]

**13.10** In exercising Revenue powers, the Director must interpret the law in line with any concession or any other document published by the Commissioners.[5]

## SOURCE OF INCOME

**13.11** To assist the Director in recovering tax due for income or gains obtained from criminal activity, he is not required, as the Inland Revenue would be, to prove the source for any income.[6] As long as he can prove that the income was received, he may make a tax assessment in respect of it. Clearly, this provision is necessary because if the source of the income can be identified, it is likely that the civil recovery powers of the Act can be utilised. Where income or profit can be identified but its source is unknown (although it must be shown that at least part of that income arises from criminal conduct for the Director to be able to adopt the Revenue's powers), it can be taxed by the Director.

**13.12** Where the Director withdraws a notice, having made an assessment for tax without specifying the source of the income, the Inland Revenue may not rely on that assessment without proving source.[7] The Director's broader powers are confined to cases where income from criminal conduct can be shown.

## APPEALS

**13.13** Appeals from the Director's exercise of revenue powers lies to the Special Commissioners, who may sit with an assessor for hearing the appeal.[8]

**13.14** Where the challenge is to a public law matter, such as the Director's jurisdiction to serve a notice under Part 6 of the PCA 2002, it would appear that challenge by way of judicial review is open to an affected party.

## HUMAN RIGHTS ISSUES

**13.15** It is difficult to categorise the powers provided by Part 6 of the PCA 2002 as anything other than ordinary revenue powers. The Director is given powers to deal

---

1    Section 318.
2    Section 317(7).
3    Section 317(4).
4    Section 317(6).
5    Section 324.
6    Section 319(1).
7    Section 319(3).
8    Section 320.

with any person in the same manner as the Inland Revenue if the income were known to it. The one exception is that the Director need not demonstrate a source for income, save that it comes at least in part from criminal conduct. It is likely that cases will arise where it will be argued that the assumption by the Director of these powers carries with it an allegation that the person subject to tax assessment is guilty of criminal conduct, thereby implicitly giving rise to a criminal charge. However, this argument may be difficult to pursue successfully.

**13.16**　　Part 6 of the PCA 2002 creates a mechanism by which tax can be claimed by the State for income and benefits arising within what might be termed the 'black economy', which might otherwise never be subjected to tax. It does not impose any additional penalty over and above what would be paid as tax if the income or benefit were from a legitimate source, neither does it record any criminal conviction. Where, however, the person or company subject to assessment challenges the Director's jurisdiction to exercise revenue powers under Part 6, he may have to prove that criminal conduct has taken place and has produced at least part of the income, gain, profit or property. It remains to be seen whether such an allegation might be construed as a criminal charge within the meaning of the Convention.

# Appendix 1

# A: EXAMPLE RESTRAINT APPLICATION

## CONFISCATION RESTRAINT APPLICATION

**TO:** The Crown Court at [*address*].

**TAKE NOTICE** that application is made for a restraint order under section 41 of the Proceeds of Crime Act 2002.

The application is made by [*name and address of prosecutor*].

The person specified in the application is [*name of defendant*].

The person specified is subject to a criminal investigation with regard to an offence[1]

**AND** there is reasonable cause to believe that the specified person has benefited from his criminal conduct.

Application is made for an order to **PROHIBIT**:

[*names of persons prohibited*]

from dealing with **ANY REALISABLE PROPERTY** held by the said person(s) and in particular:

[*list of restrained property*]

**SAVE** that exception is made as follows:

[*exceptions for reasonable living expenses, reasonable legal expenses or for the purpose of enabling a person to carry on any trade, business, profession or occupation*].

Signed .................................................... Date ....................................................

---

1    See the other triggering conditions in s 40.

# B: EXAMPLE SEARCH AND SEIZURE APPLICATION

## CONFISCATION SEARCH AND SEIZURE APPLICATION

**TO:** The Crown Court at [*address*].

**TAKE NOTICE** that application is made for a search and seizure warrant under section 352 of the Proceeds of Crime Act 2002. The application is made by:

[*name and address of appropriate officer*], an appropriate officer for the purposes of the Proceeds of Crime Act 2002.

The person [*or property*] specified in the application is
[*name and address of person subject to the confiscation or money laundering investigation; or identification of the property that is the subject of the civil recovery investigation*]

who is a person subject to a confiscation/money laundering investigation

[*which is the subject of a civil recovery investigation*].

This warrant is sought for the purposes of that investigation.

Application is made for an order that the following appropriate persons:

[*names of searching officers*]

**BETWEEN** [*dates*] **TO ENTER:** [*address of premises*]

**AND** to **SEARCH** the premises and to **SEIZE** and **RETAIN** material found there which is likely to be of substantial value (whether or not by itself) to the investigation.

The **SPECIFIED MATERIAL** is: [*identification of the specified material*] or

[*cannot be identified but, there are reasonable grounds for believing that there is material that:*

*(in a **confiscation investigation**) relates to the question of whether the specified person has benefited from criminal conduct, or the extent or whereabouts of that benefit; or*

*(in a **civil recovery investigation**) relates to the question of whether it is recoverable or associated property, the property specified in the application is recoverable or associated property;*

*(in a **money laundering investigation**) whether it relates to the person specified, or whether he has committed a money laundering offence.*

*AND is likely to be of substantial value to the investigation*].

Signed ..................................................... Date .....................................................

# Appendix 2

# PROCEEDS OF CRIME ACT 2002[1]

## PART 1    ASSETS RECOVERY AGENCY

### 1[2]    The Agency and its Director

(1) There shall be an Assets Recovery Agency (referred to in this Act as the Agency).

(2) The Secretary of State must appoint a Director of the Agency (referred to in this Act as the Director).

(3) The Director is a corporation sole.

(4) The Director may –

  (a)  appoint such persons as members of staff of the Agency, and
  (b)  make such arrangements for the provision of services,

as he considers appropriate for or in connection with the exercise of his functions.

(5) But the Director must obtain the approval of the Minister for the Civil Service as to the number of staff appointed under subsection (4)(a).

(6) Anything which the Director is authorised or required to do may be done by –

  (a)  a member of staff of the Agency, or
  (b)  a person providing services under arrangements made by the Director,

if authorised by the Director (generally or specifically) for that purpose.

(7) Schedule 1 contains further provisions about the Agency and the Director.

### 2[3]    Director's functions: general

(1) The Director must exercise his functions in the way which he considers is best calculated to contribute to the reduction of crime.

(2) In exercising his functions as required by subsection (1) the Director must –

  (a)  act efficiently and effectively;

---

1    Act reference: 2002 c 29.
     Royal Assent: 24 July 2002.
     Long title: An Act to establish the Assets Recovery Agency and make provision about the appointment of its Director and his functions (including Revenue functions), to provide for confiscation orders in relation to persons who benefit from criminal conduct and for restraint orders to prohibit dealing with property, to allow the recovery of property which is or represents property obtained through unlawful conduct or which is intended to be used in unlawful conduct, to make provision about money laundering, to make provision about investigations relating to benefit from criminal conduct or to property which is or represents property obtained through unlawful conduct or to money laundering, to make provision to give effect to overseas requests and orders made where property is found or believed to be obtained through criminal conduct, and for connected purposes.

2    Information: Commencement: Not yet in force.
3    Information: Commencement: Not yet in force.

(b) have regard to his current annual plan (as approved by the Secretary of State in accordance with Schedule 1).

(3) The Director may do anything (including the carrying out of investigations) which he considers is –

(a) appropriate for facilitating, or
(b) incidental or conducive to,

the exercise of his functions.

(4) But subsection (3) does not allow the Director to borrow money.

(5) In considering under subsection (1) the way which is best calculated to contribute to the reduction of crime the Director must have regard to any guidance given to him by the Secretary of State.

(6) The guidance must indicate that the reduction of crime is in general best secured by means of criminal investigations and criminal proceedings.

## 3[1]   Accreditation and training

(1) The Director must establish a system for the accreditation of financial investigators.

(2) The system of accreditation must include provision for –

(a) the monitoring of the performance of accredited financial investigators, and
(b) the withdrawal of accreditation from any person who contravenes or fails to comply with any condition subject to which he was accredited.

(3) A person may be accredited –

(a) in relation to this Act;
(b) in relation to particular provisions of this Act.

(4) But the accreditation may be limited to specified purposes.

(5) A reference in this Act to an accredited financial investigator is to be construed accordingly.

(6) The Director may charge a person –

(a) for being accredited as a financial investigator, and
(b) for the monitoring of his performance as an accredited financial investigator.

(7) The Director must make provision for the training of persons in –

(a) financial investigation, and
(b) the operation of this Act.

(8) The Director may charge the persons who receive the training.

## 4[2]   Co-operation

(1) Persons who have functions relating to the investigation or prosecution of offences must co-operate with the Director in the exercise of his functions.

(2) The Director must co-operate with those persons in the exercise of functions they have under this Act.

---

1     Information: Commencement: Not yet in force.
2     Information: Commencement: Not yet in force.

## 5[1]  Advice and assistance

The Director must give the Secretary of State advice and assistance which he reasonably requires and which –

(a) relate to matters connected with the operation of this Act, and
(b) are designed to help the Secretary of State to exercise his functions so as to reduce crime.

## PART 2   CONFISCATION: ENGLAND AND WALES

### *Confiscation orders*

## 6[2]  Making of order

(1) The Crown Court must proceed under this section if the following two conditions are satisfied.

(2) The first condition is that a defendant falls within any of the following paragraphs –

(a) he is convicted of an offence or offences in proceedings before the Crown Court;
(b) he is committed to the Crown Court for sentence in respect of an offence or offences under section 3, 4 or 6 of the Sentencing Act;
(c) he is committed to the Crown Court in respect of an offence or offences under section 70 below (committal with a view to a confiscation order being considered).

(3) The second condition is that –

(a) the prosecutor or the Director asks the court to proceed under this section, or
(b) the court believes it is appropriate for it to do so.

(4) The court must proceed as follows –

(a) it must decide whether the defendant has a criminal lifestyle;
(b) if it decides that he has a criminal lifestyle it must decide whether he has benefited from his general criminal conduct;
(c) if it decides that he does not have a criminal lifestyle it must decide whether he has benefited from his particular criminal conduct.

(5) If the court decides under subsection (4)(b) or (c) that the defendant has benefited from the conduct referred to it must –

(a) decide the recoverable amount, and
(b) make an order (a confiscation order) requiring him to pay that amount.

(6) But the court must treat the duty in subsection (5) as a power if it believes that any victim of the conduct has at any time started or intends to start proceedings against the defendant in respect of loss, injury or damage sustained in connection with the conduct.

(7) The court must decide any question arising under subsection (4) or (5) on a balance of probabilities.

(8) The first condition is not satisfied if the defendant absconds (but section 27 may apply).

(9) References in this Part to the offence (or offences) concerned are to the offence (or offences) mentioned in subsection (2).

---

1     Information: Commencement: Not yet in force.
2     Information: Commencement: Not yet in force.

## 7[1]  Recoverable amount

(1) The recoverable amount for the purposes of section 6 is an amount equal to the defendant's benefit from the conduct concerned.

(2) But if the defendant shows that the available amount is less than that benefit the recoverable amount is –

  (a)  the available amount, or
  (b)  a nominal amount, if the available amount is nil.

(3) But if section 6(6) applies the recoverable amount is such amount as –

  (a)  the court believes is just, but
  (b)  does not exceed the amount found under subsection (1) or (2) (as the case may be).

(4) In calculating the defendant's benefit from the conduct concerned for the purposes of subsection (1), any property in respect of which –

  (a)  a recovery order is in force under section 266, or
  (b)  a forfeiture order is in force under section 298(2),

must be ignored.

(5) If the court decides the available amount, it must include in the confiscation order a statement of its findings as to the matters relevant for deciding that amount.

## 8[2]  Defendant's benefit

(1) If the court is proceeding under section 6 this section applies for the purpose of –

  (a)  deciding whether the defendant has benefited from conduct, and
  (b)  deciding his benefit from the conduct.

(2) The court must –

  (a)  take account of conduct occurring up to the time it makes its decision;
  (b)  take account of property obtained up to that time.

(3) Subsection (4) applies if –

  (a)  the conduct concerned is general criminal conduct,
  (b)  a confiscation order mentioned in subsection (5) has at an earlier time been made against the defendant, and
  (c)  his benefit for the purposes of that order was benefit from his general criminal conduct.

(4) His benefit found at the time the last confiscation order mentioned in subsection (3)(c) was made against him must be taken for the purposes of this section to be his benefit from his general criminal conduct at that time.

(5) If the conduct concerned is general criminal conduct the court must deduct the aggregate of the following amounts –

  (a)  the amount ordered to be paid under each confiscation order previously made against the defendant;

---

1    Information: Commencement: Not yet in force.
2    Information: Commencement: Not yet in force.

(b) the amount ordered to be paid under each confiscation order previously made against him under any of the provisions listed in subsection (7).

(6) But subsection (5) does not apply to an amount which has been taken into account for the purposes of a deduction under that subsection on any earlier occasion.

(7) These are the provisions –

(a) the Drug Trafficking Offences Act 1986;
(b) Part 1 of the Criminal Justice (Scotland) Act 1987;
(c) Part 6 of the Criminal Justice Act 1988;
(d) the Criminal Justice (Confiscation) (Northern Ireland) Order 1990 (SI 1990/2588 (NI 17));
(e) Part 1 of the Drug Trafficking Act 1994;
(f) Part 1 of the Proceeds of Crime (Scotland) Act 1995;
(g) the Proceeds of Crime (Northern Ireland) Order 1996 (SI 1996/1299 (NI 9));
(h) Part 3 or 4 of this Act.

(8) The reference to general criminal conduct in the case of a confiscation order made under any of the provisions listed in subsection (7) is a reference to conduct in respect of which a court is required or entitled to make one or more assumptions for the purpose of assessing a person's benefit from the conduct.

## 9[1]  Available amount

(1) For the purposes of deciding the recoverable amount, the available amount is the aggregate of –

(a) the total of the values (at the time the confiscation order is made) of all the free property then held by the defendant minus the total amount payable in pursuance of obligations which then have priority, and
(b) the total of the values (at that time) of all tainted gifts.

(2) An obligation has priority if it is an obligation of the defendant –

(a) to pay an amount due in respect of a fine or other order of a court which was imposed or made on conviction of an offence and at any time before the time the confiscation order is made, or
(b) to pay a sum which would be included among the preferential debts if the defendant's bankruptcy had commenced on the date of the confiscation order or his winding up had been ordered on that date.

(3) 'Preferential debts' has the meaning given by section 386 of the Insolvency Act 1986.

## 10[2]  Assumptions to be made in case of criminal lifestyle

(1) If the court decides under section 6 that the defendant has a criminal lifestyle it must make the following four assumptions for the purpose of –

(a) deciding whether he has benefited from his general criminal conduct, and
(b) deciding his benefit from the conduct.

(2) The first assumption is that any property transferred to the defendant at any time after the relevant day was obtained by him –

---

1    Information: Commencement: Not yet in force.
2    Information: Commencement: Not yet in force.

(a)  as a result of his general criminal conduct, and

(b)  at the earliest time he appears to have held it.

(3)  The second assumption is that any property held by the defendant at any time after the date of conviction was obtained by him –

(a)  as a result of his general criminal conduct, and

(b)  at the earliest time he appears to have held it.

(4)  The third assumption is that any expenditure incurred by the defendant at any time after the relevant day was met from property obtained by him as a result of his general criminal conduct.

(5)  The fourth assumption is that, for the purpose of valuing any property obtained (or assumed to have been obtained) by the defendant, he obtained it free of any other interests in it.

(6)  But the court must not make a required assumption in relation to particular property or expenditure if –

(a)  the assumption is shown to be incorrect, or

(b)  there would be a serious risk of injustice if the assumption were made.

(7)  If the court does not make one or more of the required assumptions it must state its reasons.

(8)  The relevant day is the first day of the period of six years ending with –

(a)  the day when proceedings for the offence concerned were started against the defendant, or

(b)  if there are two or more offences and proceedings for them were started on different days, the earliest of those days.

(9)  But if a confiscation order mentioned in section 8(3)(c) has been made against the defendant at any time during the period mentioned in subsection (8) –

(a)  the relevant day is the day when the defendant's benefit was calculated for the purposes of the last such confiscation order;

(b)  the second assumption does not apply to any property which was held by him on or before the relevant day.

(10)  The date of conviction is –

(a)  the date on which the defendant was convicted of the offence concerned, or

(b)  if there are two or more offences and the convictions were on different dates, the date of the latest.

## 11[1]   Time for payment

(1)  The amount ordered to be paid under a confiscation order must be paid on the making of the order; but this is subject to the following provisions of this section.

(2)  If the defendant shows that he needs time to pay the amount ordered to be paid, the court making the confiscation order may make an order allowing payment to be made in a specified period.

(3)  The specified period –

(a)  must start with the day on which the confiscation order is made, and

---

1     Information: Commencement: Not yet in force.

(b)  must not exceed six months.

(4) If within the specified period the defendant applies to the Crown Court for the period to be extended and the court believes there are exceptional circumstances, it may make an order extending the period.

(5)  The extended period –

(a)  must start with the day on which the confiscation order is made, and
(b)  must not exceed 12 months.

(6)  An order under subsection (4) –

(a)  may be made after the end of the specified period, but
(b)  must not be made after the end of the period of 12 months starting with the day on which the confiscation order is made.

(7)  The court must not make an order under subsection (2) or (4) unless it gives –

(a)  the prosecutor, or
(b)  if the Director was appointed as the enforcement authority for the order under section 34, the Director,

an opportunity to make representations.

## 12[1]  Interest on unpaid sums

(1) If the amount required to be paid by a person under a confiscation order is not paid when it is required to be paid, he must pay interest on the amount for the period for which it remains unpaid.

(2)  The rate of interest is the same rate as that for the time being specified in section 17 of the Judgments Act 1838 (interest on civil judgment debts).

(3) For the purposes of this section no amount is required to be paid under a confiscation order if –

(a)  an application has been made under section 11(4),
(b)  the application has not been determined by the court, and
(c)  the period of 12 months starting with the day on which the confiscation order was made has not ended.

(4) In applying this Part the amount of the interest must be treated as part of the amount to be paid under the confiscation order.

## 13[2]  Effect of order on court's other powers

(1) If the court makes a confiscation order it must proceed as mentioned in subsections (2) and (4) in respect of the offence or offences concerned.

(2)  The court must take account of the confiscation order before –

(a)  it imposes a fine on the defendant, or
(b)  it makes an order falling within subsection (3).

---

1    Information: Commencement: Not yet in force.
2    Information: Commencement: Not yet in force.

(3) These orders fall within this subsection –

    (a)  an order involving payment by the defendant, other than an order under section 130 of the Sentencing Act (compensation orders);

    (b)  an order under section 27 of the Misuse of Drugs Act 1971 (forfeiture orders);

    (c)  an order under section 143 of the Sentencing Act (deprivation orders);

    (d)  an order under section 23 of the Terrorism Act 2000 (forfeiture orders).

(4) Subject to subsection (2), the court must leave the confiscation order out of account in deciding the appropriate sentence for the defendant.

(5) Subsection (6) applies if –

    (a)  the Crown Court makes both a confiscation order and an order for the payment of compensation under section 130 of the Sentencing Act against the same person in the same proceedings, and

    (b)  the court believes he will not have sufficient means to satisfy both the orders in full.

(6) In such a case the court must direct that so much of the compensation as it specifies is to be paid out of any sums recovered under the confiscation order; and the amount it specifies must be the amount it believes will not be recoverable because of the insufficiency of the person's means.

*Procedural matters*

## 14[1]  Postponement

(1) The court may –

    (a)  proceed under section 6 before it sentences the defendant for the offence (or any of the offences) concerned, or

    (b)  postpone proceedings under section 6 for a specified period.

(2) A period of postponement may be extended.

(3) A period of postponement (including one as extended) must not end after the permitted period ends.

(4) But subsection (3) does not apply if there are exceptional circumstances.

(5) The permitted period is the period of two years starting with the date of conviction.

(6) But if –

    (a)  the defendant appeals against his conviction for the offence (or any of the offences) concerned, and

    (b)  the period of three months (starting with the day when the appeal is determined or otherwise disposed of) ends after the period found under subsection (5),

the permitted period is that period of three months.

(7) A postponement or extension may be made –

    (a)  on application by the defendant;

    (b)  on application by the prosecutor or the Director (as the case may be);

    (c)  by the court of its own motion.

(8) If –

    (a)  proceedings are postponed for a period, and

---

1    Information: Commencement: Not yet in force.

    (b)   an application to extend the period is made before it ends,

the application may be granted even after the period ends.

(9)  The date of conviction is –

    (a)   the date on which the defendant was convicted of the offence concerned, or

    (b)   if there are two or more offences and the convictions were on different dates, the date of the latest.

(10) References to appealing include references to applying under section 111 of the Magistrates' Courts Act 1980 (statement of case).

(11) A confiscation order must not be quashed only on the ground that there was a defect or omission in the procedure connected with the application for or the granting of a postponement.

(12) But subsection (11) does not apply if before it made the confiscation order the court –

    (a)   imposed a fine on the defendant;

    (b)   made an order falling within section 13(3);

    (c)   made an order under section 130 of the Sentencing Act (compensation orders).

## 15[1]  Effect of postponement

(1) If the court postpones proceedings under section 6 it may proceed to sentence the defendant for the offence (or any of the offences) concerned.

(2) In sentencing the defendant for the offence (or any of the offences) concerned in the postponement period the court must not –

    (a)   impose a fine on him,

    (b)   make an order falling within section 13(3), or

    (c)   make an order for the payment of compensation under section 130 of the Sentencing Act.

(3) If the court sentences the defendant for the offence (or any of the offences) concerned in the postponement period, after that period ends it may vary the sentence by –

    (a)   imposing a fine on him,

    (b)   making an order falling within section 13(3), or

    (c)   making an order for the payment of compensation under section 130 of the Sentencing Act.

(4) But the court may proceed under subsection (3) only within the period of 28 days which starts with the last day of the postponement period.

(5) For the purposes of –

    (a)   section 18(2) of the Criminal Appeal Act 1968 (time limit for notice of appeal or of application for leave to appeal), and

    (b)   paragraph 1 of Schedule 3 to the Criminal Justice Act 1988 (time limit for notice of application for leave to refer a case under section 36 of that Act),

the sentence must be regarded as imposed or made on the day on which it is varied under subsection (3).

(6) If the court proceeds to sentence the defendant under subsection (1), section 6 has effect as if the defendant's particular criminal conduct included conduct which constitutes offences which

---

1    Information: Commencement: Not yet in force.

the court has taken into consideration in deciding his sentence for the offence or offences concerned.

(7) The postponement period is the period for which proceedings under section 6 are postponed.

## 16[1]  Statement of information

(1) If the court is proceeding under section 6 in a case where section 6(3)(a) applies, the prosecutor or the Director (as the case may be) must give the court a statement of information within the period the court orders.

(2) If the court is proceeding under section 6 in a case where section 6(3)(b) applies and it orders the prosecutor to give it a statement of information, the prosecutor must give it such a statement within the period the court orders.

(3) If the prosecutor or the Director (as the case may be) believes the defendant has a criminal lifestyle the statement of information is a statement of matters the prosecutor or the Director believes are relevant in connection with deciding these issues –

(a)  whether the defendant has a criminal lifestyle;
(b)  whether he has benefited from his general criminal conduct;
(c)  his benefit from the conduct.

(4) A statement under subsection (3) must include information the prosecutor or Director believes is relevant –

(a)  in connection with the making by the court of a required assumption under section 10;
(b)  for the purpose of enabling the court to decide if the circumstances are such that it must not make such an assumption.

(5) If the prosecutor or the Director (as the case may be) does not believe the defendant has a criminal lifestyle the statement of information is a statement of matters the prosecutor or the Director believes are relevant in connection with deciding these issues –

(a)  whether the defendant has benefited from his particular criminal conduct;
(b)  his benefit from the conduct.

(6) If the prosecutor or the Director gives the court a statement of information –

(a)  he may at any time give the court a further statement of information;
(b)  he must give the court a further statement of information if it orders him to do so, and he must give it within the period the court orders.

(7) If the court makes an order under this section it may at any time vary it by making another one.

## 17[2]  Defendant's response to statement of information

(1) If the prosecutor or the Director gives the court a statement of information and a copy is served on the defendant, the court may order the defendant –

(a)  to indicate (within the period it orders) the extent to which he accepts each allegation in the statement, and
(b)  so far as he does not accept such an allegation, to give particulars of any matters he proposes to rely on.

---

1    Information: Commencement: Not yet in force.
2    Information: Commencement: Not yet in force.

(2) If the defendant accepts to any extent an allegation in a statement of information the court may treat his acceptance as conclusive of the matters to which it relates for the purpose of deciding the issues referred to in section 16(3) or (5) (as the case may be).

(3) If the defendant fails in any respect to comply with an order under subsection (1) he may be treated for the purposes of subsection (2) as accepting every allegation in the statement of information apart from –

    (a)  any allegation in respect of which he has complied with the requirement;

    (b)  any allegation that he has benefited from his general or particular criminal conduct.

(4) For the purposes of this section an allegation may be accepted or particulars may be given in a manner ordered by the court.

(5) If the court makes an order under this section it may at any time vary it by making another one.

(6) No acceptance under this section that the defendant has benefited from conduct is admissible in evidence in proceedings for an offence.

## 18[1]   Provision of information by defendant

(1) This section applies if –

    (a)  the court is proceeding under section 6 in a case where section 6(3)(a) applies, or

    (b)  it is proceeding under section 6 in a case where section 6(3)(b) applies or it is considering whether to proceed.

(2) For the purpose of obtaining information to help it in carrying out its functions the court may at any time order the defendant to give it information specified in the order.

(3) An order under this section may require all or a specified part of the information to be given in a specified manner and before a specified date.

(4) If the defendant fails without reasonable excuse to comply with an order under this section the court may draw such inference as it believes is appropriate.

(5) Subsection (4) does not affect any power of the court to deal with the defendant in respect of a failure to comply with an order under this section.

(6) If the prosecutor or the Director (as the case may be) accepts to any extent an allegation made by the defendant –

    (a)  in giving information required by an order under this section, or

    (b)  in any other statement given to the court in relation to any matter relevant to deciding the available amount under section 9,

the court may treat the acceptance as conclusive of the matters to which it relates.

(7) For the purposes of this section an allegation may be accepted in a manner ordered by the court.

(8) If the court makes an order under this section it may at any time vary it by making another one.

(9) No information given under this section which amounts to an admission by the defendant that he has benefited from criminal conduct is admissible in evidence in proceedings for an offence.

---

1    Information: Commencement: Not yet in force.

*Reconsideration*

## 19[1]   No order made: reconsideration of case

(1) This section applies if –

    (a)  the first condition in section 6 is satisfied but no court has proceeded under that section,

    (b)  there is evidence which was not available to the prosecutor on the relevant date,

    (c)  before the end of the period of six years starting with the date of conviction the prosecutor or the Director applies to the Crown Court to consider the evidence, and

    (d)  after considering the evidence the court believes it is appropriate for it to proceed under section 6.

(2) If this section applies the court must proceed under section 6, and when it does so subsections (3) to (8) below apply.

(3) If the court has already sentenced the defendant for the offence (or any of the offences) concerned, section 6 has effect as if his particular criminal conduct included conduct which constitutes offences which the court has taken into consideration in deciding his sentence for the offence or offences concerned.

(4) Section 8(2) does not apply, and the rules applying instead are that the court must –

    (a)  take account of conduct occurring before the relevant date;

    (b)  take account of property obtained before that date;

    (c)  take account of property obtained on or after that date if it was obtained as a result of or in connection with conduct occurring before that date.

(5) In section 10 –

    (a)  the first and second assumptions do not apply with regard to property first held by the defendant on or after the relevant date;

    (b)  the third assumption does not apply with regard to expenditure incurred by him on or after that date;

    (c)  the fourth assumption does not apply with regard to property obtained (or assumed to have been obtained) by him on or after that date.

(6) The recoverable amount for the purposes of section 6 is such amount as –

    (a)  the court believes is just, but

    (b)  does not exceed the amount found under section 7.

(7) In arriving at the just amount the court must have regard in particular to –

    (a)  the amount found under section 7;

    (b)  any fine imposed on the defendant in respect of the offence (or any of the offences) concerned;

    (c)  any order which falls within section 13(3) and has been made against him in respect of the offence (or any of the offences) concerned and has not already been taken into account by the court in deciding what is the free property held by him for the purposes of section 9;

    (d)  any order which has been made against him in respect of the offence (or any of the offences) concerned under section 130 of the Sentencing Act (compensation orders).

---

1    Information: Commencement: Not yet in force.

(8) If an order for the payment of compensation under section 130 of the Sentencing Act has been made against the defendant in respect of the offence or offences concerned, section 13(5) and (6) above do not apply.

(9) The relevant date is –

    (a)   if the court made a decision not to proceed under section 6, the date of the decision;

    (b)   if the court did not make such a decision, the date of conviction.

(10) The date of conviction is –

    (a)   the date on which the defendant was convicted of the offence concerned, or

    (b)   if there are two or more offences and the convictions were on different dates, the date of the latest.

## 20[1]  No order made: reconsideration of benefit

(1) This section applies if the following two conditions are satisfied.

(2) The first condition is that in proceeding under section 6 the court has decided that –

    (a)   the defendant has a criminal lifestyle but has not benefited from his general criminal conduct, or

    (b)   the defendant does not have a criminal lifestyle and has not benefited from his particular criminal conduct.

(3) If the court proceeded under section 6 because the Director asked it to, the second condition is that –

    (a)   the Director has evidence which was not available to him when the court decided that the defendant had not benefited from his general or particular criminal conduct,

    (b)   before the end of the period of six years starting with the date of conviction the Director applies to the Crown Court to consider the evidence, and

    (c)   after considering the evidence the court concludes that it would have decided that the defendant had benefited from his general or particular criminal conduct (as the case may be) if the evidence had been available to it.

(4) If the court proceeded under section 6 because the prosecutor asked it to or because it believed it was appropriate for it to do so, the second condition is that –

    (a)   there is evidence which was not available to the prosecutor when the court decided that the defendant had not benefited from his general or particular criminal conduct,

    (b)   before the end of the period of six years starting with the date of conviction the prosecutor or the Director applies to the Crown Court to consider the evidence, and

    (c)   after considering the evidence the court concludes that it would have decided that the defendant had benefited from his general or particular criminal conduct (as the case may be) if the evidence had been available to it.

(5) If this section applies the court –

    (a)   must make a fresh decision under section 6(4)(b) or (c) whether the defendant has benefited from his general or particular criminal conduct (as the case may be);

    (b)   may make a confiscation order under that section.

(6) Subsections (7) to (12) below apply if the court proceeds under section 6 in pursuance of this section.

---

1    Information: Commencement: Not yet in force.

(7) If the court has already sentenced the defendant for the offence (or any of the offences) concerned, section 6 has effect as if his particular criminal conduct included conduct which constitutes offences which the court has taken into consideration in deciding his sentence for the offence or offences concerned.

(8) Section 8(2) does not apply, and the rules applying instead are that the court must –

 (a) take account of conduct occurring before the date of the original decision that the defendant had not benefited from his general or particular criminal conduct;
 (b) take account of property obtained before that date;
 (c) take account of property obtained on or after that date if it was obtained as a result of or in connection with conduct occurring before that date.

(9) In section 10 –

 (a) the first and second assumptions do not apply with regard to property first held by the defendant on or after the date of the original decision that the defendant had not benefited from his general or particular criminal conduct;
 (b) the third assumption does not apply with regard to expenditure incurred by him on or after that date;
 (c) the fourth assumption does not apply with regard to property obtained (or assumed to have been obtained) by him on or after that date.

(10) The recoverable amount for the purposes of section 6 is such amount as –

 (a) the court believes is just, but
 (b) does not exceed the amount found under section 7.

(11) In arriving at the just amount the court must have regard in particular to –

 (a) the amount found under section 7;
 (b) any fine imposed on the defendant in respect of the offence (or any of the offences) concerned;
 (c) any order which falls within section 13(3) and has been made against him in respect of the offence (or any of the offences) concerned and has not already been taken into account by the court in deciding what is the free property held by him for the purposes of section 9;
 (d) any order which has been made against him in respect of the offence (or any of the offences) concerned under section 130 of the Sentencing Act (compensation orders).

(12) If an order for the payment of compensation under section 130 of the Sentencing Act has been made against the defendant in respect of the offence or offences concerned, section 13(5) and (6) above do not apply.

(13) The date of conviction is the date found by applying section 19(10).

## 21[1] Order made: reconsideration of benefit

(1) This section applies if –

 (a) a court has made a confiscation order,
 (b) there is evidence which was not available to the prosecutor or the Director at the relevant time,
 (c) the prosecutor or the Director believes that if the court were to find the amount of the defendant's benefit in pursuance of this section it would exceed the relevant amount,

---

1 Information: Commencement: Not yet in force.

(d) before the end of the period of six years starting with the date of conviction the prosecutor or the Director applies to the Crown Court to consider the evidence, and

(e) after considering the evidence the court believes it is appropriate for it to proceed under this section.

(2) The court must make a new calculation of the defendant's benefit from the conduct concerned, and when it does so subsections (3) to (6) below apply.

(3) If a court has already sentenced the defendant for the offence (or any of the offences) concerned section 6 has effect as if his particular criminal conduct included conduct which constitutes offences which the court has taken into consideration in deciding his sentence for the offence or offences concerned.

(4) Section 8(2) does not apply, and the rules applying instead are that the court must –

(a) take account of conduct occurring up to the time it decided the defendant's benefit for the purposes of the confiscation order;

(b) take account of property obtained up to that time;

(c) take account of property obtained after that time if it was obtained as a result of or in connection with conduct occurring before that time.

(5) In applying section 8(5) the confiscation order must be ignored.

(6) In section 10 –

(a) the first and second assumptions do not apply with regard to property first held by the defendant after the time the court decided his benefit for the purposes of the confiscation order;

(b) the third assumption does not apply with regard to expenditure incurred by him after that time;

(c) the fourth assumption does not apply with regard to property obtained (or assumed to have been obtained) by him after that time.

(7) If the amount found under the new calculation of the defendant's benefit exceeds the relevant amount the court –

(a) must make a new calculation of the recoverable amount for the purposes of section 6, and

(b) if it exceeds the amount required to be paid under the confiscation order, may vary the order by substituting for the amount required to be paid such amount as it believes is just.

(8) In applying subsection (7)(a) the court must –

(a) take the new calculation of the defendant's benefit;

(b) apply section 9 as if references to the time the confiscation order is made were to the time of the new calculation of the recoverable amount and as if references to the date of the confiscation order were to the date of that new calculation.

(9) In applying subsection (7)(b) the court must have regard in particular to –

(a) any fine imposed on the defendant for the offence (or any of the offences) concerned;

(b) any order which falls within section 13(3) and has been made against him in respect of the offence (or any of the offences) concerned and has not already been taken into account by the court in deciding what is the free property held by him for the purposes of section 9;

(c) any order which has been made against him in respect of the offence (or any of the offences) concerned under section 130 of the Sentencing Act (compensation orders).

(10) But in applying subsection (7)(b) the court must not have regard to an order falling within subsection (9)(c) if a court has made a direction under section 13(6).

(11) In deciding under this section whether one amount exceeds another the court must take account of any change in the value of money.

(12) The relevant time is –

    (a)   when the court calculated the defendant's benefit for the purposes of the confiscation order, if this section has not applied previously;

    (b)   when the court last calculated the defendant's benefit in pursuance of this section, if this section has applied previously.

(13) The relevant amount is –

    (a)   the amount found as the defendant's benefit for the purposes of the confiscation order, if this section has not applied previously;

    (b)   the amount last found as the defendant's benefit in pursuance of this section, if this section has applied previously.

(14) The date of conviction is the date found by applying section 19(10).

## 22[1]   Order made: reconsideration of available amount

(1) This section applies if –

    (a)   a court has made a confiscation order,

    (b)   the amount required to be paid was the amount found under section 7(2), and

    (c)   an applicant falling within subsection (2) applies to the Crown Court to make a new calculation of the available amount.

(2) These applicants fall within this subsection –

    (a)   the prosecutor;

    (b)   the Director;

    (c)   a receiver appointed under section 50 or 52.

(3) In a case where this section applies the court must make the new calculation, and in doing so it must apply section 9 as if references to the time the confiscation order is made were to the time of the new calculation and as if references to the date of the confiscation order were to the date of the new calculation.

(4) If the amount found under the new calculation exceeds the relevant amount the court may vary the order by substituting for the amount required to be paid such amount as –

    (a)   it believes is just, but

    (b)   does not exceed the amount found as the defendant's benefit from the conduct concerned.

(5) In deciding what is just the court must have regard in particular to –

    (a)   any fine imposed on the defendant for the offence (or any of the offences) concerned;

    (b)   any order which falls within section 13(3) and has been made against him in respect of the offence (or any of the offences) concerned and has not already been taken into account by the court in deciding what is the free property held by him for the purposes of section 9;

---

1    Information: Commencement: Not yet in force.

(c) any order which has been made against him in respect of the offence (or any of the offences) concerned under section 130 of the Sentencing Act (compensation orders).

(6) But in deciding what is just the court must not have regard to an order falling within subsection (5)(c) if a court has made a direction under section 13(6).

(7) In deciding under this section whether one amount exceeds another the court must take account of any change in the value of money.

(8) The relevant amount is –

(a) the amount found as the available amount for the purposes of the confiscation order, if this section has not applied previously;
(b) the amount last found as the available amount in pursuance of this section, if this section has applied previously.

(9) The amount found as the defendant's benefit from the conduct concerned is –

(a) the amount so found when the confiscation order was made, or
(b) if one or more new calculations of the defendant's benefit have been made under section 21 the amount found on the occasion of the last such calculation.

## 23[1]   Inadequacy of available amount: variation of order

(1) This section applies if –

(a) a court has made a confiscation order, and
(b) the defendant, or a receiver appointed under section 50 or 52, applies to the Crown Court to vary the order under this section.

(2) In such a case the court must calculate the available amount, and in doing so it must apply section 9 as if references to the time the confiscation order is made were to the time of the calculation and as if references to the date of the confiscation order were to the date of the calculation.

(3) If the court finds that the available amount (as so calculated) is inadequate for the payment of any amount remaining to be paid under the confiscation order it may vary the order by substituting for the amount required to be paid such smaller amount as the court believes is just.

(4) If a person has been adjudged bankrupt or his estate has been sequestrated, or if an order for the winding up of a company has been made, the court must take into account the extent to which realisable property held by that person or that company may be distributed among creditors.

(5) The court may disregard any inadequacy which it believes is attributable (wholly or partly) to anything done by the defendant for the purpose of preserving property held by the recipient of a tainted gift from any risk of realisation under this Part.

(6) In subsection (4) 'company' means any company which may be wound up under the Insolvency Act 1986 or the Insolvency (Northern Ireland) Order 1989 (SI 1989/2405 (NI 19)).

## 24[2]   Inadequacy of available amount: discharge of order

(1) This section applies if –

(a) a court has made a confiscation order,

---

1    Information: Commencement: Not yet in force.
2    Information: Commencement: Not yet in force.

   (b)   a justices' chief executive applies to the Crown Court for the discharge of the order, and

   (c)   the amount remaining to be paid under the order is less than £1,000.

(2) In such a case the court must calculate the available amount, and in doing so it must apply section 9 as if references to the time the confiscation order is made were to the time of the calculation and as if references to the date of the confiscation order were to the date of the calculation.

(3) If the court –

   (a)   finds that the available amount (as so calculated) is inadequate to meet the amount remaining to be paid, and

   (b)   is satisfied that the inadequacy is due wholly to a specified reason or a combination of specified reasons,

it may discharge the confiscation order.

(4) The specified reasons are –

   (a)   in a case where any of the realisable property consists of money in a currency other than sterling, that fluctuations in currency exchange rates have occurred;

   (b)   any reason specified by the Secretary of State by order.

(5) The Secretary of State may by order vary the amount for the time being specified in subsection (1)(c).

## 25[1]  Small amount outstanding: discharge of order

(1) This section applies if –

   (a)   a court has made a confiscation order,

   (b)   a justices' chief executive applies to the Crown Court for the discharge of the order, and

   (c)   the amount remaining to be paid under the order is £50 or less.

(2) In such a case the court may discharge the order.

(3) The Secretary of State may by order vary the amount for the time being specified in subsection (1)(c).

## 26[2]  Information

(1) This section applies if –

   (a)   the court proceeds under section 6 in pursuance of section 19 or 20, or

   (b)   the prosecutor or the Director applies under section 21.

(2) In such a case –

   (a)   the prosecutor or the Director (as the case may be) must give the court a statement of information within the period the court orders;

   (b)   section 16 applies accordingly (with appropriate modifications where the prosecutor or the Director applies under section 21);

   (c)   section 17 applies accordingly;

   (d)   section 18 applies as it applies in the circumstances mentioned in section 18(1).

---

1    Information: Commencement: Not yet in force.
2    Information: Commencement: Not yet in force.

*Defendant absconds*

## 27¹   Defendant convicted or committed

(1) This section applies if the following two conditions are satisfied.

(2) The first condition is that a defendant absconds after –

    (a)  he is convicted of an offence or offences in proceedings before the Crown Court,

    (b)  he is committed to the Crown Court for sentence in respect of an offence or offences under section 3, 4 or 6 of the Sentencing Act, or

    (c)  he is committed to the Crown Court in respect of an offence or offences under section 70 below (committal with a view to a confiscation order being considered).

(3) The second condition is that –

    (a)  the prosecutor or the Director applies to the Crown Court to proceed under this section, and

    (b)  the court believes it is appropriate for it to do so.

(4) If this section applies the court must proceed under section 6 in the same way as it must proceed if the two conditions there mentioned are satisfied; but this is subject to subsection (5).

(5) If the court proceeds under section 6 as applied by this section, this Part has effect with these modifications –

    (a)  any person the court believes is likely to be affected by an order under section 6 is entitled to appear before the court and make representations;

    (b)  the court must not make an order under section 6 unless the prosecutor or the Director (as the case may be) has taken reasonable steps to contact the defendant;

    (c)  section 6(9) applies as if the reference to subsection (2) were to subsection (2) of this section;

    (d)  sections 10, 16(4), 17 and 18 must be ignored;

    (e)  sections 19, 20 and 21 must be ignored while the defendant is still an absconder.

(6) Once the defendant ceases to be an absconder section 19 has effect as if subsection (1)(a) read –

    '(a)  at a time when the first condition in section 27 was satisfied the court did not proceed under section 6,.'

(7) If the court does not believe it is appropriate for it to proceed under this section, once the defendant ceases to be an absconder section 19 has effect as if subsection (1)(b) read –

    '(b)  there is evidence which was not available to the prosecutor or the Director on the relevant date,.'

## 28²   Defendant neither convicted nor acquitted

(1) This section applies if the following two conditions are satisfied.

(2) The first condition is that –

    (a)  proceedings for an offence or offences are started against a defendant but are not concluded,

    (b)  he absconds, and

---

1    Information: Commencement: Not yet in force.
2    Information: Commencement: Not yet in force.

(c) the period of two years (starting with the day the court believes he absconded) has ended.

(3) The second condition is that –

(a) the prosecutor or the Director applies to the Crown Court to proceed under this section, and
(b) the court believes it is appropriate for it to do so.

(4) If this section applies the court must proceed under section 6 in the same way as it must proceed if the two conditions there mentioned are satisfied; but this is subject to subsection (5).

(5) If the court proceeds under section 6 as applied by this section, this Part has effect with these modifications –

(a) any person the court believes is likely to be affected by an order under section 6 is entitled to appear before the court and make representations;
(b) the court must not make an order under section 6 unless the prosecutor or the Director (as the case may be) has taken reasonable steps to contact the defendant;
(c) section 6(9) applies as if the reference to subsection (2) were to subsection (2) of this section;
(d) sections 10, 16(4) and 17 to 20 must be ignored;
(e) section 21 must be ignored while the defendant is still an absconder.

(6) Once the defendant has ceased to be an absconder section 21 has effect as if references to the date of conviction were to –

(a) the day when proceedings for the offence concerned were started against the defendant, or
(b) if there are two or more offences and proceedings for them were started on different days, the earliest of those days.

(7) If –

(a) the court makes an order under section 6 as applied by this section, and
(b) the defendant is later convicted in proceedings before the Crown Court of the offence (or any of the offences) concerned,

section 6 does not apply so far as that conviction is concerned.

## 29[1]   Variation of order

(1) This section applies if –

(a) the court makes a confiscation order under section 6 as applied by section 28,
(b) the defendant ceases to be an absconder,
(c) he is convicted of an offence (or any of the offences) mentioned in section 28(2)(a),
(d) he believes that the amount required to be paid was too large (taking the circumstances prevailing when the amount was found for the purposes of the order), and
(e) before the end of the relevant period he applies to the Crown Court to consider the evidence on which his belief is based.

(2) If (after considering the evidence) the court concludes that the defendant's belief is well founded –

---

1    Information: Commencement: Not yet in force.

(a) it must find the amount which should have been the amount required to be paid (taking the circumstances prevailing when the amount was found for the purposes of the order), and

(b) it may vary the order by substituting for the amount required to be paid such amount as it believes is just.

(3) The relevant period is the period of 28 days starting with –

(a) the date on which the defendant was convicted of the offence mentioned in section 28(2)(a), or

(b) if there are two or more offences and the convictions were on different dates, the date of the latest.

(4) But in a case where section 28(2)(a) applies to more than one offence the court must not make an order under this section unless it is satisfied that there is no possibility of any further proceedings being taken or continued in relation to any such offence in respect of which the defendant has not been convicted.

## 30[1]  Discharge of order

(1) Subsection (2) applies if –

(a) the court makes a confiscation order under section 6 as applied by section 28,

(b) the defendant is later tried for the offence or offences concerned and acquitted on all counts, and

(c) he applies to the Crown Court to discharge the order.

(2) In such a case the court must discharge the order.

(3) Subsection (4) applies if –

(a) the court makes a confiscation order under section 6 as applied by section 28,

(b) the defendant ceases to be an absconder,

(c) subsection (1)(b) does not apply, and

(d) he applies to the Crown Court to discharge the order.

(4) In such a case the court may discharge the order if it finds that –

(a) there has been undue delay in continuing the proceedings mentioned in section 28(2), or

(b) the prosecutor does not intend to proceed with the prosecution.

(5) If the court discharges a confiscation order under this section it may make such a consequential or incidental order as it believes is appropriate.

*Appeals*

## 31[2]  Appeal by prosecutor or Director

(1) If the Crown Court makes a confiscation order the prosecutor or the Director may appeal to the Court of Appeal in respect of the order.

(2) If the Crown Court decides not to make a confiscation order the prosecutor or the Director may appeal to the Court of Appeal against the decision.

---

1    Information: Commencement: Not yet in force.
2    Information: Commencement: Not yet in force.

(3) Subsections (1) and (2) do not apply to an order or decision made by virtue of section 19, 20, 27 or 28.

## 32[1]   Court's powers on appeal

(1) On an appeal under section 31(1) the Court of Appeal may confirm, quash or vary the confiscation order.

(2) On an appeal under section 31(2) the Court of Appeal may confirm the decision, or if it believes the decision was wrong it may –

  (a)   itself proceed under section 6 (ignoring subsections (1) to (3)), or
  (b)   direct the Crown Court to proceed afresh under section 6.

(3) In proceeding afresh in pursuance of this section the Crown Court must comply with any directions the Court of Appeal may make.

(4) If a court makes or varies a confiscation order under this section or in pursuance of a direction under this section it must –

  (a)   have regard to any fine imposed on the defendant in respect of the offence (or any of the offences) concerned;
  (b)   have regard to any order which falls within section 13(3) and has been made against him in respect of the offence (or any of the offences) concerned, unless the order has already been taken into account by a court in deciding what is the free property held by the defendant for the purposes of section 9.

(5) If the Court of Appeal proceeds under section 6 or the Crown Court proceeds afresh under that section in pursuance of a direction under this section subsections (6) to (10) apply.

(6) If a court has already sentenced the defendant for the offence (or any of the offences) concerned, section 6 has effect as if his particular criminal conduct included conduct which constitutes offences which the court has taken into consideration in deciding his sentence for the offence or offences concerned.

(7) If an order has been made against the defendant in respect of the offence (or any of the offences) concerned under section 130 of the Sentencing Act (compensation orders) –

  (a)   the court must have regard to it, and
  (b)   section 13(5) and (6) above do not apply.

(8) Section 8(2) does not apply, and the rules applying instead are that the court must –

  (a)   take account of conduct occurring before the relevant date;
  (b)   take account of property obtained before that date;
  (c)   take account of property obtained on or after that date if it was obtained as a result of or in connection with conduct occurring before that date.

(9) In section 10 –

  (a)   the first and second assumptions do not apply with regard to property first held by the defendant on or after the relevant date;
  (b)   the third assumption does not apply with regard to expenditure incurred by him on or after that date;
  (c)   the fourth assumption does not apply with regard to property obtained (or assumed to have been obtained) by him on or after that date.

---

1    Information: Commencement: Not yet in force.

(10) Section 26 applies as it applies in the circumstances mentioned in subsection (1) of that section.

(11) The relevant date is the date on which the Crown Court decided not to make a confiscation order.

## 33[1] Appeal to House of Lords

(1) An appeal lies to the House of Lords from a decision of the Court of Appeal on an appeal under section 31.

(2) An appeal under this section lies at the instance of –

(a) the defendant or the prosecutor (if the prosecutor appealed under section 31);
(b) the defendant or the Director (if the Director appealed under section 31).

(3) On an appeal from a decision of the Court of Appeal to confirm, vary or make a confiscation order the House of Lords may confirm, quash or vary the order.

(4) On an appeal from a decision of the Court of Appeal to confirm the decision of the Crown Court not to make a confiscation order or from a decision of the Court of Appeal to quash a confiscation order the House of Lords may –

(a) confirm the decision, or
(b) direct the Crown Court to proceed afresh under section 6 if it believes the decision was wrong.

(5) In proceeding afresh in pursuance of this section the Crown Court must comply with any directions the House of Lords may make.

(6) If a court varies a confiscation order under this section or makes a confiscation order in pursuance of a direction under this section it must –

(a) have regard to any fine imposed on the defendant in respect of the offence (or any of the offences) concerned;
(b) have regard to any order which falls within section 13(3) and has been made against him in respect of the offence (or any of the offences) concerned, unless the order has already been taken into account by a court in deciding what is the free property held by the defendant for the purposes of section 9.

(7) If the Crown Court proceeds afresh under section 6 in pursuance of a direction under this section subsections (8) to (12) apply.

(8) If a court has already sentenced the defendant for the offence (or any of the offences) concerned, section 6 has effect as if his particular criminal conduct included conduct which constitutes offences which the court has taken into consideration in deciding his sentence for the offence or offences concerned.

(9) If an order has been made against the defendant in respect of the offence (or any of the offences) concerned under section 130 of the Sentencing Act (compensation orders) –

(a) the Crown Court must have regard to it, and
(b) section 13(5) and (6) above do not apply.

(10) Section 8(2) does not apply, and the rules applying instead are that the Crown Court must –

(a) take account of conduct occurring before the relevant date;
(b) take account of property obtained before that date;

---

1    Information: Commencement: Not yet in force.

    (c)   take account of property obtained on or after that date if it was obtained as a result of or in connection with conduct occurring before that date.

(11) In section 10 –

    (a)   the first and second assumptions do not apply with regard to property first held by the defendant on or after the relevant date;

    (b)   the third assumption does not apply with regard to expenditure incurred by him on or after that date;

    (c)   the fourth assumption does not apply with regard to property obtained (or assumed to have been obtained) by him on or after that date.

(12) Section 26 applies as it applies in the circumstances mentioned in subsection (1) of that section.

(13) The relevant date is –

    (a)   in a case where the Crown Court made a confiscation order which was quashed by the Court of Appeal, the date on which the Crown Court made the order;

    (b)   in any other case, the date on which the Crown Court decided not to make a confiscation order.

*Enforcement authority*

## 34[1]  Enforcement authority

(1) Subsection (2) applies if a court makes a confiscation order and any of the following paragraphs applies –

    (a)   the court proceeded under section 6 after being asked to do so by the Director;

    (b)   the court proceeded under section 6 by virtue of an application by the Director under section 19, 20, 27 or 28;

    (c)   the court proceeded under section 6 as a result of an appeal by the Director under section 31(2) or 33;

    (d)   before the court made the order the Director applied to the court to appoint him as the enforcement authority for the order.

(2) In any such case the court must appoint the Director as the enforcement authority for the order.

*Enforcement as fines etc*

## 35[2]  Director not appointed as enforcement authority

(1) This section applies if a court –

    (a)   makes a confiscation order, and

    (b)   does not appoint the Director as the enforcement authority for the order.

(2) Sections 139(2) to (4) and (9) and 140(1) to (4) of the Sentencing Act (functions of court as to fines and enforcing fines) apply as if the amount ordered to be paid were a fine imposed on the defendant by the court making the confiscation order.

---

1    Information: Commencement: Not yet in force.
2    Information: Commencement: Not yet in force.

(3) In the application of Part 3 of the Magistrates' Courts Act 1980 to an amount payable under a confiscation order –

    (a)  ignore section 75 of that Act (power to dispense with immediate payment);

    (b)  such an amount is not a sum adjudged to be paid by a conviction for the purposes of section 81 (enforcement of fines imposed on young offenders) or a fine for the purposes of section 85 (remission of fines) of that Act;

    (c)  in section 87 of that Act ignore subsection (3) (inquiry into means).

## 36[1]  Director appointed as enforcement authority

(1) This section applies if a court –

    (a)  makes a confiscation order, and

    (b)  appoints the Director as the enforcement authority for the order.

(2) Section 139(2) to (4) and (9) of the Sentencing Act (functions of court as to fines) applies as if the amount ordered to be paid were a fine imposed on the defendant by the court making the confiscation order.

## 37[2]  Director's application for enforcement

(1) If the Director believes that the conditions set out in subsection (2) are satisfied he may make an ex parte application to the Crown Court for the issue of a summons against the defendant.

(2) The conditions are that –

    (a)  a confiscation order has been made;

    (b)  the Director has been appointed as the enforcement authority for the order;

    (c)  because of the defendant's wilful refusal or culpable neglect the order is not satisfied;

    (d)  the order is not subject to appeal;

    (e)  the Director has done all that is practicable (apart from this section) to enforce the order.

(3) If it appears to the Crown Court that the conditions are satisfied it may issue a summons ordering the defendant to appear before the court at the time and place specified in the summons.

(4) If the defendant fails to appear before the Crown Court in pursuance of the summons the court may issue a warrant for his arrest.

(5) If –

    (a)  the defendant appears before the Crown Court in pursuance of the summons or of a warrant issued under subsection (4), and

    (b)  the court is satisfied that the conditions set out in subsection (2) are satisfied,

it may issue a warrant committing the defendant to prison or detention for default in payment of the amount ordered to be paid by the confiscation order.

(6) Subsection (7) applies if the amount remaining to be paid under the confiscation order when the warrant under subsection (5) is issued is less than the amount ordered to be paid.

(7) In such a case the court must substitute for the term of imprisonment or detention fixed in respect of the order under section 139(2) of the Sentencing Act such term as bears to the original term the same proportion as the amount remaining to be paid bears to the amount ordered to be paid.

---

1    Information: Commencement: Not yet in force.
2    Information: Commencement: Not yet in force.

(8) Subsections (9) and (10) apply if –

    (a)   the defendant has been committed to prison or detention in pursuance of a warrant issued under subsection (5), and

    (b)   a payment is made in respect of some or all of the amount remaining to be paid under the confiscation order.

(9) If the payment is for the whole amount remaining to be paid the defendant must be released unless he is in custody for another reason.

(10) If the payment is for less than that amount, the period of commitment is reduced so that it bears to the term fixed under section 139(2) of the Sentencing Act the same proportion as the amount remaining to be paid bears to the amount ordered to be paid.

## 38[1]   Provisions about imprisonment or detention

(1) Subsection (2) applies if –

    (a)   a warrant committing the defendant to prison or detention is issued for a default in payment of an amount ordered to be paid under a confiscation order in respect of an offence or offences, and

    (b)   at the time the warrant is issued the defendant is liable to serve a term of custody in respect of the offence (or any of the offences).

(2) In such a case the term of imprisonment or of detention under section 108 of the Sentencing Act (detention of persons aged 18 to 20 for default) to be served in default of payment of the amount does not begin to run until after the term mentioned in subsection (1)(b) above.

(3) The reference in subsection (1)(b) to the term of custody the defendant is liable to serve in respect of the offence (or any of the offences) is a reference to the term of imprisonment, or detention in a young offender institution, which he is liable to serve in respect of the offence (or any of the offences).

(4) For the purposes of subsection (3) consecutive terms and terms which are wholly or partly concurrent must be treated as a single term and the following must be ignored –

    (a)   any sentence suspended under section 118(1) of the Sentencing Act which has not taken effect at the time the warrant is issued;

    (b)   in the case of a sentence of imprisonment passed with an order under section 47(1) of the Criminal Law Act 1977 (sentences of imprisonment partly served and partly suspended) any part of the sentence which the defendant has not at that time been required to serve in prison;

    (c)   any term of imprisonment or detention fixed under section 139(2) of the Sentencing Act (term to be served in default of payment of fine etc) for which a warrant committing the defendant to prison or detention has not been issued at that time.

(5) If the defendant serves a term of imprisonment or detention in default of paying any amount due under a confiscation order, his serving that term does not prevent the confiscation order from continuing to have effect so far as any other method of enforcement is concerned.

## 39[2]   Reconsideration etc: variation of prison term

(1) Subsection (2) applies if –

    (a)   a court varies a confiscation order under section 21, 22, 23, 29, 32 or 33,

---

1    Information: Commencement: Not yet in force.
2    Information: Commencement: Not yet in force.

(b)  the effect of the variation is to vary the maximum period applicable in relation to the order under section 139(4) of the Sentencing Act, and

(c)  the result is that that maximum period is less than the term of imprisonment or detention fixed in respect of the order under section 139(2) of the Sentencing Act.

(2) In such a case the court must fix a reduced term of imprisonment or detention in respect of the confiscation order under section 139(2) of the Sentencing Act in place of the term previously fixed.

(3) Subsection (4) applies if paragraphs (a) and (b) of subsection (1) apply but paragraph (c) does not.

(4) In such a case the court may amend the term of imprisonment or detention fixed in respect of the confiscation order under section 139(2) of the Sentencing Act.

(5) If the effect of section 12 is to increase the maximum period applicable in relation to a confiscation order under section 139(4) of the Sentencing Act, on the application of the appropriate person the Crown Court may amend the term of imprisonment or detention fixed in respect of the order under section 139(2) of that Act.

(6) The appropriate person is –

(a)  the Director, if he was appointed as the enforcement authority for the order under section 34;

(b)  the prosecutor, in any other case.

*Restraint orders*

## 40[1]   Conditions for exercise of powers

(1) The Crown Court may exercise the powers conferred by section 41 if any of the following conditions is satisfied.

(2) The first condition is that –

(a)  a criminal investigation has been started in England and Wales with regard to an offence, and

(b)  there is reasonable cause to believe that the alleged offender has benefited from his criminal conduct.

(3) The second condition is that –

(a)  proceedings for an offence have been started in England and Wales and not concluded, and

(b)  there is reasonable cause to believe that the defendant has benefited from his criminal conduct.

(4) The third condition is that –

(a)  an application by the prosecutor or the Director has been made under section 19, 20, 27 or 28 and not concluded, or the court believes that such an application is to be made, and

(b)  there is reasonable cause to believe that the defendant has benefited from his criminal conduct.

---

1    Information: Commencement: Not yet in force.

(5) The fourth condition is that –

   (a)   an application by the prosecutor or the Director has been made under section 21 and not concluded, or the court believes that such an application is to be made, and
   (b)   there is reasonable cause to believe that the court will decide under that section that the amount found under the new calculation of the defendant's benefit exceeds the relevant amount (as defined in that section).

(6) The fifth condition is that –

   (a)   an application by the prosecutor or the Director has been made under section 22 and not concluded, or the court believes that such an application is to be made, and
   (b)   there is reasonable cause to believe that the court will decide under that section that the amount found under the new calculation of the available amount exceeds the relevant amount (as defined in that section).

(7) The second condition is not satisfied if the court believes that –

   (a)   there has been undue delay in continuing the proceedings, or
   (b)   the prosecutor does not intend to proceed.

(8) If an application mentioned in the third, fourth or fifth condition has been made the condition is not satisfied if the court believes that –

   (a)   there has been undue delay in continuing the application, or
   (b)   the prosecutor or the Director (as the case may be) does not intend to proceed.

(9) If the first condition is satisfied –

   (a)   references in this Part to the defendant are to the alleged offender;
   (b)   references in this Part to the prosecutor are to the person the court believes is to have conduct of any proceedings for the offence;
   (c)   section 77(9) has effect as if proceedings for the offence had been started against the defendant when the investigation was started.

## 41[1]   Restraint orders

(1) If any condition set out in section 40 is satisfied the Crown Court may make an order (a restraint order) prohibiting any specified person from dealing with any realisable property held by him.

(2) A restraint order may provide that it applies –

   (a)   to all realisable property held by the specified person whether or not the property is described in the order;
   (b)   to realisable property transferred to the specified person after the order is made.

(3) A restraint order may be made subject to exceptions, and an exception may in particular –

   (a)   make provision for reasonable living expenses and reasonable legal expenses;
   (b)   make provision for the purpose of enabling any person to carry on any trade, business, profession or occupation;
   (c)   be made subject to conditions.

(4) But an exception to a restraint order must not make provision for any legal expenses which –

   (a)   relate to an offence which falls within subsection (5), and
   (b)   are incurred by the defendant or by a recipient of a tainted gift.

---

1    Information: Commencement: Not yet in force.

(5) These offences fall within this subsection –

    (a)   the offence mentioned in section 40(2) or (3), if the first or second condition (as the case may be) is satisfied;

    (b)   the offence (or any of the offences) concerned, if the third, fourth or fifth condition is satisfied.

(6) Subsection (7) applies if –

    (a)   a court makes a restraint order, and

    (b)   the applicant for the order applies to the court to proceed under subsection (7) (whether as part of the application for the restraint order or at any time afterwards).

(7) The court may make such order as it believes is appropriate for the purpose of ensuring that the restraint order is effective.

(8) A restraint order does not affect property for the time being subject to a charge under any of these provisions –

    (a)   section 9 of the Drug Trafficking Offences Act 1986;

    (b)   section 78 of the Criminal Justice Act 1988;

    (c)   Article 14 of the Criminal Justice (Confiscation) (Northern Ireland) Order 1990 (SI 1990/2588 (NI 17));

    (d)   section 27 of the Drug Trafficking Act 1994;

    (e)   Article 32 of the Proceeds of Crime (Northern Ireland) Order 1996 (SI 1996/1299 (NI 9)).

(9) Dealing with property includes removing it from England and Wales.

## 42[1]   Application, discharge and variation

(1) A restraint order –

    (a)   may be made only on an application by an applicant falling within subsection (2);

    (b)   may be made on an ex parte application to a judge in chambers.

(2) These applicants fall within this subsection –

    (a)   the prosecutor;

    (b)   the Director;

    (c)   an accredited financial investigator.

(3) An application to discharge or vary a restraint order or an order under section 41(7) may be made to the Crown Court by –

    (a)   the person who applied for the order;

    (b)   any person affected by the order.

(4) Subsections (5) to (7) apply to an application under subsection (3).

(5) The court –

    (a)   may discharge the order;

    (b)   may vary the order.

(6) If the condition in section 40 which was satisfied was that proceedings were started or an application was made, the court must discharge the order on the conclusion of the proceedings or of the application (as the case may be).

---

1    Information: Commencement: Not yet in force.

(7) If the condition in section 40 which was satisfied was that an investigation was started or an application was to be made, the court must discharge the order if within a reasonable time proceedings for the offence are not started or the application is not made (as the case may be).

## 43[1]   Appeal to Court of Appeal

(1) If on an application for a restraint order the court decides not to make one, the person who applied for the order may appeal to the Court of Appeal against the decision.

(2) If an application is made under section 42(3) in relation to a restraint order or an order under section 41(7) the following persons may appeal to the Court of Appeal in respect of the Crown Court's decision on the application –

>    (a)   the person who applied for the order;
>    (b)   any person affected by the order.

(3) On an appeal under subsection (1) or (2) the Court of Appeal may –

>    (a)   confirm the decision, or
>    (b)   make such order as it believes is appropriate.

## 44[2]   Appeal to House of Lords

(1) An appeal lies to the House of Lords from a decision of the Court of Appeal on an appeal under section 43.

(2) An appeal under this section lies at the instance of any person who was a party to the proceedings before the Court of Appeal.

(3) On an appeal under this section the House of Lords may –

>    (a)   confirm the decision of the Court of Appeal, or
>    (b)   make such order as it believes is appropriate.

## 45[3]   Seizure

(1) If a restraint order is in force a constable or a customs officer may seize any realisable property to which it applies to prevent its removal from England and Wales.

(2) Property seized under subsection (1) must be dealt with in accordance with the directions of the court which made the order.

## 46[4]   Hearsay evidence

(1) Evidence must not be excluded in restraint proceedings on the ground that it is hearsay (of whatever degree).

(2) Sections 2 to 4 of the Civil Evidence Act 1995 apply in relation to restraint proceedings as those sections apply in relation to civil proceedings.

(3) Restraint proceedings are proceedings –

>    (a)   for a restraint order;
>    (b)   for the discharge or variation of a restraint order;

---

1     Information: Commencement: Not yet in force.
2     Information: Commencement: Not yet in force.
3     Information: Commencement: Not yet in force.
4     Information: Commencement: Not yet in force.

(c)   on an appeal under section 43 or 44.

(4)  Hearsay is a statement which is made otherwise than by a person while giving oral evidence in the proceedings and which is tendered as evidence of the matters stated.

(5)  Nothing in this section affects the admissibility of evidence which is admissible apart from this section.

## 47[1]   Supplementary

(1)  The registration Acts –

    (a)   apply in relation to restraint orders as they apply in relation to orders which affect land and are made by the court for the purpose of enforcing judgments or recognisances;

    (b)   apply in relation to applications for restraint orders as they apply in relation to other pending land actions.

(2)  The registration Acts are –

    (a)   the Land Registration Act 1925;

    (b)   the Land Charges Act 1972;

    (c)   the Land Registration Act 2002.

(3)  But no notice may be entered in the register of title under the Land Registration Act 2002 in respect of a restraint order.

(4)  The person applying for a restraint order must be treated for the purposes of section 57 of the Land Registration Act 1925 (inhibitions) as a person interested in relation to any registered land to which –

    (a)   the application relates, or

    (b)   a restraint order made in pursuance of the application relates.

*Management receivers*

## 48[2]   Appointment

(1)  Subsection (2) applies if –

    (a)   the Crown Court makes a restraint order, and

    (b)   the applicant for the restraint order applies to the court to proceed under subsection (2) (whether as part of the application for the restraint order or at any time afterwards).

(2)  The Crown Court may by order appoint a receiver in respect of any realisable property to which the restraint order applies.

## 49[3]   Powers

(1)  If the court appoints a receiver under section 48 it may act under this section on the application of the person who applied for the restraint order.

(2)  The court may by order confer on the receiver the following powers in relation to any realisable property to which the restraint order applies –

    (a)   power to take possession of the property;

---

1    Information: Commencement: Not yet in force.
2    Information: Commencement: Not yet in force.
3    Information: Commencement: Not yet in force.

(b) power to manage or otherwise deal with the property;

(c) power to start, carry on or defend any legal proceedings in respect of the property;

(d) power to realise so much of the property as is necessary to meet the receiver's remuneration and expenses.

(3) The court may by order confer on the receiver power to enter any premises in England and Wales and to do any of the following –

(a) search for or inspect anything authorised by the court;

(b) make or obtain a copy, photograph or other record of anything so authorised;

(c) remove anything which the receiver is required or authorised to take possession of in pursuance of an order of the court.

(4) The court may by order authorise the receiver to do any of the following for the purpose of the exercise of his functions –

(a) hold property;

(b) enter into contracts;

(c) sue and be sued;

(d) employ agents;

(e) execute powers of attorney, deeds or other instruments;

(f) take any other steps the court thinks appropriate.

(5) The court may order any person who has possession of realisable property to which the restraint order applies to give possession of it to the receiver.

(6) The court –

(a) may order a person holding an interest in realisable property to which the restraint order applies to make to the receiver such payment as the court specifies in respect of a beneficial interest held by the defendant or the recipient of a tainted gift;

(b) may (on the payment being made) by order transfer, grant or extinguish any interest in the property.

(7) Subsections (2), (5) and (6) do not apply to property for the time being subject to a charge under any of these provisions –

(a) section 9 of the Drug Trafficking Offences Act 1986;

(b) section 78 of the Criminal Justice Act 1988;

(c) Article 14 of the Criminal Justice (Confiscation) (Northern Ireland) Order 1990 (SI 1990/2588 (NI 17));

(d) section 27 of the Drug Trafficking Act 1994;

(e) Article 32 of the Proceeds of Crime (Northern Ireland) Order 1996 (SI 1996/1299 (NI 9)).

(8) The court must not –

(a) confer the power mentioned in subsection (2)(b) or (d) in respect of property, or

(b) exercise the power conferred on it by subsection (6) in respect of property,

unless it gives persons holding interests in the property a reasonable opportunity to make representations to it.

(9) The court may order that a power conferred by an order under this section is subject to such conditions and exceptions as it specifies.

(10) Managing or otherwise dealing with property includes –

   (a)   selling the property or any part of it or interest in it;

   (b)   carrying on or arranging for another person to carry on any trade or business the assets of which are or are part of the property;

   (c)   incurring capital expenditure in respect of the property.

*Enforcement receivers*

## 50[1]  Appointment

(1) This section applies if –

   (a)   a confiscation order is made,

   (b)   it is not satisfied, and

   (c)   it is not subject to appeal.

(2) On the application of the prosecutor the Crown Court may by order appoint a receiver in respect of realisable property.

## 51[2]  Powers

(1) If the court appoints a receiver under section 50 it may act under this section on the application of the prosecutor.

(2) The court may by order confer on the receiver the following powers in relation to the realisable property –

   (a)   power to take possession of the property;

   (b)   power to manage or otherwise deal with the property;

   (c)   power to realise the property, in such manner as the court may specify;

   (d)   power to start, carry on or defend any legal proceedings in respect of the property.

(3) The court may by order confer on the receiver power to enter any premises in England and Wales and to do any of the following –

   (a)   search for or inspect anything authorised by the court;

   (b)   make or obtain a copy, photograph or other record of anything so authorised;

   (c)   remove anything which the receiver is required or authorised to take possession of in pursuance of an order of the court.

(4) The court may by order authorise the receiver to do any of the following for the purpose of the exercise of his functions –

   (a)   hold property;

   (b)   enter into contracts;

   (c)   sue and be sued;

   (d)   employ agents;

   (e)   execute powers of attorney, deeds or other instruments;

   (f)   take any other steps the court thinks appropriate.

(5) The court may order any person who has possession of realisable property to give possession of it to the receiver.

(6) The court –

---

1    Information: Commencement: Not yet in force.
2    Information: Commencement: Not yet in force.

(a)  may order a person holding an interest in realisable property to make to the receiver such payment as the court specifies in respect of a beneficial interest held by the defendant or the recipient of a tainted gift;

(b)  may (on the payment being made) by order transfer, grant or extinguish any interest in the property.

(7) Subsections (2), (5) and (6) do not apply to property for the time being subject to a charge under any of these provisions –

(a)  section 9 of the Drug Trafficking Offences Act 1986;

(b)  section 78 of the Criminal Justice Act 1988;

(c)  Article 14 of the Criminal Justice (Confiscation) (Northern Ireland) Order 1990 (SI 1990/2588 (NI 17));

(d)  section 27 of the Drug Trafficking Act 1994;

(e)  Article 32 of the Proceeds of Crime (Northern Ireland) Order 1996 (SI 1996/1299 (NI 9)).

(8) The court must not –

(a)  confer the power mentioned in subsection (2)(b) or (c) in respect of property, or

(b)  exercise the power conferred on it by subsection (6) in respect of property,

unless it gives persons holding interests in the property a reasonable opportunity to make representations to it.

(9) The court may order that a power conferred by an order under this section is subject to such conditions and exceptions as it specifies.

(10) Managing or otherwise dealing with property includes –

(a)  selling the property or any part of it or interest in it;

(b)  carrying on or arranging for another person to carry on any trade or business the assets of which are or are part of the property;

(c)  incurring capital expenditure in respect of the property.

*Director's receivers*

## 52[1]  Appointment

(1) This section applies if –

(a)  a confiscation order is made, and

(b)  the Director is appointed as the enforcement authority for the order under section 34.

(2) But this section does not apply if –

(a)  the confiscation order was made by the Court of Appeal, and

(b)  when the Crown Court comes to proceed under this section the confiscation order has been satisfied.

(3) If this section applies the Crown Court must make an order for the appointment of a receiver in respect of realisable property.

(4) An order under subsection (3) –

(a)  must confer power on the Director to nominate the person who is to be the receiver, and

---

1    Information: Commencement: Not yet in force.

(b) takes effect when the Director nominates that person.

(5) The Director must not nominate a person under subsection (4) unless at the time he does so the confiscation order –

(a) is not satisfied, and
(b) is not subject to appeal.

(6) A person nominated to be the receiver under subsection (4) may be –

(a) a member of the staff of the Agency;
(b) a person providing services under arrangements made by the Director.

(7) If this section applies section 50 does not apply.

## 53¹ Powers

(1) If the court makes an order for the appointment of a receiver under section 52 it may act under this section on the application of the Director.

(2) The court may by order confer on the receiver the following powers in relation to the realisable property –

(a) power to take possession of the property;
(b) power to manage or otherwise deal with the property;
(c) power to realise the property, in such manner as the court may specify;
(d) power to start, carry on or defend any legal proceedings in respect of the property.

(3) The court may by order confer on the receiver power to enter any premises in England and Wales and to do any of the following –

(a) search for or inspect anything authorised by the court;
(b) make or obtain a copy, photograph or other record of anything so authorised;
(c) remove anything which the receiver is required or authorised to take possession of in pursuance of an order of the court.

(4) The court may by order authorise the receiver to do any of the following for the purpose of the exercise of his functions –

(a) hold property;
(b) enter into contracts;
(c) sue and be sued;
(d) employ agents;
(e) execute powers of attorney, deeds or other instruments;
(f) take any other steps the court thinks appropriate.

(5) The court may order any person who has possession of realisable property to give possession of it to the receiver.

(6) The court –

(a) may order a person holding an interest in realisable property to make to the receiver such payment as the court specifies in respect of a beneficial interest held by the defendant or the recipient of a tainted gift;
(b) may (on the payment being made) by order transfer, grant or extinguish any interest in the property.

---

1    Information: Commencement: Not yet in force.

(7) Subsections (2), (5) and (6) do not apply to property for the time being subject to a charge under any of these provisions –

    (a)   section 9 of the Drug Trafficking Offences Act 1986;

    (b)   section 78 of the Criminal Justice Act 1988;

    (c)   Article 14 of the Criminal Justice (Confiscation) (Northern Ireland) Order 1990 (SI 1990/2588 (NI 17));

    (d)   section 27 of the Drug Trafficking Act 1994;

    (e)   Article 32 of the Proceeds of Crime (Northern Ireland) Order 1996 (SI 1996/1299 (NI 9)).

(8) The court must not –

    (a)   confer the power mentioned in subsection (2)(b) or (c) in respect of property, or

    (b)   exercise the power conferred on it by subsection (6) in respect of property,

unless it gives persons holding interests in the property a reasonable opportunity to make representations to it.

(9) The court may order that a power conferred by an order under this section is subject to such conditions and exceptions as it specifies.

(10) Managing or otherwise dealing with property includes –

    (a)   selling the property or any part of it or interest in it;

    (b)   carrying on or arranging for another person to carry on any trade or business the assets of which are or are part of the property;

    (c)   incurring capital expenditure in respect of the property.

*Application of sums*

## 54[1]   Enforcement receivers

(1) This section applies to sums which are in the hands of a receiver appointed under section 50 if they are –

    (a)   the proceeds of the realisation of property under section 51;

    (b)   sums (other than those mentioned in paragraph (a)) in which the defendant holds an interest.

(2) The sums must be applied as follows –

    (a)   first, they must be applied in payment of such expenses incurred by a person acting as an insolvency practitioner as are payable under this subsection by virtue of section 432;

    (b)   second, they must be applied in making any payments directed by the Crown Court;

    (c)   third, they must be applied on the defendant's behalf towards satisfaction of the confiscation order.

(3) If the amount payable under the confiscation order has been fully paid and any sums remain in the receiver's hands he must distribute them –

    (a)   among such persons who held (or hold) interests in the property concerned as the Crown Court directs, and

    (b)   in such proportions as it directs.

(4) Before making a direction under subsection (3) the court must give persons who held (or hold) interests in the property concerned a reasonable opportunity to make representations to it.

---

1    Information: Commencement: Not yet in force.

(5) For the purposes of subsections (3) and (4) the property concerned is –

    (a)   the property represented by the proceeds mentioned in subsection (1)(a);

    (b)   the sums mentioned in subsection (1)(b).

(6) The receiver applies sums as mentioned in subsection (2)(c) by paying them to the appropriate justices' chief executive on account of the amount payable under the order.

(7) The appropriate justices' chief executive is the one for the magistrates' court responsible for enforcing the confiscation order as if the amount ordered to be paid were a fine.

## 55[1]   Sums received by justices' chief executive

(1) This section applies if a justices' chief executive receives sums on account of the amount payable under a confiscation order (whether the sums are received under section 54 or otherwise).

(2) The chief executive's receipt of the sums reduces the amount payable under the order, but he must apply the sums received as follows.

(3) First he must apply them in payment of such expenses incurred by a person acting as an insolvency practitioner as –

    (a)   are payable under this subsection by virtue of section 432, but

    (b)   are not already paid under section 54(2)(a).

(4) If the justices' chief executive received the sums under section 54 he must next apply them –

    (a)   first, in payment of the remuneration and expenses of a receiver appointed under section 48, to the extent that they have not been met by virtue of the exercise by that receiver of a power conferred under section 49(2)(d);

    (b)   second, in payment of the remuneration and expenses of the receiver appointed under section 50.

(5) If a direction was made under section 13(6) for an amount of compensation to be paid out of sums recovered under the confiscation order, the justices' chief executive must next apply the sums in payment of that amount.

(6) If any amount remains after the justices' chief executive makes any payments required by the preceding provisions of this section, the amount must be treated for the purposes of section 60 of the Justices of the Peace Act 1997 (application of fines etc) as if it were a fine imposed by a magistrates' court.

(7) Subsection (4) does not apply if the receiver is a member of the staff of the Crown Prosecution Service or of the Commissioners of Customs and Excise; and it is immaterial whether he is a permanent or temporary member or he is on secondment from elsewhere.

## 56[2]   Director's receivers

(1) This section applies to sums which are in the hands of a receiver appointed under section 52 if they are –

    (a)   the proceeds of the realisation of property under section 53;

---

1    Information: Commencement: Not yet in force.
2    Information: Commencement: Not yet in force.

    (b)   sums (other than those mentioned in paragraph (a)) in which the defendant holds an interest.

(2) The sums must be applied as follows –

    (a)   first, they must be applied in payment of such expenses incurred by a person acting as an insolvency practitioner as are payable under this subsection by virtue of section 432;
    (b)   second, they must be applied in making any payments directed by the Crown Court;
    (c)   third, they must be applied on the defendant's behalf towards satisfaction of the confiscation order by being paid to the Director on account of the amount payable under it.

(3) If the amount payable under the confiscation order has been fully paid and any sums remain in the receiver's hands he must distribute them –

    (a)   among such persons who held (or hold) interests in the property concerned as the Crown Court directs, and
    (b)   in such proportions as it directs.

(4) Before making a direction under subsection (3) the court must give persons who held (or hold) interests in the property concerned a reasonable opportunity to make representations to it.

(5) For the purposes of subsections (3) and (4) the property concerned is –

    (a)   the property represented by the proceeds mentioned in subsection (1)(a);
    (b)   the sums mentioned in subsection (1)(b).

## 57[1]  Sums received by Director

(1) This section applies if the Director receives sums on account of the amount payable under a confiscation order (whether the sums are received under section 56 or otherwise).

(2) The Director's receipt of the sums reduces the amount payable under the order, but he must apply the sums received as follows.

(3) First he must apply them in payment of such expenses incurred by a person acting as an insolvency practitioner as –

    (a)   are payable under this subsection by virtue of section 432, but
    (b)   are not already paid under section 56(2)(a).

(4) If the Director received the sums under section 56 he must next apply them –

    (a)   first, in payment of the remuneration and expenses of a receiver appointed under section 48, to the extent that they have not been met by virtue of the exercise by that receiver of a power conferred under section 49(2)(d);
    (b)   second, in payment of the remuneration and expenses of the receiver appointed under section 52.

(5) If a direction was made under section 13(6) for an amount of compensation to be paid out of sums recovered under the confiscation order, the Director must next apply the sums in payment of that amount.

(6) Subsection (4) does not apply if the receiver is a member of the staff of the Agency or a person providing services under arrangements made by the Director.

---

1    Information: Commencement: Not yet in force.

*Restrictions*

## 58[1]  Restraint orders

(1) Subsections (2) to (4) apply if a court makes a restraint order.

(2) No distress may be levied against any realisable property to which the order applies except with the leave of the Crown Court and subject to any terms the Crown Court may impose.

(3) If the order applies to a tenancy of any premises, no landlord or other person to whom rent is payable may exercise a right within subsection (4) except with the leave of the Crown Court and subject to any terms the Crown Court may impose.

(4) A right is within this subsection if it is a right of forfeiture by peaceable re-entry in relation to the premises in respect of any failure by the tenant to comply with any term or condition of the tenancy.

(5) If a court in which proceedings are pending in respect of any property is satisfied that a restraint order has been applied for or made in respect of the property, the court may either stay the proceedings or allow them to continue on any terms it thinks fit.

(6) Before exercising any power conferred by subsection (5), the court must give an opportunity to be heard to –

    (a)   the applicant for the restraint order, and
    (b)   any receiver appointed in respect of the property under section 48, 50 or 52.

## 59[2]  Enforcement receivers

(1) Subsections (2) to (4) apply if a court makes an order under section 50 appointing a receiver in respect of any realisable property.

(2) No distress may be levied against the property except with the leave of the Crown Court and subject to any terms the Crown Court may impose.

(3) If the receiver is appointed in respect of a tenancy of any premises, no landlord or other person to whom rent is payable may exercise a right within subsection (4) except with the leave of the Crown Court and subject to any terms the Crown Court may impose.

(4) A right is within this subsection if it is a right of forfeiture by peaceable re-entry in relation to the premises in respect of any failure by the tenant to comply with any term or condition of the tenancy.

(5) If a court in which proceedings are pending in respect of any property is satisfied that an order under section 50 appointing a receiver in respect of the property has been applied for or made, the court may either stay the proceedings or allow them to continue on any terms it thinks fit.

(6) Before exercising any power conferred by subsection (5), the court must give an opportunity to be heard to –

    (a)   the prosecutor, and
    (b)   the receiver (if the order under section 50 has been made).

---

1    Information: Commencement: Not yet in force.
2    Information: Commencement: Not yet in force.

## 60[1]   Director's receivers

(1) Subsections (2) to (4) apply if –

    (a)  the Crown Court has made an order under section 52 for the appointment of a receiver in respect of any realisable property, and

    (b)  the order has taken effect.

(2) No distress may be levied against the property except with the leave of the Crown Court and subject to any terms the Crown Court may impose.

(3) If the order is for the appointment of a receiver in respect of a tenancy of any premises, no landlord or other person to whom rent is payable may exercise a right within subsection (4) except with the leave of the Crown Court and subject to any terms the Crown Court may impose.

(4) A right is within this subsection if it is a right of forfeiture by peaceable re-entry in relation to the premises in respect of any failure by the tenant to comply with any term or condition of the tenancy.

(5) If a court (whether the Crown Court or any other court) in which proceedings are pending in respect of any property is satisfied that an order under section 52 for the appointment of a receiver in respect of the property has taken effect, the court may either stay the proceedings or allow them to continue on any terms it thinks fit.

(6) Before exercising any power conferred by subsection (5), the court must give an opportunity to be heard to –

    (a)  the Director, and

    (b)  the receiver.

*Receivers: further provisions*

## 61[2]   Protection

If a receiver appointed under section 48, 50 or 52 –

    (a)  takes action in relation to property which is not realisable property,

    (b)  would be entitled to take the action if it were realisable property, and

    (c)  believes on reasonable grounds that he is entitled to take the action,

he is not liable to any person in respect of any loss or damage resulting from the action, except so far as the loss or damage is caused by his negligence.

## 62[3]   Further applications

(1) This section applies to a receiver appointed under section 48, 50 or 52.

(2) The receiver may apply to the Crown Court for an order giving directions as to the exercise of his powers.

(3) The following persons may apply to the Crown Court –

    (a)  any person affected by action taken by the receiver;

---

1    Information: Commencement: Not yet in force.
2    Information: Commencement: Not yet in force.
3    Information: Commencement: Not yet in force.

(b) any person who may be affected by action the receiver proposes to take.

(4) On an application under this section the court may make such order as it believes is appropriate.

## 63[1] Discharge and variation

(1) The following persons may apply to the Crown Court to vary or discharge an order made under any of sections 48 to 53 –

(a) the receiver;
(b) the person who applied for the order or (if the order was made under section 52 or 53) the Director;
(c) any person affected by the order.

(2) On an application under this section the court –

(a) may discharge the order;
(b) may vary the order.

(3) But in the case of an order under section 48 or 49 –

(a) if the condition in section 40 which was satisfied was that proceedings were started or an application was made, the court must discharge the order on the conclusion of the proceedings or of the application (as the case may be);
(b) if the condition which was satisfied was that an investigation was started or an application was to be made, the court must discharge the order if within a reasonable time proceedings for the offence are not started or the application is not made (as the case may be).

## 64[2] Management receivers: discharge

(1) This section applies if –

(a) a receiver stands appointed under section 48 in respect of realisable property (the management receiver), and
(b) the court appoints a receiver under section 50 or makes an order for the appointment of a receiver under section 52.

(2) The court must order the management receiver to transfer to the other receiver all property held by the management receiver by virtue of the powers conferred on him by section 49.

(3) But in a case where the court makes an order under section 52 its order under subsection (2) above does not take effect until the order under section 52 takes effect.

(4) Subsection (2) does not apply to property which the management receiver holds by virtue of the exercise by him of his power under section 49(2)(d).

(5) If the management receiver complies with an order under subsection (2) he is discharged –

(a) from his appointment under section 48;
(b) from any obligation under this Act arising from his appointment.

(6) If this section applies the court may make such a consequential or incidental order as it believes is appropriate.

---

1    Information: Commencement: Not yet in force.
2    Information: Commencement: Not yet in force.

## 65[1]   Appeal to Court of Appeal

(1) If on an application for an order under any of sections 48 to 51 or section 53 the court decides not to make one, the person who applied for the order may appeal to the Court of Appeal against the decision.

(2) If the court makes an order under any of sections 48 to 51 or section 53, the following persons may appeal to the Court of Appeal in respect of the court's decision –

   (a)  the person who applied for the order;
   (b)  any person affected by the order.

(3) If on an application for an order under section 62 the court decides not to make one, the person who applied for the order may appeal to the Court of Appeal against the decision.

(4) If the court makes an order under section 62, the following persons may appeal to the Court of Appeal in respect of the court's decision –

   (a)  the person who applied for the order;
   (b)  any person affected by the order;
   (c)  the receiver.

(5) The following persons may appeal to the Court of Appeal against a decision of the court on an application under section 63 –

   (a)  the person who applied for the order in respect of which the application was made or (if the order was made under section 52 or 53) the Director;
   (b)  any person affected by the court's decision;
   (c)  the receiver.

(6) On an appeal under this section the Court of Appeal may –

   (a)  confirm the decision, or
   (b)  make such order as it believes is appropriate.

## 66[2]   Appeal to House of Lords

(1) An appeal lies to the House of Lords from a decision of the Court of Appeal on an appeal under section 65.

(2) An appeal under this section lies at the instance of any person who was a party to the proceedings before the Court of Appeal.

(3) On an appeal under this section the House of Lords may –

   (a)  confirm the decision of the Court of Appeal, or
   (b)  make such order as it believes is appropriate.

*Seized money*

## 67[3]   Seized money

(1) This section applies to money which –

   (a)  is held by a person, and

---

1   Information: Commencement: Not yet in force.
2   Information: Commencement: Not yet in force.
3   Information: Commencement: Not yet in force.

   (b)  is held in an account maintained by him with a bank or a building society.

(2) This section also applies to money which is held by a person and which –

   (a)  has been seized by a constable under section 19 of the Police and Criminal Evidence Act 1984 (general power of seizure etc), and

   (b)  is held in an account maintained by a police force with a bank or a building society.

(3) This section also applies to money which is held by a person and which –

   (a)  has been seized by a customs officer under section 19 of the 1984 Act as applied by order made under section 114(2) of that Act, and

   (b)  is held in an account maintained by the Commissioners of Customs and Excise with a bank or a building society.

(4) This section applies if the following conditions are satisfied –

   (a)  a restraint order has effect in relation to money to which this section applies;

   (b)  a confiscation order is made against the person by whom the money is held;

   (c)  the Director has not been appointed as the enforcement authority for the confiscation order;

   (d)  a receiver has not been appointed under section 50 in relation to the money;

   (e)  any period allowed under section 11 for payment of the amount ordered to be paid under the confiscation order has ended.

(5) In such a case a magistrates' court may order the bank or building society to pay the money to the justices' chief executive for the court on account of the amount payable under the confiscation order.

(6) If a bank or building society fails to comply with an order under subsection (5) –

   (a)  the magistrates' court may order it to pay an amount not exceeding £5,000, and

   (b)  for the purposes of the Magistrates' Courts Act 1980 the sum is to be treated as adjudged to be paid by a conviction of the court.

(7) In order to take account of changes in the value of money the Secretary of State may by order substitute another sum for the sum for the time being specified in subsection (6)(a).

(8) For the purposes of this section –

   (a)  a bank is a deposit-taking business within the meaning of the Banking Act 1987;

   (b)  'building society' has the same meaning as in the Building Societies Act 1986.

*Financial investigators*

## 68[1]  Applications and appeals

(1) Subsections (2) and (3) apply to –

   (a)  an application under section 41, 42, 48, 49 or 63;

   (b)  an appeal under section 43, 44, 65 or 66.

(2) An accredited financial investigator must not make such an application or bring such an appeal unless he falls within subsection (3).

(3) An accredited financial investigator falls within this subsection if he is one of the following or is authorised for the purposes of this section by one of the following –

---

1    Information: Commencement: Not yet in force.

(a)   a police officer who is not below the rank of superintendent,

(b)   a customs officer who is not below such grade as is designated by the Commissioners of Customs and Excise as equivalent to that rank,

(c)   an accredited financial investigator who falls within a description specified in an order made for the purposes of this paragraph by the Secretary of State under section 453.

(4) If such an application is made or appeal brought by an accredited financial investigator any subsequent step in the application or appeal or any further application or appeal relating to the same matter may be taken, made or brought by a different accredited financial investigator who falls within subsection (3).

(5) If –

(a)   an application for a restraint order is made by an accredited financial investigator, and

(b)   a court is required under section 58(6) to give the applicant for the order an opportunity to be heard,

the court may give the opportunity to a different accredited financial investigator who falls within subsection (3).

*Exercise of powers*

### 69[1]   Powers of court and receiver

(1) This section applies to –

(a)   the powers conferred on a court by sections 41 to 60 and sections 62 to 67;

(b)   the powers of a receiver appointed under section 48, 50 or 52.

(2) The powers –

(a)   must be exercised with a view to the value for the time being of realisable property being made available (by the property's realisation) for satisfying any confiscation order that has been or may be made against the defendant;

(b)   must be exercised, in a case where a confiscation order has not been made, with a view to securing that there is no diminution in the value of realisable property;

(c)   must be exercised without taking account of any obligation of the defendant or a recipient of a tainted gift if the obligation conflicts with the object of satisfying any confiscation order that has been or may be made against the defendant;

(d)   may be exercised in respect of a debt owed by the Crown.

(3) Subsection (2) has effect subject to the following rules –

(a)   the powers must be exercised with a view to allowing a person other than the defendant or a recipient of a tainted gift to retain or recover the value of any interest held by him;

(b)   in the case of realisable property held by a recipient of a tainted gift, the powers must be exercised with a view to realising no more than the value for the time being of the gift;

(c)   in a case where a confiscation order has not been made against the defendant, property must not be sold if the court so orders under subsection (4).

(4) If on an application by the defendant, or by the recipient of a tainted gift, the court decides that property cannot be replaced it may order that it must not be sold.

(5) An order under subsection (4) may be revoked or varied.

---

1    Information: Commencement: Not yet in force.

*Committal*

## 70¹   Committal by magistrates' court

(1) This section applies if –

    (a)  a defendant is convicted of an offence by a magistrates' court, and

    (b)  the prosecutor asks the court to commit the defendant to the Crown Court with a view to a confiscation order being considered under section 6.

(2) In such a case the magistrates' court –

    (a)  must commit the defendant to the Crown Court in respect of the offence, and

    (b)  may commit him to the Crown Court in respect of any other offence falling within subsection (3).

(3) An offence falls within this subsection if –

    (a)  the defendant has been convicted of it by the magistrates' court or any other court, and

    (b)  the magistrates' court has power to deal with him in respect of it.

(4) If a committal is made under this section in respect of an offence or offences –

    (a)  section 6 applies accordingly, and

    (b)  the committal operates as a committal of the defendant to be dealt with by the Crown Court in accordance with section 71.

(5) If a committal is made under this section in respect of an offence for which (apart from this section) the magistrates' court could have committed the defendant for sentence under section 3(2) of the Sentencing Act (offences triable either way) the court must state whether it would have done so.

(6) A committal under this section may be in custody or on bail.

## 71²   Sentencing by Crown Court

(1) If a defendant is committed to the Crown Court under section 70 in respect of an offence or offences, this section applies (whether or not the court proceeds under section 6).

(2) In the case of an offence in respect of which the magistrates' court has stated under section 70(5) that it would have committed the defendant for sentence, the Crown Court –

    (a)  must inquire into the circumstances of the case, and

    (b)  may deal with the defendant in any way in which it could deal with him if he had just been convicted of the offence on indictment before it.

(3) In the case of any other offence the Crown Court –

    (a)  must inquire into the circumstances of the case, and

    (b)  may deal with the defendant in any way in which the magistrates' court could deal with him if it had just convicted him of the offence.

---

1    Information: Commencement: Not yet in force.
2    Information: Commencement: Not yet in force.

*Compensation*

## 72[1]  Serious default

(1) If the following three conditions are satisfied the Crown Court may order the payment of such compensation as it believes is just.

(2) The first condition is satisfied if a criminal investigation has been started with regard to an offence and proceedings are not started for the offence.

(3) The first condition is also satisfied if proceedings for an offence are started against a person and –

(a)  they do not result in his conviction for the offence, or
(b)  he is convicted of the offence but the conviction is quashed or he is pardoned in respect of it.

(4) If subsection (2) applies the second condition is that –

(a)  in the criminal investigation there has been a serious default by a person mentioned in subsection (9), and
(b)  the investigation would not have continued if the default had not occurred.

(5) If subsection (3) applies the second condition is that –

(a)  in the criminal investigation with regard to the offence or in its prosecution there has been a serious default by a person who is mentioned in subsection (9), and
(b)  the proceedings would not have been started or continued if the default had not occurred.

(6) The third condition is that an application is made under this section by a person who held realisable property and has suffered loss in consequence of anything done in relation to it by or in pursuance of an order under this Part.

(7) The offence referred to in subsection (2) may be one of a number of offences with regard to which the investigation is started.

(8) The offence referred to in subsection (3) may be one of a number of offences for which the proceedings are started.

(9) Compensation under this section is payable to the applicant and –

(a)  if the person in default was or was acting as a member of a police force, the compensation is payable out of the police fund from which the expenses of that force are met;
(b)  if the person in default was a member of the Crown Prosecution Service or was acting on its behalf, the compensation is payable by the Director of Public Prosecutions;
(c)  if the person in default was a member of the Serious Fraud Office, the compensation is payable by the Director of that Office;
(d)  if the person in default was a customs officer, the compensation is payable by the Commissioners of Customs and Excise;
(e)  if the person in default was an officer of the Commissioners of Inland Revenue, the compensation is payable by those Commissioners.

---

1    Information: Commencement: Not yet in force.

## 73[1]  Order varied or discharged

(1) This section applies if –

    (a)  the court varies a confiscation order under section 29 or discharges one under section 30, and

    (b)  an application is made to the Crown Court by a person who held realisable property and has suffered loss as a result of the making of the order.

(2) The court may order the payment of such compensation as it believes is just.

(3) Compensation under this section is payable –

    (a)  to the applicant;

    (b)  by the Lord Chancellor.

*Enforcement abroad*

## 74[2]  Enforcement abroad

(1) This section applies if –

    (a)  any of the conditions in section 40 is satisfied,

    (b)  the prosecutor or the Director believes that realisable property is situated in a country or territory outside the United Kingdom (the receiving country), and

    (c)  the prosecutor or the Director (as the case may be) sends a request for assistance to the Secretary of State with a view to it being forwarded under this section.

(2) In a case where no confiscation order has been made, a request for assistance is a request to the government of the receiving country to secure that any person is prohibited from dealing with realisable property.

(3) In a case where a confiscation order has been made and has not been satisfied, discharged or quashed, a request for assistance is a request to the government of the receiving country to secure that –

    (a)  any person is prohibited from dealing with realisable property;

    (b)  realisable property is realised and the proceeds are applied in accordance with the law of the receiving country.

(4) No request for assistance may be made for the purposes of this section in a case where a confiscation order has been made and has been satisfied, discharged or quashed.

(5) If the Secretary of State believes it is appropriate to do so he may forward the request for assistance to the government of the receiving country.

(6) If property is realised in pursuance of a request under subsection (3) the amount ordered to be paid under the confiscation order must be taken to be reduced by an amount equal to the proceeds of realisation.

(7) A certificate purporting to be issued by or on behalf of the requested government is admissible as evidence of the facts it states if it states –

    (a)  that property has been realised in pursuance of a request under subsection (3),

---

1    Information: Commencement: Not yet in force.
2    Information: Commencement: Not yet in force.

   (b)   the date of realisation, and

   (c)   the proceeds of realisation.

(8) If the proceeds of realisation made in pursuance of a request under subsection (3) are expressed in a currency other than sterling, they must be taken to be the sterling equivalent calculated in accordance with the rate of exchange prevailing at the end of the day of realisation.

*Interpretation*

## 75[1]  Criminal lifestyle

(1) A defendant has a criminal lifestyle if (and only if) the following condition is satisfied.

(2) The condition is that the offence (or any of the offences) concerned satisfies any of these tests –

   (a)   it is specified in Schedule 2;

   (b)   it constitutes conduct forming part of a course of criminal activity;

   (c)   it is an offence committed over a period of at least six months and the defendant has benefited from the conduct which constitutes the offence.

(3) Conduct forms part of a course of criminal activity if the defendant has benefited from the conduct and –

   (a)   in the proceedings in which he was convicted he was convicted of three or more other offences, each of three or more of them constituting conduct from which he has benefited, or

   (b)   in the period of six years ending with the day when those proceedings were started (or, if there is more than one such day, the earliest day) he was convicted on at least two separate occasions of an offence constituting conduct from which he has benefited.

(4) But an offence does not satisfy the test in subsection (2)(b) or (c) unless the defendant obtains relevant benefit of not less than £5000.

(5) Relevant benefit for the purposes of subsection (2)(b) is –

   (a)   benefit from conduct which constitutes the offence;

   (b)   benefit from any other conduct which forms part of the course of criminal activity and which constitutes an offence of which the defendant has been convicted;

   (c)   benefit from conduct which constitutes an offence which has been or will be taken into consideration by the court in sentencing the defendant for an offence mentioned in paragraph (a) or (b).

(6) Relevant benefit for the purposes of subsection (2)(c) is –

   (a)   benefit from conduct which constitutes the offence;

   (b)   benefit from conduct which constitutes an offence which has been or will be taken into consideration by the court in sentencing the defendant for the offence mentioned in paragraph (a).

(7) The Secretary of State may by order amend Schedule 2.

(8) The Secretary of State may by order vary the amount for the time being specified in subsection (4).

---

1   Information: Commencement: Not yet in force.

## 76¹   Conduct and benefit

(1) Criminal conduct is conduct which –

    (a)   constitutes an offence in England and Wales, or

    (b)   would constitute such an offence if it occurred in England and Wales.

(2) General criminal conduct of the defendant is all his criminal conduct, and it is immaterial –

    (a)   whether conduct occurred before or after the passing of this Act;

    (b)   whether property constituting a benefit from conduct was obtained before or after the passing of this Act.

(3) Particular criminal conduct of the defendant is all his criminal conduct which falls within the following paragraphs –

    (a)   conduct which constitutes the offence or offences concerned;

    (b)   conduct which constitutes offences of which he was convicted in the same proceedings as those in which he was convicted of the offence or offences concerned;

    (c)   conduct which constitutes offences which the court will be taking into consideration in deciding his sentence for the offence or offences concerned.

(4) A person benefits from conduct if he obtains property as a result of or in connection with the conduct.

(5) If a person obtains a pecuniary advantage as a result of or in connection with conduct, he is to be taken to obtain as a result of or in connection with the conduct a sum of money equal to the value of the pecuniary advantage.

(6) References to property or a pecuniary advantage obtained in connection with conduct include references to property or a pecuniary advantage obtained both in that connection and some other.

(7) If a person benefits from conduct his benefit is the value of the property obtained.

## 77²   Tainted gifts

(1) Subsections (2) and (3) apply if –

    (a)   no court has made a decision as to whether the defendant has a criminal lifestyle, or

    (b)   a court has decided that the defendant has a criminal lifestyle.

(2) A gift is tainted if it was made by the defendant at any time after the relevant day.

(3) A gift is also tainted if it was made by the defendant at any time and was of property –

    (a)   which was obtained by the defendant as a result of or in connection with his general criminal conduct, or

    (b)   which (in whole or part and whether directly or indirectly) represented in the defendant's hands property obtained by him as a result of or in connection with his general criminal conduct.

(4) Subsection (5) applies if a court has decided that the defendant does not have a criminal lifestyle.

(5) A gift is tainted if it was made by the defendant at any time after –

    (a)   the date on which the offence concerned was committed, or

---

1     Information: Commencement: Not yet in force.

2     Information: Commencement: Not yet in force.

(b)  if his particular criminal conduct consists of two or more offences and they were committed on different dates, the date of the earliest.

(6)  For the purposes of subsection (5) an offence which is a continuing offence is committed on the first occasion when it is committed.

(7)  For the purposes of subsection (5) the defendant's particular criminal conduct includes any conduct which constitutes offences which the court has taken into consideration in deciding his sentence for the offence or offences concerned.

(8)  A gift may be a tainted gift whether it was made before or after the passing of this Act.

(9)  The relevant day is the first day of the period of six years ending with –

(a)  the day when proceedings for the offence concerned were started against the defendant, or
(b)  if there are two or more offences and proceedings for them were started on different days, the earliest of those days.

## 78[1]   Gifts and their recipients

(1)  If the defendant transfers property to another person for a consideration whose value is significantly less than the value of the property at the time of the transfer, he is to be treated as making a gift.

(2)  If subsection (1) applies the property given is to be treated as such share in the property transferred as is represented by the fraction –

(a)  whose numerator is the difference between the two values mentioned in subsection (1), and
(b)  whose denominator is the value of the property at the time of the transfer.

(3)  References to a recipient of a tainted gift are to a person to whom the defendant has made the gift.

## 79[2]   Value: the basic rule

(1)  This section applies for the purpose of deciding the value at any time of property then held by a person.

(2)  Its value is the market value of the property at that time.

(3)  But if at that time another person holds an interest in the property its value, in relation to the person mentioned in subsection (1), is the market value of his interest at that time, ignoring any charging order under a provision listed in subsection (4).

(4)  The provisions are –

(a)  section 9 of the Drug Trafficking Offences Act 1986;
(b)  section 78 of the Criminal Justice Act 1988;
(c)  Article 14 of the Criminal Justice (Confiscation) (Northern Ireland) Order 1990 (SI 1990/2588 (NI 17));
(d)  section 27 of the Drug Trafficking Act 1994;
(e)  Article 32 of the Proceeds of Crime (Northern Ireland) Order 1996 (SI 1996/1299 (NI 9)).

---

1     Information: Commencement: Not yet in force.
2     Information: Commencement: Not yet in force.

(5) This section has effect subject to sections 80 and 81.

## 80[1]   Value of property obtained from conduct

(1) This section applies for the purpose of deciding the value of property obtained by a person as a result of or in connection with his criminal conduct; and the material time is the time the court makes its decision.

(2) The value of the property at the material time is the greater of the following –

    (a)   the value of the property (at the time the person obtained it) adjusted to take account of later changes in the value of money;

    (b)   the value (at the material time) of the property found under subsection (3).

(3) The property found under this subsection is as follows –

    (a)   if the person holds the property obtained, the property found under this subsection is that property;

    (b)   if he holds no part of the property obtained, the property found under this subsection is any property which directly or indirectly represents it in his hands;

    (c)   if he holds part of the property obtained, the property found under this subsection is that part and any property which directly or indirectly represents the other part in his hands.

(4) The references in subsection (2)(a) and (b) to the value are to the value found in accordance with section 79.

## 81[2]   Value of tainted gifts

(1) The value at any time (the material time) of a tainted gift is the greater of the following –

    (a)   the value (at the time of the gift) of the property given, adjusted to take account of later changes in the value of money;

    (b)   the value (at the material time) of the property found under subsection (2).

(2) The property found under this subsection is as follows –

    (a)   if the recipient holds the property given, the property found under this subsection is that property;

    (b)   if the recipient holds no part of the property given, the property found under this subsection is any property which directly or indirectly represents it in his hands;

    (c)   if the recipient holds part of the property given, the property found under this subsection is that part and any property which directly or indirectly represents the other part in his hands.

(3) The references in subsection (1)(a) and (b) to the value are to the value found in accordance with section 79.

## 82[3]   Free property

Property is free unless an order is in force in respect of it under any of these provisions –

    (a)   section 27 of the Misuse of Drugs Act 1971 (forfeiture orders);

---

1     Information: Commencement: Not yet in force.

2     Information: Commencement: Not yet in force.

3     Information: Commencement: Not yet in force.

    (b)   Article 11 of the Criminal Justice (Northern Ireland) Order 1994 (SI 1994/2795 (NI 15)) (deprivation orders);

    (c)   Part 2 of the Proceeds of Crime (Scotland) Act 1995 (forfeiture of property used in crime);

    (d)   section 143 of the Sentencing Act (deprivation orders);

    (e)   section 23 or 111 of the Terrorism Act 2000 (forfeiture orders);

    (f)   section 246, 266, 295(2) or 298(2) of this Act.

## 83[1]   Realisable property

Realisable property is –

    (a)   any free property held by the defendant;

    (b)   any free property held by the recipient of a tainted gift.

## 84[2]   Property: general provisions

(1) Property is all property wherever situated and includes –

    (a)   money;

    (b)   all forms of real or personal property;

    (c)   things in action and other intangible or incorporeal property.

(2) The following rules apply in relation to property –

    (a)   property is held by a person if he holds an interest in it;

    (b)   property is obtained by a person if he obtains an interest in it;

    (c)   property is transferred by one person to another if the first one transfers or grants an interest in it to the second;

    (d)   references to property held by a person include references to property vested in his trustee in bankruptcy, permanent or interim trustee (within the meaning of the Bankruptcy (Scotland) Act 1985) or liquidator;

    (e)   references to an interest held by a person beneficially in property include references to an interest which would be held by him beneficially if the property were not so vested;

    (f)   references to an interest, in relation to land in England and Wales or Northern Ireland, are to any legal estate or equitable interest or power;

    (g)   (*applies to Scotland only*)

    (h)   references to an interest, in relation to property other than land, include references to a right (including a right to possession).

## 85[3]   Proceedings

(1) Proceedings for an offence are started –

    (a)   when a justice of the peace issues a summons or warrant under section 1 of the Magistrates' Courts Act 1980 in respect of the offence;

    (b)   when a person is charged with the offence after being taken into custody without a warrant;

    (c)   when a bill of indictment is preferred under section 2 of the Administration of Justice (Miscellaneous Provisions) Act 1933 in a case falling within subsection (2)(b) of that section (preferment by Court of Appeal or High Court judge).

---

1    Information: Commencement: Not yet in force.
2    Information: Commencement: Not yet in force.
3    Information: Commencement: Not yet in force.

(2) If more than one time is found under subsection (1) in relation to proceedings they are started at the earliest of them.

(3) If the defendant is acquitted on all counts in proceedings for an offence, the proceedings are concluded when he is acquitted.

(4) If the defendant is convicted in proceedings for an offence and the conviction is quashed or the defendant is pardoned before a confiscation order is made, the proceedings are concluded when the conviction is quashed or the defendant is pardoned.

(5) If a confiscation order is made against the defendant in proceedings for an offence (whether the order is made by the Crown Court or the Court of Appeal) the proceedings are concluded –

    (a)   when the order is satisfied or discharged, or
    (b)   when the order is quashed and there is no further possibility of an appeal against the decision to quash the order.

(6) If the defendant is convicted in proceedings for an offence but the Crown Court decides not to make a confiscation order against him, the following rules apply –

    (a)   if an application for leave to appeal under section 31(2) is refused, the proceedings are concluded when the decision to refuse is made;
    (b)   if the time for applying for leave to appeal under section 31(2) expires without an application being made, the proceedings are concluded when the time expires;
    (c)   if on appeal under section 31(2) the Court of Appeal confirms the Crown Court's decision, and an application for leave to appeal under section 33 is refused, the proceedings are concluded when the decision to refuse is made;
    (d)   if on appeal under section 31(2) the Court of Appeal confirms the Crown Court's decision, and the time for applying for leave to appeal under section 33 expires without an application being made, the proceedings are concluded when the time expires;
    (e)   if on appeal under section 31(2) the Court of Appeal confirms the Crown Court's decision, and on appeal under section 33 the House of Lords confirms the Court of Appeal's decision, the proceedings are concluded when the House of Lords confirms the decision;
    (f)   if on appeal under section 31(2) the Court of Appeal directs the Crown Court to reconsider the case, and on reconsideration the Crown Court decides not to make a confiscation order against the defendant, the proceedings are concluded when the Crown Court makes that decision;
    (g)   if on appeal under section 33 the House of Lords directs the Crown Court to reconsider the case, and on reconsideration the Crown Court decides not to make a confiscation order against the defendant, the proceedings are concluded when the Crown Court makes that decision.

(7) In applying subsection (6) any power to extend the time for making an application for leave to appeal must be ignored.

(8) In applying subsection (6) the fact that a court may decide on a later occasion to make a confiscation order against the defendant must be ignored.

## 86[1]  Applications

(1) An application under section 19, 20, 27 or 28 is concluded –

    (a)   in a case where the court decides not to make a confiscation order against the defendant, when it makes the decision;

---

1    Information: Commencement: Not yet in force.

  (b) in a case where a confiscation order is made against him as a result of the application, when the order is satisfied or discharged, or when the order is quashed and there is no further possibility of an appeal against the decision to quash the order;

  (c) in a case where the application is withdrawn, when the person who made the application notifies the withdrawal to the court to which the application was made.

(2) An application under section 21 or 22 is concluded –

  (a) in a case where the court decides not to vary the confiscation order concerned, when it makes the decision;

  (b) in a case where the court varies the confiscation order as a result of the application, when the order is satisfied or discharged, or when the order is quashed and there is no further possibility of an appeal against the decision to quash the order;

  (c) in a case where the application is withdrawn, when the person who made the application notifies the withdrawal to the court to which the application was made.

## 87[1] Confiscation orders

(1) A confiscation order is satisfied when no amount is due under it.

(2) A confiscation order is subject to appeal until there is no further possibility of an appeal on which the order could be varied or quashed; and for this purpose any power to grant leave to appeal out of time must be ignored.

## 88[2] Other interpretative provisions

(1) A reference to the offence (or offences) concerned must be construed in accordance with section 6(9).

(2) A criminal investigation is an investigation which police officers or other persons have a duty to conduct with a view to it being ascertained whether a person should be charged with an offence.

(3) A defendant is a person against whom proceedings for an offence have been started (whether or not he has been convicted).

(4) A reference to sentencing the defendant for an offence includes a reference to dealing with him otherwise in respect of the offence.

(5) The Sentencing Act is the Powers of Criminal Courts (Sentencing) Act 2000.

(6) The following paragraphs apply to references to orders –

  (a) a confiscation order is an order under section 6;

  (b) a restraint order is an order under section 41.

(7) Sections 75 to 87 and this section apply for the purposes of this Part.

*General*

## 89[3] Procedure on appeal to the Court of Appeal

(1) An appeal to the Court of Appeal under this Part lies only with the leave of that Court.

(2) Subject to rules of court made under section 53(1) of the Supreme Court Act 1981

---

1  Information: Commencement: Not yet in force.
2  Information: Commencement: Not yet in force.
3  Information: Commencement: Not yet in force.

(distribution of business between civil and criminal divisions) the criminal division of the Court of Appeal is the division –

    (a)   to which an appeal to that Court under this Part is to lie, and

    (b)   which is to exercise that Court's jurisdiction under this Part.

(3)  In relation to appeals to the Court of Appeal under this Part, the Secretary of State may make an order containing provision corresponding to any provision in the Criminal Appeal Act 1968 (subject to any specified modifications).

## 90[1]   Procedure on appeal to the House of Lords

(1)  Section 33(3) of the Criminal Appeal Act 1968 (limitation on appeal from criminal division of the Court of Appeal) does not prevent an appeal to the House of Lords under this Part.

(2)  In relation to appeals to the House of Lords under this Part, the Secretary of State may make an order containing provision corresponding to any provision in the Criminal Appeal Act 1968 (subject to any specified modifications).

## 91[2]   Crown Court Rules

In relation to –

    (a)   proceedings under this Part, or

    (b)   receivers appointed under this Part,

Crown Court Rules may make provision corresponding to provision in Civil Procedure Rules.

****[3]

# PART 5   CIVIL RECOVERY OF THE PROCEEDS ETC OF UNLAWFUL CONDUCT

## CHAPTER 1   INTRODUCTORY

## 240[4]   General purpose of this Part

(1)  This Part has effect for the purposes of –

    (a)   enabling the enforcement authority to recover, in civil proceedings before the High Court or Court of Session, property which is, or represents, property obtained through unlawful conduct,

    (b)   enabling cash which is, or represents, property obtained through unlawful conduct, or which is intended to be used in unlawful conduct, to be forfeited in civil proceedings before a magistrates' court or (in Scotland) the sheriff.

(2)  The powers conferred by this Part are exercisable in relation to any property (including cash) whether or not any proceedings have been brought for an offence in connection with the property.

---

1    Information: Commencement: Not yet in force.

2    Information: Commencement: Not yet in force.

3    Omission: Parts 3, 4 (ss 92–239) not reproduced.

4    Information: Commencement: Not yet in force.

## 241[1]  'Unlawful conduct'

(1) Conduct occurring in any part of the United Kingdom is unlawful conduct if it is unlawful under the criminal law of that part.

(2) Conduct which –

   (a)  occurs in a country outside the United Kingdom and is unlawful under the criminal law of that country, and
   (b)  if it occurred in a part of the United Kingdom, would be unlawful under the criminal law of that part,

is also unlawful conduct.

(3) The court or sheriff must decide on a balance of probabilities whether it is proved –

   (a)  that any matters alleged to constitute unlawful conduct have occurred, or
   (b)  that any person intended to use any cash in unlawful conduct.

## 242[2]  'Property obtained through unlawful conduct'

(1) A person obtains property through unlawful conduct (whether his own conduct or another's) if he obtains property by or in return for the conduct.

(2) In deciding whether any property was obtained through unlawful conduct –

   (a)  it is immaterial whether or not any money, goods or services were provided in order to put the person in question in a position to carry out the conduct,
   (b)  it is not necessary to show that the conduct was of a particular kind if it is shown that the property was obtained through conduct of one of a number of kinds, each of which would have been unlawful conduct.

### CHAPTER 2   CIVIL RECOVERY IN THE HIGH COURT OR COURT OF SESSION

*Proceedings for recovery orders*

## 243[3]  Proceedings for recovery orders in England and Wales or Northern Ireland

(1) Proceedings for a recovery order may be taken by the enforcement authority in the High Court against any person who the authority thinks holds recoverable property.

(2) The enforcement authority must serve the claim form –

   (a)  on the respondent, and
   (b)  unless the court dispenses with service, on any other person who the authority thinks holds any associated property which the authority wishes to be subject to a recovery order,

wherever domiciled, resident or present.

---

1    Information: Commencement: Not yet in force.
2    Information: Commencement: Not yet in force.
3    Information: Commencement: Not yet in force.

(3) If any property which the enforcement authority wishes to be subject to a recovery order is not specified in the claim form it must be described in the form in general terms; and the form must state whether it is alleged to be recoverable property or associated property.

(4) The references above to the claim form include the particulars of claim, where they are served subsequently.

\*\*\*\*[1]

## 245[2] 'Associated property'

(1) 'Associated property' means property of any of the following descriptions (including property held by the respondent) which is not itself the recoverable property –

(a)  any interest in the recoverable property,

(b)  any other interest in the property in which the recoverable property subsists,

(c)  if the recoverable property is a tenancy in common, the tenancy of the other tenant,

(d)  (*applies to Scotland only*)

(e)  if the recoverable property is part of a larger property, but not a separate part, the remainder of that property.

(2) References to property being associated with recoverable property are to be read accordingly.

(3) No property is to be treated as associated with recoverable property consisting of rights under a pension scheme (within the meaning of sections 273 to 275).

*Interim receiving orders (England and Wales and Northern Ireland)*

## 246[3]  Application for interim receiving order

(1) Where the enforcement authority may take proceedings for a recovery order in the High Court, the authority may apply to the court for an interim receiving order (whether before or after starting the proceedings).

(2) An interim receiving order is an order for –

(a)  the detention, custody or preservation of property, and

(b)  the appointment of an interim receiver.

(3) An application for an interim receiving order may be made without notice if the circumstances are such that notice of the application would prejudice any right of the enforcement authority to obtain a recovery order in respect of any property.

(4) The court may make an interim receiving order on the application if it is satisfied that the conditions in subsections (5) and, where applicable, (6) are met.

(5) The first condition is that there is a good arguable case –

(a)  that the property to which the application for the order relates is or includes recoverable property, and

(b)  that, if any of it is not recoverable property, it is associated property.

(6) The second condition is that, if –

---

1    Omission: Section 244 not reproduced.

2    Information: Commencement: Not yet in force.

3    Information: Commencement: Not yet in force.

(a)  the property to which the application for the order relates includes property alleged to be associated property, and

(b)  the enforcement authority has not established the identity of the person who holds it,

the authority has taken all reasonable steps to do so.

(7)  In its application for an interim receiving order, the enforcement authority must nominate a suitably qualified person for appointment as interim receiver, but the nominee may not be a member of the staff of the Agency.

(8)  The extent of the power to make an interim receiving order is not limited by sections 247 to 255.

## 247[1]  Functions of interim receiver

(1)  An interim receiving order may authorise or require the interim receiver –

(a)  to exercise any of the powers mentioned in Schedule 6,
(b)  to take any other steps the court thinks appropriate,

for the purpose of securing the detention, custody or preservation of the property to which the order applies or of taking any steps under subsection (2).

(2)  An interim receiving order must require the interim receiver to take any steps which the court thinks necessary to establish –

(a)  whether or not the property to which the order applies is recoverable property or associated property,
(b)  whether or not any other property is recoverable property (in relation to the same unlawful conduct) and, if it is, who holds it.

(3)  If –

(a)  the interim receiver deals with any property which is not property to which the order applies, and
(b)  at the time he deals with the property he believes on reasonable grounds that he is entitled to do so in pursuance of the order,

the interim receiver is not liable to any person in respect of any loss or damage resulting from his dealing with the property except so far as the loss or damage is caused by his negligence.

## 248[2]  Registration

(1)  The registration Acts –

(a)  apply in relation to interim receiving orders as they apply in relation to orders which affect land and are made by the court for the purpose of enforcing judgements or recognisances,
(b)  apply in relation to applications for interim receiving orders as they apply in relation to other pending land actions.

(2)  The registration Acts are –

(a)  *the Land Registration Act 1925, . . .*[3]

---

1    Information: Commencement: Not yet in force.
2    Information: Commencement: Not yet in force.
3    Prospective amendment: Paragraph in italics prospectively repealed by Proceeds of Crime Act 2002, s 457, Sch 12, from a date to be appointed.

(b)  the Land Charges Act 1972, and

(c)  the Land Registration Act 2002.

(3) But no notice may be entered in the register of title under the Land Registration Act 2002 in respect of an interim receiving order.

*(4)  A person applying for an interim receiving order must be treated for the purposes of section 57 of the Land Registration Act 1925 (inhibitions) as a person interested in relation to any registered land to which –*

*(a)  the application relates, or*

*(b)  an interim receiving order made in pursuance of the application relates. . . .*[1]

\*\*\*\*[2]

## 250[3]  Duties of respondent etc

(1) An interim receiving order may require any person to whose property the order applies –

(a)  to bring the property to a place (in England and Wales or, as the case may be, Northern Ireland) specified by the interim receiver or place it in the custody of the interim receiver (if, in either case, he is able to do so),

(b)  to do anything he is reasonably required to do by the interim receiver for the preservation of the property.

(2) An interim receiving order may require any person to whose property the order applies to bring any documents relating to the property which are in his possession or control to a place (in England and Wales or, as the case may be, Northern Ireland) specified by the interim receiver or to place them in the custody of the interim receiver.

'Document' means anything in which information of any description is recorded.

## 251[4]  Supervision of interim receiver and variation of order

(1) The interim receiver, any party to the proceedings and any person affected by any action taken by the interim receiver, or who may be affected by any action proposed to be taken by him, may at any time apply to the court for directions as to the exercise of the interim receiver's functions.

(2) Before giving any directions under subsection (1), the court must (as well as giving the parties to the proceedings an opportunity to be heard) give such an opportunity to the interim receiver and to any person who may be interested in the application.

(3) The court may at any time vary or set aside an interim receiving order.

(4) Before exercising any power under this Chapter to vary or set aside an interim receiving order, the court must (as well as giving the parties to the proceedings an opportunity to be heard) give such an opportunity to the interim receiver and to any person who may be affected by the court's decision.

---

1    Prospective amendment: Subsection in italics prospectively repealed by Proceeds of Crime Act 2002, s 457, Sch 12, from a date to be appointed.

2    Omission: Section 249 not reproduced.

3    Information: Commencement: Not yet in force.

4    Information: Commencement: Not yet in force.

## 252[1]   Restrictions on dealing etc with property

(1) An interim receiving order must, subject to any exclusions made in accordance with this section, prohibit any person to whose property the order applies from dealing with the property.

(2) Exclusions may be made when the interim receiving order is made or on an application to vary the order.

(3) An exclusion may, in particular, make provision for the purpose of enabling any person –

   (a)   to meet his reasonable living expenses, or
   (b)   to carry on any trade, business, profession or occupation,

and may be made subject to conditions.

(4) But an exclusion may not be made for the purpose of enabling any person to meet any legal expenses in respect of proceedings under this Part.

(5) If the excluded property is not specified in the order it must be described in the order in general terms.

(6) The power to make exclusions must be exercised with a view to ensuring, so far as practicable, that the satisfaction of any right of the enforcement authority to recover the property obtained through unlawful conduct is not unduly prejudiced.

## 253[2]   Restriction on proceedings and remedies

(1) While an interim receiving order has effect –

   (a)   the court may stay any action, execution or other legal process in respect of the property to which the order applies,
   (b)   no distress may be levied against the property to which the order applies except with the leave of the court and subject to any terms the court may impose.

(2) If a court (whether the High Court or any other court) in which proceedings are pending in respect of any property is satisfied that an interim receiving order has been applied for or made in respect of the property, the court may either stay the proceedings or allow them to continue on any terms it thinks fit.

(3) If the interim receiving order applies to a tenancy of any premises, no landlord or other person to whom rent is payable may exercise any right of forfeiture by peaceable re-entry in relation to the premises in respect of any failure by the tenant to comply with any term or condition of the tenancy, except with the leave of the court and subject to any terms the court may impose.

(4) Before exercising any power conferred by this section, the court must (as well as giving the parties to any of the proceedings in question an opportunity to be heard) give such an opportunity to the interim receiver (if appointed) and any person who may be affected by the court's decision.

## 254[3]   Exclusion of property which is not recoverable etc

(1) If the court decides that any property to which an interim receiving order applies is neither recoverable property nor associated property, it must vary the order so as to exclude it.

---

1     Information: Commencement: Not yet in force.
2     Information: Commencement: Not yet in force.
3     Information: Commencement: Not yet in force.

(2) The court may vary an interim receiving order so as to exclude from the property to which the order applies any property which is alleged to be associated property if the court thinks that the satisfaction of any right of the enforcement authority to recover the property obtained through unlawful conduct will not be prejudiced.

(3) The court may exclude any property within subsection (2) on any terms or conditions, applying while the interim receiving order has effect, which the court thinks necessary or expedient.

## 255[1] Reporting

(1) An interim receiving order must require the interim receiver to inform the enforcement authority and the court as soon as reasonably practicable if he thinks that –

    (a) any property to which the order applies by virtue of a claim that it is recoverable property is not recoverable property,

    (b) any property to which the order applies by virtue of a claim that it is associated property is not associated property,

    (c) any property to which the order does not apply is recoverable property (in relation to the same unlawful conduct) or associated property, or

    (d) any property to which the order applies is held by a person who is different from the person it is claimed holds it,

or if he thinks that there has been any other material change of circumstances.

(2) An interim receiving order must require the interim receiver –

    (a) to report his findings to the court,

    (b) to serve copies of his report on the enforcement authority and on any person who holds any property to which the order applies or who may otherwise be affected by the report.

****[2]

*Vesting and realisation of recoverable property*

## 266[3] Recovery orders

(1) If in proceedings under this Chapter the court is satisfied that any property is recoverable, the court must make a recovery order.

(2) The recovery order must vest the recoverable property in the trustee for civil recovery.

(3) But the court may not make in a recovery order –

    (a) any provision in respect of any recoverable property if each of the conditions in subsection (4) or (as the case may be) (5) is met and it would not be just and equitable to do so, or

    (b) any provision which is incompatible with any of the Convention rights (within the meaning of the Human Rights Act 1998).

(4) In relation to a court in England and Wales or Northern Ireland, the conditions referred to in subsection (3)(a) are that –

---

1    Information: Commencement: Not yet in force.
2    Omission: Sections 256–265 not reproduced.
3    Information: Commencement: Not yet in force.

(a)   the respondent obtained the recoverable property in good faith,

(b)   he took steps after obtaining the property which he would not have taken if he had not obtained it or he took steps before obtaining the property which he would not have taken if he had not believed he was going to obtain it,

(c)   when he took the steps, he had no notice that the property was recoverable,

(d)   if a recovery order were made in respect of the property, it would, by reason of the steps, be detrimental to him.

(5)  (*applies to Scotland only*)

(6)  In deciding whether it would be just and equitable to make the provision in the recovery order where the conditions in subsection (4) or (as the case may be) (5) are met, the court must have regard to –

(a)   the degree of detriment that would be suffered by the respondent if the provision were made,

(b)   the enforcement authority's interest in receiving the realised proceeds of the recoverable property.

(7)  A recovery order may sever any property.

(8)  A recovery order may impose conditions as to the manner in which the trustee for civil recovery may deal with any property vested by the order for the purpose of realising it.

(9)  This section is subject to sections 270 to 278.

## 267[1]   Functions of the trustee for civil recovery

(1)  The trustee for civil recovery is a person appointed by the court to give effect to a recovery order.

(2)  The enforcement authority must nominate a suitably qualified person for appointment as the trustee.

(3)  The functions of the trustee are –

(a)   to secure the detention, custody or preservation of any property vested in him by the recovery order,

(b)   in the case of property other than money, to realise the value of the property for the benefit of the enforcement authority, and

(c)   to perform any other functions conferred on him by virtue of this Chapter.

(4)  In performing his functions, the trustee acts on behalf of the enforcement authority and must comply with any directions given by the authority.

(5)  The trustee is to realise the value of property vested in him by the recovery order, so far as practicable, in the manner best calculated to maximise the amount payable to the enforcement authority.

(6)  The trustee has the powers mentioned in Schedule 7.

(7)  References in this section to a recovery order include an order under section 276 and references to property vested in the trustee by a recovery order include property vested in him in pursuance of an order under section 276.

****[2]

---

1      Information: Commencement: Not yet in force.

2      Omission: Section 268 not reproduced.

## 269[1]  Rights of pre-emption, etc

(1) A recovery order is to have effect in relation to any property despite any provision (of whatever nature) which would otherwise prevent, penalise or restrict the vesting of the property.

(2) A right of pre-emption, right of irritancy, right of return or other similar right does not operate or become exercisable as a result of the vesting of any property under a recovery order.

A right of return means any right under a provision for the return or reversion of property in specified circumstances.

(3) Where property is vested under a recovery order, any such right is to have effect as if the person in whom the property is vested were the same person in law as the person who held the property and as if no transfer of the property had taken place.

(4) References to rights in subsections (2) and (3) do not include any rights in respect of which the recovery order was made.

(5) This section applies in relation to the creation of interests, or the doing of anything else, by a recovery order as it applies in relation to the vesting of property.

## 270[2]  Associated and joint property

(1) Sections 271 and 272 apply if the court makes a recovery order in respect of any recoverable property in a case within subsection (2) or (3).

(2) A case is within this subsection if –

    (a)  the property to which the proceedings relate includes property which is associated with the recoverable property and is specified or described in the claim form or (in Scotland) application, and

    (b)  if the associated property is not the respondent's property, the claim form or application has been served on the person whose property it is or the court has dispensed with service.

(3) A case is within this subsection if –

    (a)  the recoverable property belongs to joint tenants, and

    (b)  one of the tenants is an excepted joint owner.

(4) An excepted joint owner is a person who obtained the property in circumstances in which it would not be recoverable as against him; and references to the excepted joint owner's share of the recoverable property are to so much of the recoverable property as would have been his if the joint tenancy had been severed.

(5) *(applies to Scotland only)*

## 271[3]  Agreements about associated and joint property

(1) Where –

    (a)  this section applies, and

    (b)  the enforcement authority (on the one hand) and the person who holds the associated property or who is the excepted joint owner (on the other) agree,

---

1    Information: Commencement: Not yet in force.
2    Information: Commencement: Not yet in force.
3    Information: Commencement: Not yet in force.

the recovery order may, instead of vesting the recoverable property in the trustee for civil recovery, require the person who holds the associated property or who is the excepted joint owner to make a payment to the trustee.

(2) A recovery order which makes any requirement under subsection (1) may, so far as required for giving effect to the agreement, include provision for vesting, creating or extinguishing any interest in property.

(3) The amount of the payment is to be the amount which the enforcement authority and that person agree represents –

    (a)   in a case within section 270(2), the value of the recoverable property,

    (b)   in a case within section 270(3), the value of the recoverable property less the value of the excepted joint owner's share.

(4) But if –

    (a)   an interim receiving order or interim administration order applied at any time to the associated property or joint tenancy, and

    (b)   the enforcement authority agrees that the person has suffered loss as a result of the interim receiving order or interim administration order,

the amount of the payment may be reduced by any amount the enforcement authority and that person agree is reasonable, having regard to that loss and to any other relevant circumstances.

(5) If there is more than one such item of associated property or excepted joint owner, the total amount to be paid to the trustee, and the part of that amount which is to be provided by each person who holds any such associated property or who is an excepted joint owner, is to be agreed between both (or all) of them and the enforcement authority.

(6) A recovery order which makes any requirement under subsection (1) must make provision for any recoverable property to cease to be recoverable.

## 272[1]   Associated and joint property: default of agreement

(1) Where this section applies, the court may make the following provision if –

    (a)   there is no agreement under section 271, and

    (b)   the court thinks it just and equitable to do so.

(2) The recovery order may provide –

    (a)   for the associated property to vest in the trustee for civil recovery or (as the case may be) for the excepted joint owner's interest to be extinguished, or

    (b)   in the case of an excepted joint owner, for the severance of his interest.

(3) A recovery order making any provision by virtue of subsection (2)(a) may provide –

    (a)   for the trustee to pay an amount to the person who holds the associated property or who is an excepted joint owner, or

    (b)   for the creation of interests in favour of that person, or the imposition of liabilities or conditions, in relation to the property vested in the trustee,

or for both.

(4) In making any provision in a recovery order by virtue of subsection (2) or (3), the court must have regard to –

---

1    Information: Commencement: Not yet in force.

(a) the rights of any person who holds the associated property or who is an excepted joint owner and the value to him of that property or, as the case may be, of his share (including any value which cannot be assessed in terms of money),

(b) the enforcement authority's interest in receiving the realised proceeds of the recoverable property.

(5) If –

(a) an interim receiving order or interim administration order applied at any time to the associated property or joint tenancy, and

(b) the court is satisfied that the person who holds the associated property or who is an excepted joint owner has suffered loss as a result of the interim receiving order or interim administration order,

a recovery order making any provision by virtue of subsection (2) or (3) may require the enforcement authority to pay compensation to that person.

(6) The amount of compensation to be paid under subsection (5) is the amount the court thinks reasonable, having regard to the person's loss and to any other relevant circumstances.

## 273[1] Payments in respect of rights under pension schemes

(1) This section applies to recoverable property consisting of rights under a pension scheme.

(2) A recovery order in respect of the property must, instead of vesting the property in the trustee for civil recovery, require the trustees or managers of the pension scheme –

(a) to pay to the trustee for civil recovery within a prescribed period the amount determined by the trustees or managers to be equal to the value of the rights, and

(b) to give effect to any other provision made by virtue of this section and the two following sections in respect of the scheme.

This subsection is subject to sections 276 to 278.

(3) A recovery order made by virtue of subsection (2) overrides the provisions of the pension scheme to the extent that they conflict with the provisions of the order.

(4) A recovery order made by virtue of subsection (2) may provide for the recovery by the trustees or managers of the scheme (whether by deduction from any amount which they are required to pay to the trustee for civil recovery or otherwise) of costs incurred by them in –

(a) complying with the recovery order, or

(b) providing information, before the order was made, to the enforcement authority, interim receiver or interim administrator.

(5) None of the following provisions applies to a court making a recovery order by virtue of subsection (2) –

(a) any provision of section 159 of the Pension Schemes Act 1993, section 155 of the Pension Schemes (Northern Ireland) Act 1993, section 91 of the Pensions Act 1995 or Article 89 of the Pensions (Northern Ireland) Order 1995 (SI 1995/3213 (NI 22)) (which prevent assignment and the making of orders that restrain a person from receiving anything which he is prevented from assigning),

(b) any provision of any enactment (whenever passed or made) corresponding to any of the provisions mentioned in paragraph (a),

---

1    Information: Commencement: Not yet in force.

(c)   any provision of the pension scheme in question corresponding to any of those provisions.

## 274[1]   Consequential adjustment of liabilities under pension schemes

(1) A recovery order made by virtue of section 273(2) must require the trustees or managers of the pension scheme to make such reduction in the liabilities of the scheme as they think necessary in consequence of the payment made in pursuance of that subsection.

(2) Accordingly, the order must require the trustees or managers to provide for the liabilities of the pension scheme in respect of the respondent's recoverable property to which section 273 applies to cease.

(3) So far as the trustees or managers are required by the recovery order to provide for the liabilities of the pension scheme in respect of the respondent's recoverable property to which section 273 applies to cease, their powers include (in particular) power to reduce the amount of –

(a)   any benefit or future benefit to which the respondent is or may be entitled under the scheme,
(b)   any future benefit to which any other person may be entitled under the scheme in respect of that property.

## 275[2]   Pension schemes: supplementary

(1) Regulations may make provision as to the exercise by trustees or managers of their powers under sections 273 and 274, including provision about the calculation and verification of the value at any time of rights or liabilities.

(2) The power conferred by subsection (1) includes power to provide for any values to be calculated or verified –

(a)   in a manner which, in the particular case, is approved by a prescribed person, or
(b)   in accordance with guidance from time to time prepared by a prescribed person.

(3) Regulations means regulations made by the Secretary of State after consultation with the Scottish Ministers; and prescribed means prescribed by regulations.

(4) A pension scheme means an occupational pension scheme or a personal pension scheme; and those expressions have the same meaning as in the Pension Schemes Act 1993 or, in relation to Northern Ireland, the Pension Schemes (Northern Ireland) Act 1993.

(5) In relation to an occupational pension scheme or a personal pension scheme, the trustees or managers means –

(a)   in the case of a scheme established under a trust, the trustees,
(b)   in any other case, the managers.

(6) References to a pension scheme include –

(a)   a retirement annuity contract (within the meaning of Part 3 of the Welfare Reform and Pensions Act 1999 or, in relation to Northern Ireland, Part 4 of the Welfare Reform and Pensions (Northern Ireland) Order 1999),
(b)   an annuity or insurance policy purchased, or transferred, for the purpose of giving effect to rights under an occupational pension scheme or a personal pension scheme,

---

1     Information: Commencement: Not yet in force.
2     Information: Commencement: Not yet in force.

(c)   an annuity purchased, or entered into, for the purpose of discharging any liability in respect of a pension credit under section 29(1)(b) of the Welfare Reform and Pensions Act 1999 or, in relation to Northern Ireland, Article 26(1)(b) of the Welfare Reform and Pensions (Northern Ireland) Order 1999.

(7) References to the trustees or managers –

(a)   in relation to a retirement annuity contract or other annuity, are to the provider of the annuity,

(b)   in relation to an insurance policy, are to the insurer.

(8) Subsections (3) to (7) have effect for the purposes of this group of sections (that is, sections 273 and 274 and this section).

## 276[1]   Consent orders

(1) The court may make an order staying (in Scotland, sisting) any proceedings for a recovery order on terms agreed by the parties for the disposal of the proceedings if each person to whose property the proceedings, or the agreement, relates is a party both to the proceedings and the agreement.

(2) An order under subsection (1) may, as well as staying (or sisting) the proceedings on terms –

(a)   make provision for any property which may be recoverable property to cease to be recoverable,

(b)   make any further provision which the court thinks appropriate.

(3) Section 280 applies to property vested in the trustee for civil recovery, or money paid to him, in pursuance of the agreement as it applies to property vested in him by a recovery order or money paid under section 271.

## 277[2]   Consent orders: pensions

(1) This section applies where recoverable property to which proceedings under this Chapter relate includes rights under a pension scheme.

(2) An order made under section 276 –

(a)   may not stay (in Scotland, sist) the proceedings on terms that the rights are vested in any other person, but

(b)   may include provision imposing the following requirement, if the trustees or managers of the scheme are parties to the agreement by virtue of which the order is made.

(3) The requirement is that the trustees or managers of the pension scheme –

(a)   make a payment in accordance with the agreement, and

(b)   give effect to any other provision made by virtue of this section in respect of the scheme.

(4) The trustees or managers of the pension scheme have power to enter into an agreement in respect of the proceedings on any terms on which an order made under section 276 may stay (in Scotland, sist) the proceedings.

(5) The following provisions apply in respect of an order under section 276, so far as it includes the requirement mentioned in subsection (3).

---

1    Information: Commencement: Not yet in force.
2    Information: Commencement: Not yet in force.

(6) The order overrides the provisions of the pension scheme to the extent that they conflict with the requirement.

(7) The order may provide for the recovery by the trustees or managers of the scheme (whether by deduction from any amount which they are required to pay in pursuance of the agreement or otherwise) of costs incurred by them in –

(a) complying with the order, or
(b) providing information, before the order was made, to the enforcement authority, interim receiver or interim administrator.

(8) Sections 273(5) and 274 (read with section 275) apply as if the requirement were included in an order made by virtue of section 273(2).

(9) Section 275(4) to (7) has effect for the purposes of this section.

## 278[1]   Limit on recovery

(1) This section applies if the enforcement authority seeks a recovery order –

(a) in respect of both property which is or represents property obtained through unlawful conduct and related property, or
(b) in respect of property which is or represents property obtained through unlawful conduct where such an order, or an order under section 276, has previously been made in respect of related property.

(2) For the purposes of this section –

(a) the original property means the property obtained through unlawful conduct,
(b) the original property, and any items of property which represent the original property, are to be treated as related to each other.

(3) The court is not to make a recovery order if it thinks that the enforcement authority's right to recover the original property has been satisfied by a previous recovery order or order under section 276.

(4) Subject to subsection (3), the court may act under subsection (5) if it thinks that –

(a) a recovery order may be made in respect of two or more related items of recoverable property, but
(b) the making of a recovery order in respect of both or all of them is not required in order to satisfy the enforcement authority's right to recover the original property.

(5) The court may in order to satisfy that right to the extent required make a recovery order in respect of –

(a) only some of the related items of property, or
(b) only a part of any of the related items of property,

or both.

(6) Where the court may make a recovery order in respect of any property, this section does not prevent the recovery of any profits which have accrued in respect of the property.

(7) If –

(a) an order is made under section 298 for the forfeiture of recoverable property, and
(b) the enforcement authority subsequently seeks a recovery order in respect of related property,

---

1     Information: Commencement: Not yet in force.

the order under section 298 is to be treated for the purposes of this section as if it were a recovery order obtained by the enforcement authority in respect of the forfeited property.

(8) If –

    (a) in pursuance of a judgment in civil proceedings (whether in the United Kingdom or elsewhere), the claimant has obtained property from the defendant ('the judgment property'),

    (b) the claim was based on the defendant's having obtained the judgment property or related property through unlawful conduct, and

    (c) the enforcement authority subsequently seeks a recovery order in respect of property which is related to the judgment property,

the judgment is to be treated for the purposes of this section as if it were a recovery order obtained by the enforcement authority in respect of the judgment property.

*(words apply to Scotland only)*

(9) If –

    (a) property has been taken into account in deciding the amount of a person's benefit from criminal conduct for the purpose of making a confiscation order, and

    (b) the enforcement authority subsequently seeks a recovery order in respect of related property,

the confiscation order is to be treated for the purposes of this section as if it were a recovery order obtained by the enforcement authority in respect of the property referred to in paragraph (a).

(10) In subsection (9), a confiscation order means –

    (a) an order under section 6, 92 or 156, or

    (b) an order under a corresponding provision of an enactment mentioned in section 8(7)(a) to (g),

and, in relation to an order mentioned in paragraph (b), the reference to the amount of a person's benefit from criminal conduct is to be read as a reference to the corresponding amount under the enactment in question.

## 279[1]   Section 278: supplementary

(1) Subsections (2) and (3) give examples of the satisfaction of the enforcement authority's right to recover the original property.

(2) If –

    (a) there is a disposal, other than a part disposal, of the original property, and

    (b) other property (the representative property) is obtained in its place,

the enforcement authority's right to recover the original property is satisfied by the making of a recovery order in respect of either the original property or the representative property.

(3) If –

    (a) there is a part disposal of the original property, and

    (b) other property (the representative property) is obtained in place of the property disposed of,

---

1    Information: Commencement: Not yet in force.

the enforcement authority's right to recover the original property is satisfied by the making of a recovery order in respect of the remainder of the original property together with either the representative property or the property disposed of.

(4) In this section –

    (a)  a part disposal means a disposal to which section 314(1) applies,

    (b)  the original property has the same meaning as in section 278.

## 280[1]   Applying realised proceeds

(1) This section applies to –

    (a)  sums which represent the realised proceeds of property which was vested in the trustee for civil recovery by a recovery order or which he obtained in pursuance of a recovery order,

    (b)  sums vested in the trustee by a recovery order or obtained by him in pursuance of a recovery order.

(2) The trustee is to make out of the sums –

    (a)  first, any payment required to be made by him by virtue of section 272,

    (b)  second, any payment of expenses incurred by a person acting as an insolvency practitioner which are payable under this subsection by virtue of section 432(10),

and any sum which remains is to be paid to the enforcement authority.

*Exemptions etc*

## 281[2]   Victims of theft, etc

(1) In proceedings for a recovery order, a person who claims that any property alleged to be recoverable property, or any part of the property, belongs to him may apply for a declaration under this section.

(2) If the applicant appears to the court to meet the following condition, the court may make a declaration to that effect.

(3) The condition is that –

    (a)  the person was deprived of the property he claims, or of property which it represents, by unlawful conduct,

    (b)  the property he was deprived of was not recoverable property immediately before he was deprived of it, and

    (c)  the property he claims belongs to him.

(4) Property to which a declaration under this section applies is not recoverable property.

## 282[3]   Other exemptions

(1) Proceedings for a recovery order may not be taken against any person in circumstances of a prescribed description; and the circumstances may relate to the person himself or to the property or to any other matter.

---

1    Information: Commencement: Not yet in force.
2    Information: Commencement: Not yet in force.
3    Information: Commencement: Not yet in force.

In this subsection, prescribed means prescribed by an order made by the Secretary of State after consultation with the Scottish Ministers.

(2) Proceedings for a recovery order may not be taken in respect of cash found at any place in the United Kingdom unless the proceedings are also taken in respect of property other than cash which is property of the same person.

(3) Proceedings for a recovery order may not be taken against the Financial Services Authority in respect of any recoverable property held by the authority.

(4) Proceedings for a recovery order may not be taken in respect of any property which is subject to any of the following charges –

    (a)  a collateral security charge, within the meaning of the Financial Markets and Insolvency (Settlement Finality) Regulations 1999 (SI 1999/2979),

    (b)  a market charge, within the meaning of Part 7 of the Companies Act 1989,

    (c)  a money market charge, within the meaning of the Financial Markets and Insolvency (Money Market) Regulations 1995 (SI 1995/2049),

    (d)  a system charge, within the meaning of the Financial Markets and Insolvency Regulations 1996 (SI 1996/1469) or the Financial Markets and Insolvency Regulations (Northern Ireland) 1996 (SR 1996/252).

(5) Proceedings for a recovery order may not be taken against any person in respect of any recoverable property which he holds by reason of his acting, or having acted, as an insolvency practitioner.

Acting as an insolvency practitioner has the same meaning as in section 433.

*Miscellaneous*

## 283[1]  Compensation

(1) If, in the case of any property to which an interim receiving order or interim administration order has at any time applied, the court does not in the course of the proceedings decide that the property is recoverable property or associated property, the person whose property it is may make an application to the court for compensation.

(2) Subsection (1) does not apply if the court –

    (a)  has made a declaration in respect of the property by virtue of section 281, or

    (b)  makes an order under section 276.

(3) If the court has made a decision by reason of which no recovery order could be made in respect of the property, the application for compensation must be made within the period of three months beginning –

    (a)  in relation to a decision of the High Court in England and Wales, with the date of the decision or, if any application is made for leave to appeal, with the date on which the application is withdrawn or refused or (if the application is granted) on which any proceedings on appeal are finally concluded,

    (b)  *(applies to Scotland and Northern Ireland only)*

(4) If, in England and Wales or Northern Ireland, the proceedings in respect of the property have been discontinued, the application for compensation must be made within the period of three months beginning with the discontinuance.

---

1    Information: Commencement: Not yet in force.

(5) If the court is satisfied that the applicant has suffered loss as a result of the interim receiving order or interim administration order, it may require the enforcement authority to pay compensation to him.

(6) If, but for section 269(2), any right mentioned there would have operated in favour of, or become exercisable by, any person, he may make an application to the court for compensation.

(7) The application for compensation under subsection (6) must be made within the period of three months beginning with the vesting referred to in section 269(2).

(8) If the court is satisfied that, in consequence of the operation of section 269, the right in question cannot subsequently operate in favour of the applicant or (as the case may be) become exercisable by him, it may require the enforcement authority to pay compensation to him.

(9) The amount of compensation to be paid under this section is the amount the court thinks reasonable, having regard to the loss suffered and any other relevant circumstances.

\*\*\*\*[1]

## 287[2]  Financial threshold

(1) At any time when an order specifying an amount for the purposes of this section has effect, the enforcement authority may not start proceedings for a recovery order unless the authority reasonably believes that the aggregate value of the recoverable property which the authority wishes to be subject to a recovery order is not less than the specified amount.

(2) The power to make an order under subsection (1) is exercisable by the Secretary of State after consultation with the Scottish Ministers.

(3) If the authority applies for an interim receiving order or interim administration order before starting the proceedings, subsection (1) applies to the application instead of to the start of the proceedings.

(4) This section does not affect the continuation of proceedings for a recovery order which have been properly started or the making or continuing effect of an interim receiving order or interim administration order which has been properly applied for.

## 288[3]  Limitation

(1) After section 27 of the Limitation Act 1980 there is inserted –

### '27A  Actions for recovery of property obtained through unlawful conduct etc

(1) None of the time limits given in the preceding provisions of this Act applies to any proceedings under Chapter 2 of Part 5 of the Proceeds of Crime Act 2002 (civil recovery of proceeds of unlawful conduct).

(2) Proceedings under that Chapter for a recovery order in respect of any recoverable property shall not be brought after the expiration of the period of twelve years from the date on which the Director's cause of action accrued.

(3) Proceedings under that Chapter are brought when –

(a) a claim form is issued, or

---

1    Omission: Sections 284–286 not reproduced.
2    Information: Commencement: Not yet in force.
3    Information: Commencement: Not yet in force.

(b)   an application is made for an interim receiving order,

whichever is the earlier.

(4)   The Director's cause of action accrues in respect of any recoverable property –

    (a)   in the case of proceedings for a recovery order in respect of property obtained through unlawful conduct, when the property is so obtained,

    (b)   in the case of proceedings for a recovery order in respect of any other recoverable property, when the property obtained through unlawful conduct which it represents is so obtained.

(5)   If –

    (a)   a person would (but for the preceding provisions of this Act) have a cause of action in respect of the conversion of a chattel, and

    (b)   proceedings are started under that Chapter for a recovery order in respect of the chattel,

section 3(2) of this Act does not prevent his asserting on an application under section 281 of that Act that the property belongs to him, or the court making a declaration in his favour under that section.

(6)   If the court makes such a declaration, his title to the chattel is to be treated as not having been extinguished by section 3(2) of this Act.

(7)   Expressions used in this section and Part 5 of that Act have the same meaning in this section as in that Part.'

(2)   After section 19A of the Prescription and Limitation (Scotland) Act 1973 there is inserted –

## '19B   Actions for recovery of property obtained through unlawful conduct etc

(1)   None of the time limits given in the preceding provisions of this Act applies to any proceedings under Chapter 2 of Part 5 of the Proceeds of Crime Act 2002 (civil recovery of proceeds of unlawful conduct).

(2)   Proceedings under that Chapter for a recovery order in respect of any recoverable property shall not be commenced after the expiration of the period of twelve years from the date on which the Scottish Ministers' right of action accrued.

(3)   Proceedings under that Chapter are commenced when –

    (a)   the proceedings are served, or

    (b)   an application is made for an interim administration order,

whichever is the earlier.

(4)   The Scottish Ministers' right of action accrues in respect of any recoverable property –

    (a)   in the case of proceedings for a recovery order in respect of property obtained through unlawful conduct, when the property is so obtained,

    (b)   in the case of proceedings for a recovery order in respect of any other recoverable property, when the property obtained through unlawful conduct which it represents is so obtained.

(5)   Expressions used in this section and Part 5 of that Act have the same meaning in this section as in that Part.'

(3) After Article 72 of the Limitation (Northern Ireland) Order 1989 (SI 1989/1339 (NI 11)) there is inserted –

### '72A    Actions for recovery of property obtained through unlawful conduct etc

(1) None of the time limits fixed by Parts II and III applies to any proceedings under Chapter 2 of Part 5 of the Proceeds of Crime Act 2002 (civil recovery of proceeds of unlawful conduct).

(2) Proceedings under that Chapter for a recovery order in respect of any recoverable property shall not be brought after the expiration of the period of twelve years from the date on which the Director's cause of action accrued.

(3) Proceedings under that Chapter are brought when –

    (a)   a claim form is issued, or
    (b)   an application is made for an interim receiving order,

whichever is the earlier.

(4) The Director's cause of action accrues in respect of any recoverable property –

    (a)   in the case of proceedings for a recovery order in respect of property obtained through unlawful conduct, when the property is so obtained,
    (b)   in the case of proceedings for a recovery order in respect of any other recoverable property, when the property obtained through unlawful conduct which it represents is so obtained.

(5) If –

    (a)   a person would (but for a time limit fixed by this Order) have a cause of action in respect of the conversion of a chattel, and
    (b)   proceedings are started under that Chapter for a recovery order in respect of the chattel,

Article 17(2) does not prevent his asserting on an application under section 281 of that Act that the property belongs to him, or the court making a declaration in his favour under that section.

(6) If the court makes such a declaration, his title to the chattel is to be treated as not having been extinguished by Article 17(2).

(7) Expressions used in this Article and Part 5 of that Act have the same meaning in this Article as in that Part.'

### CHAPTER 3    RECOVERY OF CASH IN SUMMARY PROCEEDINGS

*Searches*

### 289[1]    Searches

(1) If a customs officer or constable who is lawfully on any premises has reasonable grounds for suspecting that there is on the premises cash –

---

1    Information: Commencement: Not yet in force.

(a) which is recoverable property or is intended by any person for use in unlawful conduct, and

(b) the amount of which is not less than the minimum amount,

he may search for the cash there.

(2) If a customs officer or constable has reasonable grounds for suspecting that a person (the suspect) is carrying cash –

(a) which is recoverable property or is intended by any person for use in unlawful conduct, and

(b) the amount of which is not less than the minimum amount,

he may exercise the following powers.

(3) The officer or constable may, so far as he thinks it necessary or expedient, require the suspect –

(a) to permit a search of any article he has with him,

(b) to permit a search of his person.

(4) An officer or constable exercising powers by virtue of subsection (3)(b) may detain the suspect for so long as is necessary for their exercise.

(5) The powers conferred by this section –

(a) are exercisable only so far as reasonably required for the purpose of finding cash,

(b) are exercisable by a customs officer only if he has reasonable grounds for suspecting that the unlawful conduct in question relates to an assigned matter (within the meaning of the Customs and Excise Management Act 1979).

(6) Cash means –

(a) notes and coins in any currency,

(b) postal orders,

(c) cheques of any kind, including travellers' cheques,

(d) bankers' drafts,

(e) bearer bonds and bearer shares,

found at any place in the United Kingdom.

(7) Cash also includes any kind of monetary instrument which is found at any place in the United Kingdom, if the instrument is specified by the Secretary of State by an order made after consultation with the Scottish Ministers.

(8) This section does not require a person to submit to an intimate search or strip search (within the meaning of section 164 of the Customs and Excise Management Act 1979).

## 290[1]   Prior approval

(1) The powers conferred by section 289 may be exercised only with the appropriate approval unless, in the circumstances, it is not practicable to obtain that approval before exercising the power.

(2) The appropriate approval means the approval of a judicial officer or (if that is not practicable in any case) the approval of a senior officer.

(3) A judicial officer means –

---

1    Information: Commencement: Not yet in force.

(a)   in relation to England and Wales and Northern Ireland, a justice of the peace,

(b)   (*applies to Scotland only*)

(4)  A senior officer means –

(a)   in relation to the exercise of the power by a customs officer, a customs officer of a rank designated by the Commissioners of Customs and Excise as equivalent to that of a senior police officer,

(b)   in relation to the exercise of the power by a constable, a senior police officer.

(5)  A senior police officer means a police officer of at least the rank of inspector.

(6)  If the powers are exercised without the approval of a judicial officer in a case where –

(a)   no cash is seized by virtue of section 294, or

(b)   any cash so seized is not detained for more than 48 hours,

the customs officer or constable who exercised the powers must give a written report to the appointed person.

(7)  The report must give particulars of the circumstances which led him to believe that –

(a)   the powers were exercisable, and

(b)   it was not practicable to obtain the approval of a judicial officer.

(8)  In this section and section 291, the appointed person means –

(a)   in relation to England and Wales and Northern Ireland, a person appointed by the Secretary of State,

(b)   (*applies to Scotland only*)

(9)  The appointed person must not be a person employed under or for the purposes of a government department or of the Scottish Administration; and the terms and conditions of his appointment, including any remuneration or expenses to be paid to him, are to be determined by the person appointing him.

## 291[1]   Report on exercise of powers

(1)  As soon as possible after the end of each financial year, the appointed person must prepare a report for that year.

'Financial year' means –

(a)   the period beginning with the day on which this section comes into force and ending with the next 31 March (which is the first financial year), and

(b)   each subsequent period of twelve months beginning with 1 April.

(2)  The report must give his opinion as to the circumstances and manner in which the powers conferred by section 289 are being exercised in cases where the customs officer or constable who exercised them is required to give a report under section 290(6).

(3)  In the report, he may make any recommendations he considers appropriate.

(4)  He must send a copy of his report to the Secretary of State or, as the case may be, the Scottish Ministers, who must arrange for it to be published.

(5)  The Secretary of State must lay a copy of any report he receives under this section before Parliament; and the Scottish Ministers must lay a copy of any report they receive under this section before the Scottish Parliament.

---

1      Information: Commencement: Not yet in force.

## 292[1]   Code of practice

(1) The Secretary of State must make a code of practice in connection with the exercise by customs officers and (in relation to England and Wales and Northern Ireland) constables of the powers conferred by virtue of section 289.

(2) Where he proposes to issue a code of practice he must –

(a)   publish a draft,

(b)   consider any representations made to him about the draft by the Scottish Ministers or any other person,

(c)   if he thinks it appropriate, modify the draft in the light of any such representations.

(3) He must lay a draft of the code before Parliament.

(4) When he has laid a draft of the code before Parliament he may bring it into operation by order.

(5) He may revise the whole or any part of the code issued by him and issue the code as revised; and subsections (2) to (4) apply to such a revised code as they apply to the original code.

(6) A failure by a customs officer or constable to comply with a provision of the code does not of itself make him liable to criminal or civil proceedings.

(7) The code is admissible in evidence in criminal or civil proceedings and is to be taken into account by a court or tribunal in any case in which it appears to the court or tribunal to be relevant.

\*\*\*\*[2]

*Seizure and detention*

## 294[3]   Seizure of cash

(1) A customs officer or constable may seize any cash if he has reasonable grounds for suspecting that it is –

(a)   recoverable property, or

(b)   intended by any person for use in unlawful conduct.

(2) A customs officer or constable may also seize cash part of which he has reasonable grounds for suspecting to be –

(a)   recoverable property, or

(b)   intended by any person for use in unlawful conduct,

if it is not reasonably practicable to seize only that part.

(3) This section does not authorise the seizure of an amount of cash if it or, as the case may be, the part to which his suspicion relates, is less than the minimum amount.

## 295[4]   Detention of seized cash

(1) While the customs officer or constable continues to have reasonable grounds for his suspicion, cash seized under section 294 may be detained initially for a period of 48 hours.

---

1   Information: Commencement: Not yet in force.
2   Omission: Section 293 not reproduced.
3   Information: Commencement: Not yet in force.
4   Information: Commencement: Not yet in force.

(2)  The period for which the cash or any part of it may be detained may be extended by an order made by a magistrates' court or (in Scotland) the sheriff; but the order may not authorise the detention of any of the cash –

(a)  beyond the end of the period of three months beginning with the date of the order,
(b)  in the case of any further order under this section, beyond the end of the period of two years beginning with the date of the first order.

(3)  A justice of the peace may also exercise the power of a magistrates' court to make the first order under subsection (2) extending the period.

(4)  An application for an order under subsection (2) –

(a)  in relation to England and Wales and Northern Ireland, may be made by the Commissioners of Customs and Excise or a constable,
(b)  *(applies to Scotland only)*

and the court, sheriff or justice may make the order if satisfied, in relation to any cash to be further detained, that either of the following conditions is met.

(5)  The first condition is that there are reasonable grounds for suspecting that the cash is recoverable property and that either –

(a)  its continued detention is justified while its derivation is further investigated or consideration is given to bringing (in the United Kingdom or elsewhere) proceedings against any person for an offence with which the cash is connected, or
(b)  proceedings against any person for an offence with which the cash is connected have been started and have not been concluded.

(6)  The second condition is that there are reasonable grounds for suspecting that the cash is intended to be used in unlawful conduct and that either –

(a)  its continued detention is justified while its intended use is further investigated or consideration is given to bringing (in the United Kingdom or elsewhere) proceedings against any person for an offence with which the cash is connected, or
(b)  proceedings against any person for an offence with which the cash is connected have been started and have not been concluded.

(7)  An application for an order under subsection (2) may also be made in respect of any cash seized under section 294(2), and the court, sheriff or justice may make the order if satisfied that –

(a)  the condition in subsection (5) or (6) is met in respect of part of the cash, and
(b)  it is not reasonably practicable to detain only that part.

(8)  An order under subsection (2) must provide for notice to be given to persons affected by it.

## 296[1]  Interest

(1)  If cash is detained under section 295 for more than 48 hours, it is at the first opportunity to be paid into an interest-bearing account and held there; and the interest accruing on it is to be added to it on its forfeiture or release.

(2)  In the case of cash detained under section 295 which was seized under section 294(2), the customs officer or constable must, on paying it into the account, release the part of the cash to which the suspicion does not relate.

---

1    Information: Commencement: Not yet in force.

(3) Subsection (1) does not apply if the cash or, as the case may be, the part to which the suspicion relates is required as evidence of an offence or evidence in proceedings under this Chapter.

## 297[1] Release of detained cash

(1) This section applies while any cash is detained under section 295.

(2) A magistrates' court or (in Scotland) the sheriff may direct the release of the whole or any part of the cash if the following condition is met.

(3) The condition is that the court or sheriff is satisfied, on an application by the person from whom the cash was seized, that the conditions in section 295 for the detention of the cash are no longer met in relation to the cash to be released.

(4) A customs officer, constable or (in Scotland) procurator fiscal may, after notifying the magistrates' court, sheriff or justice under whose order cash is being detained, release the whole or any part of it if satisfied that the detention of the cash to be released is no longer justified.

*Forfeiture*

## 298[2] Forfeiture

(1) While cash is detained under section 295, an application for the forfeiture of the whole or any part of it may be made –

    (a) to a magistrates' court by the Commissioners of Customs and Excise or a constable,

    (b) *(applies to Scotland only)*

(2) The court or sheriff may order the forfeiture of the cash or any part of it if satisfied that the cash or part –

    (a) is recoverable property, or

    (b) is intended by any person for use in unlawful conduct.

(3) But in the case of recoverable property which belongs to joint tenants, one of whom is an excepted joint owner, the order may not apply to so much of it as the court thinks is attributable to the excepted joint owner's share.

(4) Where an application for the forfeiture of any cash is made under this section, the cash is to be detained (and may not be released under any power conferred by this Chapter) until any proceedings in pursuance of the application (including any proceedings on appeal) are concluded.

## 299[3] Appeal against forfeiture

(1) Any party to proceedings in which an order is made under section 298 for the forfeiture of cash who is aggrieved by the order may appeal –

    (a) in relation to England and Wales, to the Crown Court,

    (b) *(applies to Scotland only)*

---

1    Information: Commencement: Not yet in force.
2    Information: Commencement: Not yet in force.
3    Information: Commencement: Not yet in force.

(c)   (*applies to Northern Ireland only*)

(2) An appeal under subsection (1) must be made within the period of 30 days beginning with the date on which the order is made.

(3) The appeal is to be by way of a rehearing.

(4) The court hearing the appeal may make any order it thinks appropriate.

(5) If the court upholds the appeal, it may order the release of the cash.

## 300[1]   Application of forfeited cash

(1) Cash forfeited under this Chapter, and any accrued interest on it –

    (a)   if forfeited by a magistrates' court in England and Wales or Northern Ireland, is to be paid into the Consolidated Fund,
    (b)   if forfeited by the sheriff, is to be paid into the Scottish Consolidated Fund.

(2) But it is not to be paid in –

    (a)   before the end of the period within which an appeal under section 299 may be made, or
    (b)   if a person appeals under that section, before the appeal is determined or otherwise disposed of.

*Supplementary*

## 301[2]   Victims and other owners

(1) A person who claims that any cash detained under this Chapter, or any part of it, belongs to him may apply to a magistrates' court or (in Scotland) the sheriff for the cash or part to be released to him.

(2) The application may be made in the course of proceedings under section 295 or 298 or at any other time.

(3) If it appears to the court or sheriff concerned that –

    (a)   the applicant was deprived of the cash to which the application relates, or of property which it represents, by unlawful conduct,
    (b)   the property he was deprived of was not, immediately before he was deprived of it, recoverable property, and
    (c)   that cash belongs to him,

the court or sheriff may order the cash to which the application relates to be released to the applicant.

(4) If –

    (a)   the applicant is not the person from whom the cash to which the application relates was seized,
    (b)   it appears to the court or sheriff that that cash belongs to the applicant,
    (c)   the court or sheriff is satisfied that the conditions in section 295 for the detention of that cash are no longer met or, if an application has been made under section 298, the court or sheriff decides not to make an order under that section in relation to that cash, and

---

1    Information: Commencement: Not yet in force.
2    Information: Commencement: Not yet in force.

(d)   no objection to the making of an order under this subsection has been made by the person from whom that cash was seized,

the court or sheriff may order the cash to which the application relates to be released to the applicant or to the person from whom it was seized.

## 302[1]   Compensation

(1) If no forfeiture order is made in respect of any cash detained under this Chapter, the person to whom the cash belongs or from whom it was seized may make an application to the magistrates' court or (in Scotland) the sheriff for compensation.

(2) If, for any period beginning with the first opportunity to place the cash in an interest-bearing account after the initial detention of the cash for 48 hours, the cash was not held in an interest-bearing account while detained, the court or sheriff may order an amount of compensation to be paid to the applicant.

(3) The amount of compensation to be paid under subsection (2) is the amount the court or sheriff thinks would have been earned in interest in the period in question if the cash had been held in an interest-bearing account.

(4) If the court or sheriff is satisfied that, taking account of any interest to be paid under section 296 or any amount to be paid under subsection (2), the applicant has suffered loss as a result of the detention of the cash and that the circumstances are exceptional, the court or sheriff may order compensation (or additional compensation) to be paid to him.

(5) The amount of compensation to be paid under subsection (4) is the amount the court or sheriff thinks reasonable, having regard to the loss suffered and any other relevant circumstances.

(6) If the cash was seized by a customs officer, the compensation is to be paid by the Commissioners of Customs and Excise.

(7) If the cash was seized by a constable, the compensation is to be paid as follows –

(a)   in the case of a constable of a police force in England and Wales, it is to be paid out of the police fund from which the expenses of the police force are met,
(b)   (*applies to Scotland only*)
(c)   in the case of a police officer within the meaning of the Police (Northern Ireland) Act 2000, it is to be paid out of money provided by the Chief Constable.

(8) If a forfeiture order is made in respect only of a part of any cash detained under this Chapter, this section has effect in relation to the other part.

## 303[2]   'The minimum amount'

(1) In this Chapter, the minimum amount is the amount in sterling specified in an order made by the Secretary of State after consultation with the Scottish Ministers.

(2) For that purpose the amount of any cash held in a currency other than sterling must be taken to be its sterling equivalent, calculated in accordance with the prevailing rate of exchange.

---

1    Information: Commencement: Not yet in force.
2    Information: Commencement: Not yet in force.

## CHAPTER 4   GENERAL

### *Recoverable property*

### 304[1]   Property obtained through unlawful conduct

(1) Property obtained through unlawful conduct is recoverable property.

(2) But if property obtained through unlawful conduct has been disposed of (since it was so obtained), it is recoverable property only if it is held by a person into whose hands it may be followed.

(3) Recoverable property obtained through unlawful conduct may be followed into the hands of a person obtaining it on a disposal by –

    (a)   the person who through the conduct obtained the property, or

    (b)   a person into whose hands it may (by virtue of this subsection) be followed.

### 305[2]   Tracing property, etc

(1) Where property obtained through unlawful conduct ('the original property') is or has been recoverable, property which represents the original property is also recoverable property.

(2) If a person enters into a transaction by which –

    (a)   he disposes of recoverable property, whether the original property or property which (by virtue of this Chapter) represents the original property, and

    (b)   he obtains other property in place of it,

the other property represents the original property.

(3) If a person disposes of recoverable property which represents the original property, the property may be followed into the hands of the person who obtains it (and it continues to represent the original property).

### 306[3]   Mixing property

(1) Subsection (2) applies if a person's recoverable property is mixed with other property (whether his property or another's).

(2) The portion of the mixed property which is attributable to the recoverable property represents the property obtained through unlawful conduct.

(3) Recoverable property is mixed with other property if (for example) it is used –

    (a)   to increase funds held in a bank account,

    (b)   in part payment for the acquisition of an asset,

    (c)   for the restoration or improvement of land,

    (d)   by a person holding a leasehold interest in the property to acquire the freehold.

### 307[4]   Recoverable property: accruing profits

(1) This section applies where a person who has recoverable property obtains further property consisting of profits accruing in respect of the recoverable property.

---

1    Information: Commencement: Not yet in force.
2    Information: Commencement: Not yet in force.
3    Information: Commencement: Not yet in force.
4    Information: Commencement: Not yet in force.

(2) The further property is to be treated as representing the property obtained through unlawful conduct.

## 308[1]   General exceptions

(1) If –

    (a)  a person disposes of recoverable property, and

    (b)  the person who obtains it on the disposal does so in good faith, for value and without notice that it was recoverable property,

the property may not be followed into that person's hands and, accordingly, it ceases to be recoverable.

(2) If recoverable property is vested, forfeited or otherwise disposed of in pursuance of powers conferred by virtue of this Part, it ceases to be recoverable.

(3) If –

    (a)  in pursuance of a judgment in civil proceedings (whether in the United Kingdom or elsewhere), the defendant makes a payment to the claimant or the claimant otherwise obtains property from the defendant,

    (b)  the claimant's claim is based on the defendant's unlawful conduct, and

    (c)  apart from this subsection, the sum received, or the property obtained, by the claimant would be recoverable property,

the property ceases to be recoverable.

*(words apply to Scotland only)*

(4) If –

    (a)  a payment is made to a person in pursuance of a compensation order under Article 14 of the Criminal Justice (Northern Ireland) Order 1994 (SI 1994/2795 (NI 15)), section 249 of the Criminal Procedure (Scotland) Act 1995 or section 130 of the Powers of Criminal Courts (Sentencing) Act 2000, and

    (b)  apart from this subsection, the sum received would be recoverable property,

the property ceases to be recoverable.

(5) If –

    (a)  a payment is made to a person in pursuance of a restitution order under section 27 of the Theft Act (Northern Ireland) 1969 or section 148(2) of the Powers of Criminal Courts (Sentencing) Act 2000 or a person otherwise obtains any property in pursuance of such an order, and

    (b)  apart from this subsection, the sum received, or the property obtained, would be recoverable property,

the property ceases to be recoverable.

(6) If –

    (a)  in pursuance of an order made by the court under section 382(3) or 383(5) of the Financial Services and Markets Act 2000 8) (restitution orders), an amount is paid to or distributed among any persons in accordance with the court's directions, and

---

1    Information: Commencement: Not yet in force.

    (b)   apart from this subsection, the sum received by them would be recoverable property,

the property ceases to be recoverable.

(7) If –

    (a)   in pursuance of a requirement of the Financial Services Authority under section 384(5) of the Financial Services and Markets Act 2000 (power of authority to require restitution), an amount is paid to or distributed among any persons, and
    (b)   apart from this subsection, the sum received by them would be recoverable property,

the property ceases to be recoverable.

(8) Property is not recoverable while a restraint order applies to it, that is –

    (a)   an order under section 41, 120 or 190, or
    (b)   an order under any corresponding provision of an enactment mentioned in section 8(7)(a) to (g).

(9) Property is not recoverable if it has been taken into account in deciding the amount of a person's benefit from criminal conduct for the purpose of making a confiscation order, that is –

    (a)   an order under section 6, 92 or 156, or
    (b)   an order under a corresponding provision of an enactment mentioned in section 8(7)(a) to (g),

and, in relation to an order mentioned in paragraph (b), the reference to the amount of a person's benefit from criminal conduct is to be read as a reference to the corresponding amount under the enactment in question.

(10) Where –

    (a)   a person enters into a transaction to which section 305(2) applies, and
    (b)   the disposal is one to which subsection (1) or (2) applies,

this section does not affect the recoverability (by virtue of section 305(2)) of any property obtained on the transaction in place of the property disposed of.

## 309[1]   Other exemptions

(1) An order may provide that property is not recoverable or (as the case may be) associated property if –

    (a)   it is prescribed property, or
    (b)   it is disposed of in pursuance of a prescribed enactment or an enactment of a prescribed description.

(2) An order may provide that if property is disposed of in pursuance of a prescribed enactment or an enactment of a prescribed description, it is to be treated for the purposes of section 278 as if it had been disposed of in pursuance of a recovery order.

(3) An order under this section may be made so as to apply to property, or a disposal of property, only in prescribed circumstances; and the circumstances may relate to the property or disposal itself or to a person who holds or has held the property or to any other matter.

(4) In this section, an order means an order made by the Secretary of State after consultation with the Scottish Ministers, and prescribed means prescribed by the order.

---

1    Information: Commencement: Not yet in force.

## 310¹  Granting interests

(1) If a person grants an interest in his recoverable property, the question whether the interest is also recoverable is to be determined in the same manner as it is on any other disposal of recoverable property.

(2) Accordingly, on his granting an interest in the property ('the property in question') –

    (a)  where the property in question is property obtained through unlawful conduct, the interest is also to be treated as obtained through that conduct,

    (b)  where the property in question represents in his hands property obtained through unlawful conduct, the interest is also to be treated as representing in his hands the property so obtained.

*Insolvency*

## 311²  Insolvency

(1) Proceedings for a recovery order may not be taken or continued in respect of property to which subsection (3) applies unless the appropriate court gives leave and the proceedings are taken or (as the case may be) continued in accordance with any terms imposed by that court.

(2) An application for an order for the further detention of any cash to which subsection (3) applies may not be made under section 295 unless the appropriate court gives leave.

(3) This subsection applies to recoverable property, or property associated with it, if –

    (a)  it is an asset of a company being wound up in pursuance of a resolution for voluntary winding up,

    (b)  it is an asset of a company and a voluntary arrangement under Part 1 of the 1986 Act, or Part 2 of the 1989 Order, has effect in relation to the company,

    (c)  an order under section 2 of the 1985 Act, section 286 of the 1986 Act or Article 259 of the 1989 Order (appointment of interim trustee or interim receiver) has effect in relation to the property,

    (d)  it is an asset comprised in the estate of an individual who has been adjudged bankrupt or, in relation to Scotland, of a person whose estate has been sequestrated,

    (e)  it is an asset of an individual and a voluntary arrangement under Part 8 of the 1986 Act, or Part 8 of the 1989 Order, has effect in relation to him, or

    (f)  *(applies to Scotland only)*

(4) An application under this section, or under any provision of the 1986 Act or the 1989 Order, for leave to take proceedings for a recovery order may be made without notice to any person.

(5) Subsection (4) does not affect any requirement for notice of an application to be given to any person acting as an insolvency practitioner or to the official receiver (whether or not acting as an insolvency practitioner).

(6) References to the provisions of the 1986 Act in sections 420 and 421 of that Act, or to the provisions of the 1989 Order in Articles 364 or 365 of that Order, (insolvent partnerships and estates of deceased persons) include subsections (1) to (3) above.

(7) In this section –

    (a)  the 1985 Act means the Bankruptcy (Scotland) Act 1985,

    (b)  the 1986 Act means the Insolvency Act 1986,

---

1    Information: Commencement: Not yet in force.
2    Information: Commencement: Not yet in force.

(c)   the 1989 Order means the Insolvency (Northern Ireland) Order 1989 (SI 1989/2405 (NI 19)),

and in subsection (8) 'the applicable enactment' means whichever enactment mentioned in paragraphs (a) to (c) is relevant to the resolution, arrangement, order or trust deed mentioned in subsection (3).

(8)  In this section –

(a)   an asset means any property within the meaning of the applicable enactment or, where the 1985 Act is the applicable enactment, any property comprised in an estate to which the 1985 Act applies,

(b)   the appropriate court means the court which, in relation to the resolution, arrangement, order or trust deed mentioned in subsection (3), is the court for the purposes of the applicable enactment or, in relation to Northern Ireland, the High Court,

(c)   acting as an insolvency practitioner has the same meaning as in section 433,

(d)   other expressions used in this section and in the applicable enactment have the same meaning as in that enactment.

*Delegation of enforcement functions*

****[1]

## 313[2]   Restriction on performance of Director's functions by police

(1)  In spite of section 1(6), nothing which the Director is authorised or required to do for the purposes of this Part may be done by –

(a)   a member of a police force,

(b)   a member of the Police Service of Northern Ireland,

(c)   a person appointed as a police member of the National Criminal Intelligence Service under section 9(1)(b) of the Police Act 1997,

(d)   a person appointed as a police member of the National Crime Squad under section 55(1)(b) of that Act.

(2)  In this section –

(a)   'member of a police force' has the same meaning as in the Police Act 1996 and includes a person who would be a member of a police force but for section 97(3) of that Act (police officers engaged on service outside their force),

(b)   'member of the Police Service of Northern Ireland' includes a person who would be a member of the Police Service of Northern Ireland but for section 27(3) of the Police (Northern Ireland) Act 1998 (members of that service engaged on other police service).

*Interpretation*

## 314[3]   Obtaining and disposing of property

(1)  References to a person disposing of his property include a reference –

(a)   to his disposing of a part of it, or

(b)   to his granting an interest in it,

---

1   Omission: Section 312 not reproduced.
2   Information: Commencement: Not yet in force.
3   Information: Commencement: Not yet in force.

(or to both); and references to the property disposed of are to any property obtained on the disposal.

(2) A person who makes a payment to another is to be treated as making a disposal of his property to the other, whatever form the payment takes.

(3) Where a person's property passes to another under a will or intestacy or by operation of law, it is to be treated as disposed of by him to the other.

(4) A person is only to be treated as having obtained his property for value in a case where he gave unexecuted consideration if the consideration has become executed consideration.

## 315[1]   Northern Ireland courts

(*applies to Northern Ireland only*)

## 316[2]   General interpretation

(1) In this Part –

'associated property' has the meaning given by section 245,

'cash' has the meaning given by section 289(6) or (7),

(*applies to Northern Ireland only*)

'country' includes territory,

'the court' (except in sections 253(2) and (3) and 262(2) and (3) and Chapter 3) means the High Court or (in relation to proceedings in Scotland) the Court of Session,

'dealing' with property includes disposing of it, taking possession of it or removing it from the United Kingdom,

'enforcement authority' –

    (a)  in relation to England and Wales and Northern Ireland, means the Director,
    (b)  (*applies to Scotland only*)

'excepted joint owner' has the meaning given by section 270(4),

'interest', in relation to land –

    (a)  in the case of land in England and Wales or Northern Ireland, means any legal estate and any equitable interest or power,
    (b)  (*applies to Scotland only*)

'interest', in relation to property other than land, includes any right (including a right to possession of the property),

'interim administration order' has the meaning given by section 256(2),

'interim receiving order' has the meaning given by section 246(2),

'the minimum amount' (in Chapter 3) has the meaning given by section 303,

'part', in relation to property, includes a portion,

'premises' has the same meaning as in the Police and Criminal Evidence Act 1984,

---

1    Information: Commencement: Not yet in force.
2    Information: Commencement: Not yet in force.

'property obtained through unlawful conduct' has the meaning given by section 242,

'recoverable property' is to be read in accordance with sections 304 to 310,

'recovery order' means an order made under section 266,

'respondent' means –

    (a)   where proceedings are brought by the enforcement authority by virtue of Chapter 2, the person against whom the proceedings are brought,

    (b)   where no such proceedings have been brought but the enforcement authority has applied for an interim receiving order or interim administration order, the person against whom he intends to bring such proceedings,

'share', in relation to an excepted joint owner, has the meaning given by section 270(4),

'unlawful conduct' has the meaning given by section 241,

'value' means market value.

(2) The following provisions apply for the purposes of this Part.

(3) For the purpose of deciding whether or not property was recoverable at any time (including times before commencement), it is to be assumed that this Part was in force at that and any other relevant time.

(4) Property is all property wherever situated and includes –

    (a)   money,

    (b)   all forms of property, real or personal, heritable or moveable,

    (c)   things in action and other intangible or incorporeal property.

(5) Any reference to a person's property (whether expressed as a reference to the property he holds or otherwise) is to be read as follows.

(6) In relation to land, it is a reference to any interest which he holds in the land.

(7) In relation to property other than land, it is a reference –

    (a)   to the property (if it belongs to him), or

    (b)   to any other interest which he holds in the property.

(8) References to the satisfaction of the enforcement authority's right to recover property obtained through unlawful conduct are to be read in accordance with section 279.

(9) Proceedings against any person for an offence are concluded when –

    (a)   the person is convicted or acquitted,

    (b)   the prosecution is discontinued or, in Scotland, the trial diet is deserted simpliciter, or

    (c)   the jury is discharged without a finding.

## PART 6   REVENUE FUNCTIONS

### *General functions*

### 317[1]   Director's general Revenue functions

(1) For the purposes of this section the qualifying condition is that the Director has reasonable grounds to suspect that –

---

1    Information: Commencement: Not yet in force.

(a) income arising or a gain accruing to a person in respect of a chargeable period is chargeable to income tax or is a chargeable gain (as the case may be) and arises or accrues as a result of the person's or another's criminal conduct (whether wholly or partly and whether directly or indirectly), or

(b) a company is chargeable to corporation tax on its profits arising in respect of a chargeable period and the profits arise as a result of the company's or another person's criminal conduct (whether wholly or partly and whether directly or indirectly).

(2) If the qualifying condition is satisfied the Director may serve on the Commissioners of Inland Revenue (the Board) a notice which –

(a) specifies the person or the company (as the case may be) and the period, and

(b) states that the Director intends to carry out, in relation to the person or the company (as the case may be) and in respect of the period, such of the general Revenue functions as are specified in the notice.

(3) Service of a notice under subsection (2) vests in the Director, in relation to the person or the company (as the case may be) and in respect of the period, such of the general Revenue functions as are specified in the notice; but this is subject to section 318.

(4) The Director –

(a) may at any time serve on the Board a notice of withdrawal of the notice under subsection (2);

(b) must serve such a notice of withdrawal on the Board if the qualifying condition ceases to be satisfied.

(5) A notice under subsection (2) and a notice of withdrawal under subsection (4) may be in respect of one or more periods.

(6) Service of a notice under subsection (4) divests the Director of the functions concerned in relation to the person or the company (as the case may be) and in respect of the period or periods specified in the notice.

(7) The vesting of a function in the Director under this section does not divest the Board or an officer of the Board of the function.

(8) If –

(a) apart from this section the Board's authorisation would be required for the exercise of a function, and

(b) the function is vested in the Director under this section,

the authorisation is not required in relation to the function as so vested.

(9) It is immaterial whether a chargeable period or any part of it falls before or after the passing of this Act.

## 318[1]  Revenue functions regarding employment

(1) Subsection (2) applies if –

(a) the Director serves a notice or notices under section 317(2) in relation to a company and in respect of a period or periods, and

(b) the company is an employer.

---

1    Information: Commencement: Not yet in force.

(2) The general Revenue functions vested in the Director do not include functions relating to any requirement which –

    (a)   is imposed on the company in its capacity as employer, and

    (b)   relates to a year of assessment which does not fall wholly within the period or periods.

(3) Subsection (4) applies if –

    (a)   the Director serves a notice or notices under section 317(2) in relation to an individual and in respect of a year or years of assessment, and

    (b)   the individual is a self-employed earner.

(4) The general Revenue functions vested in the Director do not include functions relating to any liability to pay Class 2 contributions in respect of a period which does not fall wholly within the year or years of assessment.

(5) In this section in its application to Great Britain –

    (a)   'self-employed earner' has the meaning given by section 2(1)(b) of the Social Security Contributions and Benefits Act 1992;

    (b)   'Class 2 contributions' must be construed in accordance with section 1(2)(c) of that Act.

(6) *(applies to Northern Ireland only)*

### 319[1]   Source of income

(1) For the purpose of the exercise by the Director of any function vested in him by virtue of this Part it is immaterial that he cannot identify a source for any income.

(2) An assessment made by the Director under section 29 of the Taxes Management Act 1970 (assessment where loss of tax discovered) in respect of income charged to tax under Case 6 of Schedule D must not be reduced or quashed only because it does not specify (to any extent) the source of the income.

(3) If the Director serves on the Board a notice of withdrawal under section 317(4), any assessment made by him under section 29 of the Taxes Management Act 1970 is invalid to the extent that it does not specify a source for the income.

(4) Subsections (2) and (3) apply in respect of years of assessment whenever occurring.

### 320[2]  Appeals

(1) An appeal in respect of the exercise by the Director of general Revenue functions shall be to the Special Commissioners.

(2) The Presiding Special Commissioner may nominate one or more assessors to assist the Special Commissioners in any appeal to be heard by them in respect of the exercise by the Director of any of his Revenue functions.

(3) An assessor nominated under subsection (2) –

    (a)   must have special knowledge and experience of the matter to which the appeal relates, and

    (b)   must be selected from a panel of persons appointed for the purposes of this section by the Lord Chancellor after consultation with the Scottish Ministers.

---

1    Information: Commencement: Not yet in force.
2    Information: Commencement: Not yet in force.

(4) Regulations made under section 56B of the Taxes Management Act 1970 may include provision as to the manner in which an assessor nominated under subsection (2) is to assist the Special Commissioners.

(5) The remuneration of an assessor nominated under subsection (2) must be paid by the Lord Chancellor and must be at such rate as he decides.

*Inheritance tax functions*

### 321[1]  Director's functions: transfers of value

(1) For the purposes of this section the qualifying condition is that the Director has reasonable grounds to suspect that –

(a) there has been a transfer of value within the meaning of the Inheritance Tax Act 1984, and
(b) the value transferred by it is attributable (in whole or part) to criminal property.

(2) If the qualifying condition is satisfied the Director may serve on the Board a notice which –

(a) specifies the transfer of value, and
(b) states that the Director intends to carry out the Revenue inheritance tax functions in relation to the transfer.

(3) Service of a notice under subsection (2) vests in the Director the Revenue inheritance tax functions in relation to the transfer.

(4) The Director –

(a) may at any time serve on the Board a notice of withdrawal of the notice under subsection (2);
(b) must serve such a notice of withdrawal on the Board if the qualifying condition ceases to be satisfied.

(5) Service of a notice under subsection (4) divests the Director of the Revenue inheritance tax functions in relation to the transfer.

(6) The vesting of a function in the Director under this section does not divest the Board or an officer of the Board of the function.

(7) It is immaterial whether a transfer of value is suspected to have occurred before or after the passing of this Act.

### 322[2]  Director's functions: certain settlements

(1) For the purposes of this section the qualifying condition is that the Director has reasonable grounds to suspect that –

(a) all or part of the property comprised in a settlement is relevant property for the purposes of Chapter 3 of Part 3 of the Inheritance Tax Act 1984 (settlements without interest in possession), and
(b) the relevant property is (in whole or part) criminal property.

(2) If the qualifying condition is satisfied the Director may serve on the Board a notice which –

(a) specifies the settlement concerned,

---

1    Information: Commencement: Not yet in force.
2    Information: Commencement: Not yet in force.

(b)   states that the Director intends to carry out the Revenue inheritance tax functions in relation to the settlement, and

(c)   states the period for which he intends to carry them out.

(3) Service of a notice under subsection (2) vests in the Director the Revenue inheritance tax functions in relation to the settlement for the period.

(4) The Director –

(a)   may at any time serve on the Board a notice of withdrawal of the notice under subsection (2);

(b)   must serve such a notice of withdrawal on the Board if the qualifying condition ceases to be satisfied.

(5) Service of a notice under subsection (4) divests the Director of the Revenue inheritance tax functions in relation to the settlement for the period.

(6) The vesting of a function in the Director under this section does not divest the Board or an officer of the Board of the function.

(7) It is immaterial whether the settlement is commenced or a charge to tax arises or a period or any part of it falls before or after the passing of this Act.

*General*

## 323[1]   Functions

(1) The general Revenue functions are such of the functions vested in the Board or in an officer of the Board as relate to any of the following matters –

(a)   income tax;

(b)   capital gains tax;

(c)   corporation tax;

(d)   national insurance contributions;

(e)   statutory sick pay;

(f)   statutory maternity pay;

(g)   statutory paternity pay;

(h)   statutory adoption pay;

(i)   student loans.

(2) The Revenue inheritance tax functions are such functions vested in the Board or in an officer of the Board as relate to inheritance tax.

(3) But the general Revenue functions and the Revenue inheritance tax functions do not include any of the following functions –

(a)   functions relating to the making of subordinate legislation (within the meaning given by section 21(1) of the Interpretation Act 1978);

(b)   the function of the prosecution of offences;

(c)   the function of authorising an officer for the purposes of section 20BA of the Taxes Management Act 1970 (orders for delivery of documents);

(d)   the function of giving information under that section;

(e)   the function of approving an officer's application for the purposes of section 20C of the Taxes Management Act 1970 (warrant to enter and search premises);

(f)   the function of applying under that section.

---

1    Information: Commencement: Not yet in force.

(4) For the purposes of this section in its application to Great Britain –

  (a) national insurance contributions are contributions payable under Part 1 of the Social Security Contributions and Benefits Act 1992;
  (b) 'statutory sick pay' must be construed in accordance with section 151(1) of that Act;
  (c) 'statutory maternity pay' must be construed in accordance with section 164(1) of that Act;
  (d) 'statutory paternity pay' must be construed in accordance with section 171ZA of that Act;
  (e) 'statutory adoption pay' must be construed in accordance with section 171ZL of that Act;
  (f) 'student loans' must be construed in accordance with the Education (Student Loans) (Repayment) Regulations 2000 (SI 2000/944).

(5) (*applies to Northern Ireland only*)

## 324[1] Exercise of Revenue functions

(1) This section applies in relation to the exercise by the Director of –

  (a) general Revenue functions;
  (b) Revenue inheritance tax functions.

(2) Paragraph (b) of section 1(6) does not apply.

(3) The Director must apply –

  (a) any interpretation of the law which has been published by the Board;
  (b) any concession which has been published by the Board and which is available generally to any person falling within its terms.

(4) The Director must also take account of any material published by the Board which does not fall within subsection (3).

(5) The Director must provide the Board with such documents and information as they consider appropriate.

(6) 'Concession' includes any practice, interpretation or other statement in the nature of a concession.

## 325[2] Declarations

(1) As soon as practicable after the appointment of a person as the Director he must make a declaration in the form set out in Schedule 8 before a member of the Board.

(2) Every member of the staff of the Agency who is authorised under section 1(6)(a) to carry out any of the functions of the Director under this Part must, as soon as practicable after being so authorised, make a declaration in the form set out in Schedule 8 before a person nominated by the Director for the purpose.

## 326[3] Interpretation

(1) Criminal conduct is conduct which –

  (a) constitutes an offence in any part of the United Kingdom, or

---

1    Information: Commencement: Not yet in force.
2    Information: Commencement: Not yet in force.
3    Information: Commencement: Not yet in force.

(b)   would constitute an offence in any part of the United Kingdom if it occurred there.

(2) But criminal conduct does not include conduct constituting an offence relating to a matter under the care and management of the Board.

(3) In applying subsection (1) it is immaterial whether conduct occurred before or after the passing of this Act.

(4) Property is criminal property if it constitutes a person's benefit from criminal conduct or it represents such a benefit (in whole or part and whether directly or indirectly); and it is immaterial –

(a)   who carried out the conduct;
(b)   who benefited from it.

(5) A person benefits from conduct if he obtains property as a result of or in connection with the conduct.

(6) If a person obtains a pecuniary advantage as a result of or in connection with conduct, he is to be taken to obtain as a result of or in connection with the conduct a sum of money equal to the value of the pecuniary advantage.

(7) References to property or a pecuniary advantage obtained in connection with conduct include references to property or a pecuniary advantage obtained in both that connection and some other.

(8) If a person benefits from conduct his benefit is the property obtained as a result of or in connection with the conduct.

(9) Property is all property wherever situated and includes –

(a)   money;
(b)   all forms of property, real or personal, heritable or moveable;
(c)   things in action and other intangible or incorporeal property.

(10) The following rules apply in relation to property –

(a)   property is obtained by a person if he obtains an interest in it;
(b)   references to an interest, in relation to land in England and Wales or Northern Ireland, are to any legal estate or equitable interest or power;
(c)   (*applies to Scotland only*)
(d)   references to an interest, in relation to property other than land, include references to a right (including a right to possession).

(11) Any reference to an officer of the Board includes a reference to –

(a)   a collector of taxes;
(b)   an inspector of taxes.

(12) Expressions used in this Part and in the Taxes Acts have the same meaning as in the Taxes Acts (within the meaning given by section 118 of the Taxes Management Act 1970).

(13) This section applies for the purposes of this Part.

## PART 7   MONEY LAUNDERING

*Offences*

### 327[1]   Concealing etc

(1) A person commits an offence if he –

    (a)   conceals criminal property;

    (b)   disguises criminal property;

    (c)   converts criminal property;

    (d)   transfers criminal property;

    (e)   removes criminal property from England and Wales or from Scotland or from Northern Ireland.

(2) But a person does not commit such an offence if –

    (a)   he makes an authorised disclosure under section 338 and (if the disclosure is made before he does the act mentioned in subsection (1)) he has the appropriate consent;

    (b)   he intended to make such a disclosure but had a reasonable excuse for not doing so;

    (c)   the act he does is done in carrying out a function he has relating to the enforcement of any provision of this Act or of any other enactment relating to criminal conduct or benefit from criminal conduct.

(3) Concealing or disguising criminal property includes concealing or disguising its nature, source, location, disposition, movement or ownership or any rights with respect to it.

### 328[2]   Arrangements

(1) A person commits an offence if he enters into or becomes concerned in an arrangement which he knows or suspects facilitates (by whatever means) the acquisition, retention, use or control of criminal property by or on behalf of another person.

(2) But a person does not commit such an offence if –

    (a)   he makes an authorised disclosure under section 338 and (if the disclosure is made before he does the act mentioned in subsection (1)) he has the appropriate consent;

    (b)   he intended to make such a disclosure but had a reasonable excuse for not doing so;

    (c)   the act he does is done in carrying out a function he has relating to the enforcement of any provision of this Act or of any other enactment relating to criminal conduct or benefit from criminal conduct.

### 329[3]   Acquisition, use and possession

(1) A person commits an offence if he –

    (a)   acquires criminal property;

    (b)   uses criminal property;

    (c)   has possession of criminal property.

(2) But a person does not commit such an offence if –

---

1     Information: Commencement: Not yet in force.

2     Information: Commencement: Not yet in force.

3     Information: Commencement: Not yet in force.

    (a)　he makes an authorised disclosure under section 338 and (if the disclosure is made before he does the act mentioned in subsection (1)) he has the appropriate consent;

    (b)　he intended to make such a disclosure but had a reasonable excuse for not doing so;

    (c)　he acquired or used or had possession of the property for adequate consideration;

    (d)　the act he does is done in carrying out a function he has relating to the enforcement of any provision of this Act or of any other enactment relating to criminal conduct or benefit from criminal conduct.

(3)　For the purposes of this section –

    (a)　a person acquires property for inadequate consideration if the value of the consideration is significantly less than the value of the property;

    (b)　a person uses or has possession of property for inadequate consideration if the value of the consideration is significantly less than the value of the use or possession;

    (c)　the provision by a person of goods or services which he knows or suspects may help another to carry out criminal conduct is not consideration.

## 330[1]　Failure to disclose: regulated sector

(1)　A person commits an offence if each of the following three conditions is satisfied.

(2)　The first condition is that he –

    (a)　knows or suspects, or

    (b)　has reasonable grounds for knowing or suspecting,

that another person is engaged in money laundering.

(3)　The second condition is that the information or other matter –

    (a)　on which his knowledge or suspicion is based, or

    (b)　which gives reasonable grounds for such knowledge or suspicion,

came to him in the course of a business in the regulated sector.

(4)　The third condition is that he does not make the required disclosure as soon as is practicable after the information or other matter comes to him.

(5)　The required disclosure is a disclosure of the information or other matter –

    (a)　to a nominated officer or a person authorised for the purposes of this Part by the Director General of the National Criminal Intelligence Service;

    (b)　in the form and manner (if any) prescribed for the purposes of this subsection by order under section 339.

(6)　But a person does not commit an offence under this section if –

    (a)　he has a reasonable excuse for not disclosing the information or other matter;

    (b)　he is a professional legal adviser and the information or other matter came to him in privileged circumstances;

    (c)　subsection (7) applies to him.

(7)　This subsection applies to a person if –

    (a)　he does not know or suspect that another person is engaged in money laundering, and

---

1　　Information: Commencement: Not yet in force.

(b)  he has not been provided by his employer with such training as is specified by the Secretary of State by order for the purposes of this section.

(8) In deciding whether a person committed an offence under this section the court must consider whether he followed any relevant guidance which was at the time concerned –

(a)  issued by a supervisory authority or any other appropriate body,
(b)  approved by the Treasury, and
(c)  published in a manner it approved as appropriate in its opinion to bring the guidance to the attention of persons likely to be affected by it.

(9) A disclosure to a nominated officer is a disclosure which –

(a)  is made to a person nominated by the alleged offender's employer to receive disclosures under this section, and
(b)  is made in the course of the alleged offender's employment and in accordance with the procedure established by the employer for the purpose.

(10) Information or other matter comes to a professional legal adviser in privileged circumstances if it is communicated or given to him –

(a)  by (or by a representative of) a client of his in connection with the giving by the adviser of legal advice to the client,
(b)  by (or by a representative of) a person seeking legal advice from the adviser, or
(c)  by a person in connection with legal proceedings or contemplated legal proceedings.

(11) But subsection (10) does not apply to information or other matter which is communicated or given with the intention of furthering a criminal purpose.

(12) Schedule 9 has effect for the purpose of determining what is –

(a)  a business in the regulated sector;
(b)  a supervisory authority.

(13) An appropriate body is any body which regulates or is representative of any trade, profession, business or employment carried on by the alleged offender.

## 331[1]   Failure to disclose: nominated officers in the regulated sector

(1) A person nominated to receive disclosures under section 330 commits an offence if the conditions in subsections (2) to (4) are satisfied.

(2) The first condition is that he –

(a)  knows or suspects, or
(b)  has reasonable grounds for knowing or suspecting,

that another person is engaged in money laundering.

(3) The second condition is that the information or other matter –

(a)  on which his knowledge or suspicion is based, or
(b)  which gives reasonable grounds for such knowledge or suspicion,

came to him in consequence of a disclosure made under section 330.

---

1    Information: Commencement: Not yet in force.

(4) The third condition is that he does not make the required disclosure as soon as is practicable after the information or other matter comes to him.

(5) The required disclosure is a disclosure of the information or other matter –

(a)   to a person authorised for the purposes of this Part by the Director General of the National Criminal Intelligence Service;

(b)   in the form and manner (if any) prescribed for the purposes of this subsection by order under section 339.

(6) But a person does not commit an offence under this section if he has a reasonable excuse for not disclosing the information or other matter.

(7) In deciding whether a person committed an offence under this section the court must consider whether he followed any relevant guidance which was at the time concerned –

(a)   issued by a supervisory authority or any other appropriate body,

(b)   approved by the Treasury, and

(c)   published in a manner it approved as appropriate in its opinion to bring the guidance to the attention of persons likely to be affected by it.

(8) Schedule 9 has effect for the purpose of determining what is a supervisory authority.

(9) An appropriate body is a body which regulates or is representative of a trade, profession, business or employment.

### 332[1]   Failure to disclose: other nominated officers

(1) A person nominated to receive disclosures under section 337 or 338 commits an offence if the conditions in subsections (2) to (4) are satisfied.

(2) The first condition is that he knows or suspects that another person is engaged in money laundering.

(3) The second condition is that the information or other matter on which his knowledge or suspicion is based came to him in consequence of a disclosure made under section 337 or 338.

(4) The third condition is that he does not make the required disclosure as soon as is practicable after the information or other matter comes to him.

(5) The required disclosure is a disclosure of the information or other matter –

(a)   to a person authorised for the purposes of this Part by the Director General of the National Criminal Intelligence Service;

(b)   in the form and manner (if any) prescribed for the purposes of this subsection by order under section 339.

(6) But a person does not commit an offence under this section if he has a reasonable excuse for not disclosing the information or other matter.

### 333[2]   Tipping off

(1) A person commits an offence if –

(a)   he knows or suspects that a disclosure falling within section 337 or 338 has been made, and

---

1     Information: Commencement: Not yet in force.
2     Information: Commencement: Not yet in force.

(b) he makes a disclosure which is likely to prejudice any investigation which might be conducted following the disclosure referred to in paragraph (a).

(2) But a person does not commit an offence under subsection (1) if –

(a) he did not know or suspect that the disclosure was likely to be prejudicial as mentioned in subsection (1);

(b) the disclosure is made in carrying out a function he has relating to the enforcement of any provision of this Act or of any other enactment relating to criminal conduct or benefit from criminal conduct;

(c) he is a professional legal adviser and the disclosure falls within subsection (3).

(3) A disclosure falls within this subsection if it is a disclosure –

(a) to (or to a representative of) a client of the professional legal adviser in connection with the giving by the adviser of legal advice to the client, or

(b) to any person in connection with legal proceedings or contemplated legal proceedings.

(4) But a disclosure does not fall within subsection (3) if it is made with the intention of furthering a criminal purpose.

## 334[1]  Penalties

(1) A person guilty of an offence under section 327, 328 or 329 is liable –

(a) on summary conviction, to imprisonment for a term not exceeding six months or to a fine not exceeding the statutory maximum or to both, or

(b) on conviction on indictment, to imprisonment for a term not exceeding 14 years or to a fine or to both.

(2) A person guilty of an offence under section 330, 331, 332 or 333 is liable –

(a) on summary conviction, to imprisonment for a term not exceeding six months or to a fine not exceeding the statutory maximum or to both, or

(b) on conviction on indictment, to imprisonment for a term not exceeding five years or to a fine or to both.

*Consent*

## 335[2]  Appropriate consent

(1) The apropriate consent is –

(a) the consent of a nominated officer to do a prohibited act if an authorised disclosure is made to the nominated officer;

(b) the consent of a constable to do a prohibited act if an authorised disclosure is made to a constable;

(c) the consent of a customs officer to do a prohibited act if an authorised disclosure is made to a customs officer.

(2) A person must be treated as having the appropriate consent if –

(a) he makes an authorised disclosure to a constable or a customs officer, and

---

1    Information: Commencement: Not yet in force.
2    Information: Commencement: Not yet in force.

(b)  the condition in subsection (3) or the condition in subsection (4) is satisfied.

(3)  The condition is that before the end of the notice period he does not receive notice from a constable or customs officer that consent to the doing of the act is refused.

(4)  The condition is that –

(a)  before the end of the notice period he receives notice from a constable or customs officer that consent to the doing of the act is refused, and
(b)  the moratorium period has expired.

(5)  The notice period is the period of seven working days starting with the first working day after the person makes the disclosure.

(6)  The moratorium period is the period of 31 days starting with the day on which the person receives notice that consent to the doing of the act is refused.

(7)  A working day is a day other than a Saturday, a Sunday, Christmas Day, Good Friday or a day which is a bank holiday under the Banking and Financial Dealings Act 1971 in the part of the United Kingdom in which the person is when he makes the disclosure.

(8)  References to a prohibited act are to an act mentioned in section 327(1), 328(1) or 329(1) (as the case may be).

(9)  A nominated officer is a person nominated to receive disclosures under section 338.

(10)  Subsections (1) to (4) apply for the purposes of this Part.

## 336[1]  Nominated officer: consent

(1)  A nominated officer must not give the appropriate consent to the doing of a prohibited act unless the condition in subsection (2), the condition in subsection (3) or the condition in subsection (4) is satisfied.

(2)  The condition is that –

(a)  he makes a disclosure that property is criminal property to a person authorised for the purposes of this Part by the Director General of the National Criminal Intelligence Service, and
(b)  such a person gives consent to the doing of the act.

(3)  The condition is that –

(a)  he makes a disclosure that property is criminal property to a person authorised for the purposes of this Part by the Director General of the National Criminal Intelligence Service, and
(b)  before the end of the notice period he does not receive notice from such a person that consent to the doing of the act is refused.

(4)  The condition is that –

(a)  he makes a disclosure that property is criminal property to a person authorised for the purposes of this Part by the Director General of the National Criminal Intelligence Service,
(b)  before the end of the notice period he receives notice from such a person that consent to the doing of the act is refused, and

---

1    Information: Commencement: Not yet in force.

(c) the moratorium period has expired.

(5) A person who is a nominated officer commits an offence if –

    (a) he gives consent to a prohibited act in circumstances where none of the conditions in subsections (2), (3) and (4) is satisfied, and

    (b) he knows or suspects that the act is a prohibited act.

(6) A person guilty of such an offence is liable –

    (a) on summary conviction, to imprisonment for a term not exceeding six months or to a fine not exceeding the statutory maximum or to both, or

    (b) on conviction on indictment, to imprisonment for a term not exceeding five years or to a fine or to both.

(7) The notice period is the period of seven working days starting with the first working day after the nominated officer makes the disclosure.

(8) The moratorium period is the period of 31 days starting with the day on which the nominated officer is given notice that consent to the doing of the act is refused.

(9) A working day is a day other than a Saturday, a Sunday, Christmas Day, Good Friday or a day which is a bank holiday under the Banking and Financial Dealings Act 1971 in the part of the United Kingdom in which the nominated officer is when he gives the appropriate consent.

(10) References to a prohibited act are to an act mentioned in section 327(1), 328(1) or 329(1) (as the case may be).

(11) A nominated officer is a person nominated to receive disclosures under section 338.

*Disclosures*

## 337[1]   **Protected disclosures**

(1) A disclosure which satisfies the following three conditions is not to be taken to breach any restriction on the disclosure of information (however imposed).

(2) The first condition is that the information or other matter disclosed came to the person making the disclosure (the discloser) in the course of his trade, profession, business or employment.

(3) The second condition is that the information or other matter –

    (a) causes the discloser to know or suspect, or

    (b) gives him reasonable grounds for knowing or suspecting,

that another person is engaged in money laundering.

(4) The third condition is that the disclosure is made to a constable, a customs officer or a nominated officer as soon as is practicable after the information or other matter comes to the discloser.

(5) A disclosure to a nominated officer is a disclosure which –

    (a) is made to a person nominated by the discloser's employer to receive disclosures under this section, and

---

1    Information: Commencement: Not yet in force.

(b)  is made in the course of the discloser's employment and in accordance with the procedure established by the employer for the purpose.

## 338[1]  Authorised disclosures

(1) For the purposes of this Part a disclosure is authorised if –

(a)  it is a disclosure to a constable, a customs officer or a nominated officer by the alleged offender that property is criminal property,
(b)  it is made in the form and manner (if any) prescribed for the purposes of this subsection by order under section 339, and
(c)  the first or second condition set out below is satisfied.

(2) The first condition is that the disclosure is made before the alleged offender does the prohibited act.

(3) The second condition is that –

(a)  the disclosure is made after the alleged offender does the prohibited act,
(b)  there is a good reason for his failure to make the disclosure before he did the act, and
(c)  the disclosure is made on his own initiative and as soon as it is practicable for him to make it.

(4) An authorised disclosure is not to be taken to breach any restriction on the disclosure of information (however imposed).

(5) A disclosure to a nominated officer is a disclosure which –

(a)  is made to a person nominated by the alleged offender's employer to receive authorised disclosures, and
(b)  is made in the course of the alleged offender's employment and in accordance with the procedure established by the employer for the purpose.

(6) References to the prohibited act are to an act mentioned in section 327(1), 328(1) or 329(1) (as the case may be).

## 339[2]  Form and manner of disclosures

(1) The Secretary of State may by order prescribe the form and manner in which a disclosure under section 330, 331, 332 or 338 must be made.

(2) An order under this section may also provide that the form may include a request to the discloser to provide additional information specified in the form.

(3) The additional information must be information which is necessary to enable the person to whom the disclosure is made to decide whether to start a money laundering investigation.

(4) A disclosure made in pursuance of a request under subsection (2) is not to be taken to breach any restriction on the disclosure of information (however imposed).

(5) The discloser is the person making a disclosure mentioned in subsection (1).

(6) Money laundering investigation must be construed in accordance with section 341(4).

(7) Subsection (2) does not apply to a disclosure made to a nominated officer.

---

1    Information: Commencement: Not yet in force.
2    Information: Commencement: Not yet in force.

*Interpretation*

## 340[1]  Interpretation

(1) This section applies for the purposes of this Part.

(2) Criminal conduct is conduct which –

   (a)  constitutes an offence in any part of the United Kingdom, or
   (b)  would constitute an offence in any part of the United Kingdom if it occurred there.

(3) Property is criminal property if –

   (a)  it constitutes a person's benefit from criminal conduct or it represents such a benefit (in whole or part and whether directly or indirectly), and
   (b)  the alleged offender knows or suspects that it constitutes or represents such a benefit.

(4) It is immaterial –

   (a)  who carried out the conduct;
   (b)  who benefited from it;
   (c)  whether the conduct occurred before or after the passing of this Act.

(5) A person benefits from conduct if he obtains property as a result of or in connection with the conduct.

(6) If a person obtains a pecuniary advantage as a result of or in connection with conduct, he is to be taken to obtain as a result of or in connection with the conduct a sum of money equal to the value of the pecuniary advantage.

(7) References to property or a pecuniary advantage obtained in connection with conduct include references to property or a pecuniary advantage obtained in both that connection and some other.

(8) If a person benefits from conduct his benefit is the property obtained as a result of or in connection with the conduct.

(9) Property is all property wherever situated and includes –

   (a)  money;
   (b)  all forms of property, real or personal, heritable or moveable;
   (c)  things in action and other intangible or incorporeal property.

(10) The following rules apply in relation to property –

   (a)  property is obtained by a person if he obtains an interest in it;
   (b)  references to an interest, in relation to land in England and Wales or Northern Ireland, are to any legal estate or equitable interest or power;
   (c)  *(applies to Scotland only)*
   (d)  references to an interest, in relation to property other than land, include references to a right (including a right to possession).

(11) Money laundering is an act which –

   (a)  constitutes an offence under section 327, 328 or 329,
   (b)  constitutes an attempt, conspiracy or incitement to commit an offence specified in paragraph (a),

---

1    Information: Commencement: Not yet in force.

    (c)   constitutes aiding, abetting, counselling or procuring the commission of an offence specified in paragraph (a), or

    (d)   would constitute an offence specified in paragraph (a), (b) or (c) if done in the United Kingdom.

(12) For the purposes of a disclosure to a nominated officer –

    (a)   references to a person's employer include any body, association or organisation (including a voluntary organisation) in connection with whose activities the person exercises a function (whether or not for gain or reward), and

    (b)   references to employment must be construed accordingly.

(13) References to a constable include references to a person authorised for the purposes of this Part by the Director General of the National Criminal Intelligence Service.

## PART 8   INVESTIGATIONS

## CHAPTER 1   INTRODUCTION

### 341[1]  Investigations

(1) For the purposes of this Part a confiscation investigation is an investigation into –

    (a)   whether a person has benefited from his criminal conduct, or

    (b)   the extent or whereabouts of his benefit from his criminal conduct.

(2) For the purposes of this Part a civil recovery investigation is an investigation into –

    (a)   whether property is recoverable property or associated property,

    (b)   who holds the property, or

    (c)   its extent or whereabouts.

(3) But an investigation is not a civil recovery investigation if –

    (a)   proceedings for a recovery order have been started in respect of the property in question,

    (b)   an interim receiving order applies to the property in question,

    (c)   an interim administration order applies to the property in question, or

    (d)   the property in question is detained under section 295.

(4) For the purposes of this Part a money laundering investigation is an investigation into whether a person has committed a money laundering offence.

### 342[2]  Offences of prejudicing investigation

(1) This section applies if a person knows or suspects that an appropriate officer or (in Scotland) a proper person is acting (or proposing to act) in connection with a confiscation investigation, a civil recovery investigation or a money laundering investigation which is being or is about to be conducted.

(2) The person commits an offence if –

    (a)   he makes a disclosure which is likely to prejudice the investigation, or

---

1    Information: Commencement: Not yet in force.
2    Information: Commencement: Not yet in force.

(b) he falsifies, conceals, destroys or otherwise disposes of, or causes or permits the falsification, concealment, destruction or disposal of, documents which are relevant to the investigation.

(3) A person does not commit an offence under subsection (2)(a) if –

(a) he does not know or suspect that the disclosure is likely to prejudice the investigation,

(b) the disclosure is made in the exercise of a function under this Act or any other enactment relating to criminal conduct or benefit from criminal conduct or in compliance with a requirement imposed under or by virtue of this Act, or

(c) he is a professional legal adviser and the disclosure falls within subsection (4).

(4) A disclosure falls within this subsection if it is a disclosure –

(a) to (or to a representative of) a client of the professional legal adviser in connection with the giving by the adviser of legal advice to the client, or

(b) to any person in connection with legal proceedings or contemplated legal proceedings.

(5) But a disclosure does not fall within subsection (4) if it is made with the intention of furthering a criminal purpose.

(6) A person does not commit an offence under subsection (2)(b) if –

(a) he does not know or suspect that the documents are relevant to the investigation, or

(b) he does not intend to conceal any facts disclosed by the documents from any appropriate officer or (in Scotland) proper person carrying out the investigation.

(7) A person guilty of an offence under subsection (2) is liable –

(a) on summary conviction, to imprisonment for a term not exceeding six months or to a fine not exceeding the statutory maximum or to both, or

(b) on conviction on indictment, to imprisonment for a term not exceeding five years or to a fine or to both.

(8) For the purposes of this section –

(a) 'appropriate officer' must be construed in accordance with section 378;

(b) 'proper person' must be construed in accordance with section 412.

## CHAPTER 2    ENGLAND AND WALES AND NORTHERN IRELAND

### *Judges and courts*

### 343[1]  **Judges**

(1) In this Chapter references to a judge in relation to an application must be construed in accordance with this section.

(2) In relation to an application for the purposes of a confiscation investigation or a money laundering investigation a judge is –

(a) in England and Wales, a judge entitled to exercise the jurisdiction of the Crown Court;

(b) *(applies to Northern Ireland only)*

(3) In relation to an application for the purposes of a civil recovery investigation a judge is a judge of the High Court.

---

1    Information: Commencement: Not yet in force.

## 344[1]   Courts

In this Chapter references to the court are to –

    (a)  the Crown Court, in relation to an order for the purposes of a confiscation investigation or a money laundering investigation;

    (b)  the High Court, in relation to an order for the purposes of a civil recovery investigation.

*Production orders*

## 345[2]   Production orders

(1) A judge may, on an application made to him by an appropriate officer, make a production order if he is satisfied that each of the requirements for the making of the order is fulfilled.

(2) The application for a production order must state that –

    (a)  a person specified in the application is subject to a confiscation investigation or a money laundering investigation, or

    (b)  property specified in the application is subject to a civil recovery investigation.

(3) The application must also state that –

    (a)  the order is sought for the purposes of the investigation;

    (b)  the order is sought in relation to material, or material of a description, specified in the application;

    (c)  a person specified in the application appears to be in possession or control of the material.

(4) A production order is an order either –

    (a)  requiring the person the application for the order specifies as appearing to be in possession or control of material to produce it to an appropriate officer for him to take away, or

    (b)  requiring that person to give an appropriate officer access to the material,

within the period stated in the order.

(5) The period stated in a production order must be a period of seven days beginning with the day on which the order is made, unless it appears to the judge by whom the order is made that a longer or shorter period would be appropriate in the particular circumstances.

## 346[3]   Requirements for making of production order

(1) These are the requirements for the making of a production order.

(2) There must be reasonable grounds for suspecting that –

    (a)  in the case of a confiscation investigation, the person the application for the order specifies as being subject to the investigation has benefited from his criminal conduct;

    (b)  in the case of a civil recovery investigation, the property the application for the order specifies as being subject to the investigation is recoverable property or associated property;

---

1    Information: Commencement: Not yet in force.
2    Information: Commencement: Not yet in force.
3    Information: Commencement: Not yet in force.

(c) in the case of a money laundering investigation, the person the application for the order specifies as being subject to the investigation has committed a money laundering offence.

(3) There must be reasonable grounds for believing that the person the application specifies as appearing to be in possession or control of the material so specified is in possession or control of it.

(4) There must be reasonable grounds for believing that the material is likely to be of substantial value (whether or not by itself) to the investigation for the purposes of which the order is sought.

(5) There must be reasonable grounds for believing that it is in the public interest for the material to be produced or for access to it to be given, having regard to –

(a) the benefit likely to accrue to the investigation if the material is obtained;
(b) the circumstances under which the person the application specifies as appearing to be in possession or control of the material holds it.

## 347[1]  Order to grant entry

(1) This section applies if a judge makes a production order requiring a person to give an appropriate officer access to material on any premises.

(2) The judge may, on an application made to him by an appropriate officer and specifying the premises, make an order to grant entry in relation to the premises.

(3) An order to grant entry is an order requiring any person who appears to an appropriate officer to be entitled to grant entry to the premises to allow him to enter the premises to obtain access to the material.

## 348[2]  Further provisions

(1) A production order does not require a person to produce, or give access to, privileged material.

(2) Privileged material is any material which the person would be entitled to refuse to produce on grounds of legal professional privilege in proceedings in the High Court.

(3) A production order does not require a person to produce, or give access to, excluded material.

(4) A production order has effect in spite of any restriction on the disclosure of information (however imposed).

(5) An appropriate officer may take copies of any material which is produced, or to which access is given, in compliance with a production order.

(6) Material produced in compliance with a production order may be retained for so long as it is necessary to retain it (as opposed to copies of it) in connection with the investigation for the purposes of which the order was made.

(7) But if an appropriate officer has reasonable grounds for believing that –

(a) the material may need to be produced for the purposes of any legal proceedings, and
(b) it might otherwise be unavailable for those purposes,

it may be retained until the proceedings are concluded.

---

1    Information: Commencement: Not yet in force.
2    Information: Commencement: Not yet in force.

## 349[1]   Computer information

(1) This section applies if any of the material specified in an application for a production order consists of information contained in a computer.

(2) If the order is an order requiring a person to produce the material to an appropriate officer for him to take away, it has effect as an order to produce the material in a form in which it can be taken away by him and in which it is visible and legible.

(3) If the order is an order requiring a person to give an appropriate officer access to the material, it has effect as an order to give him access to the material in a form in which it is visible and legible.

## 350[2]   Government departments

(1) A production order may be made in relation to material in the possession or control of an authorised government department.

(2) An order so made may require any officer of the department (whether named in the order or not) who may for the time being be in possession or control of the material to comply with it.

(3) An order containing such a requirement must be served as if the proceedings were civil proceedings against the department.

(4) If an order contains such a requirement –

  (a)   the person on whom it is served must take all reasonable steps to bring it to the attention of the officer concerned;
  (b)   any other officer of the department who is in receipt of the order must also take all reasonable steps to bring it to the attention of the officer concerned.

(5) If the order is not brought to the attention of the officer concerned within the period stated in the order (in pursuance of section 345(4)) the person on whom it is served must report the reasons for the failure to –

  (a)   a judge entitled to exercise the jurisdiction of the Crown Court or (in Northern Ireland) a Crown Court judge, in the case of an order made for the purposes of a confiscation investigation or a money laundering investigation;
  (b)   a High Court judge, in the case of an order made for the purposes of a civil recovery investigation.

(6) An authorised government department is a government department, or a Northern Ireland department, which is an authorised department for the purposes of the Crown Proceedings Act 1947.

## 351[3]   Supplementary

(1) An application for a production order or an order to grant entry may be made ex parte to a judge in chambers.

(2) Rules of court may make provision as to the practice and procedure to be followed in connection with proceedings relating to production orders and orders to grant entry.

(3) An application to discharge or vary a production order or an order to grant entry may be made to the court by –

---

1      Information: Commencement: Not yet in force.
2      Information: Commencement: Not yet in force.
3      Information: Commencement: Not yet in force.

(a) the person who applied for the order;

(b) any person affected by the order.

(4) The court –

(a) may discharge the order;

(b) may vary the order.

(5) If an accredited financial investigator, a constable or a customs officer applies for a production order or an order to grant entry, an application to discharge or vary the order need not be by the same accredited financial investigator, constable or customs officer.

(6) References to a person who applied for a production order or an order to grant entry must be construed accordingly.

(7) Production orders and orders to grant entry have effect as if they were orders of the court.

(8) Subsections (2) to (7) do not apply to orders made in England and Wales for the purposes of a civil recovery investigation.

*Search and seizure warrants*

## 352[1] Search and seizure warrants

(1) A judge may, on an application made to him by an appropriate officer, issue a search and seizure warrant if he is satisfied that either of the requirements for the issuing of the warrant is fulfilled.

(2) The application for a search and seizure warrant must state that –

(a) a person specified in the application is subject to a confiscation investigation or a money laundering investigation, or

(b) property specified in the application is subject to a civil recovery investigation.

(3) The application must also state –

(a) that the warrant is sought for the purposes of the investigation;

(b) that the warrant is sought in relation to the premises specified in the application;

(c) that the warrant is sought in relation to material specified in the application, or that there are reasonable grounds for believing that there is material falling within section 353(6), (7) or (8) on the premises.

(4) A search and seizure warrant is a warrant authorising an appropriate person –

(a) to enter and search the premises specified in the application for the warrant, and

(b) to seize and retain any material found there which is likely to be of substantial value (whether or not by itself) to the investigation for the purposes of which the application is made.

(5) An appropriate person is –

(a) a constable or a customs officer, if the warrant is sought for the purposes of a confiscation investigation or a money laundering investigation;

(b) a named member of the staff of the Agency, if the warrant is sought for the purposes of a civil recovery investigation.

---

1 Information: Commencement: Not yet in force.

(6)  The requirements for the issue of a search and seizure warrant are –

    (a)   that a production order made in relation to material has not been complied with and there are reasonable grounds for believing that the material is on the premises specified in the application for the warrant, or

    (b)   that section 353 is satisfied in relation to the warrant.

## 353[1]   Requirements where production order not available

(1)  This section is satisfied in relation to a search and seizure warrant if –

    (a)   subsection (2) applies, and

    (b)   either the first or the second set of conditions is complied with.

(2)  This subsection applies if there are reasonable grounds for suspecting that –

    (a)   in the case of a confiscation investigation, the person specified in the application for the warrant has benefited from his criminal conduct;

    (b)   in the case of a civil recovery investigation, the property specified in the application for the warrant is recoverable property or associated property;

    (c)   in the case of a money laundering investigation, the person specified in the application for the warrant has committed a money laundering offence.

(3)  The first set of conditions is that there are reasonable grounds for believing that –

    (a)   any material on the premises specified in the application for the warrant is likely to be of substantial value (whether or not by itself) to the investigation for the purposes of which the warrant is sought,

    (b)   it is in the public interest for the material to be obtained, having regard to the benefit likely to accrue to the investigation if the material is obtained, and

    (c)   it would not be appropriate to make a production order for any one or more of the reasons in subsection (4).

(4)  The reasons are –

    (a)   that it is not practicable to communicate with any person against whom the production order could be made;

    (b)   that it is not practicable to communicate with any person who would be required to comply with an order to grant entry to the premises;

    (c)   that the investigation might be seriously prejudiced unless an appropriate person is able to secure immediate access to the material.

(5)  The second set of conditions is that –

    (a)   there are reasonable grounds for believing that there is material on the premises specified in the application for the warrant and that the material falls within subsection (6), (7) or (8),

    (b)   there are reasonable grounds for believing that it is in the public interest for the material to be obtained, having regard to the benefit likely to accrue to the investigation if the material is obtained, and

    (c)   any one or more of the requirements in subsection (9) is met.

(6)  In the case of a confiscation investigation, material falls within this subsection if it cannot be identified at the time of the application but it –

---

1    Information: Commencement: Not yet in force.

(a) relates to the person specified in the application, the question whether he has benefited from his criminal conduct or any question as to the extent or whereabouts of his benefit from his criminal conduct, and

(b) is likely to be of substantial value (whether or not by itself) to the investigation for the purposes of which the warrant is sought.

(7) In the case of a civil recovery investigation, material falls within this subsection if it cannot be identified at the time of the application but it –

(a) relates to the property specified in the application, the question whether it is recoverable property or associated property, the question as to who holds any such property, any question as to whether the person who appears to hold any such property holds other property which is recoverable property, or any question as to the extent or whereabouts of any property mentioned in this paragraph, and

(b) is likely to be of substantial value (whether or not by itself) to the investigation for the purposes of which the warrant is sought.

(8) In the case of a money laundering investigation, material falls within this subsection if it cannot be identified at the time of the application but it –

(a) relates to the person specified in the application or the question whether he has committed a money laundering offence, and

(b) is likely to be of substantial value (whether or not by itself) to the investigation for the purposes of which the warrant is sought.

(9) The requirements are –

(a) that it is not practicable to communicate with any person entitled to grant entry to the premises;

(b) that entry to the premises will not be granted unless a warrant is produced;

(c) that the investigation might be seriously prejudiced unless an appropriate person arriving at the premises is able to secure immediate entry to them.

(10) An appropriate person is –

(a) a constable or a customs officer, if the warrant is sought for the purposes of a confiscation investigation or a money laundering investigation;

(b) a member of the staff of the Agency, if the warrant is sought for the purposes of a civil recovery investigation.

## 354[1]   Further provisions: general

(1) A search and seizure warrant does not confer the right to seize privileged material.

(2) Privileged material is any material which a person would be entitled to refuse to produce on grounds of legal professional privilege in proceedings in the High Court.

(3) A search and seizure warrant does not confer the right to seize excluded material.

## 355[2]   Further provisions: confiscation and money laundering

(1) This section applies to –

(a) search and seizure warrants sought for the purposes of a confiscation investigation or a money laundering investigation, and

---

1    Information: Commencement: Not yet in force.
2    Information: Commencement: Not yet in force.

(b)   powers of seizure under them.

(2) In relation to such warrants and powers, the Secretary of State may make an order which applies the provisions to which subsections (3) and (4) apply subject to any specified modifications.

(3) This subsection applies to the following provisions of the Police and Criminal Evidence Act 1984 –

(a)   section 15 (search warrants – safeguards);
(b)   section 16 (execution of warrants);
(c)   section 21 (access and copying);
(d)   section 22 (retention).

(4) This subsection applies to the following provisions of the Police and Criminal Evidence (Northern Ireland) Order 1989 (SI 1989/1341 (NI 12)) –

(a)   Article 17 (search warrants – safeguards);
(b)   Article 18 (execution of warrants);
(c)   Article 23 (access and copying);
(d)   Article 24 (retention).

## 356[1]   Further provisions: civil recovery

(1) This section applies to search and seizure warrants sought for the purposes of civil recovery investigations.

(2) An application for a warrant may be made ex parte to a judge in chambers.

(3) A warrant may be issued subject to conditions.

(4) A warrant continues in force until the end of the period of one month starting with the day on which it is issued.

(5) A warrant authorises the person it names to require any information which is held in a computer and is accessible from the premises specified in the application for the warrant, and which the named person believes relates to any matter relevant to the investigation, to be produced in a form –

(a)   in which it can be taken away, and
(b)   in which it is visible and legible.

(6) If –

(a)   the Director gives written authority for members of staff of the Agency to accompany the person a warrant names when executing it, and
(b)   a warrant is issued,

the authorised members have the same powers under it as the person it names.

(7) A warrant may include provision authorising a person who is exercising powers under it to do other things which –

(a)   are specified in the warrant, and
(b)   need to be done in order to give effect to it.

---

1    Information: Commencement: Not yet in force.

(8) Copies may be taken of any material seized under a warrant.

(9) Material seized under a warrant may be retained for so long as it is necessary to retain it (as opposed to copies of it) in connection with the investigation for the purposes of which the warrant was issued.

(10) But if the Director has reasonable grounds for believing that –

(a) the material may need to be produced for the purposes of any legal proceedings, and
(b) it might otherwise be unavailable for those purposes,

it may be retained until the proceedings are concluded.

*Disclosure orders*

## 357[1]  Disclosure orders

(1) A judge may, on an application made to him by the Director, make a disclosure order if he is satisfied that each of the requirements for the making of the order is fulfilled.

(2) No application for a disclosure order may be made in relation to a money laundering investigation.

(3) The application for a disclosure order must state that –

(a) a person specified in the application is subject to a confiscation investigation which is being carried out by the Director and the order is sought for the purposes of the investigation, or
(b) property specified in the application is subject to a civil recovery investigation and the order is sought for the purposes of the investigation.

(4) A disclosure order is an order authorising the Director to give to any person the Director considers has relevant information notice in writing requiring him to do, with respect to any matter relevant to the investigation for the purposes of which the order is sought, any or all of the following –

(a) answer questions, either at a time specified in the notice or at once, at a place so specified;
(b) provide information specified in the notice, by a time and in a manner so specified;
(c) produce documents, or documents of a description, specified in the notice, either at or by a time so specified or at once, and in a manner so specified.

(5) Relevant information is information (whether or not contained in a document) which the Director considers to be relevant to the investigation.

(6) A person is not bound to comply with a requirement imposed by a notice given under a disclosure order unless evidence of authority to give the notice is produced to him.

## 358[2]  Requirements for making of disclosure order

(1) These are the requirements for the making of a disclosure order.

(2) There must be reasonable grounds for suspecting that –

(a) in the case of a confiscation investigation, the person specified in the application for the order has benefited from his criminal conduct;

---

1  Information: Commencement: Not yet in force.
2  Information: Commencement: Not yet in force.

(b)  in the case of a civil recovery investigation, the property specified in the application for the order is recoverable property or associated property.

(3) There must be reasonable grounds for believing that information which may be provided in compliance with a requirement imposed under the order is likely to be of substantial value (whether or not by itself) to the investigation for the purposes of which the order is sought.

(4) There must be reasonable grounds for believing that it is in the public interest for the information to be provided, having regard to the benefit likely to accrue to the investigation if the information is obtained.

## 359[1]  Offences

(1) A person commits an offence if without reasonable excuse he fails to comply with a requirement imposed on him under a disclosure order.

(2) A person guilty of an offence under subsection (1) is liable on summary conviction to –

(a)  imprisonment for a term not exceeding six months,
(b)  a fine not exceeding level 5 on the standard scale, or
(c)  both.

(3) A person commits an offence if, in purported compliance with a requirement imposed on him under a disclosure order, he –

(a)  makes a statement which he knows to be false or misleading in a material particular, or
(b)  recklessly makes a statement which is false or misleading in a material particular.

(4) A person guilty of an offence under subsection (3) is liable –

(a)  on summary conviction, to imprisonment for a term not exceeding six months or to a fine not exceeding the statutory maximum or to both, or
(b)  on conviction on indictment, to imprisonment for a term not exceeding two years or to a fine or to both.

## 360[2]  Statements

(1) A statement made by a person in response to a requirement imposed on him under a disclosure order may not be used in evidence against him in criminal proceedings.

(2) But subsection (1) does not apply –

(a)  in the case of proceedings under Part 2 or 4,
(b)  on a prosecution for an offence under section 359(1) or (3),
(c)  on a prosecution for an offence under section 5 of the Perjury Act 1911 or Article 10 of the Perjury (Northern Ireland) Order 1979 (SI 1979/1714 (NI 19)) (false statements), or
(d)  on a prosecution for some other offence where, in giving evidence, the person makes a statement inconsistent with the statement mentioned in subsection (1).

(3) A statement may not be used by virtue of subsection (2)(d) against a person unless –

(a)  evidence relating to it is adduced, or

---

1     Information: Commencement: Not yet in force.
2     Information: Commencement: Not yet in force.

(b) a question relating to it is asked,

by him or on his behalf in the proceedings arising out of the prosecution.

## 361[1]  Further provisions

(1) A disclosure order does not confer the right to require a person to answer any privileged question, provide any privileged information or produce any privileged document, except that a lawyer may be required to provide the name and address of a client of his.

(2) A privileged question is a question which the person would be entitled to refuse to answer on grounds of legal professional privilege in proceedings in the High Court.

(3) Privileged information is any information which the person would be entitled to refuse to provide on grounds of legal professional privilege in proceedings in the High Court.

(4) Privileged material is any material which the person would be entitled to refuse to produce on grounds of legal professional privilege in proceedings in the High Court.

(5) A disclosure order does not confer the right to require a person to produce excluded material.

(6) A disclosure order has effect in spite of any restriction on the disclosure of information (however imposed).

(7) The Director may take copies of any documents produced in compliance with a requirement to produce them which is imposed under a disclosure order.

(8) Documents so produced may be retained for so long as it is necessary to retain them (as opposed to a copy of them) in connection with the investigation for the purposes of which the order was made.

(9) But if the Director has reasonable grounds for believing that –

(a)  the documents may need to be produced for the purposes of any legal proceedings, and
(b)  they might otherwise be unavailable for those purposes,

they may be retained until the proceedings are concluded.

## 362[2]  Supplementary

(1) An application for a disclosure order may be made ex parte to a judge in chambers.

(2) Rules of court may make provision as to the practice and procedure to be followed in connection with proceedings relating to disclosure orders.

(3) An application to discharge or vary a disclosure order may be made to the court by –

(a)  the Director;
(b)  any person affected by the order.

(4) The court –

(a)  may discharge the order;
(b)  may vary the order.

(5) Subsections (2) to (4) do not apply to orders made in England and Wales for the purposes of a civil recovery investigation.

---

1    Information: Commencement: Not yet in force.
2    Information: Commencement: Not yet in force.

*Customer information orders*

## 363[1] Customer information orders

(1) A judge may, on an application made to him by an appropriate officer, make a customer information order if he is satisfied that each of the requirements for the making of the order is fulfilled.

(2) The application for a customer information order must state that –

    (a) a person specified in the application is subject to a confiscation investigation or a money laundering investigation, or

    (b) property specified in the application is subject to a civil recovery investigation and a person specified in the application appears to hold the property.

(3) The application must also state that –

    (a) the order is sought for the purposes of the investigation;

    (b) the order is sought against the financial institution or financial institutions specified in the application.

(4) An application for a customer information order may specify –

    (a) all financial institutions,

    (b) a particular description, or particular descriptions, of financial institutions, or

    (c) a particular financial institution or particular financial institutions.

(5) A customer information order is an order that a financial institution covered by the application for the order must, on being required to do so by notice in writing given by an appropriate officer, provide any such customer information as it has relating to the person specified in the application.

(6) A financial institution which is required to provide information under a customer information order must provide the information to an appropriate officer in such manner, and at or by such time, as an appropriate officer requires.

(7) If a financial institution on which a requirement is imposed by a notice given under a customer information order requires the production of evidence of authority to give the notice, it is not bound to comply with the requirement unless evidence of the authority has been produced to it.

## 364[2] Meaning of customer information

(1) 'Customer information', in relation to a person and a financial institution, is information whether the person holds, or has held, an account or accounts at the financial institution (whether solely or jointly with another) and (if so) information as to –

    (a) the matters specified in subsection (2) if the person is an individual;

    (b) the matters specified in subsection (3) if the person is a company or limited liability partnership or a similar body incorporated or otherwise established outside the United Kingdom.

(2) The matters referred to in subsection (1)(a) are –

    (a) the account number or numbers;

    (b) the person's full name;

---

1    Information: Commencement: Not yet in force.
2    Information: Commencement: Not yet in force.

(c) his date of birth;

(d) his most recent address and any previous addresses;

(e) the date or dates on which he began to hold the account or accounts and, if he has ceased to hold the account or any of the accounts, the date or dates on which he did so;

(f) such evidence of his identity as was obtained by the financial institution under or for the purposes of any legislation relating to money laundering;

(g) the full name, date of birth and most recent address, and any previous addresses, of any person who holds, or has held, an account at the financial institution jointly with him;

(h) the account number or numbers of any other account or accounts held at the financial institution to which he is a signatory and details of the person holding the other account or accounts.

(3) The matters referred to in subsection (1)(b) are –

(a) the account number or numbers;

(b) the person's full name;

(c) a description of any business which the person carries on;

(d) the country or territory in which it is incorporated or otherwise established and any number allocated to it under the Companies Act 1985 or the Companies (Northern Ireland) Order 1986 (SI 1986/ 1032 (NI 6)) or corresponding legislation of any country or territory outside the United Kingdom;

(e) any number assigned to it for the purposes of value added tax in the United Kingdom;

(f) its registered office, and any previous registered offices, under the Companies Act 1985 or the Companies (Northern Ireland) Order 1986 (SI 1986/1032 (NI 6)) or anything similar under corresponding legislation of any country or territory outside the United Kingdom;

(g) its registered office, and any previous registered offices, under the Limited Liability Partnerships Act 2000 or anything similar under corresponding legislation of any country or territory outside Great Britain;

(h) the date or dates on which it began to hold the account or accounts and, if it has ceased to hold the account or any of the accounts, the date or dates on which it did so;

(i) such evidence of its identity as was obtained by the financial institution under or for the purposes of any legislation relating to money laundering;

(j) the full name, date of birth and most recent address and any previous addresses of any person who is a signatory to the account or any of the accounts.

(4) The Secretary of State may by order provide for information of a description specified in the order –

(a) to be customer information, or

(b) no longer to be customer information.

(5) Money laundering is an act which –

(a) constitutes an offence under section 327, 328 or 329 of this Act or section 18 of the Terrorism Act 2000, or

(b) would constitute an offence specified in paragraph (a) if done in the United Kingdom.

## 365[1] Requirements for making of customer information order

(1) These are the requirements for the making of a customer information order.

(2) In the case of a confiscation investigation, there must be reasonable grounds for suspecting that the person specified in the application for the order has benefited from his criminal conduct.

---

1    Information: Commencement: Not yet in force.

(3) In the case of a civil recovery investigation, there must be reasonable grounds for suspecting that –

    (a)   the property specified in the application for the order is recoverable property or associated property;
    (b)   the person specified in the application holds all or some of the property.

(4) In the case of a money laundering investigation, there must be reasonable grounds for suspecting that the person specified in the application for the order has committed a money laundering offence.

(5) In the case of any investigation, there must be reasonable grounds for believing that customer information which may be provided in compliance with the order is likely to be of substantial value (whether or not by itself) to the investigation for the purposes of which the order is sought.

(6) In the case of any investigation, there must be reasonable grounds for believing that it is in the public interest for the customer information to be provided, having regard to the benefit likely to accrue to the investigation if the information is obtained.

## 366[1]  Offences

(1) A financial institution commits an offence if without reasonable excuse it fails to comply with a requirement imposed on it under a customer information order.

(2) A financial institution guilty of an offence under subsection (1) is liable on summary conviction to a fine not exceeding level 5 on the standard scale.

(3) A financial institution commits an offence if, in purported compliance with a customer information order, it –

    (a)   makes a statement which it knows to be false or misleading in a material particular, or
    (b)   recklessly makes a statement which is false or misleading in a material particular.

(4) A financial institution guilty of an offence under subsection (3) is liable –

    (a)   on summary conviction, to a fine not exceeding the statutory maximum, or
    (b)   on conviction on indictment, to a fine.

## 367[2]  Statements

(1) A statement made by a financial institution in response to a customer information order may not be used in evidence against it in criminal proceedings.

(2) But subsection (1) does not apply –

    (a)   in the case of proceedings under Part 2 or 4,
    (b)   on a prosecution for an offence under section 366(1) or (3), or
    (c)   on a prosecution for some other offence where, in giving evidence, the financial institution makes a statement inconsistent with the statement mentioned in subsection (1).

(3) A statement may not be used by virtue of subsection (2)(c) against a financial institution unless –

---

1    Information: Commencement: Not yet in force.
2    Information: Commencement: Not yet in force.

    (a)  evidence relating to it is adduced, or

    (b)  a question relating to it is asked,

by or on behalf of the financial institution in the proceedings arising out of the prosecution.

## 368[1]  Disclosure of information

A customer information order has effect in spite of any restriction on the disclosure of information (however imposed).

## 369[2]  Supplementary

(1) An application for a customer information order may be made ex parte to a judge in chambers.

(2) Rules of court may make provision as to the practice and procedure to be followed in connection with proceedings relating to customer information orders.

(3) An application to discharge or vary a customer information order may be made to the court by –

    (a)  the person who applied for the order;

    (b)  any person affected by the order.

(4) The court –

    (a)  may discharge the order;

    (b)  may vary the order.

(5) If an accredited financial investigator, a constable or a customs officer applies for a customer information order, an application to discharge or vary the order need not be by the same accredited financial investigator, constable or customs officer.

(6) References to a person who applied for a customer information order must be construed accordingly.

(7) An accredited financial investigator, a constable or a customs officer may not make an application for a customer information order or an application to vary such an order unless he is a senior appropriate officer or he is authorised to do so by a senior appropriate officer.

(8) Subsections (2) to (6) do not apply to orders made in England and Wales for the purposes of a civil recovery investigation.

*Account monitoring orders*

## 370[3]  Account monitoring orders

(1) A judge may, on an application made to him by an appropriate officer, make an account monitoring order if he is satisfied that each of the requirements for the making of the order is fulfilled.

(2) The application for an account monitoring order must state that –

---

1    Information: Commencement: Not yet in force.
2    Information: Commencement: Not yet in force.
3    Information: Commencement: Not yet in force.

(a) a person specified in the application is subject to a confiscation investigation or a money laundering investigation, or

(b) property specified in the application is subject to a civil recovery investigation and a person specified in the application appears to hold the property.

(3) The application must also state that –

(a) the order is sought for the purposes of the investigation;

(b) the order is sought against the financial institution specified in the application in relation to account information of the description so specified.

(4) Account information is information relating to an account or accounts held at the financial institution specified in the application by the person so specified (whether solely or jointly with another).

(5) The application for an account monitoring order may specify information relating to –

(a) all accounts held by the person specified in the application for the order at the financial institution so specified,

(b) a particular description, or particular descriptions, of accounts so held, or

(c) a particular account, or particular accounts, so held.

(6) An account monitoring order is an order that the financial institution specified in the application for the order must, for the period stated in the order, provide account information of the description specified in the order to an appropriate officer in the manner, and at or by the time or times, stated in the order.

(7) The period stated in an account monitoring order must not exceed the period of 90 days beginning with the day on which the order is made.

## 371[1] Requirements for making of account monitoring order

(1) These are the requirements for the making of an account monitoring order.

(2) In the case of a confiscation investigation, there must be reasonable grounds for suspecting that the person specified in the application for the order has benefited from his criminal conduct.

(3) In the case of a civil recovery investigation, there must be reasonable grounds for suspecting that –

(a) the property specified in the application for the order is recoverable property or associated property;

(b) the person specified in the application holds all or some of the property.

(4) In the case of a money laundering investigation, there must be reasonable grounds for suspecting that the person specified in the application for the order has committed a money laundering offence.

(5) In the case of any investigation, there must be reasonable grounds for believing that account information which may be provided in compliance with the order is likely to be of substantial value (whether or not by itself) to the investigation for the purposes of which the order is sought.

(6) In the case of any investigation, there must be reasonable grounds for believing that it is in the public interest for the account information to be provided, having regard to the benefit likely to accrue to the investigation if the information is obtained.

---

1    Information: Commencement: Not yet in force.

## 372[1]  Statements

(1) A statement made by a financial institution in response to an account monitoring order may not be used in evidence against it in criminal proceedings.

(2) But subsection (1) does not apply –

  (a)  in the case of proceedings under Part 2 or 4,
  (b)  in the case of proceedings for contempt of court, or
  (c)  on a prosecution for an offence where, in giving evidence, the financial institution makes a statement inconsistent with the statement mentioned in subsection (1).

(3) A statement may not be used by virtue of subsection (2)(c) against a financial institution unless –

  (a)  evidence relating to it is adduced, or
  (b)  a question relating to it is asked,

by or on behalf of the financial institution in the proceedings arising out of the prosecution.

## 373[2]  Applications

An application for an account monitoring order may be made ex parte to a judge in chambers.

## 374[3]  Disclosure of information

An account monitoring order has effect in spite of any restriction on the disclosure of information (however imposed).

## 375[4]  Supplementary

(1) Rules of court may make provision as to the practice and procedure to be followed in connection with proceedings relating to account monitoring orders.

(2) An application to discharge or vary an account monitoring order may be made to the court by –

  (a)  the person who applied for the order;
  (b)  any person affected by the order.

(3) The court –

  (a)  may discharge the order;
  (b)  may vary the order.

(4) If an accredited financial investigator, a constable or a customs officer applies for an account monitoring order, an application to discharge or vary the order need not be by the same accredited financial investigator, constable or customs officer.

(5) References to a person who applied for an account monitoring order must be construed accordingly.

(6) Account monitoring orders have effect as if they were orders of the court.

(7) This section does not apply to orders made in England and Wales for the purposes of a civil recovery investigation.

---

1    Information: Commencement: Not yet in force.
2    Information: Commencement: Not yet in force.
3    Information: Commencement: Not yet in force.
4    Information: Commencement: Not yet in force.

*Evidence overseas*

## 376[1]   Evidence overseas

(1) This section applies if the Director is carrying out a confiscation investigation.

(2) A judge on the application of the Director or a person subject to the investigation may issue a letter of request if he thinks that there is evidence in a country or territory outside the United Kingdom –

   (a)  that such a person has benefited from his criminal conduct, or
   (b)  of the extent or whereabouts of that person's benefit from his criminal conduct.

(3) The Director may issue a letter of request if he thinks that there is evidence in a country or territory outside the United Kingdom –

   (a)  that a person subject to the investigation has benefited from his criminal conduct, or
   (b)  of the extent or whereabouts of that person's benefit from his criminal conduct.

(4) A letter of request is a letter requesting assistance in obtaining outside the United Kingdom such evidence as is specified in the letter for use in the investigation.

(5) The person issuing a letter of request must send it to the Secretary of State.

(6) If the Secretary of State believes it is appropriate to do so he may forward a letter received under subsection (5) –

   (a)  to a court or tribunal which is specified in the letter and which exercises jurisdiction in the place where the evidence is to be obtained, or
   (b)  to an authority recognised by the government of the country or territory concerned as the appropriate authority for receiving letters of request.

(7) But in a case of urgency the person issuing the letter of request may send it directly to the court or tribunal mentioned in subsection (6)(a).

(8) Evidence obtained in pursuance of a letter of request must not be used –

   (a)  by any person other than the Director or a person subject to the investigation;
   (b)  for any purpose other than that for which it is obtained.

(9) Subsection (8) does not apply if the authority mentioned in subsection (6)(b) consents to the use.

(10) Evidence includes documents and other articles.

(11) Rules of court may make provision as to the practice and procedure to be followed in connection with proceedings relating to the issue of letters of request by a judge under this section.

*Code of practice*

## 377[2]   Code of practice

(1) The Secretary of State must prepare a code of practice as to the exercise by all of the following of functions they have under this Chapter –

   (a)  the Director;

---

1    Information: Commencement: Not yet in force.
2    Information: Commencement: Not yet in force.

(b)  members of the staff of the Agency;
(c)  accredited financial investigators;
(d)  constables;
(e)  customs officers.

(2) After preparing a draft of the code the Secretary of State –

(a)  must publish the draft;
(b)  must consider any representations made to him about the draft;
(c)  may amend the draft accordingly.

(3) After the Secretary of State has proceeded under subsection (2) he must lay the code before Parliament.

(4) When he has done so the Secretary of State may bring the code into operation on such day as he may appoint by order.

(5) A person specified in subsection (1)(a) to (e) must comply with a code of practice which is in operation under this section in the exercise of any function he has under this Chapter.

(6) If such a person fails to comply with any provision of such a code of practice he is not by reason only of that failure liable in any criminal or civil proceedings.

(7) But the code of practice is admissible in evidence in such proceedings and a court may take account of any failure to comply with its provisions in determining any question in the proceedings.

(8) The Secretary of State may from time to time revise a code previously brought into operation under this section; and the preceding provisions of this section apply to a revised code as they apply to the code as first prepared.

(9) The following provisions do not apply to an appropriate officer in the exercise of any function he has under this Chapter –

(a)  section 67(9) of the Police and Criminal Evidence Act 1984 (application of codes of practice under that Act to persons other than police officers);
(b)  Article 66(8) of the Police and Criminal Evidence (Northern Ireland) Order 1989 (SI 1989/1341 (NI 12)) (which makes similar provision for Northern Ireland).

*Interpretation*

## 378[1]  Officers

(1) In relation to a confiscation investigation these are appropriate officers –

(a)  the Director;
(b)  an accredited financial investigator;
(c)  a constable;
(d)  a customs officer.

(2) In relation to a confiscation investigation these are senior appropriate officers –

(a)  the Director;
(b)  a police officer who is not below the rank of superintendent;

---

1    Information: Commencement: Not yet in force.

    (c)   a customs officer who is not below such grade as is designated by the Commissioners of Customs and Excise as equivalent to that rank;

    (d)   an accredited financial investigator who falls within a description specified in an order made for the purposes of this paragraph by the Secretary of State under section 453.

(3) In relation to a civil recovery investigation the Director (and only the Director) is –

    (a)   an appropriate officer;

    (b)   a senior appropriate officer.

(4) In relation to a money laundering investigation these are appropriate officers –

    (a)   an accredited financial investigator;

    (b)   a constable;

    (c)   a customs officer.

(5) For the purposes of section 342, in relation to a money laundering investigation a person authorised for the purposes of money laundering investigations by the Director General of the National Criminal Intelligence Service is also an appropriate officer.

(6) In relation to a money laundering investigation these are senior appropriate officers –

    (a)   a police officer who is not below the rank of superintendent;

    (b)   a customs officer who is not below such grade as is designated by the Commissioners of Customs and Excise as equivalent to that rank;

    (c)   an accredited financial investigator who falls within a description specified in an order made for the purposes of this paragraph by the Secretary of State under section 453.

(7) But a person is not an appropriate officer or a senior appropriate officer in relation to a money laundering investigation if he is –

    (a)   a member of the staff of the Agency, or

    (b)   a person providing services under arrangements made by the Director.

## 379[1]  Miscellaneous

'Document', 'excluded material' and 'premises' have the same meanings as in the Police and Criminal Evidence Act 1984 or (in relation to Northern Ireland) the Police and Criminal Evidence (Northern Ireland) Order 1989 (SI 1989/1341 (NI 12)).

\*\*\*\*[2]

## CHAPTER 4  INTERPRETATION

## 413[3]  Criminal conduct

(1) Criminal conduct is conduct which –

    (a)   constitutes an offence in any part of the United Kingdom, or

    (b)   would constitute an offence in any part of the United Kingdom if it occurred there.

(2) A person benefits from conduct if he obtains property or a pecuniary advantage as a result of or in connection with the conduct.

---

1    Information: Commencement: Not yet in force.
2    Omission: Chapter 3 (ss 380–412) not reproduced.
3    Information: Commencement: Not yet in force.

(3) References to property or a pecuniary advantage obtained in connection with conduct include references to property or a pecuniary advantage obtained in both that connection and some other.

(4) If a person benefits from conduct his benefit is the property or pecuniary advantage obtained as a result of or in connection with the conduct.

(5) It is immaterial –

    (a)   whether conduct occurred before or after the passing of this Act, and

    (b)   whether property or a pecuniary advantage constituting a benefit from conduct was obtained before or after the passing of this Act.

## 414¹ Property

(1) Property is all property wherever situated and includes –

    (a)   money;

    (b)   all forms of property, real or personal, heritable or moveable;

    (c)   things in action and other intangible or incorporeal property.

(2) 'Recoverable property' and 'associated property' have the same meanings as in Part 5.

(3) The following rules apply in relation to property –

    (a)   property is obtained by a person if he obtains an interest in it;

    (b)   references to an interest, in relation to land in England and Wales or Northern Ireland, are to any legal estate or equitable interest or power;

    (c)   (*applies to Scotland only*)

    (d)   references to an interest, in relation to property other than land, include references to a right (including a right to possession).

## 415² Money laundering offences

(1) An offence under section 327, 328 or 329 is a money laundering offence.

(2) Each of the following is a money laundering offence –

    (a)   an attempt, conspiracy or incitement to commit an offence specified in subsection (1);

    (b)   aiding, abetting, counselling or procuring the commission of an offence specified in subsection (1).

## 416³ Other interpretative provisions

(1) These expressions are to be construed in accordance with these provisions of this Part –

civil recovery investigation: section 341(2) and (3)

confiscation investigation: section 341(1)

money laundering investigation: section 341(4)

(2) In the application of this Part to England and Wales and Northern Ireland, these expressions are to be construed in accordance with these provisions of this Part –

account information: section 370(4)

---

1    Information: Commencement: Not yet in force.

2    Information: Commencement: Not yet in force.

3    Information: Commencement: Not yet in force.

account monitoring order: section 370(6)

appropriate officer: section 378

customer information: section 364

customer information order: section 363(5)

disclosure order: section 357(4)

document: section 379

order to grant entry: section 347(3)

production order: section 345(4)

search and seizure warrant: section 352(4)

senior appropriate officer: section 378.

(3) (*applies to Scotland only*)

(4) 'Financial institution' means a person carrying on a business in the regulated sector.

(5) But a person who ceases to carry on a business in the regulated sector (whether by virtue of paragraph 5 of Schedule 9 or otherwise) is to continue to be treated as a financial institution for the purposes of any requirement under –

 (a) a customer information order, or
 (b) an account monitoring order,

to provide information which relates to a time when the person was a financial institution.

(6) References to a business in the regulated sector must be construed in accordance with Schedule 9.

(7) 'Recovery order', 'interim receiving order' and 'interim administration order' have the same meanings as in Part 5.

(8) References to notice in writing include references to notice given by electronic means.

(9) This section and sections 413 to 415 apply for the purposes of this Part.

## PART 9 INSOLVENCY ETC

*Bankruptcy in England and Wales*

### 417[1] Modifications of the 1986 Act

(1) This section applies if a person is adjudged bankrupt in England and Wales.

(2) The following property is excluded from his estate for the purposes of Part 9 of the 1986 Act –

 (a) property for the time being subject to a restraint order which was made under section 41, 120 or 190 before the order adjudging him bankrupt;

---

1 Information: Commencement: Not yet in force.

(b) any property in respect of which an order under section 50 or 52 is in force;

(c) any property in respect of which an order under section 128(3) is in force;

(d) any property in respect of which an order under section 198 or 200 is in force.

(3) (*applies to Scotland only*)

(4) If in the case of a debtor an interim receiver stands at any time appointed under section 286 of the 1986 Act and any property of the debtor is then subject to a restraint order made under section 41, 120 or 190 the powers conferred on the receiver by virtue of that Act do not apply to property then subject to the restraint order.

## 418[1]  Restriction of powers

(1) If a person is adjudged bankrupt in England and Wales the powers referred to in subsection (2) must not be exercised in relation to the property referred to in subsection (3).

(2) These are the powers –

(a) the powers conferred on a court by sections 41 to 67 and the powers of a receiver appointed under section 48, 50 or 52;

(b) the powers conferred on a court by sections 120 to 136 and Schedule 3 and the powers of an administrator appointed under section 125 or 128(3);

(c) the powers conferred on a court by sections 190 to 215 and the powers of a receiver appointed under section 196, 198 or 200.

(3) This is the property –

(a) property which is for the time being comprised in the bankrupt's estate for the purposes of Part 9 of the 1986 Act;

(b) property in respect of which his trustee in bankruptcy may (without leave of the court) serve a notice under section 307, 308 or 308A of the 1986 Act (after-acquired property, tools, tenancies etc);

(c) property which is to be applied for the benefit of creditors of the bankrupt by virtue of a condition imposed under section 280(2)(c) of the 1986 Act;

(d) in a case where a confiscation order has been made under section 6 or 156 of this Act, any sums remaining in the hands of a receiver appointed under section 50, 52, 198 or 200 of this Act after the amount required to be paid under the confiscation order has been fully paid;

(e) in a case where a confiscation order has been made under section 92 of this Act, any sums remaining in the hands of an administrator appointed under section 128 of this Act after the amount required to be paid under the confiscation order has been fully paid.

(4) But nothing in the 1986 Act must be taken to restrict (or enable the restriction of) the powers referred to in subsection (2).

(5) In a case where a petition in bankruptcy was presented or a receiving order or adjudication in bankruptcy was made before 29 December 1986 (when the 1986 Act came into force) this section has effect with these modifications –

(a) for the reference in subsection (3)(a) to the bankrupt's estate for the purposes of Part 9 of that Act substitute a reference to the property of the bankrupt for the purposes of the 1914 Act;

---

1    Information: Commencement: Not yet in force.

(b) omit subsection (3)(b);

(c) for the reference in subsection (3)(c) to section 280(2)(c) of the 1986 Act substitute a reference to section 26(2) of the 1914 Act;

(d) for the reference in subsection (4) to the 1986 Act substitute a reference to the 1914 Act.

## 419[1] Tainted gifts

(1) This section applies if a person who is adjudged bankrupt in England and Wales has made a tainted gift (whether directly or indirectly).

(2) No order may be made under section 339, 340 or 423 of the 1986 Act (avoidance of certain transactions) in respect of the making of the gift at any time when –

(a) any property of the recipient of the tainted gift is subject to a restraint order under section 41, 120 or 190, or

(b) there is in force in respect of such property an order under section 50, 52, 128(3), 198 or 200.

(3) Any order made under section 339, 340 or 423 of the 1986 Act after an order mentioned in subsection (2)(a) or (b) is discharged must take into account any realisation under Part 2, 3 or 4 of this Act of property held by the recipient of the tainted gift.

(4) A person makes a tainted gift for the purposes of this section if he makes a tainted gift within the meaning of Part 2, 3 or 4.

(5) In a case where a petition in bankruptcy was presented or a receiving order or adjudication in bankruptcy was made before 29 December 1986 (when the 1986 Act came into force) this section has effect with the substitution for a reference to section 339, 340 or 423 of the 1986 Act of a reference to section 27, 42 or 44 of the 1914 Act.

****[2]

*Winding up in England and Wales and Scotland*

## 426[3] Winding up under the 1986 Act

(1) In this section 'company' means any company which may be wound up under the 1986 Act.

(2) If an order for the winding up of a company is made or it passes a resolution for its voluntary winding up, the functions of the liquidator (or any provisional liquidator) are not exercisable in relation to the following property –

(a) property for the time being subject to a restraint order which was made under section 41, 120 or 190 before the relevant time;

(b) any property in respect of which an order under section 50 or 52 is in force;

(c) any property in respect of which an order under section 128(3) is in force;

(d) any property in respect of which an order under section 198 or 200 is in force.

(3) (*applies to Scotland only*)

(4) If an order for the winding up of a company is made or it passes a resolution for its voluntary winding up the powers referred to in subsection (5) must not be exercised in the way mentioned in subsection (6) in relation to any property –

---

1     Information: Commencement: Not yet in force.

2     Omission: Sections 420–425 not reproduced.

3     Information: Commencement: Not yet in force.

(a) which is held by the company, and

(b) in relation to which the functions of the liquidator are exercisable.

(5) These are the powers –

(a) the powers conferred on a court by sections 41 to 67 and the powers of a receiver appointed under section 48, 50 or 52;

(b) the powers conferred on a court by sections 120 to 136 and Schedule 3 and the powers of an administrator appointed under section 125 or 128(3);

(c) the powers conferred on a court by sections 190 to 215 and the powers of a receiver appointed under section 196, 198 or 200.

(6) The powers must not be exercised –

(a) so as to inhibit the liquidator from exercising his functions for the purpose of distributing property to the company's creditors;

(b) so as to prevent the payment out of any property of expenses (including the remuneration of the liquidator or any provisional liquidator) properly incurred in the winding up in respect of the property.

(7) But nothing in the 1986 Act must be taken to restrict (or enable the restriction of) the exercise of the powers referred to in subsection (5).

(8) For the purposes of the application of Parts 4 and 5 of the 1986 Act (winding up) to a company which the Court of Session has jurisdiction to wind up, a person is not a creditor in so far as any sum due to him by the company is due in respect of a confiscation order made under section 6, 92 or 156.

(9) The relevant time is –

(a) if no order for the winding up of the company has been made, the time of the passing of the resolution for voluntary winding up;

(b) if such an order has been made, but before the presentation of the petition for the winding up of the company by the court such a resolution has been passed by the company, the time of the passing of the resolution;

(c) if such an order has been made, but paragraph (b) does not apply, the time of the making of the order.

(10) In a case where a winding up of a company commenced or is treated as having commenced before 29 December 1986, this section has effect with the following modifications –

(a) in subsections (1) and (7) for 'the 1986 Act' substitute 'the Companies Act 1985';

(b) in subsection (8) for 'Parts 4 and 5 of the 1986 Act' substitute 'Parts 20 and 21 of the Companies Act 1985'.

## 427[1]  Tainted gifts

(1) In this section 'company' means any company which may be wound up under the 1986 Act.

(2) This section applies if –

(a) an order for the winding up of a company is made or it passes a resolution for its voluntary winding up, and

(b) it has made a tainted gift (whether directly or indirectly).

(3) No order may be made under section 238, 239 or 423 of the 1986 Act (avoidance of certain transactions) and no decree may be granted under section 242 or 243 of that Act (gratuitous

---

1    Information: Commencement: Not yet in force.

alienations and unfair preferences), or otherwise, in respect of the making of the gift at any time when –

    (a)  any property of the recipient of the tainted gift is subject to a restraint order under section 41, 120 or 190, or

    (b)  there is in force in respect of such property an order under section 50, 52, 128(3), 198 or 200.

(4) Any order made under section 238, 239 or 423 of the 1986 Act or decree granted under section 242 or 243 of that Act, or otherwise, after an order mentioned in subsection (3)(a) or (b) is discharged must take into account any realisation under Part 2, 3 or 4 of this Act of property held by the recipient of the tainted gift.

(5) A person makes a tainted gift for the purposes of this section if he makes a tainted gift within the meaning of Part 2, 3 or 4.

(6) In a case where the winding up of a company commenced or is treated as having commenced before 29 December 1986 this section has effect with the substitution –

    (a)  for references to section 239 of the 1986 Act of references to section 615 of the Companies Act 1985;

    (b)  for references to section 242 of the 1986 Act of references to section 615A of the Companies Act 1985;

    (c)  for references to section 243 of the 1986 Act of references to section 615B of the Companies Act 1985.

****[1]

## Floating charges

### 430[2]  Floating charges

(1) In this section 'company' means a company which may be wound up under

    (a)  the 1986 Act, or

    (b)  the 1989 Order.

(2) If a company holds property which is subject to a floating charge, and a receiver has been appointed by or on the application of the holder of the charge, the functions of the receiver are not exercisable in relation to the following property –

    (a)  property for the time being subject to a restraint order which was made under section 41, 120 or 190 before the appointment of the receiver;

    (b)  any property in respect of which an order under section 50 or 52 is in force;

    (c)  any property in respect of which an order under section 128(3) is in force;

    (d)  any property in respect of which an order under section 198 or 200 is in force.

(3) (*applies to Scotland only*)

(4) If a company holds property which is subject to a floating charge, and a receiver has been appointed by or on the application of the holder of the charge, the powers referred to in subsection (5) must not be exercised in the way mentioned in subsection (6) in relation to any property –

    (a)  which is held by the company, and

---

1    Omission: Sections 428, 429 not reproduced.

2    Information: Commencement: Not yet in force.

(b)   in relation to which the functions of the receiver are exercisable.

(5)  These are the powers –

(a)   the powers conferred on a court by sections 41 to 67 and the powers of a receiver appointed under section 48, 50 or 52;

(b)   the powers conferred on a court by sections 120 to 136 and Schedule 3 and the powers of an administrator appointed under section 125 or 128(3);

(c)   the powers conferred on a court by sections 190 to 215 and the powers of a receiver appointed under section 196, 198 or 200.

(6)  The powers must not be exercised –

(a)   so as to inhibit the receiver from exercising his functions for the purpose of distributing property to the company's creditors;

(b)   so as to prevent the payment out of any property of expenses (including the remuneration of the receiver) properly incurred in the exercise of his functions in respect of the property.

(7)  But nothing in the 1986 Act or the 1989 Order must be taken to restrict (or enable the restriction of) the exercise of the powers referred to in subsection (5).

(8)  In this section 'floating charge' includes a floating charge within the meaning of section 462 of the Companies Act 1985.

*Limited liability partnerships*

## 431[1]   Limited liability partnerships

(1)  In sections 426, 427 and 430 'company' includes a limited liability partnership which may be wound up under the 1986 Act.

(2)  A reference in those sections to a company passing a resolution for its voluntary winding up is to be construed in relation to a limited liability partnership as a reference to the partnership making a determination for its voluntary winding up.

*Insolvency practitioners*

## 432[2]   Insolvency practitioners

(1)  Subsections (2) and (3) apply if a person acting as an insolvency practitioner seizes or disposes of any property in relation to which his functions are not exercisable because –

(a)   it is for the time being subject to a restraint order made under section 41, 120 or 190, or

(b)   it is for the time being subject to an interim receiving order made under section 246 or an interim administration order made under section 256,

and at the time of the seizure or disposal he believes on reasonable grounds that he is entitled (whether in pursuance of an order of a court or otherwise) to seize or dispose of the property.

(2)  He is not liable to any person in respect of any loss or damage resulting from the seizure or disposal, except so far as the loss or damage is caused by his negligence.

---

1     Information: Commencement: Not yet in force.
2     Information: Commencement: Not yet in force.

(3) He has a lien on the property or the proceeds of its sale –

    (a)  for such of his expenses as were incurred in connection with the liquidation, bankruptcy, sequestration or other proceedings in relation to which he purported to make the seizure or disposal, and

    (b)  for so much of his remuneration as may reasonably be assigned to his acting in connection with those proceedings.

(4) Subsection (2) does not prejudice the generality of any provision of the 1985 Act, the 1986 Act, the 1989 Order or any other Act or Order which confers protection from liability on him.

(5) Subsection (7) applies if –

    (a)  property is subject to a restraint order made under section 41, 120 or 190,

    (b)  a person acting as an insolvency practitioner incurs expenses in respect of property subject to the restraint order, and

    (c)  he does not know (and has no reasonable grounds to believe) that the property is subject to the restraint order.

(6) Subsection (7) also applies if –

    (a)  property is subject to a restraint order made under section 41, 120 or 190,

    (b)  a person acting as an insolvency practitioner incurs expenses which are not ones in respect of property subject to the restraint order, and

    (c)  the expenses are ones which (but for the effect of the restraint order) might have been met by taking possession of and realising property subject to it.

(7) Whether or not he has seized or disposed of any property, he is entitled to payment of the expenses under –

    (a)  section 54(2), 55(3), 56(2) or 57(3) if the restraint order was made under section 41;

    (b)  section 130(3) or 131(3) if the restraint order was made under section 120;

    (c)  section 202(2), 203(3), 204(2) or 205(3) if the restraint order was made under section 190.

(8) Subsection (10) applies if –

    (a)  property is subject to an interim receiving order made under section 246 or an interim administration order made under section 256,

    (b)  a person acting as an insolvency practitioner incurs expenses in respect of property subject to the order, and

    (c)  he does not know (and has no reasonable grounds to believe) that the property is subject to the order.

(9) Subsection (10) also applies if –

    (a)  property is subject to an interim receiving order made under section 246 or an interim administration order made under section 256,

    (b)  a person acting as an insolvency practitioner incurs expenses which are not ones in respect of property subject to the order, and

    (c)  the expenses are ones which (but for the effect of the order) might have been met by taking possession of and realising property subject to it.

(10) Whether or not he has seized or disposed of any property, he is entitled to payment of the expenses under section 280.

## 433¹ Meaning of insolvency practitioner

(1) This section applies for the purposes of section 432.

(2) A person acts as an insolvency practitioner if he so acts within the meaning given by section 388 of the 1986 Act or Article 3 of the 1989 Order; but this is subject to subsections (3) to (5).

(3) The expression 'person acting as an insolvency practitioner' includes the official receiver acting as receiver or manager of the property concerned.

(4) In applying section 388 of the 1986 Act under subsection (2) above –

    (a)  the reference in section 388(2)(a) to a permanent or interim trustee in sequestration must be taken to include a reference to a trustee in sequestration;

    (b)  section 388(5) (which includes provision that nothing in the section applies to anything done by the official receiver or the Accountant in Bankruptcy) must be ignored.

(5) In applying Article 3 of the 1989 Order under subsection (2) above, paragraph (5) (which includes provision that nothing in the Article applies to anything done by the official receiver) must be ignored.

*Interpretation*

## 434² Interpretation

(1) The following paragraphs apply to references to Acts or Orders –

    (a)  the 1913 Act is the Bankruptcy (Scotland) Act 1913;
    (b)  the 1914 Act is the Bankruptcy Act 1914;
    (c)  the 1985 Act is the Bankruptcy (Scotland) Act 1985;
    (d)  the 1986 Act is the Insolvency Act 1986;
    (e)  the 1989 Order is the Insolvency (Northern Ireland) Order 1989 (SI 1989/2405 (NI 19)).

(2) An award of sequestration is made on the date of sequestration within the meaning of section 12(4) of the 1985 Act.

(3) This section applies for the purposes of this Part.

## PART 10    INFORMATION

*England and Wales and Northern Ireland*

## 435³ Use of information by Director

Information obtained by or on behalf of the Director in connection with the exercise of any of his functions may be used by him in connection with his exercise of any of his other functions.

---

1    Information: Commencement: Not yet in force.
2    Information: Commencement: Not yet in force.
3    Information: Commencement: Not yet in force.

## 436[1]   Disclosure of information to Director

(1) Information which is held by or on behalf of a permitted person (whether it was obtained before or after the coming into force of this section) may be disclosed to the Director for the purpose of the exercise by the Director of his functions.

(2) A disclosure under this section is not to be taken to breach any restriction on the disclosure of information (however imposed).

(3) But nothing in this section authorises the making of a disclosure –

    (a)   which contravenes the Data Protection Act 1998;
    (b)   which is prohibited by Part 1 of the Regulation of Investigatory Powers Act 2000.

(4) This section does not affect a power to disclose which exists apart from this section.

(5) These are permitted persons –

    (a)   a constable;
    (b)   the Director General of the National Criminal Intelligence Service;
    (c)   the Director General of the National Crime Squad;
    (d)   the Director of the Serious Fraud Office;
    (e)   the Commissioners of Inland Revenue;
    (f)   the Commissioners of Customs and Excise;
    (g)   the Director of Public Prosecutions;
    (h)   *(applies to Northern Ireland only)*

(6) The Secretary of State may by order designate as permitted persons other persons who exercise functions which he believes are of a public nature.

(7) But an order under subsection (6) must specify the functions in respect of which the designation is made.

(8) Information must not be disclosed under this section on behalf of the Commissioners of Inland Revenue or on behalf of the Commissioners of Customs and Excise unless the Commissioners concerned authorise the disclosure.

(9) The power to authorise a disclosure under subsection (8) may be delegated (either generally or for a specified purpose) –

    (a)   in the case of the Commissioners of Inland Revenue, to an officer of the Board of Inland Revenue;
    (b)   in the case of the Commissioners of Customs and Excise, to a customs officer.

## 437[2]   Further disclosure

(1) Subsection (2) applies to information obtained under section 436 from the Commissioners of Inland Revenue or from the Commissioners of Customs and Excise or from a person acting on behalf of either of them.

(2) Such information must not be further disclosed except –

    (a)   for a purpose connected with the exercise of the Director's functions, and
    (b)   with the consent of the Commissioners concerned.

(3) Consent under subsection (2) may be given –

---

1    Information: Commencement: Not yet in force.
2    Information: Commencement: Not yet in force.

    (a)   in relation to a particular disclosure;

    (b)   in relation to disclosures made in circumstances specified or described in the consent.

(4)  The power to consent to further disclosure under subsection (2)(b) may be delegated (either generally or for a specified purpose) –

    (a)   in the case of the Commissioners of Inland Revenue, to an officer of the Board of Inland Revenue;

    (b)   in the case of the Commissioners of Customs and Excise, to a customs officer.

(5)  Subsection (6) applies to information obtained under section 436 from a permitted person other than the Commissioners of Inland Revenue or the Commissioners of Customs and Excise or a person acting on behalf of either of them.

(6)  A permitted person who discloses such information to the Director may make the disclosure subject to such conditions as to further disclosure by the Director as the permitted person thinks appropriate; and the information must not be further disclosed in contravention of the conditions.

## 438[1]   Disclosure of information by Director

(1)  Information obtained by or on behalf of the Director in connection with the exercise of any of his functions may be disclosed by him if the disclosure is for the purposes of any of the following –

    (a)   any criminal investigation which is being or may be carried out, whether in the United Kingdom or elsewhere;

    (b)   any criminal proceedings which have been or may be started, whether in the United Kingdom or elsewhere;

    (c)   the exercise of the Director's functions;

    (d)   the exercise by the prosecutor of functions under Parts 2, 3 and 4;

    (e)   the exercise by the Scottish Ministers of their functions under Part 5;

    (f)   the exercise by a customs officer or a constable of his functions under Chapter 3 of Part 5;

    (g)   safeguarding national security;

    (h)   investigations or proceedings outside the United Kingdom which have led or may lead to the making of an external order within the meaning of section 447;

    (i)   the exercise of a designated function.

(2)  Subsection (1) does not apply to information obtained by the Director or on his behalf in connection with the exercise of his functions under Part 6.

(3)  But such information may be disclosed by the Director –

    (a)   to the Commissioners of Inland Revenue;

    (b)   to the Lord Advocate for the purpose of the exercise by the Lord Advocate of his functions under Part 3.

(4)  Information disclosed to the Lord Advocate under subsection (3)(b) may be further disclosed by him only to the Scottish Ministers for the purpose of the exercise by them of their functions under Part 5.

(5)  If the Director makes a disclosure of information for a purpose specified in subsection (1) he may make any further disclosure of the information by the person to whom he discloses it subject to such conditions as he thinks fit.

---

1    Information: Commencement: Not yet in force.

(6) Such a person must not further disclose the information in contravention of the conditions.

(7) A disclosure under this section is not to be taken to breach any restriction on the disclosure of information (however imposed).

(8) But nothing in this section authorises the making of a disclosure –

(a)   which contravenes the Data Protection Act 1998;
(b)   which is prohibited by Part 1 of the Regulation of Investigatory Powers Act 2000.

(9) A designated function is a function which the Secretary of State thinks is a function of a public nature and which he designates by order.

****[1]

*Overseas purposes*

## 442[2]   Restriction on disclosure for overseas purposes

(1) Section 18 of the Anti-terrorism, Crime and Security Act 2001 (restrictions on disclosure of information for overseas purposes) applies to a disclosure of information authorised by section 438(1)(a) or (b) or 441(2)(a) or (b).

(2) In the application of section 18 of the Anti-terrorism, Crime and Security Act 2001 by virtue of subsection (1) section 20 of that Act must be ignored and the following subsection is substituted for subsection (2) of section 18 of that Act –

'(2)   In subsection (1) the reference, in relation to a direction, to a relevant disclosure is a reference to a disclosure which –

(a)   is made for a purpose authorised by section 438(1)(a) or (b) or 441(2)(a) or (b) of the Proceeds of Crime Act 2002, and
(b)   is of any such information as is described in the direction.'.

## PART 11   CO-OPERATION

## 443[3]   Enforcement in different parts of the United Kingdom

(1) Her Majesty may by Order in Council make provision –

(a)   for an order made by a court under Part 2 to be enforced in Scotland or Northern Ireland;
(b)   for an order made by a court under Part 3 to be enforced in England and Wales or Northern Ireland;
(c)   for an order made by a court under Part 4 to be enforced in England and Wales or Scotland;
(d)   for an order made under Part 8 in one part of the United Kingdom to be enforced in another part;
(e)   for a warrant issued under Part 8 in one part of the United Kingdom to be executed in another part.

(2) Her Majesty may by Order in Council make provision –

---

1    Omission: Sections 439–441 not reproduced.
2    Information: Commencement: Not yet in force.
3    Information: Commencement: Not yet in force.

(a) for a function of a receiver appointed in pursuance of Part 2 to be exercisable in Scotland or Northern Ireland;

(b) for a function of an administrator appointed in pursuance of Part 3 to be exercisable in England and Wales or Northern Ireland;

(c) for a function of a receiver appointed in pursuance of Part 4 to be exercisable in England and Wales or Scotland.

(3) An Order under this section may include –

(a) provision conferring and imposing functions on the prosecutor and the Director;

(b) provision about the registration of orders and warrants;

(c) provision allowing directions to be given in one part of the United Kingdom about the enforcement there of an order made or warrant issued in another part;

(d) provision about the authentication in one part of the United Kingdom of an order made or warrant issued in another part.

(4) An Order under this section may –

(a) amend an enactment;

(b) apply an enactment (with or without modifications).

## 444[1]  External requests and orders

(1) Her Majesty may by Order in Council –

(a) make provision for a prohibition on dealing with property which is the subject of an external request;

(b) make provision for the realisation of property for the purpose of giving effect to an external order.

(2) An Order under this section may include provision which (subject to any specified modifications) corresponds to any provision of Part 2, 3 or 4 or Part 5 except Chapter 3.

(3) An Order under this section may include –

(a) provision about the functions of the Secretary of State, the Lord Advocate, the Scottish Ministers and the Director in relation to external requests and orders;

(b) provision about the registration of external orders;

(c) provision about the authentication of any judgment or order of an overseas court, and of any other document connected with such a judgment or order or any proceedings relating to it;

(d) provision about evidence (including evidence required to establish whether proceedings have been started or are likely to be started in an overseas court);

(e) provision to secure that any person affected by the implementation of an external request or the enforcement of an external order has an opportunity to make representations to a court in the part of the United Kingdom where the request is being implemented or the order is being enforced.

## 445[2]  External investigations

(1) Her Majesty may by Order in Council make –

(a) provision to enable orders equivalent to those under Part 8 to be made, and warrants equivalent to those under Part 8 to be issued, for the purposes of an external investigation;

---

1    Information: Commencement: Not yet in force.
2    Information: Commencement: Not yet in force.

   (b)  provision creating offences in relation to external investigations which are equivalent to offences created by Part 8.

(2) An Order under this section may include –

   (a)  provision corresponding to any provision of Part 8 (subject to any specified modifications);

   (b)  provision about the functions of the Secretary of State, the Lord Advocate, the Scottish Ministers, the Director, the Director General of the National Criminal Intelligence Service, the Director of the Serious Fraud Office, constables and customs officers;

   (c)  provision about evidence (including evidence required to establish whether an investigation is being carried out in a country or territory outside the United Kingdom).

(3) But an Order under this section must not provide for a disclosure order to be made for the purposes of an external investigation into whether a money laundering offence has been committed.

## 446[1]  Rules of court

Rules of court may make such provision as is necessary or expedient to give effect to an Order in Council made under this Part (including provision about the exercise of functions of a judge conferred or imposed by the Order).

## 447[2]  Interpretation

(1) An external request is a request by an overseas authority to prohibit dealing with relevant property which is identified in the request.

(2) An external order is an order which –

   (a)  is made by an overseas court where property is found or believed to have been obtained as a result of or in connection with criminal conduct, and

   (b)  is for the recovery of specified property or a specified sum of money.

(3) An external investigation is an investigation by an overseas authority into –

   (a)  whether property has been obtained as a result of or in connection with criminal conduct, or

   (b)  whether a money laundering offence has been committed.

(4) Property is all property wherever situated and includes –

   (a)  money;

   (b)  all forms of property, real or personal, heritable or moveable;

   (c)  things in action and other intangible or incorporeal property.

(5) Property is obtained by a person if he obtains an interest in it.

(6) References to an interest, in relation to property other than land, include references to a right (including a right to possession).

(7) Property is relevant property if there are reasonable grounds to believe that it may be needed to satisfy an external order which has been or which may be made.

---

1    Information: Commencement: Not yet in force.
2    Information: Commencement: Not yet in force.

(8) Criminal conduct is conduct which –

    (a)    constitutes an offence in any part of the United Kingdom, or

    (b)    would constitute an offence in any part of the United Kingdom if it occurred there.

(9) A money laundering offence is conduct carried out in a country or territory outside the United Kingdom and which if carried out in the United Kingdom would constitute any of the following offences –

    (a)    an offence under section 327, 328 or 329;

    (b)    an attempt, conspiracy or incitement to commit an offence specified in paragraph (a);

    (c)    aiding, abetting, counselling or procuring the commission of an offence specified in paragraph (a).

(10) An overseas court is a court of a country or territory outside the United Kingdom.

(11) An overseas authority is an authority which has responsibility in a country or territory outside the United Kingdom –

    (a)    for making a request to an authority in another country or territory (including the United Kingdom) to prohibit dealing with relevant property,

    (b)    for carrying out an investigation into whether property has been obtained as a result of or in connection with criminal conduct, or

    (c)    for carrying out an investigation into whether a money laundering offence has been committed.

(12) This section applies for the purposes of this Part.

## PART 12   MISCELLANEOUS AND GENERAL

*Miscellaneous*

### 448[1]  Tax

Schedule 10 contains provisions about tax.

### 449[2]  Agency staff: pseudonyms

(1) This section applies to a member of the staff of the Agency if –

    (a)    he is authorised (generally or specifically) by the Director to do anything for the purposes of this Act, and

    (b)    it is necessary or expedient for the purpose of doing the thing for the member of the staff of the Agency to identify himself by name.

(2) The Director may direct that such a member of the staff of the Agency may for that purpose identify himself by means of a pseudonym.

(3) For the purposes of any proceedings or application under this Act a certificate signed by the Director which sufficiently identifies the member of the staff of the Agency by reference to the pseudonym is conclusive evidence that that member of the staff of the Agency is authorised to use the pseudonym.

---

1    Information: Commencement: Not yet in force.
2    Information: Commencement: Not yet in force.

(4) In any proceedings or application under this Act a member of the staff of the Agency in respect of whom a direction under this section is in force must not be asked (and if asked is not required to answer) any question which is likely to reveal his true identity.

(5) Section 1(6) does not apply to anything done by the Director under this section.

****[1]

## 451[2]   Customs and Excise prosecutions

(1) Proceedings for a specified offence may be started by order of the Commissioners of Customs and Excise (the Commissioners).

(2) Such proceedings must be brought in the name of a customs officer.

(3) If the customs officer in whose name the proceedings are brought –

   (a)   dies,
   (b)   is removed or discharged, or
   (c)   is absent,

the proceedings may be continued by a different customs officer.

(4) If the Commissioners investigate, or propose to investigate, any matter to help them to decide –

   (a)   whether there are grounds for believing that a specified offence has been committed, or
   (b)   whether a person is to be prosecuted for such an offence,

the matter must be treated as an assigned matter within the meaning of the Customs and Excise Management Act 1979.

(5) This section –

   (a)   does not prevent any person (including a customs officer) who has power to arrest, detain or prosecute a person for a specified offence from doing so;
   (b)   does not prevent a court from dealing with a person brought before it following his arrest by a customs officer for a specified offence, even if the proceedings were not started by an order under subsection (1).

(6) The following are specified offences –

   (a)   an offence under Part 7;
   (b)   an offence under section 342;
   (c)   an attempt, conspiracy or incitement to commit an offence specified in paragraph (a) or (b);
   (d)   aiding, abetting, counselling or procuring the commission of an offence specified in paragraph (a) or (b).

(7) (*applies to Scotland only*)

## 452[3]   Crown servants

(1) The Secretary of State may by regulations provide that any of the following provisions apply to persons in the public service of the Crown.

---

1    Omission: Section 450 not reproduced.
2    Information: Commencement: Not yet in force.
3    Information: Commencement: Not yet in force.

(2) The provisions are –

    (a)  the provisions of Part 7;

    (b)  section 342.

## 453[1]  References to financial investigators

(1) The Secretary of State may by order provide that a specified reference in this Act to an accredited financial investigator is a reference to such an investigator who falls within a specified description.

(2) A description may be framed by reference to a grade designated by a specified person.

## 454[2]  Customs officers

For the purposes of this Act a customs officer is a person commissioned by the Commissioners of Customs and Excise under section 6(3) of the Customs and Excise Management Act 1979.

## 455[3]  Enactment

In this Act (except in section 460(1)) a reference to an enactment includes a reference to –

    (a)  an Act of the Scottish Parliament;

    (b)  Northern Ireland legislation.

*General*

## 456[4]  Amendments

Schedule 11 contains miscellaneous and consequential amendments.

## 457[5]  Repeals and revocations

Schedule 12 contains repeals and revocations.

## 458[6]  Commencement

(1) The preceding provisions of this Act (except the provisions specified in subsection (3)) come into force in accordance with provision made by the Secretary of State by order.

(2) But no order may be made which includes provision for the commencement of Part 5, 8 or 10 unless the Secretary of State has consulted the Scottish Ministers.

(3) The following provisions come into force in accordance with provision made by the Scottish Ministers by order after consultation with the Secretary of State –

    (a)  Part 3;

    (b)  this Part, to the extent that it relates to Part 3.

---

1    Information: Commencement: Not yet in force.
2    Information: Commencement: Not yet in force.
3    Information: Commencement: Not yet in force.
4    Information: Commencement: Not yet in force.
5    Information: Commencement: Not yet in force.
6    Information: Commencement: 24 July 2002 (Royal Assent).

## 459[1]  Orders and regulations

(1) References in this section to subordinate legislation are to –

(a)  any Order in Council under this Act;
(b)  any order under this Act (other than one falling to be made by a court);
(c)  any regulations under this Act.

(2) Subordinate legislation –

(a)  may make different provision for different purposes;
(b)  may include supplementary, incidental, saving or transitional provisions.

(3) Any power to make subordinate legislation is exercisable by statutory instrument.

(4) A statutory instrument is subject to annulment in pursuance of a resolution of either House of Parliament if it contains subordinate legislation other than –

(a)  an order under section 75(7) or (8), 223(7) or (8), 282, 292(4), 309, 364(4), 377(4), 436(6), 438(9) or 458;
(b), (c) (*apply to Scotland only*)

(5) (*applies to Scotland only*)

(6) No order may be made –

(a)  by the Secretary of State under section 75(7) or (8), 223(7) or (8), 282, 292(4), 309, 364(4), 377(4), 436(6) or 438(9) unless a draft of the order has been laid before Parliament and approved by a resolution of each House;
(b)  by the Scottish Ministers under section 142(6) or (7), 293(4), 398(4), 410(4), 439(6) or 441(9) unless a draft of the order has been laid before and approved by a resolution of the Scottish Parliament.

(7) The Scottish Ministers must lay before the Scottish Parliament a copy of every statutory instrument containing an Order in Council made under section 444 or 445.

## 460[2]  Finance

(1) The following are to be paid out of money provided by Parliament –

(a)  any expenditure incurred by any Minister of the Crown under this Act;
(b)  any increase attributable to this Act in the sums payable out of money so provided under any other enactment.

(2) Any sums received by the Secretary of State in consequence of this Act are to be paid into the Consolidated Fund.

## 461[3]  Extent

(1) Part 2 extends to England and Wales only.

(2) In Part 8, Chapter 2 extends to England and Wales and Northern Ireland only.

(3) (*applies to Scotland only*)

(4) (*applies to Northern Ireland only*)

---

1    Information: Commencement: 24 July 2002 (Royal Assent).
2    Information: Commencement: 24 July 2002 (Royal Assent).
3    Information: Commencement: 24 July 2002 (Royal Assent).

(5) The amendments in Schedule 11 have the same extent as the provisions amended.

(6) The repeals and revocations in Schedule 12 have the same extent as the provisions repealed or revoked.

## 462[1]  Short title

This Act may be cited as the Proceeds of Crime Act 2002.

---

1    Information: Commencement: 24 July 2002 (Royal Assent).

# SCHEDULES

## SCHEDULE 1[1]   ASSETS RECOVERY AGENCY

### Director's terms of appointment

**1** (1) The Director holds office for the period determined by the Secretary of State on his appointment (or re-appointment) to the office.

(2) But –

    (a)  the Director may at any time resign by giving notice to the Secretary of State;

    (b)  the Secretary of State may at any time remove the Director from office if satisfied that he is unable or unfit to exercise his functions.

**2** Subject to that, the Director holds office on the terms determined by the Secretary of State with the approval of the Minister for the Civil Service.

### Staff

**3** (1) The members of staff of the Agency must include –

    (a)  a deputy to the Director who is to act as Director during any vacancy in that office or if the Director is absent, subject to suspension or unable to act, and

    (b)  an assistant to the Director with responsibilities in relation to the exercise of the Director's functions in Northern Ireland.

(2) But the Director must not appoint a person under sub-paragraph (1)(b) unless he first consults the Secretary of State.

**4** The members of staff of the Agency hold office on the terms determined by the Director with the approval of the Minister for the Civil Service.

### Finances

**5** (1) These amounts are to be paid out of money provided by Parliament –

    (a)  the remuneration of the Director and the staff of the Agency;

    (b)  any expenses incurred by the Director or any of the staff in the exercise of his or their functions.

(2) Subject to anything in this Act any sums received by the Director are to be paid into the Consolidated Fund.

### Annual plan

**6** (1) The Director must, before the beginning of each financial year apart from the first, prepare a plan setting out how he intends to exercise his functions during the financial year (an annual plan).

(2) The annual plan must, in particular, set out how the Director intends to exercise his functions in Northern Ireland.

(3) The annual plan must also include a statement of –

    (a)  the Director's objectives for the financial year;

    (b)  any performance targets which he has for the financial year (whether or not relating to his objectives);

    (c)  his priorities for the financial year;

---

1    Information: Commencement: Not yet in force.

(d)  the financial resources expected to be available to him for the financial year;

(e)  his proposed allocation of those resources.

(4) Once the annual plan has been prepared the Director must send a copy to the Secretary of State for his approval.

(5) If the Secretary of State does not approve the annual plan –

(a)  he must give the Director his reasons for not approving it, and

(b)  he may require the Director to revise it in the manner specified by the Secretary of State.

(6) The Director must revise the annual plan, but if sub-paragraph (5)(b) applies he must do so in the manner specified by the Secretary of State.

(7) The Director must send a copy of the revised annual plan to the Secretary of State for his approval.

## Annual report

7 (1)  The Director must, as soon as possible after the end of each financial year, prepare a report on how he has exercised his functions during the financial year.

(2) The report for any financial year apart from the first must include –

(a)  the Director's annual plan for the financial year, and

(b)  an assessment of the extent to which it has been carried out.

(3) The Director must send a copy of each report to the Secretary of State who must –

(a)  lay a copy of it before each House of Parliament, and

(b)  arrange for it to be published.

## Meaning of 'financial year'

8 In this Schedule 'financial year' means –

(a)  the period beginning with the day on which section 1 comes into force and ending with the next 31 March (which is the first financial year), and

(b)  each subsequent period of twelve months beginning with 1 April.

## SCHEDULE 2[1]   LIFESTYLE OFFENCES: ENGLAND AND WALES

### Drug trafficking

1 (1)  An offence under any of the following provisions of the Misuse of Drugs Act 1971 –

(a)  section 4(2) or (3) (unlawful production or supply of controlled drugs);

(b)  section 5(3) (possession of controlled drug with intent to supply);

(c)  section 8 (permitting certain activities relating to controlled drugs);

(d)  section 20 (assisting in or inducing the commission outside the UK of an offence punishable under a corresponding law).

(2) An offence under any of the following provisions of the Customs and Excise Management Act 1979 if it is committed in connection with a prohibition or restriction on importation or exportation which has effect by virtue of section 3 of the Misuse of Drugs Act 1971 –

---

1    Information: Commencement: Not yet in force.

    (a)   section 50(2) or (3) (improper importation of goods);

    (b)   section 68(2) (exploration of prohibited or restricted goods);

    (c)   section 170 (fraudulent evasion).

(3) An offence under either of the following provisions of the Criminal Justice (International Co-operation) Act 1990 –

    (a)   section 12 (manufacture or supply of a substance for the time being specified in Schedule 2 to that Act);

    (b)   section 19 (using a ship for illicit traffic in controlled drugs).

## Money laundering

**2** An offence under either of the following provisions of this Act –

    (a)   section 327 (concealing etc criminal property);

    (b)   section 328 (assisting another to retain criminal property).

## Directing terrorism

**3** An offence under section 56 of the Terrorism Act 2000 (directing the activities of a terrorist organisation).

## People trafficking

**4** An offence under section 25(1) of the Immigration Act 1971 (assisting illegal entry etc).

## Arms trafficking

**5** (1) An offence under either of the following provisions of the Customs and Excise Management Act 1979 if it is committed in connection with a firearm or ammunition –

    (a)   section 68(2) (exportation of prohibited goods);

    (b)   section 170 (fraudulent evasion).

(2) An offence under section 3(1) of the Firearms Act 1968 (dealing in firearms or ammunition by way of trade or business).

(3) In this paragraph 'firearm' and 'ammunition' have the same meanings as in section 57 of the Firearms Act 1968.

## Counterfeiting

**6** An offence under any of the following provisions of the Forgery and Counterfeiting Act 1981 –

    (a)   section 14 (making counterfeit notes or coins);

    (b)   section 15 (passing etc counterfeit notes or coins);

    (c)   section 16 (having counterfeit notes or coins);

    (d)   section 17 (making or possessing materials or equipment for counterfeiting).

## Intellectual property

**7** (1) An offence under any of the following provisions of the Copyright, Designs and Patents Act 1988 –

    (a)   section 107(1) (making or dealing in an article which infringes copyright);

    (b)   section 107(2) (making or possessing an article designed or adapted for making a copy of a copyright work);

(c)  section 198(1) (making or dealing in an illicit recording);

(d)  section 297A (making or dealing in unauthorised decoders).

(2)  An offence under section 92(1), (2) or (3) of the Trade Marks Act 1994 (unauthorised use etc of trade mark).

## Pimps and brothels

**8** (1)  An offence under any of the following provisions of the Sexual Offences Act 1956 –

(a)  section 2 (procuring a woman by threats);

(b)  section 3 (procuring a woman by false pretences);

(c)  section 9 (procuring a defective woman to have sexual intercourse);

(d)  section 22 (procuring a woman for prostitution);

(e)  section 24 (detaining a woman in a brothel);

(f)  section 28 (causing or encouraging prostitution etc of girl under 16);

(g)  section 29 (causing or encouraging prostitution of defective woman);

(h)  section 30 (man living on earnings of prostitution);

(i)  section 31 (woman exercising control over prostitute);

(j)  section 33 (keeping a brothel);

(k)  section 34 (letting premises for use as brothel).

(2)  An offence under section 5 of the Sexual Offences Act 1967 (living on the earnings of male prostitute).

## Blackmail

**9**  An offence under section 21 of the Theft Act 1968 (blackmail).

## Inchoate offences

**10** (1)  An offence of attempting, conspiring or inciting the commission of an offence specified in this Schedule.

(2)  An offence of aiding, abetting, counselling or procuring the commission of such an offence.

## SCHEDULE 3¹   ADMINISTRATORS: FURTHER PROVISION

## General

**1**  In this Schedule, unless otherwise expressly provided –

(a)  references to an administrator are to an administrator appointed under section 125 or 128(3);

(b)  references to realisable property are to the realisable property in respect of which the administrator is appointed.

## Appointment etc

**2** (1)  If the office of administrator is vacant, for whatever reason, the court must appoint a new administrator.

(2)  Any property vested in the previous administrator by virtue of paragraph 5(4) vests in the new administrator.

---

1    Information: Commencement: Not yet in force.

(3) Any order under section 125 or 128(7) in relation to the previous administrator applies in relation to the new administrator when he gives written notice of his appointment to the person subject to the order.

(4) The administration of property by an administrator must be treated as continuous despite any temporary vacancy in that office.

(5) The appointment of an administrator is subject to such conditions as to caution as the accountant of court may impose.

(6) The premium of any bond of caution or other security required by such conditions must be treated as part of the administrator's expenses in the exercise of his functions.

## Functions

3 (1) An administrator –

    (a)  may, if appointed under section 125, and
    (b)  must, if appointed under section 128(3),

as soon as practicable take possession of the realisable property and of the documents mentioned in sub-paragraph (2).

(2) Those documents are any document which –

    (a)  is in the possession or control of the person ('A') in whom the property is vested (or would be vested but for an order made under paragraph 5(4)), and
    (b)  relates to the property or to A's assets, business or financial affairs.

(3) An administrator is entitled to have access to, and to copy, any document relating to the property or to A's assets, business or financial affairs and not falling within sub-paragraph (2)(a).

(4) An administrator may bring, defend or continue any legal proceedings relating to the property.

(5) An administrator may borrow money so far as it is necessary to do so to safeguard the property and may for the purposes of such borrowing create a security over any part of the property.

(6) An administrator may, if he considers that it would be beneficial for the management or realisation of the property –

    (a)  carry on any business of A;
    (b)  exercise any right of A as holder of securities in a company;
    (c)  grant a lease of the property or take on lease any other property;
    (d)  enter into any contract, or execute any deed, as regards the property or as regards A's business.

(7) An administrator may, where any right, option or other power forms part of A's estate, make payments or incur liabilities with a view to –

    (a)  obtaining property which is the subject of, or
    (b)  maintaining,

the right, option or power.

(8) An administrator may effect or maintain insurance policies as regards the property on A's business.

(9) An administrator may, if appointed under section 128(3), complete any uncompleted title which A has to any heritable estate; but completion of title in A's name does not validate by accretion any unperfected right in favour of any person other than the administrator.

(10) An administrator may sell, purchase or exchange property or discharge any security for an obligation due to A; but it is incompetent for the administrator or an associate of his (within the meaning of section 74 of the Bankruptcy (Scotland) Act 1985) to purchase any of A's property in pursuance of this sub-paragraph.

(11) An administrator may claim, vote and draw dividends in the sequestration of the estate (or bankruptcy or liquidation) of a debtor of A and may accede to a voluntary trust deed for creditors of such a debtor.

(12) An administrator may discharge any of his functions through agents or employees, but is personally liable to meet the fees and expenses of any such agent or employee out of such remuneration as is payable to the administrator on a determination by the accountant of court.

(13) An administrator may take such professional advice as he considers necessary in connection with the exercise of his functions.

(14) An administrator may at any time apply to the court for directions as regards the exercise of his functions.

(15) An administrator may exercise any power specifically conferred on him by the court, whether conferred on his appointment or subsequently.

(16) An administrator may –

    (a)   enter any premises;
    (b)   search for or inspect anything authorised by the court;
    (c)   make or obtain a copy, photograph or other record of anything so authorised;
    (d)   remove anything which the administrator is required or authorised to take possession of in pursuance of an order of the court.

(17) An administrator may do anything incidental to the powers and duties listed in the previous provisions of this paragraph.

## Consent of accountant of court

**4** An administrator proposing to exercise any power conferred by paragraph 3(4) to (17) must first obtain the consent of the accountant of court.

## Dealings in good faith with administrator

**5** (1) A person dealing with an administrator in good faith and for value is not concerned to enquire whether the administrator is acting within the powers mentioned in paragraph 3.

(2) Sub-paragraph (1) does not apply where the administrator or an associate purchases property in contravention of paragraph 3(10).

(3) The validity of any title is not challengeable by reason only of the administrator having acted outwith the powers mentioned in paragraph 3.

(4) The exercise of a power mentioned in paragraph 3(4) to (11) must be in A's name except where and in so far as an order made by the court under this sub-paragraph vests the property in the administrator (or in a previous administrator).

(5) The court may make an order under sub-paragraph (4) on the application of the administrator or on its own motion.

## Money received by administrator

**6** (1) All money received by an administrator in the exercise of his functions must be deposited by him, in the name (unless vested in the administrator by virtue of paragraph 5(4)) of the holder of the property realised, in an appropriate bank or institution.

(2) But the administrator may at any time retain in his hands a sum not exceeding £200 or such other sum as may be prescribed by the Scottish Ministers by regulations.

(3) In sub-paragraph (1), 'appropriate bank or institution' means a bank or institution mentioned in section 3(1) of the Banking Act 1987 or for the time being specified in Schedule 2 to that Act.

## Effect of appointment of administrator on diligence

**7** (1) An arrestment or poinding of realisable property executed on or after the appointment of an administrator does not create a preference for the arrester or poinder.

(2) Any realisable property so arrested or poinded, or (if the property has been sold) the proceeds of sale, must be handed over to the administrator.

(3) A poinding of the ground in respect of realisable property on or after such appointment is ineffectual in a question with the administrator except for the interest mentioned in sub-paragraph (4).

(4) That interest is –

    (a)  interest on the debt of a secured creditor for the current half-yearly term, and
    (b)  arrears of interest on that debt for one year immediately before the commencement of that term.

(5) On and after such appointment no other person may raise or insist in an adjudication against realisable property or be confirmed as executor-creditor on that property.

(6) An inhibition on realisable property which takes effect on or after such appointment does not create a preference for the inhibitor in a question with the administrator.

(7) This paragraph is without prejudice to sections 123 and 124.

(8) In this paragraph, the reference to an administrator is to an administrator appointed under section 128(3).

## Supervision

**8** (1) If the accountant of court reports to the court that an administrator has failed to perform any duty imposed on him, the court may, after giving the administrator an opportunity to be heard as regards the matter –

    (a)  remove him from office,
    (b)  censure him, or
    (c)  make such other order as it thinks fit.

(2) Section 6 of the Judicial Factors (Scotland) Act 1889 (supervision of judicial factors) does not apply in relation to an administrator.

## Accounts and remuneration

**9** (1) Not later than two weeks after the issuing of any determination by the accountant of court as to the remuneration and expenses payable to the administrator, the administrator or the Lord Advocate may appeal against it to the court.

(2) The amount of remuneration payable to the administrator must be determined on the basis of the value of the work reasonably undertaken by him, regard being had to the extent of the responsibilities involved.

(3) The accountant of court may authorise the administrator to pay without taxation an account in respect of legal services incurred by the administrator.

## Discharge of administrator

**10** (1) After an administrator has lodged his final accounts under paragraph 9(1), he may apply to the accountant of court to be discharged from office.

(2) A discharge, if granted, frees the administrator from all liability (other than liability arising from fraud) in respect of any act or omission of his in exercising his functions as administrator.

\*\*\*\*[1]

# SCHEDULE 6[2]   POWERS OF INTERIM RECEIVER OR ADMINISTRATOR

## Seizure

**1** Power to seize property to which the order applies.

## Information

**2** (1) Power to obtain information or to require a person to answer any question.

(2) A requirement imposed in the exercise of the power has effect in spite of any restriction on the disclosure of information (however imposed).

(3) An answer given by a person in pursuance of such a requirement may not be used in evidence against him in criminal proceedings.

(4) Sub-paragraph (3) does not apply –

  (a) on a prosecution for an offence under section 5 of the Perjury Act 1911, section 44(2) of the Criminal Law (Consolidation) (Scotland) Act 1995 or Article 10 of the Perjury (Northern Ireland) Order 1979 (false statements), or
  (b) on a prosecution for some other offence where, in giving evidence, he makes a statement inconsistent with it.

(5) But an answer may not be used by virtue of sub-paragraph (4)(b) against a person unless –

  (a) evidence relating to it is adduced, or
  (b) a question relating to it is asked,

by him or on his behalf in the proceedings arising out of the prosecution.

## Entry, search, etc

**3** (1) Power to –

  (a) enter any premises in the United Kingdom to which the interim order applies, and
  (b) take any of the following steps.

(2) Those steps are –

---

1    Omission: Schedules 4, 5 not reproduced.
2    Information: Commencement: Not yet in force.

(a)   to carry out a search for or inspection of anything described in the order,

(b)   to make or obtain a copy, photograph or other record of anything so described,

(c)   to remove anything which he is required to take possession of in pursuance of the order or which may be required as evidence in the proceedings under Chapter 2 of Part 5.

(3)  The order may describe anything generally, whether by reference to a class or otherwise.

## Supplementary

**4** (1)  An order making any provision under paragraph 2 or 3 must make provision in respect of legal professional privilege (in Scotland, legal privilege within the meaning of Chapter 3 of Part 8).

(2)  An order making any provision under paragraph 3 may require any person –

(a)   to give the interim receiver or administrator access to any premises which he may enter in pursuance of paragraph 3,

(b)   to give the interim receiver or administrator any assistance he may require for taking the steps mentioned in that paragraph.

## Management

**5** (1)  Power to manage any property to which the order applies.

(2)  Managing property includes –

(a)   selling or otherwise disposing of assets comprised in the property which are perishable or which ought to be disposed of before their value diminishes,

(b)   where the property comprises assets of a trade or business, carrying on, or arranging for another to carry on, the trade or business,

(c)   incurring capital expenditure in respect of the property.

## SCHEDULE 7[1]   POWERS OF TRUSTEE FOR CIVIL RECOVERY

## Sale

**1** Power to sell the property or any part of it or interest in it.

## Expenditure

**2** Power to incur expenditure for the purpose of –

(a)   acquiring any part of the property, or any interest in it, which is not vested in him,

(b)   discharging any liabilities, or extinguishing any rights, to which the property is subject.

## Management

**3** (1)  Power to manage property.

(2)  Managing property includes doing anything mentioned in paragraph 5(2) of Schedule 6.

## Legal proceedings

**4** Power to start, carry on or defend any legal proceedings in respect of the property.

---

1     Information: Commencement: Not yet in force.

## Compromise

**5** Power to make any compromise or other arrangement in connection with any claim relating to the property.

## Supplementary

**6** (1) For the purposes of, or in connection with, the exercise of any of his powers –

(a) power by his official name to do any of the things mentioned in sub-paragraph (2),
(b) power to do any other act which is necessary or expedient.

(2) Those things are –

(a) holding property,
(b) entering into contracts,
(c) suing and being sued,
(d) employing agents,
(e) executing a power of attorney, deed or other instrument.

## SCHEDULE 8[1]   FORMS OF DECLARATIONS

### The Director

'I, AB, do solemnly declare that I will not disclose any information received by me in carrying out my functions under Part 6 of the Proceeds of Crime Act 2002 except for the purposes of those functions or for the purposes of any prosecution for an offence relating to inland revenue, or in such other cases as may be required or permitted by law.'

### Members of The Staff of the Agency

'I, AB, do solemnly declare that I will not disclose any information received by me in carrying out the functions under Part 6 of the Proceeds of Crime Act 2002 which I may from time to time be authorised by the Director of the Assets Recovery Agency to carry out except for the purposes of those functions, or to the Director or in accordance with his instructions, or for the purposes of any prosecution for an offence relating to inland revenue, or in such other cases as may be required or permitted by law.'

## SCHEDULE 9[2]   REGULATED SECTOR AND SUPERVISORY AUTHORITIES

### PART 1   REGULATED SECTOR

### Business in the regulated sector

**1** (1) A business is in the regulated sector to the extent that it engages in any of the following activities –

(a) accepting deposits by a person with permission under Part 4 of the Financial Services and Markets Act 2000 to accept deposits (including, in the case of a building society, the raising of money from members of the society by the issue of shares);
(b) the business of the National Savings Bank;

---

1    Information: Commencement: Not yet in force.
2    Information: Commencement: Not yet in force.

(c)   business carried on by a credit union;

(d)   any home-regulated activity carried on by a European institution in respect of which the establishment conditions in paragraph 13 of Schedule 3 to the Financial Services and Markets Act 2000, or the service conditions in paragraph 14 of that Schedule, are satisfied;

(e)   any activity carried on for the purpose of raising money authorised to be raised under the National Loans Act 1968 under the auspices of the Director of Savings;

(f)   the activity of operating a bureau de change, transmitting money (or any representation of monetary value) by any means or cashing cheques which are made payable to customers;

(g)   any activity falling within sub-paragraph (2);

(h)   any of the activities in points 1 to 12 or 14 of Annex 1 to the Banking Consolidation Directive, ignoring an activity described in any of sub-paragraphs (a) to (g) above;

(i)   business which consists of effecting or carrying out contracts of long term insurance by a person who has received official authorisation pursuant to Article 6 or 27 of the First Life Directive.

(2) An activity falls within this sub-paragraph if it constitutes any of the following kinds of regulated activity in the United Kingdom –

(a)   dealing in investments as principal or as agent;

(b)   arranging deals in investments;

(c)   managing investments;

(d)   safeguarding and administering investments;

(e)   sending dematerialised instructions;

(f)   establishing (and taking other steps in relation to) collective investment schemes;

(g)   advising on investments.

(3) Paragraphs (a) and (i) of sub-paragraph (1) and sub-paragraph (2) must be read with section 22 of the Financial Services and Markets Act 2000, any relevant order under that section and Schedule 2 to that Act.

2 (1) This paragraph has effect for the purposes of paragraph 1.

(2) 'Building society' has the meaning given by the Building Societies Act 1986.

(3) 'Credit union' has the meaning given by the Credit Unions Act 1979 or the Credit Unions (Northern Ireland) Order 1985 (SI 1985/1205 (NI 12)).

(4) 'European institution' means an EEA firm of the kind mentioned in paragraph 5(b) or (c) of Schedule 3 to the Financial Services and Markets Act 2000 which qualifies for authorisation for the purposes of that Act under paragraph 12 of that Schedule.

(5) 'Home-regulated activity' in relation to a European institution, means an activity –

(a)   which is specified in Annex 1 to the Banking Consolidation Directive and in respect of which a supervisory authority in the home State of the institution has regulatory functions, and

(b)   if the institution is an EEA firm of the kind mentioned in paragraph 5(c) of Schedule 3 to the Financial Services and Markets Act 2000, which the institution carries on in its home State.

(6) 'Home State', in relation to a person incorporated in or formed under the law of another member State, means that State.

(7) The Banking Consolidation Directive is the Directive of the European Parliament and Council relating to the taking up and pursuit of the business of credit institutions (No. 2000/12 EC).

(8) The First Life Directive is the First Council Directive on the co-ordination of laws, regulations and administrative provisions relating to the taking up and pursuit of the business of direct life assurance (No. 79/267/EEC).

## Excluded activities

3 A business is not in the regulated sector to the extent that it engages in any of the following activities –

    (a)   the issue of withdrawable share capital within the limit set by section 6 of the Industrial and Provident Societies Act 1965 by a society registered under that Act;

    (b)   the acceptance of deposits from the public within the limit set by section 7(3) of that Act by such a society;

    (c)   the issue of withdrawable share capital within the limit set by section 6 of the Industrial and Provident Societies Act (Northern Ireland) 1969 by a society registered under that Act;

    (d)   the acceptance of deposits from the public within the limit set by section 7(3) of that Act by such a society;

    (e)   activities carried on by the Bank of England;

    (f)   any activity in respect of which an exemption order under section 38 of the Financial Services and Markets Act 2000 has effect if it is carried on by a person who is for the time being specified in the order or falls within a class of persons so specified.

## PART 2    SUPERVISORY AUTHORITIES

4 (1) Each of the following is a supervisory authority –

    (a)   the Bank of England;

    (b)   the Financial Services Authority;

    (c)   the Council of Lloyd's;

    (d)   the Director General of Fair Trading;

    (e)   a body which is a designated professional body for the purposes of Part 20 of the Financial Services and Markets Act 2000.

(2) The Secretary of State is also a supervisory authority in the exercise, in relation to a person carrying on a business in the regulated sector, of his functions under the enactments relating to companies or insolvency or under the Financial Services and Markets Act 2000.

(3) The Treasury are also a supervisory authority in the exercise, in relation to a person carrying on a business in the regulated sector, of their functions under the enactments relating to companies or insolvency or under the Financial Services and Markets Act 2000.

## PART 3    POWER TO AMEND

5 The Treasury may by order amend Part 1 or 2 of this Schedule.

## SCHEDULE 10[1]    TAX

## PART 1    GENERAL

1 Sections 75 and 77 of the Taxes Management Act 1970 (receivers: income tax and capital gains tax) shall not apply in relation to –

    (a)   a receiver appointed under section 48, 50 or 52;

---

1    Information: Commencement: Not yet in force.

    (b)   an administrator appointed under section 125 or 128;

    (c)   a receiver appointed under section 196, 198 or 200;

    (d)   an interim receiver appointed under section 246;

    (e)   an interim administrator appointed under section 256.

## PART 2    PROVISIONS RELATING TO PART 5

### *Introductory*

**2** (1)  The vesting of property in the trustee for civil recovery or any other person by a recovery order or in pursuance of an order under section 276 is referred to as a Part 5 transfer.

(2)  The person who holds the property immediately before the vesting is referred to as the transferor; and the person in whom the property is vested is referred to as the transferee.

(3)  Any amount paid in respect of the transfer by the trustee for civil recovery, or another, to a person who holds the property immediately before the vesting is referred to (in relation to that person) as a compensating payment.

(4)  If the recovery order provides or (as the case may be) the terms on which the order under section 276 is made provide for the creation of any interest in favour of a person who holds the property immediately before the vesting, he is to be treated instead as receiving (in addition to any payment referred to in sub-paragraph (3)) a compensating payment of an amount equal to the value of the interest.

(5)  Where the property belongs to joint tenants immediately before the vesting and a compensating payment is made to one or more (but not both or all) of the joint tenants, this Part has effect separately in relation to each joint tenant.

(6)  Expressions used in this paragraph have the same meaning as in Part 5 of this Act.

(7)  'The Taxes Act 1988' means the Income and Corporation Taxes Act 1988, and 'the Allowances Act 2001' means the Capital Allowances Act 2001.

(8)  This paragraph applies for the purposes of this Part.

### *Capital Gains Tax*

**3** (1)  If a gain attributable to a Part 5 transfer accrues to the transferor, it is not a chargeable gain.

(2)  But if a compensating payment is made to the transferor –

    (a)   sub-paragraph (1) does not apply, and

    (b)   the consideration for the transfer is the amount of the compensating payment.

(3)  If a gain attributable to the forfeiture under section 298 of property consisting of –

    (a)   notes or coins in any currency other than sterling,

    (b)   anything mentioned in section 289(6)(b) to (d), if expressed in any currency other than sterling, or

    (c)   bearer bonds or bearer shares,

accrues to the person who holds the property immediately before the forfeiture, it is not a chargeable gain.

(4)  This paragraph has effect as if it were included in Chapter 1 of Part 2 of the Taxation of Chargeable Gains Act 1992.

*Income Tax and Corporation Tax*

## Accrued income scheme

**4** If a Part 5 transfer is a transfer of securities within the meaning of sections 711 to 728 of the Taxes Act 1988 (transfers with or without accrued interest), sections 713(2) and (3) and 716 of that Act do not apply to the transfer.

## Discounted securities

**5** In the case of a Part 5 transfer of property consisting of a relevant discounted security (within the meaning of Schedule 13 to the Finance Act 1996), it is not to be treated as a transfer for the purposes of that Schedule.

## Rights to receive amounts stated in certificates of deposit etc

**6** In the case of a Part 5 transfer of property consisting of a right to which section 56(2) of the Taxes Act 1988 applies, or a right mentioned in section 56A(1) of that Act, (rights stated in certificates of deposit etc) it is not to be treated as a disposal of the right for the purposes of section 56(2) of that Act.

## Non-qualifying offshore funds

**7** In the case of a Part 5 transfer of property consisting of an asset mentioned in section 757(1)(a) or (b) of the Taxes Act 1988 (interests in non-qualifying offshore funds etc), it is not to be treated as a disposal for the purposes of that section.

## Futures and options

**8** In the case of a Part 5 transfer of property consisting of futures or options (within the meaning of paragraph 4 of Schedule 5AA to the Taxes Act 1988), it is not to be treated as a disposal of the futures or options for the purposes of that Schedule.

## Loan relationships

**9** (1) Sub-paragraph (2) applies if, apart from this paragraph, a Part 5 transfer would be a related transaction for the purposes of section 84 of the Finance Act 1996 (debits and credits brought into account for the purpose of taxing loan relationships under Chapter 2 of Part 4 of that Act).

(2) The Part 5 transfer is to be disregarded for the purposes of that Chapter, except for the purpose of identifying any person in whose case any debit or credit not relating to the transaction is to be brought into account.

## Exception from paragraphs 4 to 9

**10** Paragraphs 4 to 9 do not apply if a compensating payment is made to the transferor.

## Trading stock

**11** (1) Sub-paragraph (2) applies, in the case of a Part 5 transfer of property consisting of the trading stock of a trade, for the purpose of computing any profits of the trade for tax purposes.

(2) If, because of the transfer, the trading stock is to be treated for that purpose as if it had been sold in the course of the trade, the amount realised on the sale is to be treated for that purpose as equal to its acquisition cost.

(3) Sub-paragraph (2) has effect in spite of anything in section 100 of the Taxes Act 1988 (valuation of trading stock at discontinuance).

(4) In this paragraph, trading stock and trade have the same meaning as in that section.

## CAPITAL ALLOWANCES

### Plant and machinery

**12** (1) If there is a Part 5 transfer of plant or machinery, Part 2 of the Allowances Act 2001 is to have effect as if a transferor who has incurred qualifying expenditure were required to bring the disposal value of the plant or machinery into account in accordance with section 61 of that Act for the chargeable period in which the transfer occurs.

(2) But the Part 5 transfer is not to be treated as a disposal event for the purposes of Part 2 of that Act other than by virtue of sub-paragraph (1).

**13** (1) If a compensating payment is made to the transferor, the disposal value to be brought into account is the amount of the payment.

(2) Otherwise, the disposal value to be brought into account is the amount which would give rise neither to a balancing allowance nor to a balancing charge.

**14** (1) Paragraph 13(2) does not apply if the qualifying expenditure has been allocated to the main pool or a class pool.

(2) Instead, the disposal value to be brought into account is the notional written-down value of the qualifying expenditure incurred by the transferor on the provision of the plant or machinery.

(3) The notional written-down value is –

$$QE — A$$

where –

QE is the qualifying expenditure incurred by the transferor on the provision of the plant or machinery,

A is the total of all allowances which could have been made to the transferor in respect of the expenditure if –

    (a)    that expenditure had been the only expenditure that had ever been taken into account in determining his available qualifying expenditure, and

    (b)    all allowances had been made in full.

(4) But if –

    (a)    the Part 5 transfer of the plant or machinery occurs in the same chargeable period as that in which the qualifying expenditure is incurred, and

    (b)    a first-year allowance is made in respect of an amount of the expenditure,

the disposal value to be brought into account is that which is equal to the balance left after deducting the first year allowance.

**15** (1) Paragraph 13 does not apply if –

    (a)    a qualifying activity is carried on in partnership,

    (b)    the Part 5 transfer is a transfer of plant or machinery which is partnership property, and

    (c)    compensating payments are made to one or more, but not both or all, of the partners.

(2) Instead, the disposal value to be brought into account is the sum of –

(a) any compensating payments made to any of the partners, and

(b) in the case of each partner to whom a compensating payment has not been made, his share of the tax-neutral amount.

(3) A partner's share of the tax-neutral amount is to be determined according to the profit-sharing arrangements for the twelve months ending immediately before the date of the Part 5 transfer.

**16** (1) Paragraph 13 does not apply if –

(a) a qualifying activity is carried on in partnership,

(b) the Part 5 transfer is a transfer of plant or machinery which is not partnership property but is owned by two or more of the partners ('the owners'),

(c) the plant or machinery is used for the purposes of the qualifying activity, and

(d) compensating payments are made to one or more, but not both or all, of the owners.

(2) Instead, the disposal value to be brought into account is the sum of –

(a) any compensating payments made to any of the owners, and

(b) in the case of each owner to whom a compensating payment has not been made, his share of the tax-neutral amount.

(3) An owner's share of the tax-neutral amount is to be determined in proportion to the value of his interest in the plant or machinery.

**17** (1) Paragraphs 12 to 16 have effect as if they were included in section 61 of the Allowances Act 2001.

(2) In paragraphs 15 and 16, the tax-neutral amount is the amount that would be brought into account as the disposal value under paragraph 13(2) or (as the case may be) 14 if the provision in question were not disapplied.

## Industrial buildings

**18** (1) If there is a Part 5 transfer of a relevant interest in an industrial building, Part 3 of the Allowances Act 2001 is to have effect as if the transfer were a balancing event within section 315(1) of that Act.

(2) But the Part 5 transfer is not to be treated as a balancing event for the purposes of Part 3 of that Act other than by virtue of sub-paragraph (1).

**19** (1) If a compensating payment is made to the transferor, the proceeds from the balancing event are the amount of the payment.

(2) Otherwise –

(a) the proceeds from the balancing event are the amount which is equal to the residue of qualifying expenditure immediately before the transfer, and

(b) no balancing adjustment is to be made as a result of the event under section 319 of the Allowances Act 2001.

**20** (1) Paragraph 19 does not apply to determine the proceeds from the balancing event if –

(a) the relevant interest in the industrial building is partnership property, and

(b) compensating payments are made to one or more, but not both or all, of the partners.

(2) Instead, the proceeds from the balancing event are the sum of –

(a) any compensating payments made to any of the partners, and

(b) in the case of each partner to whom a compensating payment has not been made, his share of the amount which is equal to the residue of qualifying expenditure immediately before the Part 5 transfer.

(3) A partner's share of that amount is to be determined according to the profit-sharing arrangements for the twelve months ending immediately before the date of the Part 5 transfer.

21 Paragraphs 18 to 20 have effect as if they were included in Part 3 of the Allowances Act 2001.

## Flat conversion

22 (1) If there is a Part 5 transfer of a relevant interest in a flat, Part 4A of the Allowances Act 2001 is to have effect as if the transfer were a balancing event within section 393N of that Act.

(2) But the Part 5 transfer is not to be treated as a balancing event for the purposes of Part 4A of that Act other than by virtue of sub-paragraph (1).

23 (1) If a compensating payment is made to the transferor, the proceeds from the balancing event are the amount of the payment.

(2) Otherwise, the proceeds from the balancing event are the amount which is equal to the residue of qualifying expenditure immediately before the transfer.

24 (1) Paragraph 23 does not apply to determine the proceeds from the balancing event if –

(a) the relevant interest in the flat is partnership property, and
(b) compensating payments are made to one or more, but not both or all, of the partners.

(2) Instead, the proceeds from the balancing event are the sum of –

(a) any compensating payments made to any of the partners, and
(b) in the case of each partner to whom a compensating payment has not been made, his share of the amount which is equal to the residue of qualifying expenditure immediately before the transfer.

(3) A partner's share of that amount is to be determined according to the profit-sharing arrangements for the twelve months ending immediately before the date of the transfer.

25 Paragraphs 22 to 24 have effect as if they were included in Part 4A of the Allowances Act 2001.

## Research and development

26 If there is a Part 5 transfer of an asset representing qualifying expenditure incurred by a person, the disposal value he is required to bring into account under section 443(1) of the Allowances Act 2001 for any chargeable period is to be determined as follows (and not in accordance with subsection (4) of that section).

27 (1) If a compensating payment is made to the transferor, the disposal value he is required to bring into account is the amount of the payment.

(2) Otherwise, the disposal value he is required to bring into account is nil.

28 (1) Paragraph 27 does not apply to determine the disposal value to be brought into account if –

(a) the asset is partnership property, and
(b) compensating payments are made to one or more, but not both or all, of the partners.

(2) Instead, the disposal value to be brought into account is equal to the sum of any compensating payments.

**29** Paragraphs 26 to 28 have effect as if they were included in Part 6 of the Allowances Act 2001.

## EMPLOYEE ETC SHARE SCHEMES

### Share options

**30** Section 135(6) of the Taxes Act 1988 (gains by directors and employees) does not make any person chargeable to tax in respect of any gain realised by the trustee for civil recovery.

### Conditional acquisition of shares

**31** Section 140A(4) of the Taxes Act 1988 (disposal etc of shares) does not make the transferor chargeable to income tax in respect of a Part 5 transfer of shares or an interest in shares.

### Shares acquired at an undervalue

**32** Section 162(5) of the Taxes Act 1988 (employee shareholdings) does not make the transferor chargeable to income tax in respect of a Part 5 transfer of shares.

### Shares in dependent subsidiaries

**33** Section 79 of the Finance Act 1988 (charge on increase in value of shares) does not make the transferor chargeable to income tax in respect of a Part 5 transfer of shares or an interest in shares.

## SCHEDULE 11[1]   AMENDMENTS

### Introduction

**1** The amendments specified in this Schedule shall have effect.

### Parliamentary Commissioner Act 1967

**2** (1)  The Parliamentary Commissioner Act 1967 is amended as follows.

(2)  In Schedule 2 (Departments etc subject to investigation) at the appropriate place insert –

'Director of the Assets Recovery Agency.'

(3)  In the Notes to that Schedule before paragraph 1 insert –

'A1  In the case of the Director of the Assets Recovery Agency an investigation under this Act may be conducted only in respect of the exercise of functions vested in him by virtue of a notice served on the Commissioners of Inland Revenue under section 317(2), 321(2) or 322(2) of the Proceeds of Crime Act 2002 (Inland Revenue functions).'

### Police (Scotland) Act 1967

**3** (1)  The Police (Scotland) Act 1967 is amended as follows.

(2)  In section 38(3B)(liability of Scottish Ministers for constables on central service) after 'central service' insert 'or on temporary service as mentioned in section 38A(1)(aa) of this Act'.

(3)  In section 38A(1) (meaning of 'relevant service') after paragraph (a) insert –

---

1    Information: Commencement: Not yet in force.

'(aa) temporary service with the Scottish Ministers in connection with their functions under Part 5 or 8 of the Proceeds of Crime Act 2002, on which a person is engaged with the consent of the appropriate authority;'.

## Criminal Appeal Act 1968

4 (1) The Criminal Appeal Act 1968 is amended as follows.

(2) In section 33 (appeal to House of Lords) after subsection (1) insert –

'(1A) In subsection (1) above the reference to the prosecutor includes a reference to the Director of the Assets Recovery Agency in a case where (and to the extent that) he is a party to the appeal to the Court of Appeal.'

(3) In section 50(1) (meaning of sentence) after paragraph (c) insert –

'(ca) a confiscation order under Part 2 of the Proceeds of Crime Act 2002;
(cb) an order which varies a confiscation order made under Part 2 of the Proceeds of Crime Act 2002 if the varying order is made under section 21, 22 or 29 of that Act (but not otherwise);'.

## Misuse of Drugs Act 1971

5 (1) Section 27 of the Misuse of Drugs Act 1971 (forfeiture) is amended as follows.

(2) In subsection (1) for 'a drug trafficking offence, as defined in section 1(3) of the Drug Trafficking Act 1994' substitute 'an offence falling within subsection (3) below'.

(3) After subsection (2) insert –

'(3) An offence falls within this subsection if it is an offence which is specified in –

(a) paragraph 1 of Schedule 2 to the Proceeds of Crime Act 2002 (drug trafficking offences), or
(b) so far as it relates to that paragraph, paragraph 10 of that Schedule.'

## Immigration Act 1971

6 In section 28L of the Immigration Act 1971, in paragraph (c) for the words '33 of the Criminal Law (Consolidation) (Scotland) Act 1995' substitute '412 of the Proceeds of Crime Act 2002'.

## Rehabilitation of Offenders Act 1974

7 In section 1 of the Rehabilitation of Offenders Act 1974 (rehabilitated persons and spent convictions) after subsection (2A) insert –

'(2B) In subsection (2)(a) above the reference to a fine or other sum adjudged to be paid by or imposed on a conviction does not include a reference to an amount payable under a confiscation order made under Part 2 or 3 of the Proceeds of Crime Act 2002.'

## Rehabilitation of Offenders (Northern Ireland) Order 1978 (SI 1978/1908 (NI 27))

8 In Article 3 of the Rehabilitation of Offenders (Northern Ireland) Order 1978 (rehabilitated persons and spent convictions) after paragraph (2) insert –

'(2A) In paragraph (2)(a) the reference to a fine or other sum adjudged to be paid by or imposed on a conviction does not include a reference to an amount payable under a confiscation order made under Part 4 of the Proceeds of Crime Act 2002.'

## Criminal Appeal (Northern Ireland) Act 1980

**9** (1) The Criminal Appeal (Northern Ireland) Act 1980 is amended as follows.

(2) In section 30(3) (meaning of sentence) omit 'and' after paragraph (b) and after paragraph (c) insert –

> (d) a confiscation order under Part 4 of the Proceeds of Crime Act 2002;
>
> (e) an order which varies a confiscation order made under Part 4 of the Proceeds of Crime Act 2002 if the varying order is made under section 171, 172 or 179 of that Act (but not otherwise).'

(3) In section 31 (appeal to House of Lords) after subsection (1) insert –

'(1A) In subsection (1) above the reference to the prosecutor includes a reference to the Director of the Assets Recovery Agency in a case where (and to the extent that) he is a party to the appeal to the Court of Appeal.'

## Legal Aid, Advice and Assistance (Northern Ireland) Order 1981 (SI 1981/228 (NI 8))

**10** (1) Part I of Schedule 1 to the Legal Aid, Advice and Assistance (Northern Ireland) Order 1981 (proceedings for which legal aid may be given under Part II of the Order) is amended as follows.

(2) After paragraph 2 insert –

'**2A** (1) The following proceedings in the Crown Court under the Proceeds of Crime Act 2002 –

> (a) proceedings which relate to a direction under section 202(3) or 204(3) as to the distribution of funds in the hands of a receiver;
>
> (b) applications under section 210 relating to action taken or proposed to be taken by a receiver;
>
> (c) applications under section 211 to vary or discharge an order under any of sections 196 to 201 for the appointment of or conferring powers on a receiver;
>
> (d) applications under section 220 or 221 for the payment of compensation;
>
> (e) applications under sections 351(3), 362(3), 369(3) or 375(2) to vary or discharge certain orders made under Part 8.

(2) But sub-paragraph (1) does not apply in relation to a defendant (within the meaning of Part 4 of that Act) in the following proceedings –

> (a) proceedings mentioned in head (b) of that sub-paragraph;
>
> (b) an application under section 221 for the payment of compensation if the confiscation order was varied under section 179.'

(3) In paragraph 3 (courts of summary jurisdiction), after sub-paragraph (i) insert –

'(j) proceedings under sections 295, 297, 298, 301 and 302 of the Proceeds of Crime Act 2002'.

(4) The amendments made by this paragraph are without prejudice to the power to make regulations under Article 10(2) of the Legal Aid, Advice and Assistance (Northern Ireland) Order 1981 amending or revoking the provisions inserted by this paragraph.

## Civil Jurisdiction and Judgments Act 1982

**11** In section 18 of the Civil Jurisdiction and Judgments Act 1982 (enforcement of United Kingdom judgments in other parts of the United Kingdom) in subsection (3) (exceptions) insert after paragraph (c) –

> '(d)   an order made under Part 2, 3 or 4 of the Proceeds of Crime Act 2002 (confiscation).'

## Civic Government (Scotland) Act 1982

**12** (1)  The Civic Government (Scotland) Act 1982 is amended as follows.

(2)  In section 86A(3) (application of Part VIIA) for 'sections 21(2) and 28(1) of the Proceeds of Crime (Scotland) Act 1995' substitute 'section 21(2) of the Proceeds of Crime (Scotland) Act 1995 and Part 3 of the Proceeds of Crime Act 2002'.

(3) In paragraph 8 of Schedule 2A (interpretation) for the definition of 'restraint order' substitute –

> ' "restraint order" means a restraint order made under Part 3 of the Proceeds of Crime Act 2002'.

## Criminal Justice Act 1982

**13** In Part 2 of Schedule 1 to the Criminal Justice Act 1982 (offences excluded from early release provisions) after the entry relating to the Drug Trafficking Act 1994 insert –

### 'PROCEEDS OF CRIME ACT 2002

> Section 327 (concealing criminal property etc).
>
> Section 328 (arrangements relating to criminal property).
>
> Section 329 (acquisition, use and possession of criminal property).'

## Police and Criminal Evidence Act 1984

**14** (1)  The Police and Criminal Evidence Act 1984 is amended as follows.

(2) In section 56 (right to have someone informed when arrested) for subsection (5A) substitute –

> '(5A)  An officer may also authorise delay where he has reasonable grounds for believing that –
>
> > (a)   the person detained for the serious arrestable offence has benefited from his criminal conduct, and
> > (b)   the recovery of the value of the property constituting the benefit will be hindered by telling the named person of the arrest.
>
> (5B)  For the purposes of subsection (5A) above the question whether a person has benefited from his criminal conduct is to be decided in accordance with Part 2 of the Proceeds of Crime Act 2002.'

(3) In section 58 (access to legal advice) for subsection (8A) substitute –

> '(8A)  An officer may also authorise delay where he has reasonable grounds for believing that –

(a) the person detained for the serious arrestable offence has benefited from his criminal conduct, and

(b) the recovery of the value of the property constituting the benefit will be hindered by the exercise of the right conferred by subsection (1) above.

(8B) For the purposes of subsection (8A) above the question whether a person has benefited from his criminal conduct is to be decided in accordance with Part 2 of the Proceeds of Crime Act 2002.'

(4) In section 116 (meaning of serious arrestable offence) in subsection (2) for paragraph (c) and the word 'and' immediately preceding it substitute –

'(c) any offence which is specified in paragraph 1 of Schedule 2 to the Proceeds of Crime Act 2002 (drug trafficking offences),

(d) any offence under section 327, 328 or 329 of that Act (certain money laundering offences).'

## Bankruptcy (Scotland) Act 1985

**15** (1) The Bankruptcy (Scotland) Act 1985 is amended as follows.

(2) In section 5(4) (meaning of 'qualified creditor') for the words from 'has the meaning' to '1995' substitute 'means a confiscation order under Part 2, 3 or 4 of the Proceeds of Crime Act 2002'.

(3) In section 7(1) (meaning of 'apparent insolvency') for the words from 'has the meaning assigned' where second occurring to 'said Act of 1994' where second occurring substitute "confiscation order' and 'restraint order' mean a confiscation order or a restraint order made under Part 2, 3 or 4 of the Proceeds of Crime Act 2002'.

(4) After section 31 (vesting of estate at date of sequestration) insert –

### '31A  Property subject to restraint order

(1) This section applies where –

(a) property is excluded from the debtor's estate by virtue of section 420(2)(a) of the Proceeds of Crime Act 2002 (property subject to a restraint order),

(b) an order under section 50, 52, 128, 198 or 200 of that Act has not been made in respect of the property, and

(c) the restraint order is discharged.

(2) On the discharge of the restraint order the property vests in the permanent trustee as part of the debtor's estate.

(3) But subsection (2) does not apply to the proceeds of property realised by a management receiver under section 49(2)(d) or 197(2)(d) of that Act (realisation of property to meet receiver's remuneration and expenses).

### 31B  Biodiesel used otherwise than as road fuel

(1) This section applies where –

(a) property is excluded from the debtor's estate by virtue of section 420(2)(b), (c) or (d) of the Proceeds of Crime Act 2002 (property in respect of which an order for the appointment of a receiver or administrator under certain provisions of that Act is in force), and

(b) a confiscation order is made under section 6, 92 or 156 of that Act,

(c)   the amount payable under the confiscation order is fully paid, and

(d)   any of the property remains in the hands of the receiver or administrator (as the case may be).

(2) The property vests in the permanent trustee as part of the debtor's estate.

### 31C   Property subject to certain orders where confiscation order discharged or quashed

(1) This section applies where –

(a)   property is excluded from the debtor's estate by virtue of section 420(2)(a), (b), (c) or (d) of the Proceeds of Crime Act 2002 (property in respect of which a restraint order or an order for the appointment of a receiver or administrator under that Act is in force),

(b)   a confiscation order is made under section 6, 92 or 156 of that Act, and

(c)   the confiscation order is discharged under section 30, 114 or 180 of that Act (as the case may be) or quashed under that Act or in pursuance of any enactment relating to appeals against conviction or sentence.

(2) Any property in the hands of a receiver appointed under Part 2 or 4 of that Act or an administrator appointed under Part 3 of that Act vests in the permanent trustee as part of the debtor's estate.

(3) But subsection (2) does not apply to the proceeds of property realised by a management receiver under section 49(2)(d) or 197(2)(d) of that Act (realisation of property to meet receiver's remuneration and expenses).'

(5) In section 55 (effect of discharge) after subsection (2) insert –

'(3) In subsection (2)(a) above the reference to a fine or other penalty due to the Crown includes a reference to a confiscation order made under Part 2, 3 or 4 of the Proceeds of Crime Act 2002.'.

## Insolvency Act 1986

**16** (1) The Insolvency Act 1986 is amended as follows.

(2) In section 281 (effect of discharge) after subsection (4) insert –

'(4A) In subsection (4) the reference to a fine includes a reference to a confiscation order under Part 2, 3 or 4 of the Proceeds of Crime Act 2002.'

(3) After section 306 insert –

### '306A   Property subject to restraint order

(1) This section applies where –

(a)   property is excluded from the bankrupt's estate by virtue of section 417(2)(a) of the Proceeds of Crime Act 2002 (property subject to a restraint order),

(b)   an order under section 50, 52, 128, 198 or 200 of that Act has not been made in respect of the property, and

(c)   the restraint order is discharged.

(2) On the discharge of the restraint order the property vests in the trustee as part of the bankrupt's estate.

(3) But subsection (2) does not apply to the proceeds of property realised by a management receiver under section 49(2)(d) or 197(2)(d) of that Act (realisation of property to meet receiver's remuneration and expenses).

### 306B  Property in respect of which receivership or administration order made

(1) This section applies where –

    (a)  property is excluded from the bankrupt's estate by virtue of section 417(2)(b), (c) or (d) of the Proceeds of Crime Act 2002 (property in respect of which an order for the appointment of a receiver or administrator under certain provisions of that Act is in force),

    (b)  a confiscation order is made under section 6, 92 or 156 of that Act,

    (c)  the amount payable under the confiscation order is fully paid, and

    (d)  any of the property remains in the hands of the receiver or administrator (as the case may be).

(2) The property vests in the trustee as part of the bankrupt's estate.

### 306C  Property subject to certain orders where confiscation order discharged or quashed

(1) This section applies where –

    (a)  property is excluded from the bankrupt's estate by virtue of section 417(2)(a), (b), (c) or (d) of the Proceeds of Crime Act 2002 (property in respect of which a restraint order or an order for the appointment of a receiver or administrator under that Act is in force),

    (b)  a confiscation order is made under section 6, 92 or 156 of that Act, and

    (c)  the confiscation order is discharged under section 30, 114 or 180 of that Act (as the case may be) or quashed under that Act or in pursuance of any enactment relating to appeals against conviction or sentence.

(2) Any such property in the hands of a receiver appointed under Part 2 or 4 of that Act or an administrator appointed under Part 3 of that Act vests in the trustee as part of the bankrupt's estate.

(3) But subsection (2) does not apply to the proceeds of property realised by a management receiver under section 49(2)(d) or 197(2)(d) of that Act (realisation of property to meet receiver's remuneration and expenses).'

## Criminal Justice Act 1988

**17** (1) The Criminal Justice Act 1988 is amended as follows.

(2) The following provisions shall cease to have effect –

    (a)  sections 71 to 102;

    (b)  Schedule 4.

(3) In section 151(4) (Customs and Excise power of arrest) omit 'and' after paragraph (a), and after paragraph (b) insert –

    '(c)  a money laundering offence;'

(4) In section 151(5) for the words after 'means' substitute 'any offence which is specified in –

(a)  paragraph 1 of Schedule 2 to the Proceeds of Crime Act 2002 (drug trafficking offences), or

(b)  so far as it relates to that paragraph, paragraph 10 of that Schedule.'

(5)  In section 151 after subsection (5) insert –

'(6)  In this section 'money laundering offence' means any offence which by virtue of section 415 of the Proceeds of Crime Act 2002 is a money laundering offence for the purposes of Part 8 of that Act.'

(6)  In section 152(4) (remands of suspected drugs offenders to customs detention) for the words after 'means' substitute 'any offence which is specified in –

(a)  paragraph 1 of Schedule 5 to the Proceeds of Crime Act 2002 (drug trafficking offences), or

(b)  so far as it relates to that paragraph, paragraph 10 of that Schedule.'

## Extradition Act 1989

18  (1)  The Extradition Act 1989 is amended as follows.

(2)  In section 22 (extension of purposes of extradition for offences under Acts giving effect to international conventions) in subsection (4)(h) –

(a)  for sub-paragraph (i) substitute –

'(i)  any offence which is specified in –
    (a)  paragraph 1 of Schedule 2 to the Proceeds of Crime Act 2002 (drug trafficking offences), or
    (b)  so far as it relates to that paragraph, paragraph 10 of that Schedule;
(ia)  any offence which by virtue of section 415 of the Proceeds of Crime Act 2002 is a money laundering offence for the purposes of Part 8 of that Act;';

(b)  for sub-paragraph (ii) substitute –

'(ii)  any offence which is specified in –
    (a)  paragraph 2 of Schedule 4 to the Proceeds of Crime Act 2002, or
    (b)  so far as it relates to that paragraph, paragraph 10 of that Schedule;
(iia)  any offence which by virtue of section 415 of the Proceeds of Crime Act 2002 is a money laundering offence for the purposes of Part 8 of that Act;';

(c)  omit 'and' after sub-paragraph (ii) and for sub-paragraph (iii) substitute –

'(iii)  any offence which is specified in –
    (a)  paragraph 1 of Schedule 5 to the Proceeds of Crime Act 2002 (drug trafficking offences), or
    (b)  so far as it relates to that paragraph, paragraph 10 of that Schedule; and
(iv)  any offence which by virtue of section 415 of the Proceeds of Crime Act 2002 is a money laundering offence for the purposes of Part 8 of that Act;'.

(3)  In paragraph 15 of Schedule 1 (deemed extension of jurisdiction of foreign states) –

(a)  for paragraph (j) substitute –

'(j)  any offence which is specified in –
    (i)  paragraph 1 of Schedule 2 to the Proceeds of Crime Act 2002 (drug trafficking offences), or
    (ii)  so far as it relates to that paragraph, paragraph 10 of that Schedule;
(ja)  any offence which by virtue of section 415 of the Proceeds of Crime Act 2002 is a money laundering offence for the purposes of Part 8 of that Act;';

  (b)  for paragraph (k) substitute –

    '(k)  any offence which is specified in –
        (i)   paragraph 2 of Schedule 4 to the Proceeds of Crime Act 2002, or
       (ii)  so far as it relates to that paragraph, paragraph 10 of that Schedule;
   (ka)  any offence which by virtue of section 415 of the Proceeds of Crime Act 2002 is a money laundering offence for the purposes of Part 8 of that Act;';

  (c)  for paragraph (m) substitute –

    '(m)  any offence which is specified in –
        (i)   paragraph 1 of Schedule 5 to the Proceeds of Crime Act 2002 (drug trafficking offences), or
       (ii)  so far as it relates to that paragraph, paragraph 10 of that Schedule;
  (ma)  any offence which by virtue of section 415 of the Proceeds of Crime Act 2002 is a money laundering offence for the purposes of Part 8 of that Act;'.

## Police and Criminal Evidence (Northern Ireland) Order 1989 (SI 1989/1341 (NI 12))

**19** (1)  The Police and Criminal Evidence (Northern Ireland) Order 1989 is amended as follows.

(2)  In Article 57 (right to have someone informed when arrested) for paragraph (5A) substitute –

'(5A)  An officer may also authorise delay where he has reasonable grounds for believing that –

    (a)  the person detained for the serious arrestable offence has benefited from his criminal conduct, and
    (b)  the recovery of the value of the property constituting the benefit will be hindered by telling the named person of the arrest.

(5B)  For the purposes of paragraph (5A) the question whether a person has benefited from his criminal conduct is to be decided in accordance with Part 4 of the Proceeds of Crime Act 2002.'

(3)  In Article 59 (access to legal advice) for paragraph (8A) substitute –

'(8A)  An officer may also authorise delay where he has reasonable grounds for believing that –

    (a)  the person detained for the serious arrestable offence has benefited from his criminal conduct, and
    (b)  the recovery of the value of the property constituting the benefit will be hindered by the exercise of the right conferred by paragraph (1).

(8B)  For the purposes of paragraph (8A) the question whether a person has benefited from his criminal conduct is to be decided in accordance with Part 4 of the Proceeds of Crime Act 2002.'

(4)  In Article 87 (meaning of serious arrestable offence) in paragraph (2) for sub-paragraph (aa) substitute –

    '(aa)  any offence which is specified in paragraph 1 of Schedule 5 to the Proceeds of Crime Act 2002 (drug trafficking offences);
    (ab)  any offence under section 327, 328 or 329 of that Act (certain money laundering offences);'.

**Insolvency (Northern Ireland) Order 1989 (SI 1989/2405 (NI 19))**

**20** (1)  The Insolvency (Northern Ireland) Order 1989 is amended as follows.

(2)  In Article 255 (effect of discharge) after paragraph (4) insert –

'(4A)  In paragraph (4) the reference to a fine includes a reference to a confiscation order under Part 2, 3 or 4 of the Proceeds of Crime Act 2002.'

(3)  After Article 279 insert –

**'279A    Property subject to restraint order**

(1)  This Article applies where –

    (a)   property is excluded from the bankrupt's estate by virtue of section 423(2)(a) of the Proceeds of Crime Act 2002 (property subject to a restraint order),

    (b)   an order under section 50, 52, 128, 198 or 200 of that Act has not been made in respect of the property, and

    (c)   the restraint order is discharged.

(2)  On the discharge of the restraint order the property vests in the trustee as part of the bankrupt's estate.

(3)  But paragraph (2) does not apply to the proceeds of property realised by a management receiver under section 49(2)(d) or 197(2)(d) of that Act (realisation of property to meet receiver's remuneration and expenses).

**279B    Property in respect of which receivership or administration order made**

(1)  This Article applies where –

    (a)   property is excluded from the bankrupt's estate by virtue of section 423(2)(b), (c) or (d) of the Proceeds of Crime Act 2002 (property in respect of which an order for the appointment of a receiver or administrator under certain provisions of that Act is in force),

    (b)   a confiscation order is made under section 6, 92 or 156 of that Act,

    (c)   the amount payable under the confiscation order is fully paid, and

    (d)   any of the property remains in the hands of the receiver or administrator (as the case may be).

(2)  The property vests in the trustee as part of the bankrupt's estate.

**279C    Property subject to certain orders where confiscation order discharged or quashed**

(1)  This Article applies where –

    (a)   property is excluded from the bankrupt's estate by virtue of section 423(2)(a), (b), (c) or (d) of the Proceeds of Crime Act 2002 (property in respect of which a restraint order or an order for the appointment of a receiver or administrator under that Act is in force),

    (b)   a confiscation order is made under section 6, 92 or 156 of that Act, and

    (c)   the confiscation order is discharged under section 30, 114 or 180 of that Act (as the case may be) or quashed under that Act or in pursuance of any enactment relating to appeals against conviction or sentence.

(2) Any such property in the hands of a receiver appointed under Part 2 or 4 of that Act or an administrator appointed under Part 3 of that Act vests in the trustee as part of the bankrupt's estate.

(3) But paragraph (2) does not apply to the proceeds of property realised by a management receiver under section 49(2)(d) or 197(2)(d) of that Act (realisation of property to meet receiver's remuneration and expenses).'

## Criminal Justice (International Co-operation) Act 1990

**21** In section 13(6) of the Criminal Justice (International Co-operation) Act 1990 (information not to be disclosed except for certain purposes) –

(a) omit 'the Drug Trafficking Act 1994 or the Criminal Justice (Scotland) Act 1987';
(b) at the end insert 'or of proceedings under Part 2, 3 or 4 of the Proceeds of Crime Act 2002'.

## Pension Schemes Act 1993

**22** (1) The Pension Schemes Act 1993 is amended as follows.

(2) In section 10 (protected rights and money purchase benefits), after subsection (5) insert –

'(6) Where, in the case of a scheme which makes such provision as is mentioned in subsection (2) or (3), any liability of the scheme in respect of a member's protected rights ceases by virtue of a civil recovery order, his protected rights are extinguished or reduced accordingly.'

(3) In section 14 (earner's guaranteed minimum), after subsection (2) insert –

'(2A) Where any liability of a scheme in respect of an earner's guaranteed minimum pension ceases by virtue of a civil recovery order, his guaranteed minimum in relation to the scheme is extinguished or reduced accordingly.'

(4) In section 47 (further provisions relating to guaranteed minimum pensions), in subsection (6), after 'but for' insert 'section 14(2A) and'.

(5) In section 68B (safeguarded rights), at the end insert 'including provision for such rights to be extinguished or reduced in consequence of a civil recovery order made in respect of such rights'.

(6) In section 181(1) (general interpretation), after the definition of 'Category A retirement pension' insert –

'"civil recovery order" means an order under section 266 of the Proceeds of Crime Act 2002 or an order under section 276 imposing the requirement mentioned in section 277(3).'

## Pension Schemes (Northern Ireland) Act 1993

**23** (1) The Pension Schemes (Northern Ireland) Act 1993 is amended as follows.

(2) In section 6 (protected rights and money purchase benefits), after subsection (5) insert –

'(6) Where, in the case of a scheme which makes such provision as is mentioned in subsection (2) or (3), any liability of the scheme in respect of a member's protected rights ceases by virtue of a civil recovery order, his protected rights are extinguished or reduced accordingly.'

(3) In section 10 (earner's guaranteed minimum), after subsection (2) insert –

'(2A) Where any liability of a scheme in respect of an earner's guaranteed minimum pension ceases by virtue of a civil recovery order, his guaranteed minimum in relation to the scheme is extinguished or reduced accordingly.'

(4) In section 43 (further provisions relating to guaranteed minimum pensions), in subsection (6), after 'but for' insert 'section 10(2A) and'.

(5) In section 64B (safeguarded rights), at the end insert 'including provision for such rights to be extinguished or reduced in consequence of a civil recovery order made in respect of such rights'.

(6) In section 176(1) (general interpretation), after the definition of 'Category A retirement pension' insert –

'"civil recovery order" means an order under section 266 of the Proceeds of Crime Act 2002 or an order under section 276 imposing the requirement mentioned in section 277(3).'

## Criminal Justice and Public Order Act 1994

24 In section 139(12) of the Criminal Justice and Public Order Act 1994 (search powers) in paragraph (b) of the definition of 'items subject to legal privilege' for 'section 40 of the Criminal Justice (Scotland) Act 1987' substitute 'section 412 of the Proceeds of Crime Act 2002'.

## Drug Trafficking Act 1994

25 (1) The Drug Trafficking Act 1994 is amended as follows.

(2) The following provisions shall cease to have effect –

  (a) sections 1 to 54;
  (b) in sections 55(4)(a) (orders to make material available) and 56(3)(a) and (4)(a) (authority for search) the words 'or has benefited from';
  (c) in section 59 (disclosure of information held by government departments), subsections (1) to (10) and in subsection (11) the words 'An order under subsection (1) above, and,';
  (d) in section 60(6) (Customs and Excise prosecution powers), in the definition of 'specified offence', in paragraph (a) the words 'Part III or' and paragraph (c) and the word 'or' immediately preceding it;
  (e) in section 60(6) the words from 'and references to the institution of proceedings' to the end;
  (f) in section 60, subsections (7) and (8);
  (g) in section 61 (extension of certain offences to the Crown), subsections (2) to (4);
  (h) sections 62, 63(1), (2) and (3)(a) and 64 (interpretation);
  (i) in section 68(2) (extent –Scotland), paragraphs (a) to (c) and in paragraph (g) the words '1, 41, 62' and '64';
  (j) in section 68(3) (extent –Northern Ireland), paragraph (a) and in paragraph (d) the word '64'.

(3) In section 59(12)(b) for the words 'referred to in subsection (1) above' substitute 'specified in an order under section 55(2)'.

(4) After section 59 insert the following section –

### '59A　Construction of sections 55 to 59

(1) This section has effect for the purposes of sections 55 to 59.

(2) A reference to a constable includes a reference to a customs officer.

(3) A customs officer is a person commissioned by the Commissioners of Customs and Excise under section 6(3) of the Customs and Excise Management Act 1979.

(4) Drug trafficking means doing or being concerned in any of the following (whether in England and Wales or elsewhere) –

    (a) producing or supplying a controlled drug where the production or supply contravenes section 4(1) of the Misuse of Drugs Act 1971 or a corresponding law;

    (b) transporting or storing a controlled drug where possession of the drug contravenes section 5(1) of that Act or a corresponding law;

    (c) importing or exporting a controlled drug where the importation or exportation is prohibited by section 3(1) of that Act or a corresponding law;

    (d) manufacturing or supplying a scheduled substance within the meaning of section 12 of the Criminal Justice (International Co-operation) Act 1990 where the manufacture or supply is an offence under that section or would be such an offence if it took place in England and Wales;

    (e) using any ship for illicit traffic in controlled drugs in circumstances which amount to the commission of an offence under section 19 of that Act.

(5) In this section 'corresponding law' has the same meaning as in the Misuse of Drugs Act 1971.'

(5) In section 60 after subsection (6) insert –

'(6A) Proceedings for an offence are instituted –

    (a) when a justice of the peace issues a summons or warrant under section 1 of the Magistrates' Courts Act 1980 (issue of summons to, or warrant for arrest of, accused) in respect of the offence;

    (b) when a person is charged with the offence after being taken into custody without a warrant;

    (c) when a bill of indictment is preferred under section 2 of the Administration of Justice (Miscellaneous Provisions) Act 1933 in a case falling within paragraph (b) of subsection (2) of that section (preferment by direction of the criminal division of the Court of Appeal or by direction, or with the consent, of a High Court judge).

(6B) Where the application of subsection (6A) would result in there being more than one time for the institution of proceedings they must be taken to have been instituted at the earliest of those times.'

(6) In section 61(1) for 'sections 49(2), 50 to 53 and 58' substitute 'section 58'.

(7) In section 68(2)(d), for '59(10)' substitute '59(11)'.

## Criminal Justice (Northern Ireland) Order 1994 (SI 1994/2795 (NI 15))

**26** In Article 16 of the Criminal Justice (Northern Ireland) Order 1994 in paragraph (a) after 'Proceeds of Crime (Northern Ireland) Order 1996' insert 'or Part 4 of the Proceeds of Crime Act 2002'.

## Proceeds of Crime Act 1995

**27** Section 15(2) and (3) of the Proceeds of Crime Act 1995 (investigation into benefit to be treated as the investigation of an offence for the purposes of sections 21 and 22 of the Police and Criminal Evidence Act 1984) shall cease to have effect.

## Proceeds of Crime (Scotland) Act 1995

**28** (1)  The Proceeds of Crime (Scotland) Act 1995 is amended as follows.

(2)  The following provisions in the Act shall cease to have effect –

- (a)  Part I, except section 2(7);
- (b)  in section 28, subsections (1)(a) and (2) and in subsection (5) the words '(including a restraint order made under and within the meaning of the 1994 Act)';
- (c)  section 29;
- (d)  in section 31, subsection (2) and in subsection (4) the words 'or (2)';
- (e)  sections 35 to 39;
- (f)  in section 40, subsections (1)(a), (2) and (4);
- (g)  in section 42, subsections (1)(a) and (b);
- (h)  in section 43, in subsection (1) the words ', confiscation order' and subsection (2);
- (i)  in section 45, subsection (1)(a);
- (j)  section 47;
- (k)  in section 49, in subsection (1) the definitions of 'the 1988 Act', 'the 1994 Act' and 'confiscation order' and subsection (4).

(3)  The following provisions in Schedule 1 to the Act shall cease to have effect –

- (a)  in paragraph 1(1)(b) the words 'or a confiscation order', in paragraph 1(2)(a) the words 'subject to paragraph (b) below', paragraph 1(2)(b) and in paragraph 1(3)(a)(i) the words 'or confiscation order';
- (b)  in paragraph 2(1)(a) the words ', and if appointed (or empowered) under paragraph 1(1)(b) above where a confiscation order has been made';
- (c)  paragraph 4;
- (d)  in paragraph 5(1) the words 'Part I of';
- (e)  in paragraph 8(2) the words ', unless in a case where a confiscation order has been made there are sums available to be applied in payment of it under paragraph 4(4)(b) above,';
- (f)  in paragraph 10(1) the words 'or the recipient of a gift caught by Part I of this Act or an implicative gift' and paragraphs 10(2) and 10(3);
- (g)  in paragraph 12(1)(a) the words 'paragraph (a) or (b) of section 4(1) or'.

(4)  The following provisions in Schedule 2 to the Act shall cease to have effect –

- (a)  in paragraph 1(2) the words 'and 35 to 38';
- (b)  in paragraph 2, in sub-paragraph (1) the words 'realisable or', in sub-paragraph (2) the words 'and 35 to 38', sub-paragraph (5).
- (c)  in paragraph 3(2) the words 'and 35 to 38' and paragraphs 3(4) and (5);
- (d)  in paragraph 4(2) the words 'and 35 to 38';
- (e)  paragraph 6(2)(a).

(5)  In section 28(9) (restraint orders) for 'Subsections (2)(a) and' substitute 'Subsection'.

(6)  In section 42 (enforcement) in subsections (2)(a), (c) and (d) for 'Part I,' substitute 'Part'.

## Criminal Procedure (Scotland) Act 1995

**29** (1)  The Criminal Procedure (Scotland) Act 1995 is amended as follows.

(2)  In section 109(1) (intimation of appeal) for 'section 10 of the Proceeds of Crime (Scotland) Act 1995 (postponed confiscation orders)' substitute 'section 99 of the Proceeds of Crime Act 2002 (postponement)'.

(3)  In section 205B(5) (minimum sentence for third drug trafficking offence) for the definition of 'drug trafficking offence' substitute –

'"drug trafficking offence" means an offence specified in paragraph 2 or (so far as it relates to that paragraph) paragraph 10 of Schedule 4 to the Proceeds of Crime Act 2002;'.

(4) In section 219(8)(b) (fines: imprisonment for non-payment) for '14(2) of the Proceeds of Crime (Scotland) Act 1995' substitute '118(2) of the Proceeds of Crime Act 2002'.

## Police Act 1996

**30** (1) Section 97 of the Police Act 1996 (police officers engaged on service outside their force) is amended as follows.

(2) In subsection (1) after paragraph (cc) insert –

> '(cd) temporary service with the Assets Recovery Agency on which a person is engaged with the consent of the appropriate authority;'.

(3) In subsection (6)(a) after '(cc)' insert '(cd)'.

(4) In subsection (8) after '(cc)' insert '(cd)'.

## Proceeds of Crime (Northern Ireland) Order 1996 (SI 1996/1299 (NI 9)

**31** (1) The Proceeds of Crime (Northern Ireland) Order 1996 is amended as follows.

(2) Parts II and III shall cease to have effect.

(3) The following provisions shall also cease to have effect –

(a) in Article 2 (interpretation) in paragraph (2) from the definition of 'charging order' to the definition of 'external confiscation order' and from the definition of 'modifications' to the definition of 'restraint order' and paragraphs (3) to (10) and (12);

(b) Article 3 (definition of 'property' etc);

(c) in Article 49 (additional investigation powers), in paragraph (1) sub-paragraph (c) and the word 'and' immediately preceding it, in paragraph (1A) sub-paragraph (c) and the word 'and' immediately preceding it, paragraph (4) and in paragraph (5) the definitions of 'customs officer' and 'relevant property';

(d) in Article 52 (supplementary provisions) in paragraph (2) sub-paragraph (b) and the word 'and' immediately preceding it, and paragraph (3);

(e) in Article 54 (disclosure of information held by government departments) paragraphs (1) to (10) and (13) and in paragraph (11) the words 'An order under paragraph (1) and,';

(f) in Article 55 (Customs and Excise prosecution powers), in paragraph (6) in the definition of 'specified offence' in paragraph (a) the words 'Part III or' and paragraph (c) and the word 'or' immediately preceding it, and paragraph (7);

(g) Article 56(2) to (4) (extension of certain offences to the Crown);

(h) in Schedule 2 paragraph 3.

(4) In Article 49(1) (additional investigation powers) –

(a) for 'county court' substitute 'Crown Court';

(b) in sub-paragraph (a) for the words from 'an investigation' to the end of head (ii) substitute 'a confiscation investigation';

(c) in sub-paragraph (b) after 'and who is' insert 'an accredited financial investigator'.

(5) In Article 49(1A) –

(a) after 'application made by' insert 'the Director of the Assets Recovery Agency or';

(b)  for 'county court' substitute 'Crown Court';

(c)  in sub-paragraph (a) for the words from 'an investigation' to the end of head (ii) substitute 'a confiscation investigation';

(d)  in sub-paragraph (b) after 'if' insert 'the Director or';

(e)  after 'authorise' insert 'the Director or';

(f)  for 'paragraphs 3 and 3A' where it twice occurs substitute 'paragraph 3A'.

(6)  In Article 49(5) insert at the appropriate place in alphabetical order –

' "accredited financial investigator" has the meaning given by section 3(5) of the Proceeds of Crime Act 2002;

"confiscation investigation" has the same meaning as it has for the purposes of Part 8 of that Act by virtue of section 341(1);'.

(7)  In Article 50(1) (order to make material available) –

(a)  for sub-paragraphs (a) and (b) substitute 'drug trafficking';

(b)  for 'county court' substitute 'Crown Court'.

(8)  In Article 50(4)(a), for heads (i) to (iii) substitute 'has carried on drug trafficking'.

(9)  In Article 50(8) for 'county court' substitute 'Crown Court'.

(10)  In Article 51(1) (authority for search) –

(a)  for sub-paragraphs (a) and (b) substitute 'drug trafficking';

(b)  for 'county court' substitute 'Crown Court'.

(11)  In Article 51(3)(a) for heads (i) to (iii) substitute 'has carried on drug trafficking'.

(12)  In Article 51(4) –

(a)  in sub-paragraph (a) for heads (i) to (iii) substitute 'has carried on drug trafficking';

(b)  in sub-paragraph (b)(i) for the words from 'the question' to the end substitute 'drug trafficking'.

(13)  In Article 52(1)(a) (supplementary provisions), for heads (i) to (ii) substitute 'drug trafficking'.

(14)  In Article 54 (disclosure of information held by government departments) in paragraph (12)(b) for 'referred to in paragraph (1)' substitute 'specified in an order under Article 50(2)'.

(15)  After Article 54 insert the following Article –

## '54A  Construction of Articles 49 to 54

(1)  This Article has effect for the purposes of Articles 49 to 54.

(2)  A reference to a constable includes a reference to a customs officer.

(3)  A customs officer is a person commissioned by the Commissioners of Customs and Excise under section 6(3) of the Customs and Excise Management Act 1979.

(4)  Drug trafficking means doing or being concerned in any of the following (whether in Northern Ireland or elsewhere) –

(a)  producing or supplying a controlled drug where the production or supply contravenes section 4(1) of the Misuse of Drugs Act 1971 or a corresponding law;

(b) transporting or storing a controlled drug where possession of the drug contravenes section 5(1) of that Act or a corresponding law;

(c) importing or exporting a controlled drug where the importation or exportation is prohibited by section 3(1) of that Act or a corresponding law;

(d) manufacturing or supplying a scheduled substance within the meaning of section 12 of the Criminal Justice (International Co-operation) Act 1990 where the manufacture or supply is an offence under that section or would be such an offence if it took place in Northern Ireland;

(e) using any ship for illicit traffic in controlled drugs in circumstances which amount to the commission of an offence under section 19 of that Act.

(5) In this Article 'corresponding law' has the same meaning as in the Misuse of Drugs Act 1971.'

(16) In Article 55 after paragraph (6) insert –

'(6A) Proceedings for an offence are instituted –

(a) when a summons or warrant is issued under Article 20 of the Magistrates' Courts (Northern Ireland) Order 1981 in respect of the offence;

(b) when a person is charged with the offence after being taken into custody without a warrant;

(c) when an indictment is preferred under section 2(2)(c), (e) or (f) of the Grand Jury (Abolition) Act (Northern Ireland) 1969.

(6B) Where the application of paragraph (6A) would result in there being more than one time for the institution of proceedings they must be taken to have been instituted at the earliest of those times.'

(17) In Article 56(1) (extension of certain offences to the Crown), for 'Articles 44, 45, 46, 47(2), 48 and' substitute 'Article'.

(18) In Schedule 2 (financial investigations) in paragraph 3A –

(a) in sub-paragraph (1) for 'any conduct to which Article 49 applies' substitute 'his criminal conduct';

(b) after that paragraph insert –

'(1A) For the purposes of sub-paragraph (1) the question whether a person has benefited from his criminal conduct is to be decided in accordance with Part 4 of the Proceeds of Crime Act 2002.'

## Crime (Sentences) Act 1997

32 (1) The Crime (Sentences) Act 1997 is amended as follows.

(2) In section 35 (fine defaulters) in subsection (1)(a) after 'Drug Trafficking Act 1994' insert 'or section 6 of the Proceeds of Crime Act 2002'.

(3) In section 40 (fine defaulters) in subsection (1)(a) after 'Drug Trafficking Act 1994' insert 'or section 6 of the Proceeds of Crime Act 2002'.

## Crime and Punishment (Scotland) Act 1997

33 The following provisions of the Crime and Punishment (Scotland) Act 1997 shall cease to have effect –

(a) section 15(3),

(b) in Schedule 1, paragraph 20.

## Police (Northern Ireland) Act 1998

**34** (1) Section 27 of the Police (Northern Ireland) Act 1998 (members of the Police Service engaged on other police service) is amended as follows.

(2) In subsection (1) after paragraph (c) insert –

'(ca) temporary service with the Assets Recovery Agency on which a member of the Police Service of Northern Ireland is engaged with the consent of the Chief Constable;'.

(3) In subsection (5)(b) after '(c)' insert '(ca)'.

(4) In subsection (7) for 'or (c)' there is substituted '(c) or (ca)'.

## Crime and Disorder Act 1998

**35** In Schedule 8 to the Crime and Disorder Act 1998 paragraphs 115 and 116 shall cease to have effect.

## Access to Justice Act 1999

**36** (1) Schedule 2 to the Access to Justice Act 1999 (services excluded from the Community Legal Service) is amended as follows.

(2) In paragraph 2(2), after paragraph (d) insert

'or

(e) under the Proceeds of Crime Act 2002 to the extent specified in paragraph 3,'

and omit the 'or' at the end of paragraph (c).

(3) In paragraph 2(3) (magistrates courts), after '2001' insert –

'(l) for an order or direction under section 295, 297, 298, 301 or 302 of the Proceeds of Crime Act 2002,'

and omit the 'or' at the end of paragraph (j).

(4) After paragraph 2 insert –

'3 (1) These are the proceedings under the Proceeds of Crime Act 2002 –

(a) an application under section 42(3) to vary or discharge a restraint order or an order under section 41(7);
(b) proceedings which relate to a direction under section 54(3) or 56(3) as to the distribution of funds in the hands of a receiver;
(c) an application under section 62 relating to action taken or proposed to be taken by a receiver;
(d) an application under section 63 to vary or discharge an order under any of sections 48 to 53 for the appointment of or conferring powers on a receiver;
(e) an application under section 72 or 73 for the payment of compensation;
(f) proceedings which relate to an order under section 298 for the forfeiture of cash;
(g) an application under section 351(3), 362(3), 369(3) or 375(2) to vary or discharge certain orders made under Part 8.

(2) But sub-paragraph (1) does not authorise the funding of the provision of services to a defendant (within the meaning of Part 1 of that Act) in relation to –

(a) proceedings mentioned in paragraph (b);

(b) an application under section 73 for the payment of compensation if the confiscation order was varied under section 29.'

## Powers of Criminal Courts (Sentencing) Act 2000

**37** (1) The Powers of Criminal Courts (Sentencing) Act 2000 is amended as follows.

(2) In section 110(5) (minimum sentence for third drug trafficking offence) for the definition of 'drug trafficking offence' there is substituted –

'"drug trafficking offence" means an offence which is specified in –

(a) paragraph 1 of Schedule 2 to the Proceeds of Crime Act 2002 (drug trafficking offences), or
(b) so far as it relates to that paragraph, paragraph 10 of that Schedule.'

(3) In section 133 (review of compensation orders) in subsection (3)(c) after 'Criminal Justice Act 1988' insert ', or Part 2 of the Proceeds of Crime Act 2002,'.

## Financial Services and Markets Act 2000

**38** In Schedule 1 to the Financial Services and Markets Act 2000 (provisions relating to the Financial Services Authority) after paragraph 19 insert –

'**19A** For the purposes of this Act anything done by an accredited financial investigator within the meaning of the Proceeds of Crime Act 2002 who is –

(a) a member of the staff of the Authority, or
(b) a person appointed by the Authority under section 97, 167 or 168 to conduct an investigation,

must be treated as done in the exercise or discharge of a function of the Authority.'

## Terrorism Act 2000

**39** (1) Schedule 8 to the Terrorism Act 2000 (detention) is amended as follows.

(2) In paragraph 8 (authorisation of delay in exercise of detained person's rights) for sub-paragraph (5) substitute –

'(5) An officer may also give an authorisation under sub-paragraph (1) if he has reasonable grounds for believing that –

(a) the detained person has benefited from his criminal conduct, and
(b) the recovery of the value of the property constituting the benefit will be hindered by –
(i) informing the named person of the detained person's detention (in the case of an authorisation under sub-paragraph (1)(a)), or
(ii) the exercise of the right under paragraph 7 (in the case of an authorisation under sub-paragraph (1)(b)).

(5A) For the purposes of sub-paragraph (5) the question whether a person has benefited from his criminal conduct is to be decided in accordance with Part 2 of the Proceeds of Crime Act 2002.'

(3) In paragraph 17(3) (grounds for authorising delay or requiring presence of senior officer), in paragraph (d) for 'Part VI of the Criminal Justice Act 1988, Part I of the Proceeds of Crime (Scotland) Act 1995' substitute 'Part 2 or 3 of the Proceeds of Crime Act 2002'.

(4) For paragraph 17(4) (further grounds for authorising delay in exercise of detained person's rights) substitute –

'(4) This sub-paragraph applies where an officer mentioned in paragraph 16(4) or (7) has reasonable grounds for believing that –

(a) the detained person has benefited from his criminal conduct, and
(b) the recovery of the value of the property constituting the benefit will be hindered by –
 (i) informing the named person of the detained person's detention (in the case of an authorisation under paragraph 16(4)), or
 (ii) the exercise of the entitlement under paragraph 16(6) (in the case of an authorisation under paragraph 16(7)).

(4A) For the purposes of sub-paragraph (4) the question whether a person has benefited from his criminal conduct is to be decided in accordance with Part 3 of the Proceeds of Crime Act 2002.'

(5) In paragraph 34 (authorisation for withholding information from detained person) for sub-paragraph (3) substitute –

'(3) A judicial authority may also make an order under sub-paragraph (1) in relation to specified information if satisfied that there are reasonable grounds for believing that –

(a) the detained person has benefited from his criminal conduct, and
(b) the recovery of the value of the property constituting the benefit would be hindered if the information were disclosed.

(3A) For the purposes of sub-paragraph (3) the question whether a person has benefited from his criminal conduct is to be decided in accordance with Part 2 or 3 of the Proceeds of Crime Act 2002.'

## Criminal Justice and Police Act 2001

**40** (1) The Criminal Justice and Police Act 2001 is amended as follows.

(2) In section 55 (obligation to return excluded and special procedure material) in subsection (5) (powers in relation to which section does not apply as regards special procedure material) omit 'and' after paragraph (b), and after paragraph (c) insert –

'and

(d) section 352(4) of the Proceeds of Crime Act 2002,'.

(3) In section 60 (cases where duty to secure seized property arises) in subsection (4) (powers in relation to which duty does not arise as regards special procedure material) omit 'or' after paragraph (b), and after paragraph (c) insert –

'or

(d) section 352(4) of the Proceeds of Crime Act 2002,'.

(4) In section 64 (meaning of appropriate judicial authority) in subsection (3) after paragraph (a) omit 'and' and insert –

'(aa) the power of seizure conferred by section 352(4) of the Proceeds of Crime Act 2002, if the power is exercisable for the purposes of a civil recovery investigation (within the meaning of Part 8 of that Act);'.

(5) In section 65 (meaning of 'legal privilege') –

(a) in subsection (1)(b) for the words '33 of the Criminal Law (Consolidation) (Scotland) Act 1995' substitute '412 of the Proceeds of Crime Act 2002';

(b) after subsection (3) insert –

'(3A) In relation to property which has been seized in exercise, or purported exercise, of –

(a) the power of seizure conferred by section 352(4) of the Proceeds of Crime Act 2002, or

(b) so much of any power of seizure conferred by section 50 as is exercisable by reference to that power,

references in this Part to an item subject to legal privilege shall be read as references to privileged material within the meaning of section 354(2) of that Act.'

(6) In Part 1 of Schedule 1 (powers of seizure to which section 50 applies) at the end add –

### 'Proceeds of Crime Act 2002

**73A** The power of seizure conferred by section 352(4) of the Proceeds of Crime Act 2002 (seizure of material likely to be of substantial value to certain investigations).'

(7) In Part 3 of Schedule 1 (powers of seizure to which section 55 applies) at the end add –

### 'Proceeds of Crime Act 2002

**110** The power of seizure conferred by section 352(4) of the Proceeds of Crime Act 2002 (seizure of material likely to be of substantial value to certain investigations).'

## SCHEDULE 12[1]   REPEALS AND REVOCATIONS

| *Short title and chapter* | *Extent of repeal or revocation* |
|---|---|
| Misuse of Drugs Act 1971 | In section 21 the words 'or section 49 of the Drug Trafficking Act 1994'. In section 23(3A) the words 'or section 49 of the Drug Trafficking Act 1994'. |
| Criminal Appeal (Northern Ireland) Act 1980 | In section 30(3) the word 'and' after paragraph (b). |
| Police and Criminal Evidence Act 1984 | In section 65 – (a) the definitions of 'drug trafficking' and 'drug trafficking offence'; (b) the words from 'references in this Part' to 'in accordance with the Drug Trafficking Act 1994'. |
| Criminal Justice Act 1988 | Sections 71 to 102. In section 151(4) the word 'and' after paragraph (a). In section 172 – (a) in subsection (2) the words from 'section 76(3)' to 'extending to Scotland'; (b) in subsection (4) the words from 'sections 90' to 'section 93E'. Schedule 4. |
| Housing Act 1988 | In Schedule 17, paragraphs 83 and 84. |

---

1   Information: Commencement: Not yet in force.

| Short title and chapter | Extent of repeal or revocation |
|---|---|
| Extradition Act 1989 | In section 22(4)(h) the word 'and' after sub-paragraph (ii). |
| Police and Criminal Evidence (Northern Ireland) Order 1989 (SI 1989/1341 (NI 12)) | In Article 53 –<br>(a) the definitions of 'drug trafficking' and 'drug trafficking offence';<br>(b) the words from 'References in this Part' to 'Order 1996'. |
| Criminal Justice (International Co-operation) Act 1990 | In section 13(6) the words 'the Drug Trafficking Act 1994 or'.<br>Section 14.<br>In Schedule 4, paragraph 1. |
| Criminal Justice (Confiscation) (Northern Ireland) Order 1990 (SI 1990/2588 (NI 17)) | In Article 37 –<br>(a) paragraph (2);<br>(b) in paragraphs (3) and (4) sub-paragraph (b) and the word 'and' before it;<br>(c) paragraph (5). |
| Criminal Justice Act 1993 | Section 21(3)(e) to (g).<br>Sections 27 to 35.<br>In Schedule 4, paragraph 3.<br>In Schedule 5, paragraph 14. |
| Criminal Justice and Public Order Act 1994 | In Schedule 9, paragraph 36. |
| Drug Trafficking Act 1994 | Sections 1 to 54.<br>In sections 55(4)(a) and 56(3)(a) and (4)(a) the words 'or has benefited from'.<br>In section 59, subsections (1) to (10) and in subsection (11) the words 'An order under subsection (1) above, and'.<br>In section 60(6), in the definition of 'specified offence', in paragraph (a) the words 'Part III or' and paragraph (c) and the word 'or' immediately preceding it.<br>In section 60(6), the words from 'and references to the institution of proceedings' to the end.<br>Section 60(7) and (8).<br>Section 61(2) to (4).<br>Sections 62, 63(1), (2) and (3)(a) and 64.<br>In section 68(2), paragraphs (a) to (c) and in paragraph (g) the words '1, 41, 62' and '64'.<br>In section 68(3), paragraph (a) and in paragraph (d) the word '64'.<br>In Schedule 1, paragraphs 3, 4(a), 8, 21 and 26. |
| Proceeds of Crime Act 1995 | Sections 1 to 13.<br>Section 15(1) to (3).<br>Section 16(2), (5) and (6).<br>Schedule 1. |
| Criminal Law (Consolidation) (Scotland) Act 1995 | Part V. |
| Criminal Procedure (Consequential Provisions) (Scotland) Act 1995 | In Schedule 3, paragraph 4(2).<br>In Schedule 4, paragraphs 69 and 94. |

| *Short title and chapter* | *Extent of repeal or revocation* |
|---|---|
| Private International Law (Miscellaneous Provisions) Act 1995 | Section 4(3). |
| Proceeds of Crime (Scotland) Act 1995 | Part I, except section 2(7).<br>In section 28, subsections (1)(a) and (2) and in subsection (5) the words '(including a restraint order made under and within the meaning of the 1994 Act)'.<br>Section 29.<br>In section 31, subsection (2), in subsection (4) the words 'or (2)'.<br>Sections 35 to 39.<br>In section 40, subsections (1)(a), (2) and (4).<br>In section 42, subsections (1)(a) and (b).<br>In section 43, in subsection (1) the words 'confiscation order', subsection (2).<br>Section 45(1)(a).<br>Section 47.<br>In section 49, in subsection (1) the definitions of 'the 1988 Act', 'the 1994 Act' and 'confiscation order' and subsection (4).<br>In Schedule 1, in paragraph 1, in sub-paragraph (1)(b) the words 'or a confiscation order', in sub-paragraph (2)(a) the words 'subject to paragraph (b) below', sub-paragraph (2)(b), in sub-paragraph (3)(a)(i) the words 'or confiscation order'.<br>In Schedule 1, in paragraph 2, in sub-paragraph (1)(a) the words ', and if appointed (or empowered) under paragraph 1(1)(b) above where a confiscation order has been made', paragraph 4, in paragraph 5(1) the words 'Part I of', in paragraph 8(2) the words from ', unless in a case where a confiscation order has been' to '4(4)(b) above,'.<br>In Schedule 1, in paragraph 10(1) the words 'or the recipient of a gift caught by Part I of this Act or an implicative gift', paragraphs 10(2) and (3), in paragraph 12(1)(a) the words 'paragraph (a) or (b) of section 4(1) or'.<br>In Schedule 2, in paragraph 1(2) the words 'and 35 to 38', in paragraph 2(1) the words 'realisable or', in paragraph 2(2) the words 'and 35 to 38', paragraph 2(5), in paragraph 3(2) the words 'and 35 to 38', paragraphs 3(4) and (5), in paragraph 4(2) the words 'and 35 to 38', paragraph 6(2)(a). |
| Proceeds of Crime (Northern Ireland) Order 1996 (SI 1996/1299 (NI 9)) | Parts II and III.<br>In Article 2 in paragraph (2) from the definition of 'charging order' to the definition of 'external confiscation order' and from the definition of 'modifications' to the definition of 'restraint order' and paragraphs (3) to (10) and (12).<br>Article 3.<br>In Article 49, in paragraph (1) sub-paragraph (c) and the word 'and' immediately preceding it, in paragraph (1A) sub-paragraph (c) and the word |

| *Short title and chapter* | *Extent of repeal or revocation* |
|---|---|
| | 'and' immediately preceding it, paragraph (4) and in paragraph (5) the definitions of 'customs officer' and 'relevant property'. |
| | In Article 52 in paragraph (2) sub-paragraph (b) and the word 'and' immediately preceding it, and paragraph (3). |
| | In Article 54 paragraphs (1) to (10) and (13) and in paragraph (11) the words 'An order under paragraph (1) and,'. |
| | In Article 55, in paragraph (6) in the definition of 'specified offence' in paragraph (a) the words 'Part III or' and paragraph (c) and the word 'or' immediately preceding it, and paragraph (7). |
| | Article 56(2) to (4). |
| | In Schedule 2– |
| |    (a)  in paragraph 1(3) '3 or'; |
| |    (b)  paragraph 3; |
| |    (c)  in paragraphs 4(2), 5(1) and 6(1) '3'. |
| | In Schedule 3, paragraphs 1 to 3 and 18. |
| Justices of the Peace Act 1997 | In Schedule 5, paragraphs 23 and 36. |
| Crime and Punishment (Scotland) Act 1997 | Section 15(3). In Schedule 1, paragraph 20. |
| Crime and Disorder Act 1998 | Section 83. In Schedule 1, paragraphs 115 and 116. In Schedule 8, paragraph 114. In Schedule 9, paragraph 8. |
| Access to Justice Act 1999 | In Schedule 2 – <br>    (a)  in paragraph 2(2) the word 'or' at the end of paragraph (c); <br>    (b)  in paragraph 2(3) the word 'or' at the end of paragraph (j). <br> In Schedule 13, paragraphs 139 and 172. |
| Powers of Criminal Courts (Sentencing) Act 2000 | In Schedule 9, paragraphs 105 to 113 and 163 to 173. |
| Terrorism Act 2000 | In Schedule 15, paragraphs 6, 10 and 11(2). |
| Criminal Justice and Police Act 2001 | In section 55(5) paragraph (a) and the word 'and' after paragraph (b). In section 60(4) paragraph (a) and the word 'or' after paragraph (b). In section 64(3) the word 'and' after paragraph (a). In Schedule 1, paragraphs 47 and 105. |
| Financial Investigations (Northern Ireland) Order 2001 (SI 2001/1866 (NI 1)) | Articles 3(2)(b) and 4(1)(a) and (c), (2), (3) and (5). |
| Land Registration Act 2002 | In Schedule 11, paragraphs 22 and 32. |
| This Act | Section 248(2)(a) and (4). |

# Appendix 3

# DRAFT
# CODE OF PRACTICE
# ISSUED UNDER SECTION 377 OF
# THE PROCEEDS OF CRIME ACT 2002

## Introduction

1.   This code of practice governs the exercise of the investigation powers in Chapter 2 of Part 8 of the Proceeds of Crime Act 2002 ('the Act'). It is issued by the Home Secretary under section 377 of the Act. The code provides guidance as to how such powers in respect of confiscation, civil recovery and money laundering investigations are to be used in England, Wales and Northern Ireland. There is a separate code of practice in respect of the Scottish powers in Chapter 3 issued by Scottish Ministers under section 410. These powers of investigation are not available where cash has been detained under chapter 3 of part 5, where an interim receiving order or administration order has been made or where civil recovery proceedings have started. They are also not available for revenue investigations (part 6).

2.   Where a person fails to comply with any provision of the code, he is not by reason only of that failure liable to any criminal or civil proceedings, but the code is admissible as evidence in such proceedings and a court may take account of any failure to comply with its provisions in determining any questions in the proceedings. Minor deviations from the provisions of the code do not constitute a breach of the code provided there has been no significant prejudice to the investigation or persons connected to the investigation.

3.   A summary of the powers and access to them is provided in the table attached to this code. Also annexed to the code are models of the warrants and orders, and information in support of applications. These act as models for appropriate officers, but are not prescribed forms.[1]

## Persons covered by the code

4.   This code of practice places obligations on all those who either apply for or execute the five powers of investigation in England, Wales and Northern Ireland. Chapter 2 has a basic framework by which appropriate officers apply for and execute the investigation powers. A definition of appropriate officer is found at section 378. These are variously the Director of the Assets Recovery Agency ('the Agency'[2]), an accredited financial investigator,[3] a constable and a customs officer. The identity of the appropriate officer in each case depends on the type of investigation and the specific power.

---

1   These documents are still under development and are liable to amendment but show the basic structure envisaged. The orders will be similar for criminal and civil investigations. The models provided are for confiscation and money laundering investigations; for civil recovery, the orders and warrants will be different, as they will be made in respect of property rather than a person. Disclosure orders will have similar templates

2   Throughout this code references to the Agency mean the Assets Recovery Agency, unless some other meaning is obviously implied.

3   An accredited financial investigator is a civilian investigator accredited by the Director of the Agency to have access to some or all of the powers of investigation. The accredited financial investigator will also have to fall within a category given in an order issued by the Home Secretary. It is envisaged that this will include financial investigators who are working for government departments, agencies and other bodies who have the existing function of investigating acquisitive crime, e.g. all types of fraud.

5.   A search and seizure warrant (sections 352(5) and 353(10)) must be executed by an appropriate person. An appropriate person is a constable or customs officer in respect of warrants issued in respect of a confiscation or money laundering investigation, and a member of the staff of the Agency in respect of a civil recovery investigation. These persons' actions will also be covered by this code of practice.

6.   The disclosure order (section 357(1)) is only available to the Director. Under section 1(6) of the Act, the Director can authorise a member of the staff of the Agency or a person providing services under arrangements to perform his functions. The code therefore also covers persons to whom the Director has delegated investigation powers. They should look for references to 'the Director' in determining their obligations. If the Director does delegate this responsibility, he or she will provide written authority, which the person must produce when acting as the Director under the Act and this code.

7.   This code of practice should be readily available at all police stations for consultation by police and members of the public. The code should also form part of the published instructions or guidance for customs officers. The Agency will also make arrangements for the code to be publicly available (whether in a hard form or electronically). Government Departments and other bodies who have accredited financial investigators operating the powers of investigation should also make arrangements for the code to be available to both their staff and members of the public.

8.   The code only applies to functions carried out under Chapter 2 of Part 8. Those carrying out functions under Part 8 do not have to have regard to other codes of practice, e.g. those issued under the Police and Criminal Evidence Act 1984 ('PACE') or section 292 of the Act.

9.   The production order and search warrant provisions under the Drug Trafficking Act 1994 still remain in respect of investigations into the **offences** of drug trafficking. This code does not relate to those provisions. However, appropriate officers and financial investigators should be aware that the powers of investigation into the **benefit** of drug trafficking under the Drug Trafficking Act are now repealed and have been replaced by the provisions of the Act, and therefore are covered by this code.[1]

## General provisions relating to all the orders and warrants

*Action to be taken before an application is made*

10.   The powers of investigation may involve significant interference with privacy of those whose premises are searched; on whom personal information is obtained; or whose personal information, material or documents are seen and/or seized by an appropriate officer or appropriate person. This places an obligation upon those operating the powers of investigation to ensure that the application for the order or warrant is fully and clearly justified. In particular, appropriate officers should consider at every stage whether the necessary objectives can be achieved by less intrusive means.

11.   Officers should be aware that the operation of the Act is subject to the Human Rights Act 1998 and consider their use of the powers of investigation accordingly. The use of the powers which impact upon individual's rights under the ECHR (European Convention on Human Rights) must be proportionate to the outcome being sought.

---

1    The order describing the accredited financial investigators will be laid and brought into force at the same time as this code.

12.   An appropriate officer will have to satisfy a judge that any infringement of, for example, a person's right to privacy under Article 8 of the ECHR is proportionate to the benefit to be gained from making an order or warrant. The appropriate officer must satisfy himself or herself of these issues, as with the other requirements for the making of orders/warrants, before an application is made. This becomes a greater consideration in respect of orders and warrants made against people who are not themselves under investigation.

13.   Before a judge can grant any of the Part 8 orders or warrants, he will have to be satisfied that the statutory requirements are met. For each order or warrant to be granted, there is a statutory requirement that there must be reasonable grounds for suspecting that a person has benefited from his criminal conduct, has committed a money laundering offence (except in the case of the disclosure order which is not available for investigation of money laundering offences) or that the property specified in the application can be recovered under Part 5 of the Act.

14.   Reasonable grounds for suspicion depend on the circumstances in each case. There must be an objective basis for that suspicion based on facts and/or information. Reasonable suspicion can never be supported on the basis of personal factors alone without reliable supporting information. Where information is received which appears to justify an application the appropriate officer concerned must take reasonable steps to check that the information is accurate, recent and has not been provided maliciously or irresponsibly. An application must not be made on the basis of information from an anonymous source unless there is corroboration.

15.   For each order or warrant to be granted, there is a statutory requirement that there must be reasonable grounds for believing that the material or information is likely to be of substantial value (whether or not by itself) to the investigation. The appropriate officer must be satisfied that the material or information will progress the investigation.

16.   There is also a statutory requirement that there must be reasonable grounds for believing that it is in the public interest that the material or information is obtained or accessed by the appropriate officer. The appropriate officer must make sure that the public interest in obtaining the order outweighs the disadvantages to the person against whom the order is being made. For example, an application for an account monitoring order against a bank should not normally be made unless the appropriate officer considers that this may lead to the identification of monies greater than the anticipated cost to the bank in complying with the order.[1]

17.   The appropriate officer must satisfy himself or herself that all of these statutory requirements are satisfied before making the application.

18.   The Act only requires appropriate officers to obtain authorisation for their applications in respect of customer information orders. However, appropriate officers should, where practicable, obtain internal authorisation in respect of applications for the other orders and warrants. The appropriate officer should therefore obtain the authorisation of a senior officer (at least inspector rank in the police or the equivalent rank of seniority within the department or agency for which the appropriate officer works). This does not apply to disclosure orders which are only available to the Director.

*Action to be taken in making an application*

19.   All the applications for the powers of investigation may be made ex parte to a judge in chambers.[2] In deciding whether the application should be ex parte, the appropriate officer should

---

1    The appropriate officer is under no obligation to divulge the anticipated cost he or she has decided.

2    This means that an appropriate officer can apply for an order or warrant without notifying the respondent that the application is being contemplated or made.

consider the benefit of not holding the proceedings inter partes.[1] The usual reason would be so as not to alert the persons connected to an investigation that such is ongoing. This may have the effect of the person moving material and thereby frustrating the investigation. However, where a production order is against a financial institution (who would be the respondent), the institution should normally be notified of the intention of making an application for an investigation order – the application hearing could then be held inter partes.

20.     An application in respect of a civil recovery investigation must be made to a High Court judge in accordance with the relevant civil procedure rules and Practice Direction.[2]

21.     The following must be included in an application for an order or warrant:–

- the name of the person who is under investigation or who holds property which is under investigation and confirmation that the information sought is for the purposes of the investigation. If the application is for an order against a different person to the one under investigation, he or she must also be named on the application and there must be an explanation of the person's connection to the investigation;
- the grounds on which the application is made; and
- confirmation that none of the material or information sought is or consists of items subject to legal privilege or excluded material (with the exception of information relating to a client's name and address which is subject to legal privilege requested under a disclosure order. This does not apply to customer information orders and account monitoring orders as the type of information requested will not be that which could be subject to legal privilege.

22.     The identity of an informant needs not be disclosed when making an application, but the appropriate officer should be prepared to deal with any questions the judge may have about the accuracy of previous information provided by that source or any other related matters.

23.     The person applying must be ready to prove to the judge that he or she is an appropriate officer (see section 378) who may apply for the order or warrant.[3]

*Action to be taken in serving an order or warrant*

24.     In all cases, the investigatory powers should be exercised courteously and with respect for the persons and property of those concerned.

25.     In deciding the method of service of the order, the appropriate officer should take into account all the circumstances of the investigation, including the possible need to prove that service was effected, and the person or body on whom the order is served. Search and seizure warrants are executed by an 'appropriate person' who must also have regard to these actions in service of the warrant.

26.     When serving the order, warrant or (in the case of a disclosure order and customer information order) notice under the order, a covering letter must be provided which includes the following information (unless it is already included in order or the notice):

---

1     Inter partes applications are those notified to the respondent of the contemplated order or warrant. They are therefore aware of the application and can be represented at the hearing.
2     Specific references to the applicable rules will be inserted into this paragraph. These have yet to be written and issued, but will be laid prior to this code coming into force. The need for Crown Court rules is still under consideration.
3     This could be a police or customs officer's warrant card. Documentation confirming the status of accredited financial investigators, the Director and persons authorised by the Director to perform his functions, is still under development.

- the name of the subject of the order or the name by which he or she is known;
- a warning in plain language that failure without reasonable excuse to comply with the requirement is an offence and could result in prosecution;
- a warning that disclosure of information about the investigation may contravene section 342 ('offences of prejudicing investigation'), and that if anyone contacts the respondent about the investigation they should report this to the appropriate officer or appropriate person;
- a general description of the investigation in connection with which the requirement is made; [it is not necessary to specify the name of the person or property subject to the investigation on the order, although this must be imparted to the judge at the application stage]; and
- that the subject of the order should seek legal advice or ask the appropriate officer about any doubts or concerns they may have, or for guidance on complying with the order.
- the duty not to falsify, conceal, destroy or otherwise dispose of, or cause or permit the falsification, concealment, destruction or disposal of relevant documents which are relevant to any confiscation, civil recovery or money laundering investigation which the subject of the order knows or suspects is being or is about to be conducted; and a warning that to do so is an offence punishable by up to five years imprisonment and an unlimited fine; and
- the duty not to disclose to any other person information or any other matter which is likely to prejudice any confiscation, civil recovery or money laundering investigation which the subject of the order knows or suspects is being or is about to be conducted and a warning to do so is an offence punishable by up to five years imprisonment and an unlimited fine.

27.   When serving a disclosure order or a customer information order, the appropriate officer must inform the subject of his right to refuse to comply with any requirement imposed on him or her unless the appropriate officer has, if required to do so, produced evidence of his authority.

28.   Where it appears to the appropriate officer or person that the recipient of an order or warrant has genuine difficulty in reading or understanding English he or she should attempt to serve a copy of the order on a person known to the recipient who, in the opinion of the appropriate officer or person, is able to explain or translate what is happening. If this not practicable the appropriate officer or person should attempt to engage an interpreter or translator to effect service of the order or warrant.

29.   Sections 359(1) and 366(1) provide that an offence is committed if without reasonable excuse, a person or financial institution fails to comply with a requirement imposed by a disclosure or customer information order. The other orders are treated as orders of the court and therefore attract contempt proceedings if they are not complied with. The recipient of the order should be warned in plain language that failure without reasonable excuse to comply with the requirement of an order is an offence that could result in prosecution, imprisonment and/or a fine.

30.   What in law amounts to a reasonable excuse may depend on the facts of each particular case and will be a matter for decision by a court. But the fact that a person has already been questioned in connection with the same or a connected investigation, that the question relates to activities outside the jurisdiction or that a truthful answer to a question would tend to incriminate the interviewee or some other person is unlikely, in itself, to amount to a reasonable excuse.

31.   Section 449 of the Act empowers the Director to direct that a member of staff of the Agency may identify himself or herself by means of a pseudonym when authorised to carry out functions

under the Act. An application may be made or service of an order or warrant may be carried out using a pseudonym. A certificate signed by the Director is sufficient to identify a member of staff of the Agency and the member of staff may not be asked any question which is likely to reveal his or her true identity. The pseudonym provision does not extend to appropriate officers working outside the Agency, for example police officers or accredited financial investigators, working for a government department.

32.    No document may be removed or accessed and no information sought which is subject to legal privilege (with the one limited exception in respect of the disclosure order as explained in that part of the code). A respondent has the right to withhold material and information sought which is subject to legal privilege The Act relies upon the evolving definition of legal privilege as in caselaw which is relied upon in High Court proceedings. The current caselaw broadly defines the concept as communications between a lawyer and his client regarding contemplated or actual legal proceedings. However such communications made in the furtherance of a criminal purpose are not privileged.

33.    None of the powers of investigation allow access to excluded material. Excluded material is defined at section 11 of PACE and includes journalistic material and medical records.

34.    Where an appropriate person is executing a search and seizure warrant, then under Part 2 of the Criminal Justice and Police Act 2001, he can seize privileged or excluded material if it is not reasonably practicable for him to determine on the premises whether the material he is seizing includes privilege or excluded material.

35.    Aside from the legal privilege provision, requirements for information made under the powers of investigation take precedence in spite of any restriction on the disclosure of information, however imposed. They therefore take precedence over any contractual duties of confidentiality and the common law duty of confidence.

*Action to be taken in receiving an application for an extension of a time limit*

36.    It is for the appropriate officer to set the time limit for replies to disclosure orders and customer information orders. Where the subject of one of these orders asks for more time to comply with one of these orders, the appropriate officer must consider the request. When he has made his decision, the appropriate officers must set out his decision and the reasons for it in a letter to the subject of the order. The type of requests that the appropriate officer should accept are those on the grounds of obtaining legal advice, difficulty in obtaining requested information and/or documents and an interviewee's unavailability. The decision letter must be served in the same way as the original notice under the order was served.

37.    Where a solicitor acting on behalf of the subject of the order makes the application for an extension of time, the letter may be served on the solicitor.

38.    Time limits for compliance with a production order and an account monitoring order are set out on the face of the order – (see sections 345(5) and 370(6)). Therefore they cannot be extended unless the subject of the order applies to the court for a variation of the order. If the appropriate officer receives a request for an extension of the time limit to comply with a production order or an account monitoring order, he or she should direct the subject of the order to the court.[1]

---

1    This underlines the importance of an appropriate officer requesting a reasonable time limit at the time of his application for a production order or an account monitoring order. The appropriate officer should liase where possible with the subject of the order. Realistic time limits in orders will reduce later applications to the court for extensions of time.

*Record of Proceedings*

39.   The appropriate officer must keep or cause to be kept a record of the exercise of the powers conferred by the provisions of Chapter 2 of Part 8.

40.   The record must, in relation to each requirements, include:

- a copy of the order or warrant and copies of notices given under an order;
- the date on which the order, warrant or notice was served;
- the date of receipt of and reason for any request for an extension of the time allowed to comply with the order;
- the decision in respect of any such request and the date on which it was notified to the subject of the order;
- the date and place that the information or documents were received in response to the order;
- receipts provided in accordance with the provisions of this code;

*Retention of documents and information*

41.   If documents or information are provided which were not required to be provided under the terms of the order, no account of that document or information must be taken of it in the investigation and it must be returned to the sender of the material.

42.   Appropriate officers should follow established local procedures on the retention and return of documents, material and information. Intelligence that arises during the appropriate officer's investigation may be passed to the National Criminal Intelligence Service, police, customs, the Assets Recovery Agency and/or other departments and agencies (provided there is a statutory gateway in place for the passing of information between those bodies for that purpose).

## Variation and discharge applications

43.   Where an appropriate officer applies to the court to vary or discharge an order or warrant made under Chapter 2 of Part 8 of the Act, he should, as far as is practicable, follow the same procedure as for the original application. There is no requirement for the same appropriate officer to make the variation or discharge application but if it is a different officer, that officer should be in a position to explain the genuine change of circumstances. These applications are inter partes.[1]

## PRODUCTION ORDERS

44.   Persons to whom this code applies must familiarise themselves with the introduction section which sets out general instructions relating to all the orders and warrants.

## Definition

45.   A production order is an order which can be served on any person or institution, for example a financial institution, requiring the production of material; this might include documents such as bank statements (section 345(4)).

---

1     Unlike an application for an investigation order, both the applicant and respondent are notified of an application for a variation or discharge of the order. They therefore both have the opportunity to be represented before the judge.

## Statutory requirements

46.   The application must specify a person who is subject to a confiscation investigation or a money laundering investigation or property which is subject to a civil recovery investigation. The application must also state that the order is sought for the purposes of a civil recovery, confiscation or money laundering investigation. It must identify the specific material sought or describe the type of material sought and it must specify a person who appears to possess or be in control of the material. It must also state whether production of the material or access to the material is required.

47.   The person named in the order must either produce the material, or provide access to it, as directed by the order. This is within a period decided at the judge's discretion, but section 345(5) provides seven days as the normal period.

## Persons who may apply for a production order

48.   As with the other orders, an application may be made by an appropriate officer; the definition depends on the type of investigation (section 378).

## Particular action to be taken before an application for a production order

49.   The appropriate officer must ascertain, as specifically as is possible in the circumstances, the nature of the material concerned and, where relevant, its location.

50.   The appropriate officer must also make enquiries to establish what, if anything, is known about the likely occupier of the premises where the material is believed to be located and the nature of the premises themselves; and to obtain any other information relevant to the application.

51.   The appropriate officer must consider whether he or she requires production of the material or access to it. In most circumstances he or she would want production, so as to retain it. There are occasions however where, for example, he or she may simply want sight of information contained in larger material, e.g. an entry in a register.

52.   The 7 day time limit for the production of material will apply unless it appears to the judge that a shorter or longer period would be appropriate. Reasons which the appropriate officer might put to the judge for changing the 7 day period are that the investigation may be prejudiced unless there is a shorter time limit, or that it would not be reasonably practicable for the subject of the production order to comply with the seven day time limit due to the nature or amount of documentation required. There will be cases when the best practice is to contact the subject of the production order (e.g. a financial institution) before the application is made to discuss a reasonable time limit.

## Particular action to be taken executing a production order

53.   When a production order is served on a person, business or institution under section 345(4)(a) of the Act, the order or the covering letter must, in addition to the matters specified in paragraph 26 of the general section, state:

- that the order was made under section 345(4)(a) of the Act;
- the material or class of material required to be furnished;
- the period of time within which such documents must be furnished;

54.   Where an order is made under section 345(4)(b) of the Act (for access to material), the order or covering letter must, in addition, state:

- that the order was made under section 345(4)(b) of the Act;

- the material or class of material required to satisfy the production order;
- the appropriate officer's right of access to such material.

55. Section 350 deals with service of a production order on a government department. Where a production order is served on a government department, it must be served in the way that civil proceedings would be served on the department. This means that officers should look at the list of government departments published by the Cabinet Office under section 17 of the Crown Proceedings Act 1947 in order to find the correct address for service. In many cases, the correct procedure may be to serve the order on the Treasury Solicitor. A production order served on a government department can contain a requirement for the person on whom the order is served and anyone else who receives to bring it to the attention of the official who holds the material even if they are unknown at that stage.

## Particular provisions relating to the handling and retention of documents produced or accessed in response to a production order

56. When executing a production order, an appropriate officer should ask for the material specified in the production order to be produced. This request may, if considered necessary, include a request to see the index of files held on the premises if there is one. The appropriate officer may inspect any files which, according to the index, appear to contain any of the material specified in the order or material falling within the class of material specified in the order.

57. When asking for material to be produced in accordance with an order the appropriate officer should direct the request to a person in authority and with responsibility for the material.

58. An appropriate officer may remove any material covered by the production order, except where the production order is made under section 345(4)(b) and only allows access to, rather than removal of, the material.

59. An appropriate officer may photograph or copy or have photographed or copied any material which he or she has power to remove.

60. Where an appropriate officer requires material to be produced from a computer in a form which may be taken away or to which access can be given in a legible form (for example a computer printout or a removable computer disk), in accordance with section 349, care should be taken to ensure that, the person producing the material in this form does not delete evidence from the computer, either deliberately or accidentally.

61. The appropriate officer should complete [unless it is impracticable to do so] a list of the articles or documents removed and give a copy of it and receipt to the occupier [and the subject of the order], if present, before leaving the premises. In any event, the appropriate officer must make or have made a record of the articles removed and or accessed in compliance with a production order. A copy of this record shall be given to the subject of the order within 7 days of the removal or access of the material.

## Order to grant entry

62. An appropriate officer should consider at the application stage if he or she considers the right to enter premises is necessary in order to satisfy the production order. It might be used, for example, to enable an appropriate officer to be granted entry to a building in circumstances where a production order had been made in respect of material in a particular company's office in that building.

63. An order to grant entry differs from a search and seizure warrant in that the order to grant entry is to overcome any physical obstacle in serving the production order. It does not include the power to search the premises.

## SEARCH AND SEIZURE WARRANTS[1]

64. Persons to whom this code applies must familiarise themselves with the introduction section which sets out general instructions relating to all the orders and warrants.

### Definition

65. A search and seizure warrant (defined at section 352(4)) can be issued in the three circumstances set out below, and enables the appropriate person to enter and search the premises specified in the warrant, and to retain material which is likely to be of substantial value to the investigation. The search and seizure warrant does not include a power to stop a person, make an arrest or to search a person. The legislation and the code only apply to searches of premises. For the purpose of this code and the legislation 'premises' is defined in section 23 of Police and Criminal Evidence Act 1984. The definition provides that premises includes any place and, in particular, includes any vehicle, vessel, aircraft or hovercraft, any offshore installation any tent or moveable structure.

66. This code does not apply to searches conducted under other legislation or section 289 of the Act, and does not apply to searches conducted with consent without a search and seizure warrant.

### Persons who can apply for and/or execute search and seizure warrants

67. As with the other powers of investigation, the code deals with appropriate officers' power to make an application for a search and seizure warrant and their right to retain material. This part of the code also deals with appropriate persons' powers to execute the warrants, namely to search the premises and seize and retain relevant material found on premises.

68. As detailed in the general section it is an appropriate officer who must make an application for a search and seizure warrant. This is defined at section 378 as the Director of the Assets Recovery Agency, an accredited financial investigator, a constable or a customs officer, depending on the type of investigation in respect of which the warrants is being requested. The person who is carrying out the investigation will normally make the application. The search warrant must be executed by an appropriate person. As detailed in the introduction, section 352(5) of the Act provides that an appropriate person is a constable or customs officer for search and seizure warrants in respect of confiscation and money laundering investigations, and a member of the staff of the Assets Recovery Agency for warrants in respect of civil recovery investigations.

### Statutory requirements

69. A search and seizure warrant may only be issued if one of three statutory requirements are met.

70. The first requirement is met if a production order has not been complied with and there are reasonable grounds for believing that the material specified in the production order is on the premises specified in the search and seizure warrant.

71. The second requirement is met if the material which is sought can be identified, but it is not practicable to communicate with the person against whom a production order might be made or

---

1  An order will be made under section 355 of the Act applying certain sections of the Police and Criminal Evidence Act 1984 to search and seizure warrants sought in respect of confiscation and money laundering investigations. A Practice Direction will be made on civil procedure relating to search and seizure warrants sought in respect of civil recovery investigations. These are not finalised, and this draft code may need to be amended after they are finalised.

with any person against whom an order to grant entry to premises might be made. This might be satisfied, for example, where the person who owns the material or who controls access to the premises on which the material is held is abroad and therefore it is not possible to communicate with that person. In such circumstances, it is clear that a production order in respect of that person would have no effect. In order for this requirement to be met, the judge must also be satisfied that the investigation might be seriously prejudiced unless immediate access to the premises is secured.

72. The third requirement is met if there are reasonable grounds for believing that there is material on the premises which cannot be identified precisely enough for the purposes of a production order and that the material relates to property or a person specified in the application (appropriate officers should look at section 353 of the Act for full details). This might be satisfied where it is impossible to describe the material in precise detail, but it is known that suspect material belonging to a person is on a premises. In order for this requirement to be met, the judge must also be satisfied that it is not practicable to communicate with anyone who might grant entry to the premises or that entry to the premises will not be granted unless a warrant is produced or that the investigation might be seriously prejudiced unless immediate access to the premises is secured.

## Particular action to be taken before an application for a search and seizure warrant

73. The appropriate officer must note that a search and seizure warrant is the most invasive of the powers of investigation.

74. The appropriate officer should consider why he needs a search and seizure warrant rather than a production order with an order to grant entry.

75. The appropriate officer must ascertain as specifically as is possible in the circumstances the nature of the material to be specified in the application and its location.

76. The appropriate officer must also make reasonable enquiries to establish what, if anything, is known about the likely occupier of the premises and the nature of the premises themselves; whether they have been previously searched and if so how recently; and obtain any other information relevant to the application.

## Particular action in making an application for a search and seizure warrant

77. An application for a search and seizure warrant must include the following information:

- the person who is subject to a confiscation investigation or a money laundering investigation or the property which is subject to a civil recovery investigation;
- that the warrant is sought for the purposes of that investigation;
- which of the conditions under section 352(6)(a), 353(3) or (5) of the Act apply to the application – and why a production order is not appropriate;
- the premises to be searched and the object of the search;
- the material which is sought or that there are reasonable grounds for believing that there is relevant material on the premises which cannot be identified;

78. If an application for a search and seizure warrant is refused, no further application may be made for a warrant to search those premises unless supported by additional grounds.

## Particular action to be taken executing a search and seizure warrant

79. If the appropriate officer who made the application is different from the appropriate person authorised to execute the warrant, the appropriate officer should explain the background and

decision to apply for the warrant to the appropriate person. The appropriate person will thereby have the relevant information which will help him to execute the warrant.

## Time of searches[1]

80.   Searches made under a warrant in respect of a civil recovery investigation must be made within one calendar month from the date of issue of the warrant.

81.   Where the extent or complexity of a search mean that it is likely to take a long time to complete, the appropriate person may wish to consider whether the seize and sift powers can appropriately be used (see paragraph 34).

## Entry other than with consent

82.   Before entering the premises, the appropriate person must first attempt to communicate with the occupier, or any other person entitled to grant access to the premises, by explaining the authority under which entry is sought to the premises, showing the warrant and asking the occupier to allow entry, unless:

- the premises to be searched are known to be unoccupied;
- the occupier and any other person entitled to grant access are known to be absent; or
- there are reasonable grounds for believing that to alert the occupier or any other person entitled to grant access by attempting to communicate with them would frustrate the object of the search or endanger the person concerned or other people.

83.   Before a search begins, the appropriate person must identify him or herself (subject to the provisions relating to pseudonyms of Agency staff) and show an official form of identification, state the purpose of the search and the grounds for undertaking it. The appropriate person does not need to comply with this provision if the circumstances detailed at paragraph 82 apply.

## Notice of powers and rights

84.   The appropriate person must, unless it is impractical to do so, provide the occupier of the premises with a copy of the warrant and a notice in a standard format:

- summarising the extent of the powers of search and seizure conferred in the Act;
- explaining the rights of the occupier of the premises and of the owner of the material seized under this code and as set out in the section 355 Order in connection with warrants issued in respect of a confiscation investigation or a money laundering investigation, or the Practice Direction applying safeguards to civil warrants in respect of a civil recovery investigation;
- stating that a copy of this code is available to be consulted and giving an address at which it can be obtained.

85.   If the occupier is present, copies of the notice mentioned above, and of the warrant must, if practicable, be given to the occupier before the search begins, unless the appropriate person reasonably believes that to do so would frustrate the object of the search or endanger the officers concerned or other people. If the occupier is not present, copies of the notice and of the warrant, should be left in a prominent place on the premises or appropriate part of the premises and endorsed with the name of the appropriate person (or, if authorised, the pseudonym used by a member of staff of the Agency) and the date and time of the search. The warrant itself must be endorsed to show that this has been done.

---

1    Ibid.

## Conduct of searches

86.   Premises may be searched only to the extent necessary to achieve the object of the search, having regard to the size and nature of whatever is sought. No search may continue once the appropriate person is satisfied that whatever is being sought is not on the premises. This does not prevent a further search of the same premises if additional grounds come to light which support a further application for a search warrant. Examples would be when as a result of new information it is believed that articles previously not found or additional articles are on the premises.

87.   Searches must be conducted with due consideration for the property and privacy of the occupier of the premises searched, and with no more disturbance than necessary. They should be conducted at a reasonable time of day unless there are reasonable grounds to suspect that this would frustrate the search. Officers might want to consider the possibility of using reasonable force as a last resort if this appears to be the only way in which to give effect to their power of search.

88.   The occupier must be asked whether he or she wishes a friend, neighbour or other person to witness the search. That person must be allowed to do so unless the appropriate person has reasonable grounds for believing that the presence of the person asked for would seriously hinder the investigation or endanger persons present. A search need not be unreasonably delayed for this purpose. A record of the action taken under this paragraph, including the grounds for refusing a request from the occupier, must be made on the premises search record (see below). This requirement also relates to business and commercial properties if practicable, as well as private addresses.

89.   A person is not required to be cautioned prior to being asked questions that are solely necessary for the purpose of furthering the proper and effective conduct of a search. Examples would include questions to discover who is the occupier of specified premises, to find a key to open a locked drawer or cupboard or to otherwise seek co-operation during the search or to determine whether a particular item is liable to be seized.

## Leaving premises

90.   If premises have been entered by force the appropriate person must, before leaving them, be satisfied that they are secure either by arranging for the occupier or the occupier's agent to be present or by any other appropriate means.

## Seizure of material

91.   An appropriate person may seize:

- anything covered by the warrant;
- anything covered by the powers in Part 2 of the Criminal Justice and Police Act 2001 ("the 2001 Act") which allow an appropriate person to seize property from premises where it is not reasonably practicable to determine on the premises whether he is entitled to seize it and retain it for sifting or examination in secure conditions elsewhere; and
- anything that the appropriate person has the power to seize not covered by the warrant which is discovered during the course of the search (e.g. cash under section 294 of the Act). However, this is incidental to the search powers, and a warrant must not be applied for to search for other material other than that specified in the application. Also, a search must not continue after it appears that there is no more material covered by the warrant on the premises, even if the appropriate person suspects that there are other items which he or she may want to seize.

92.   Appropriate persons must be aware of section 59 of the Criminal Justice and Police Act 2001 which allows persons with a relevant interest in material which has been seized to make an

application to a judicial authority for the return of the material. Appropriate persons must also be aware of the subsequent duty to secure in section 60.

93.   An appropriate person may photograph, image or copy, or have photographed, copied or imaged, any material which he has power to seize.[1] An appropriate person must have regard to his or her statutory obligation to not to retain an original material when a photograph or copy would be sufficient.[2]

94.   Where an appropriate person considers that information which is held in a computer and is accessible from the premises specified in the warrant is relevant to the investigation, the officer may require the information to be produced from the computer in a form which can be taken away (for example a computed printout or a removable computer disk). Care should be taken to ensure that the person producing the material in this form does not delete evidence from the computer, either deliberately or accidentally.

## Particular record of proceedings in executing a search and seizure warrant

95. Where premises have been searched under a warrant issued under Chapter 2 of Part 8 of the Act, the appropriate person must make or have made a record of the search. The record shall include:

- the address of the premises searched;
- the date, time and duration of the search;
- the warrant under which the search was made (a copy of the warrant shall be appended to the record or kept in a place identified in the record);
- subject to the provisions relating to pseudonyms of Agency staff, the name of the appropriate person and the names of all other persons involved in the search;
- the names of any people on the premises if they are known;
- any grounds for refusing the occupier's request to have someone present during the search as set out in paragraph 88;
- either a list of any material seized or a note of where such a list is kept and, if not covered by a warrant, the grounds for their seizure;
- whether force was used, and, if so, the reason why it was used; and
- details of any damage caused during the search, and the circumstances in which it was caused.
- confirmation that premises were left secured and by what means.

96.   The warrant must be endorsed by the appropriate person to show:

- whether any material was seized;
- the date and time at which it was executed;
- subject to the provisions relating to pseudonyms of Agency staff, the name of the appropriate person who executed it; and
- whether a copy of the warrant, together with a copy of the Notice of Powers and Rights, was handed to the occupier; or whether it was endorsed and left on the premises together with the copy notice and, if so, where.

## Search register

97.   A search register must be maintained at each sub-divisional or equivalent police station, each Customs office and at the Assets Recovery Agency. All search records which are required to

---

1     In respect of warrants issued for a confiscation investigation or money laundering investigation, the provision to copy will be dependant on the section 355 Order. In respect of warrants issued for a civil recovery investigation, see section 356.

2     Ibid.

be made shall be made, copied, or referred to in the register.[1] However, police stations are not required to set up a separate register in addition to the one maintained for searches covered by the PACE Codes of Practice.

## Specific procedures for seize and sift powers

98.    Part 2 of the Criminal Justice and Police Act 2001 provides persons who are lawfully on any premises and exercising powers of search and seizure with limited powers to seize material from premises so that they can sift through it or otherwise examine it elsewhere. These powers may be exercised where it is not reasonably practicable to determine on the premises whether or not the person is entitled to seize it. All appropriate persons conducting searches under the Act are permitted to use these powers. Appropriate persons must be careful that they only exercise these powers where it is essential to do so and that they do not remove any more material than is absolutely necessary. The removal of large volumes of material, much of which may not ultimately be retainable, may have serious implications for the owners, particularly where they are involved in business. Appropriate persons must always give careful consideration to whether removing copies or images of relevant material or data would be a satisfactory alternative to removing the originals. Where originals are taken, appropriate persons must always be prepared to facilitate the provision of copies or images for the owners where that is reasonably practicable.

99.    Property seized under section 50 of the 2001 Act must be kept securely and separately from any other material seized under other powers. Section 51 is not relevant as the search and seizure powers under the Act do not extend to seizing material from the person. An examination under section 53 to determine what material may be retained in accordance with the Act must be carried out at soon as practicable, allowing the person from whom the material was seized, or a person with an interest in the material, an opportunity of being present or represented. The appropriate person must ensure that he or she has the facilities for the sift to be conducted in suitable surroundings and that persons from whom the material was seized or who have an interest in the material or their representative can be present.

100.    It is the responsibility of the appropriate person to ensure that, where appropriate, property is returned in accordance with sections 53 to 55 of the 2001 Act. Material which is not retainable (i.e. because it is legally privileged material, excluded material or falls outside the terms of the warrant) must be separated from the rest of the seized property and returned as soon as reasonably practicable after the examination of all the seized property has been completed. Delay is only warranted if very clear and compelling reasons exist. For example, the unavailability of the person to whom the material is to be returned or the need to agree a convenient time to return a very large volume of material. Legally privileged or excluded material which cannot be retained must be returned as soon as reasonably practicable and without waiting for the whole examination to be completed. As set out in section 58 of the 2001 Act, material must be returned to the person from whom it was seized, except where it is clear that some other person has a better right to it. Unlike most other legislation, the Proceeds of Crime Act allows for the seizure and retention of special procedure material. Special procedure material is defined at section 14 of the Police and Criminal Evidence Act 1984 and refers to journalistic and other confidential material acquired or created in the course of a trade, business, profession or unpaid office.

101.    Where an officer involved in the investigation has reasonable grounds to believe that a person with a relevant interest in property seized under section 50 of the 2001 Act intends to

---

1    The government accepts that searches should be recorded to some detail for statistical purposes and potentially for monitoring trends of the use and outcomes of searches. The precise detail of the material held on the search register held by Police, Customs and the Assets Recovery Agency has yet to be fully developed.

make an application under section 59 for the return of any legally privileged or excluded material, the officer in charge of the investigation must be informed and the material seized must be kept secure in accordance with section 61.

102.    The responsibility for ensuring property is properly secured rests ultimately with the appropriate person and the appropriate officer, even if there is a separate person delegated with this specific task. Securing involves making sure that the property is not examined, copied or put to any other use except with the consent of the applicant or in accordance with the directions of the appropriate judicial authority. Any such consent or directions must be recorded in writing and signed by both the applicant or judicial authority and the appropriate person.

103.    Where an appropriate person exercises a power of seizure conferred by section 50 of the 2001 Act that appropriate person must at the earliest opportunity and unless it is impracticable to do so, provide the occupier of the premises or the person from whom the property was seized with a written notice:

- specifying what has been seized in reliance on the powers conferred by that section;
- specifying the grounds on which those powers have been exercised;
- setting out the effect of sections 59 to 61 of the 2001 Act which cover the grounds on which a person with a relevant interest in seized property may apply to a judicial authority for its return and the duty of officers to secure property in certain circumstances where such an application is made;
- specifying the name and address of the person to whom notice of an application to the appropriate judicial authority in respect of any of the seized property must be given; and
- specifying the name and address of the person to whom an application may be made to be allowed to attend the initial examination of the property (i.e. police station, customs office, office of the accredited financial investigator or an Agency building).

104.    If the occupier is not present but there is some other person there who is in charge of the premises, the notice must be given to that person. If there is no one on the premises to whom the notice may appropriately be given, it should either be left in a prominent place on the premises or attached to the exterior of the premises so that it will easily be found.

## Retention[1]

105.    Anything which has been seized in accordance with the above provisions may be retained only for as long as is necessary in connection with the investigation for the purposes of which the warrant was issued or (in the case of confiscation or money laundering investigations) in order to establish its lawful owner, where there are reasonable grounds for believing that it has been obtained in consequence of the commission of an offence.

106.    Property must not be retained if a photograph or copy would suffice for the purposes of evidence in the prospective court proceedings following the investigation.

## Rights of owners etc.[2]

107.    If property is retained, the occupier of the premises on which it was seized or the person who had custody or control of it immediately prior to its seizure must on request be provided with a list or description of the property within a reasonable time.

---

1    In respect of warrants issued for a confiscation investigation or money laundering investigation, the provision to retain will be dependant on the section 355 Order. In respect of warrants issued for a civil recovery investigation, see section 356.
2    In respect of warrants issued for a confiscation investigation or money laundering investigation, the provision to retain will be dependant on the section 355 Order.

108.  That person or their representative must be allowed supervised access to the property to examine it or have it photographed or copied, or must be provided with a photograph or copy, in either case within a reasonable time of any request and at their own expense, unless the appropriate officer has reasonable grounds for believing that this would prejudice the investigation or any proceedings. A record of the grounds must be made in any case where access is denied.

## CUSTOMER INFORMATION ORDERS

109.  Persons to whom this code applies must familiarise themselves with the introduction section which sets out general instructions relating to all the orders and warrants.

### Definition

110.  A customer information order compels a financial institution covered by the application to provide any 'customer information' it has relating to the person specified in the application. 'Customer information' is defined at section 364 of the Act. A 'financial institution' means a person carrying on a business in the regulated sector. Regulated sector is defined at Schedule 9 to the Act.

### Persons who can apply for a customer information order

111.  An appropriate officer must have the authorisation of a senior appropriate officer to make an application for a customer information order. A senior appropriate officer for a confiscation investigation is the Director or a police officer who is not below the rank of superintendent, a customs officer at Pay Band 9 or above or a financial investigator accredited for the function of authorising such applications. For money laundering investigations, a senior appropriate officer is a police officer who is not below the rank of superintendent, a customs officer at Pay Band 9 or above or a financial investigator accredited for the function of authorising such applications. For civil recovery investigations, the senior appropriate officer is the Director. If an investigator is accredited to both apply for and authorise the making of an application for a customer information order, he or she can make such an application without an additional separate authorisation. A police officer who is not below the rank of superintendent, an customs officer at Pay Band 9 or above or the Director can also make such an application without an additional separate authorisation.

### Statutory requirements

112.  The application must specify a person who is subject to a confiscation investigation or money laundering investigation or a person who holds property subject to a civil recovery investigation. It must state that the order is sought for the purposes of that investigation. It must specify the financial institutions from which the appropriate officer wishes to obtain customer information, whether this is done by a list or a description of financial institution. A description of financial institutions may include all financial institutions within a specific geographical area or who specialise in a particular form of account.

### Particular action to be taken before an application for a customer information order is made

113.  The appropriate officer must carefully consider his existing evidence and information so as to limit the number or scope of financial institutions. This would include researching his own force or agency's intelligence systems, the Police National Computer and the National Criminal Intelligence Service. He or she should consider what benefit the customer information he or she

may obtain may have, either in itself or as the lead to other avenues of investigation. He or she should also consider whether the information he or she wishes to gain could not be acquired as effectively and efficiently from material which could be obtained by way of a production order. The appropriate officer should consider the cost both to himself or herself and the financial institutions.

114.   A customer information order should only be sought where there is an ongoing financial investigation of a relatively serious nature. It would therefore be appropriate, as with all other serious operations, that the application should be notified to the National Criminal Intelligence Service.

115.   On receiving a request for authorisation for an application for a customer information order, the senior appropriate officer must consider similar issues. He or she should particularly consider the proportionality of requesting the customer information, against the believed benefit to the investigation. The senior appropriate officer should also consider the broader issues of law enforcement such as the benefit to the community of removing the suspected proceeds from circulation.

## Particular action to be taken executing a customer information order

116.   Section 363(5) of the Act requires a financial institution to provide any customer information which it has relating to the person specified in the application if it is given notice in writing by an appropriate officer. Section 363(6) gives the appropriate office power to request the manner and the time by which the financial institution provides the information. The appropriate officer is expected to impose a reasonable time limit depending on the nature of the institution and the information which is requested. There will be cases when the best practice is to contact the financial institution before the notice is served to discuss a reasonable time limit.

117.   A notice given under a customer information order should include the following:

- the name of the financial institution;
- the name of the person about whom customer information is sought;
- the financial institution's right to refuse to comply with any requirement made of them unless the appropriate officer has, if asked to do so, produced evidence of his authority;
- the period of time within which the customer information must be furnished;
- the manner in which such information must be furnished;
- the place at which the information is to be furnished;
- where the appropriate officer thinks that the customer information includes information in relation to accounts held in any other name which it appears to the appropriate officer that the specified person may have used, that other name;
- where the appropriate officer thinks that the customer information includes information in relation to accounts held in the name of any company or limited liability partnership, which the specified person is or in which it appears to the appropriate officer that the specified person has or had an interest, the name and all known addresses of that company or limited liability partnership;
- all addresses known by the appropriate officer to have been used by the specified person possibly relating to accounts that may have been or are held by the financial institution;
- the date of birth or approximate age of that person if an individual, or any known identification information in respect of a company or limited liability partnership ;
- such other information as the appropriate officer considers would assist the respondent in complying with the requirement; and
- the financial institution's right not to have information furnished used in evidence against it in criminal proceedings other than in the circumstances specified in section 367(2).

## Particular record of proceedings under a customer information order

118. The appropriate officer should keep a copy of the customer information order and all the notices issued to financial institutions under a customer information order. He or she should also keep a record of all the information supplied in response to the notices.

119. The appropriate officer should consider the customer information he or she has obtained and consider whether a production order or account monitoring order would be the next step to obtain further information and material to support the investigation.

## ACCOUNT MONITORING ORDERS

120. Persons to whom this code applies must familiarise themselves with the introduction section which sets out general instructions relating to all the orders and warrants.

## Definition

121. An account monitoring order is an order that requires a specified financial institution to provide account information on a specified account for a specified period, up to 90 days in the manner and at or by the times specified in the order. 'Account information' is information relating to an account held at a financial institution – this would most commonly be transaction details. There is no bar on an appropriate officer making a repeat application for an account monitoring order immediately after an account monitoring order has expired.

## Persons who can apply for an account monitoring order

122. As with the other orders, an application may be made by an appropriate officer; the definition depends on the type of investigation (see section 378 of the Act).

## Statutory requirements

123. The application must specify a person who is subject to a confiscation investigation or money laundering investigation or a person who holds property subject to a civil recovery investigation. It must state that the order is sought for the purposes of that investigation. It must specify the financial institution from which the appropriate officer wishes to obtain the account information. The application must state that the order is sought in relation to account information about the specified person. It must specify the account information which is sought, whether by reference to specific accounts or accounts of a general description.

124. The order also sets the manner and deadline by which the financial institution must produce account information and the period for which the order should last.

## Particular action to be taken before an application for an account monitoring order

125. The appropriate officer has to consider to his investigation the benefit of obtaining information from an account, and whether this information could be as easily obtained by using a production order. He should consider whether in relation to a confiscation investigation he should consider making (or where he is not an accredited financial investigator, asking someone else to make) an application for a restraint order on the account (under section 42 or 191).

126. The appropriate officer should also consider what account information he or she should request. If, for example, the appropriate officer requires information on certain transactions, he or she should consider whether he or she could meaningfully limit the information he or she requires to amounts over a certain threshold or identity of the source of the deposit or destination of a withdrawal.

127.   The period to be specified for compliance with any requirement shall be set by the judge on the order. A reasonable time limit to suggest to the judge might be that the information should be provided within 24 hours on all transactions unless it appears that it would not be reasonably practicable for the subject of the account monitoring order to comply with this time limit. There will be cases when the best practice is to contact the subject of the account monitoring order (i.e. the relevant financial institution) before the application is made to discuss types of transaction and the reporting process.

128.   Appropriate officers should consider if the time period they wish the account monitoring order to cover. The appropriate officer should not treat the 90 day maximum as the standard time limit. They must carefully consider and justify to the judge the requirement for the time period requested.

### Particular action to be taken executing an account monitoring order

129.   When an account monitoring orders is served on a financial institution, the covering letter should include the following (unless it is already included in the order):

- the name of the financial institution;
- the identity of the person(s) who hold the account to be monitored, including as much identity information as is known by the appropriate officer;
- the accounts in relation to which the information is required, whether this is a specific account or a general description of accounts;
- the account information required (in as specific detail as possible, for example a general description of the nature of the transactions);
- the period for which the account monitoring order will have effect;
- the period of time within which such information must be furnished to the appropriate officer (e.g. within 24 hours of a particular transaction taking place);
- the manner in which such information must be furnished;
- such other information as the appropriate officer considers would assist the respondent in complying with the requirements of the account monitoring order;
- the financial institution's right not to have information furnished used in evidence against it in criminal proceedings other than in the circumstances specified in section 367(2).

*Particular record of proceedings under an account monitoring order*

130.   The appropriate officer should keep a record of all the account information supplied in response to the order.

## DISCLOSURE ORDERS

131.   The Director must familiarise himself or herself with the introduction section which sets out general instructions relating to all the orders and warrants.

### Introduction

132.   This part of the code only applies to the Director, due to the disclosure order only being available to the Director. However, under section 1(6) of the Act, the Director can authorise a member of staff of the Agency or a person providing services under arrangements to perform his functions. This part of the code therefore also covers persons to whom the Director has delegated the power to apply for and perform functions under a disclosure order. These delegated persons should be guided by references in the Act to "the Director" in determining their obligations. In the passage relating to interviews, the code uses the term 'person conducting the interview' to clarify that the interview can be undertaken by the Director or a person delegated to perform this function.

## Definition

133. A disclosure order is an order authorising the Director to give notice in writing to any person requiring him or her to answer questions, to provide information or to produce documents with respect to any matter relevant to the investigation in relation to which the order is sought.

134. Once a disclosure order has been made, the Director may use the extensive powers set out in section 357(4) of the Act throughout his investigation. Thus, unlike the other orders which have to be applied for separately on each occasion, a disclosure order gives the Director continuing powers for the purposes of the investigation. The Director must serve a notice on any person he wishes to question or to ask to provide information or documents. The disclosure order is only available for confiscation and civil recovery investigations. The disclosure order is not available for money laundering investigations. In keeping with the other powers the disclosure order is not available for revenue investigations under Part 6 of the Act.

135. Under section 357(6), where a person is given a notice under a disclosure order, he can require that evidence of the authority to give the notice be provided. Where this happens, a copy of the disclosure order should be given to the person.

## Persons who can apply for a disclosure order

136. Only the Director of the Assets Recovery Agency can apply for a disclosure order, and only in respect of his own investigations. He or she cannot apply for and execute a disclosure order on behalf of another agency (i.e. police, customs or other body with the power to conduct a confiscation investigation).

## Statutory requirements

137. The Director has to satisfy the judge that a civil recovery or confiscation investigation is going on and the order is sought for the purposes of that investigation.

## Particular action to be taken in making an application

138. An application for a disclosure order must include the following information:

- the person who is subject to a confiscation investigation or the property which is subject to a civil recovery investigation;
- that the order is sought for the purposes of that investigation;
- if it is a confiscation investigation, that the investigation is being undertaken by the Director or by one of his staff;
- whether the Director is likely to require answers to questions and/or information and/or documents;
- if practicable, the person or persons against whom the power may be used; and
- the grounds on which the application is made (including details of the investigation);
- why a disclosure order is required in preference to the other powers of investigation.

## Particular action to be taken in executing a disclosure order

*Providing of information and production of documents*

139. Production of documents or information in response to a disclosure order should follow similar processes to those set out for production orders. The Director must give notice in writing

to anyone whom he wishes to provide information or documents. In addition to the general requirements at paragraph 26, this notice should include, where applicable:

- whether the Director wants the respondent to provide information under section 357(4)(b) or produce documents under section 357(4)(c) of the Act;
- if the Director requires information, a description of the information required;
- if the Director requires documents, the documents or class of documents required.

### Interview

140.   The disclosure order also contains a power to ask questions. The preferred course of asking questions is to conduct a formalised interview in accordance with the procedure set out below.

### Invitation to interview

141.   The Director must send the interviewee a notice served under the disclosure order which must contain:

- the right of the Director to interview the interviewee under section 357(4)(a) of the Act;
- the purpose of the interview, which may be as detailed as the Director thinks necessary;
- the interviewee's right not to have statements made by him used in evidence in criminal proceedings against him or her other than in the circumstances specified in section 360(2);
- his or her right to be accompanied at any interview by a solicitor and/or a qualified accountant;
- his or her right, if he or she is a juvenile,[1] is mentally disordered or mentally handicapped, to be accompanied at any interview by an appropriate adult;
- details of the place at which the interview is to take place, and
- where attendance is not required at once, the time and date of the interview.

### Legal and Financial advice

142.   In this code, a 'solicitor' means a solicitor who holds a current practising certificate, a trainee solicitor, a duty solicitor representative or an accredited representative included on the register of representatives maintained by the Legal Services Commission. A 'qualified accountant' means a person who is a member or fellow of the Institute of Chartered Accountants in England and Wales, or the Institute of Chartered Accountants of Scotland, or the Institute of Chartered Accountants in Ireland, or the Association of Chartered Certified Accountants or who would, for the purposes of the audit of company accounts be regarded by virtue of section 33 of the Companies Act 1989, as holding an approved overseas qualification.

143.   In urgent cases a person who is not suspected of any unlawful conduct may be prepared to answer questions without the presence of a solicitor and/or qualified account. If a person to be interviewed requests access to legal or financial advice before complying with a requirement to be interviewed in a notice served under a disclosure order, the Director should normally consent and set a reasonable time limit for obtaining such advice. In the exceptional cases set out below the Director can refuse such a request depending on the circumstances of the case and the information or material which is being requested.

144.   A person who requests legal and/or financial advice may not be interviewed or continue to be interviewed until they have received such advice unless:

(a) the person conducting the interview has reasonable grounds for believing that:

---

1    If anyone appears to be under the age of 17 then he or she shall be treated as a juvenile for the purposes of this code in the absence of clear evidence to show that he or she is older.

(i) the consequent delay would be likely to lead to interference with or harm to evidence connected with the investigation; or

(ii) the delay would alert another person whom the person conducting the interview thinks might have information relevant to the investigation and alerting that person would prejudice the investigation;

(b) a solicitor and/or qualified accountant has been contacted and has agreed to attend but the Director considers that awaiting their arrival would cause unreasonable delay to the process of investigation This decision must be made by the Director him or herself and cannot be taken by a person delegated to perform his or her functions under section 1(6) of the Act;

(c) the solicitor and/or qualified accountant whom the person has nominated:

(i) cannot be contacted; or

(ii) has previously indicated that they do not wish to be contacted; or

(iii) having been contacted, has declined to attend and the person being interviewed declines to consult another solicitor and/or qualified accountant;

(c) the person who wanted legal and/or financial advice changes his or her mind.

145. In a case falling within paragraph (a), once sufficient information has been obtained to avert the risk of interference or harm to evidence or of alerting another person so as to prejudice the investigation, questioning must cease until the interviewee has received legal or financial advice.

146. In a case falling within paragraph (c), the interview may be started or continued without further delay provided that the person has given his or her agreement in writing to being interviewed without receiving legal or financial advice and that the person conducting the interview has inquired into the person's reasons for the change of mind and has given authority for the interview to proceed. Confirmation of the person's agreement, his or her change of mind and his or her reasons (where given) must be recorded in the written interview record at the beginning or re-commencement of interview.

If a solicitor wishes to send a non-accredited or probationary representative to provide advice on his behalf, then that person is also recognised as a 'legal adviser' and must be admitted to the interview unless the Director considers that this will hinder the investigation.

147. If a solicitor wishes to send a non-accredited or probationary representative to provide advice on his behalf, then that person is also recognised as a 'legal adviser' and must be admitted to the interview unless the Director considers that this will hinder the investigation.

148. In exercising his discretion as to whether to admit a legal adviser who is not a solicitor, the person conducting the interview should take into account in particular whether the identity and status of the non-accredited or probationary representative have been satisfactorily established; whether he or she is of suitable character to provide legal advice (a person with a criminal record is unlikely to be suitable unless the conviction was for a minor offence and is not recent); and any other matters in any written letter of authorisation provided by the solicitor on whose behalf the person is attending.

149. If the person conducting the interview refuses access to a non-accredited or probationary representative or a decision is taken that such a person should not be permitted to remain at an interview, he or she must forthwith notify a solicitor on whose behalf the non-accredited or probationary representative was to have acted or was acting, and give him or her an opportunity to make alternative arrangements. The interviewee must also be informed.

## Persons who may be present at interviews

150. Interviews must be conducted in private by the person conducting the interview. Another member of the Agency must be present at all times. Only persons whose presence is sanctioned

by this code should be present. It is up to the interviewee to arrange the presence of any solicitor and/or qualified accountant. When doing so he or she should ensure that the person he or she selects is available to attend. Where the provisions of this code require the presence of an appropriate adult or an interpreter and no such person attends with the interviewee the person conducting the interview must, before commencing or restarting any interview, secure the attendance of such a person.

151.    The person conducting the interview may be accompanied by a person to assist in handling documents and carrying out such other support tasks as will assist the person conducting the interview to perform his duties. Such a person has no power to require the interviewee to do anything and need not disclose his name or address provided a record of these is made by the person conducting the interview.

152.    If the person conducting the interview has any suspicion, or is told in good faith, that a person is or appears to be (without clear evidence to the contrary):

- under seventeen years of age;
- mentally disordered;
- mentally handicapped; or
- mentally incapable of understanding the significance of questions put to him or her or his or her replies[1]

he or she shall not be interviewed unless an appropriate adult is present.

## The 'appropriate adult'

153.    In this code 'the appropriate adult' means:
   (a) in the case of a juvenile:
       (i)   his or her parent or guardian (or, if the juvenile is in care a member of staff of the care authority/agency or voluntary organisation. The term 'in care' is used in this code to cover all cases in which a juvenile is 'looked after' by a local authority under the terms of the Children Act 1989);
       (ii)  a social worker;
       (iii) failing either of the above, another responsible adult aged 18 or over who is not a member of staff of the Agency or any law enforcement or prosecuting body.
   (b) in the case of a person who is mentally disordered or mentally handicapped:
       (i)   a relative, guardian or other person responsible for his or her care and custody;
       (ii)  someone who has experience of working with mentally disordered or mentally handicapped people but who is not a member of staff of the Agency or any law enforcement or prosecuting body (such as an approved social worker as defined by the Mental Health Act 1983, a specialist social worker or a community psychiatric nurse); or
       (iii) failing either of the above, some other responsible adult aged 18 or over who is not a member of staff of the Agency or any law enforcement or prosecuting body.

154.    A person, including a parent or guardian, should not be an appropriate adult if he or she is suspected of involvement in the unlawful conduct to which the civil recovery investigation relates or the criminal conduct to which the confiscation investigation relates is involved in the

---

1    'Mental disorder' is defined in section 1(2) of the Mental Health Act 1983 as 'mental illness, arrested or incomplete development of mind, psychopathic disorder and any other disorder or disability of the mind'. Where the person conducting the interview has any doubt about the mental state or capacity of an interviewee, that person should be treated as mentally vulnerable and an appropriate adult should be called.

investigation or has received admissions from the juvenile prior to attending to act as the appropriate adult. If the parent of a juvenile is estranged from the juvenile, he or she should not be asked to act as the appropriate adult if the juvenile expressly and specifically objects to his presence.

155. A person should always be given an opportunity, when an appropriate adult is called to the interview, to consult privately with a solicitor and/or a qualified accountant in the absence of the appropriate adult if they wish to do so.

## Role of persons who may be present at interviews

### Solicitor and Qualified Accountant

156. The main role of any solicitor or qualified accountant is to see that it is conducted in a fair and proper manner. He or she may not answer questions on behalf of the interviewee but he or she may intervene:

- to seek clarification of questions put during the interview;
- to challenge a question put by the Director which he or she considers improper;
- to challenge the manner in which a question is put;
- if the client may have a reasonable excuse for failure to comply with the disclosure order, to advise him or her whether or not to reply to a question; or
- give the interviewee advice.

157. Any request for legal or financial advice and the action taken on it shall be recorded on the record and/or taped. If a person has asked for legal or financial advice and an interview is begun in the absence of a solicitor or qualified accountant (or the solicitor or qualified accountant has been required to leave an interview), a note shall be made in the interview record.

158. The solicitor or qualified accountant may read any documents shown to, or produced by, the interviewee at the interview.

### Appropriate Adult

159. Where the appropriate adult is present at an interview, he or she shall be informed that he or she is not expected to act simply as an observer, and that the purposes of their presence are, first, to advise the person being questioned and to observe whether or not the interview is being conducted properly and fairly, and secondly, to facilitate communication with the person being interviewed.

### Physical Disability

160. A person who is blind or seriously visually impaired may be accompanied by his guide dog. The person conducting the interview shall ensure that the person who is blind or seriously visually impaired has his or her solicitor, relative, the appropriate adult or some other person likely to take an interest in him or her (and not involved in the investigation) available to help in the checking of any documentation. Where this code requires written consent then the person who is assisting may be asked to sign instead if the interviewee so wishes.

161. An interviewee who is seriously physically impaired may be accompanied by an able-bodied adult aged 18 or over to provide such physical assistance, as the interviewee requires. Such a person may take no part in the interview and has none of the rights of an appropriate adult.

*Interpreters*

162.   A person must not be interviewed in the absence of a person capable of acting as interpreter if:

- he or she has difficulty in understanding English and the person conducting the interview cannot speak the person's own language; or
- he or she is deaf or has difficulty with hearing or speaking,

unless the interviewee agrees in writing that the interview may proceed without an interpreter.

163.   An interpreter shall also be called if a juvenile is interviewed and the appropriate adult appears to be deaf or there is doubt about his or her hearing or speaking ability, unless he or she agrees in writing that the interview should proceeds without one.

164.   The interpreter must be provided at the Director's expense. The person conducting the interview must ascertain, as far as is practicable, that the interpreter and interviewee understand each other, and this must be noted on the interview record. An appropriate adult may not act as the interpreter.

165.   The interviewing officer must ensure that the interpreter makes a note of the interview at the time in the language of the person being interviewed for use in the event of his or her being called to give evidence, and certifies its accuracy. The person conducting the interview shall allow sufficient time for the interpreter to make a note of each question and answer after each question and answer has been put or given and interpreted. The interviewee shall be given the opportunity to read it or, in the case of an interviewee who is not deaf or has difficulty in hearing, have it read to him and sign it as correct or to indicate the respects in which he considers it inaccurate.[1]

166.   Action taken to call an interpreter under this section and any agreement to be interviewed in the absence of an interpreter must be recorded in writing and or taped.

*Excluding Persons from the Interview*

167.   The person conducting the interview may exclude from the interview a person whose presence is authorised[2] by the provisions of this code if it appears to the person conducting the interview that the person is mentally disordered (see footnote 20).

168.   Subject to paragraph 167, the person conducting the interview may exclude from the interview a person whose presence is authorised[3] only if he or she has reason to believe that the person is personally involved in the matter under investigation or that the person has, by improper conduct, hindered the proper conduct of the interview. Before excluding any person the person conducting the interview shall state his or her reason and note this on the interview record. What amounts to improper conduct will depend on the circumstances of each case. It would almost always be improper conduct for a person to prompt the interviewee, to provide the interviewee with written answers to the questions, to answer questions on behalf of the interviewee or to interrupt the interview for any reason other than to make a proper representation. Exclusion of any person from an interview is a serious matter which may be subject to comment in court. The person conducting the interview should therefore be prepared to justify his decision.

---

1   The interpreter must make a note of the interview even if it is also being tape-recorded.
2   Persons whose presence is authorised are a solicitor, a qualified accountant, an appropriate adult, a person providing assistance and an interpreter.
3   Ibid.

169.   If the person conducting the interview has excluded a person from the interview room under paragraph 167 or 168, he or she should adjourn the interview. The interviewee must then be informed that he has the right to seek another person to act in the same role as the person who was excluded. If the interviewee wished the interview to continue, then the interviewer should record this decision and continue with the interview.

170.   If the person conducting the interview considers that a solicitor or qualified accountant is acting in such a way, he or she must stop the interview. After speaking to the solicitor or qualified accountant, the person conducting the interview must decide whether or not the interview should continue in the presence of that solicitor or qualified accountant. If he or she decides that it should not, the interviewee must be given the opportunity to consult another solicitor or qualified accountant before the interview continues and that solicitor must be given an opportunity to be present at the interview.

171.   The removal of a solicitor from an interview is a serious step and, if it occurs, the person conducting the interview must consider whether the incident should be reported to the Law Society.

## Conduct of interviews

172.   As far as practicable interviews should take place in interview rooms which must be adequately heated, lit and ventilated.

173.   People being questioned or making statements must not be required to stand.

174.   Breaks from interviewing must be made at recognised meal times. Short breaks for refreshment must also be provided at intervals of approximately two hours, subject to the interviewer's discretion to delay a break if there are reasonable grounds for believing that it would prejudice the outcome of the investigation.

175.   Where an interview, is adjourned for any reason and is to be resumed at the same place later the same day it shall be sufficient for the person conducting the interview to inform the interviewee of the time or resumption and no notice in writing requiring attendance at that time shall be necessary. The details of the adjournment should be noted in the interview record

176.   Where an interview, is adjourned for any reason and is to be resumed either at a different place or on a different day the person conducting the interview must serve another notice under the disclosure order on the interviewee requiring him to attend at that place or on that day.

## The interviewer's obligations at the interview

177.   The person conducting the interview must then caution the interviewee as follows:

'You are required by law to answer all the questions I put to you unless you have a reasonable excuse for not doing so. If you fail, without reasonable excuse, to answer a question or if you knowingly or recklessly make a statement which is false you will be committing an offence for which you may be prosecuted. Do you understand?'

The person conducting the interview should also inform the interviewee that this is not a criminal caution and any responses will not be used to incriminate the interviewee.

178.   The person conducting the interview must, if asked to do so, produce evidence of his authority to require the interviewee to answer questions under the disclosure order.

179.   The person conducting the interview may ask such further questions as appear to him or her to be necessary to ascertain the entitlement of any person to be present.

180.   The person conducting the interview must ask the interviewee whether he or she suffers from any condition which may impair his ability to understand what is taking place or if he or she

is due to take any medication before the time at which the Director estimates that the interview will end. The interviewee must be free to take medication during a routine break in the interview. When a break is to be taken during the interview, the fact that a break is to be taken, the reason for it and the time shall be recorded.

181.    The person conducting the interview must offer the interviewee the opportunity to ask any questions to clarify the purpose, structure and conduct of the interview.

182.    Before concluding the interview the person conducting the interview must ask the interviewee if he or she has any complaint to make about anything which has taken place at the interview.

183.    If a question and answer record has been taken of the interview because it was not tape-recorded, the person conducting the interview must afford the interviewee the opportunity to read the record. If the interviewee is for any reason unable to read the note or if the interviewee declines to do so the person conducting the interview must read, or cause it to be read, aloud. The person conducting the interview must invite the interviewee to comment on the note and will add to it any comments made. The interviewee must be invited to sign the note. The person conducting the interview must then record the time in the presence of the interviewee. If the interviewee is unable for any reason to sign the note he or she may authorise any person, present at the interview to sign it on his behalf. Where the interviewee refuses to sign the note, or to have it signed on his behalf; the person conducting the interview must record that fact and any reason given for the refusal on the note.

184.    Whenever this code requires a person to be given certain information he or she does not have to be given it if he or she is incapable at the time of understanding what is said to him or her, or is violent or likely to become violent or is in urgent need of medical attention, but he or she must be given it as soon as practicable.

## Tape Recording

185.    Interviews should be tape-recorded. A record of certain matters arising from the interview should also be made contemporaneously. The matters to be recorded in the note are listed at the end of this section.

### Recording and the sealing of master tapes

186.    Tape recording of interviews must be carried out openly to instil confidence in its reliability as an impartial and accurate record of the interview.

187.    One tape that shall be the master tape must be sealed before it leaves the presence of the interviewee. A second tape will be used as a working copy. The master tape is either one of the two tapes used in a twin deck machine or the only tape used in a single deck machine. The working copy is either the second tape used in a twin deck machine or a copy of the master tape made by a single deck machine.

### Interviews to be taped recorded

188.    The person conducting the interview may authorise that the interview not be taped where it is not reasonably practicable to do so. This could be due to failure of the equipment or lack of a suitable interview room or recorder if the person conducting the interview has reasonable grounds for considering that the interview should not be delayed until the failure has been rectified or a suitable room or recorder becomes available.

189.    In such cases the interview must be recorded in writing. In all cases the person conducting the interview shall make a note in specific terms of the reasons for not tape recording.

*Commencement of interviews*

190.   When the interviewee is brought into the interview room the person conducting the interview must without delay, but in the sight of the interviewee, load the tape recorder with clean tapes and set it to record. The tapes must be unwrapped or otherwise opened in the presence of the interviewee.

191.   The person conducting the interview must:

- inform the interviewee that he or she is the Director or has delegated authority (see section 1(6) of the Act);
- give his or her name and that of any other persons present (subject to the provision on pseudonyms of Agency staff);
- inform the interviewee of the purpose for which any person accompanying the person conducting the interview is present;
- ask the interviewee to state his full name and address and date of birth;
- ask any person present with the interviewee to state their name, business address[1] and capacity in which he or she is present; and
- state the date, time of commencement and place of the interview;
- state that the interviewee has the opportunity to request legal and/or financial advice;
- inform the interviewee of his or her right:
  - (a) to consult in private at any time with any solicitor, qualified accountant or appropriate adult present with him or her at any interview;
  - (b) to be questioned fairly
  - (c) to be given an opportunity at the end of the interview to clarify anything he or she has said or to say anything further if he or she wishes;
  - (d) to be allowed a break in any interview which last for more than two hours.
- say that the interview is being tape-recorded;
- state that the interviewee will be given a notice about what will happen to the tapes.
- attempt to estimate the likely length of the interview and inform the interviewee.

*Objections and complaints by the suspect*

192.   If the interviewee raises objections to the interview being tape-recorded either at the outset or during the interview or during a break in the interview, the person conducting the interview must explain the fact that the interview is being tape-recorded and that the provisions of this code require that the interviewee's objections shall be recorded on tape. When any objections have been recorded on tape or the interviewee has refused to have their objections recorded, the person conducting the interview may turn off the recorder. In this eventuality the person conducting the interview must say that he or she is turning off the recorder, give his or her reasons for doing so and then turn it off. The person conducting the interview must then make a written record of the interview. If, however, the person conducting the interview reasonably considers that he or she may proceed to put questions to the interviewee with the tape recorder still on, the person conducting the interview may do so.

*Changing tapes*

193.   When the recorder indicates that the tapes have only a short time left to run, the person conducting the interview must tell the interviewee that the tapes are coming to an end and round off that part of the interview. If the person conducting the interview wishes to continue the

---

1     If persons present do not have a business address (e.g. a parent) , they should provide a home address.

interview but does not already have a second set of tapes, he or she must obtain a set. The interviewee must not be left unattended in the interview room. The person conducting the interview must remove the tapes from the tape recorder and insert the new tapes, which must be unwrapped or otherwise opened in the interviewee's presence. The tape recorder must then be set to record on the new tapes. Care must be taken, particularly when a number of sets of tapes have been used, to ensure that there is no confusion between the tapes. This may be done by marking the tapes with an identification number immediately they are removed from the tape recorder.

*Taking a break during interview*

194.　When a break is to be taken during the course of an interview and the interview room is to be vacated by the interviewee, the fact that a break is to be taken, the reason for it and the time must be recorded on tape. The tapes must then be removed from the tape recorder and the procedures for the conclusion of an interview set out in paragraphs 200 to 203 below followed.

195.　When a break is to be a short one and both the interviewee and the person conducting the interview are to remain in the interview room the fact that a break is to be taken, the reasons for it and the time must be recorded on tape. The tape recorder may be turned off. There is, however, no need to remove the tapes and when the interview is recommenced the tape recording shall be continued on the same tapes. The time at which the interview recommences must be recorded on tape.

*Failure of recording equipment*

196.　If there is a failure of equipment, which can be rectified quickly, for example by inserting new tapes, the appropriate procedures set out in paragraph 193 shall be followed. When the recording is resumed the person conducting the interview must explain what has happened and record the time the interview recommences. If, however, it will not be possible to continue recording on that particular tape recorder and no replacement recorder or recorder in another interview room is readily available, the interview may continue without being tape-recorded.

## Removing tapes from the recorder

197.　Where tapes are removed from the recorder in the course of an interview, they must be retained and the procedures set out in paragraphs 200 to 203 below followed.

## Conclusion of interview

198.　The person conducting the interview must inform the interviewee that he or she has no further questions and offer the interviewee an opportunity to clarify anything he or she has said and to say anything further he or she wishes. Any solicitor, qualified accountant or appropriate adult present at the interview along with the interviewee, must be given the opportunity to ask the interviewee any question the purpose of which is to clarify any ambiguity in an answer given by the interviewee or to give the interviewee an opportunity to answer any question which he or she has refused previously to answer.

199.　At the conclusion of the interview, including the taking and reading back of any written statement, the time must be recorded and the tape recorder switched off. The master tape must be sealed with a master tape label. The Director must sign the label and ask the interviewee and any appropriate adult and other third party present during the interview to sign it also. If the interviewee or the appropriate adult refuses to sign the label, the person conducting the interview must sign it.

200. The interviewee must be handed a notice, which explains the use, which will be made of the tape recording and the arrangements for access to it. A copy of the tape must be supplied as soon as practicable to the interviewee, if court proceedings are connected to interview are commenced (i.e. a confiscation or civil recovery proceedings).

## *After the interview*

201. Where the interview is not subsequently used in confiscation or civil recovery proceedings the tapes must nevertheless be kept securely in accordance with the provisions below.

## *Tape security*

202. The person conducting the interview must make arrangements for master tapes to be kept securely and their movements accounted for.

203. The person conducting the interview has no authority to break the seal on a master tape, which may be required for civil recovery or confiscation proceedings. If it is necessary to gain access to the master tape, the person conducting the interview must arrange for its seal to be broken in the presence of another member of the Agency. The interviewee or his legal adviser must be informed and given a reasonable opportunity to be present. If the interviewee or his legal representative is present he or she must be invited to reseal and sign the master tape. If either refuses or neither is present another member of the Agency shall do this.

204. Where no court proceedings result, it is the responsibility of the Director to establish arrangements for the breaking of the seal on the master tape, where this becomes necessary.

## Particular record of action taken under a disclosure order

205. In addition to the general provisions on taking records, the Director shall also keep copies of notices in writing issued under a disclosure order (see section 357(4)) together with full details of their issue and response.

206. The record of an interview should contain the following, as appropriate:

- a copy of the invitation to interview letter;
- the date and place and time of the interview;
- the time the interview began and ended, the time of any breaks in the interview and, subject to the provisions relating to pseudonyms of Agency staff, the names of all those present;
- any request made for financial or legal advice, and action taken on that request;
- that the person conducting the interview told the interviewee everything he was required to tell him or her under this code;
- the name of person(s) excluded from the interview room, and the reason for that decision;
- the presence of an interpreter, and the reason for this.

207. In respect of interviews conducted under the authority of section 357(4)(a), the record of the interview should be held with a transcript of the interview. Documents produced at the interview should also be listed on a note of the action taken under disclosure order. Receipts should be given to the interviewee and this should also be recorded.

208. In respect of requests for information under section 357(4)(b) or documents under section 357(4)(c) he or she should keep a copy of the disclosure order together with all the notices requesting information and/or documents under the disclosure order. The Director should also keep a record of all the documents and information submitted in response to the notices. Receipts should be sent to the supplier of the material if requested.

## SUMMARY OF THE POWERS OF INVESTIGATION UNDER THE PROCEEDS OF CRIME ACT 2002

| | Purpose of power | Who can apply for it – confiscation investigation? | Who can apply for it – money laundering investigation? | Who can apply for it – civil recovery investigation? |
|---|---|---|---|---|
| **Production order** | Obtain material already in existence relating to a known account in control of a known person e.g. bank statements and correspondence | (1) Director of the Agency (2) Any constable (3) Any customs officer (4) AFI with relevant accreditation[1] | (1) Any constable (2) Any customs officer (3) AFI with relevant accreditation | Director of the Agency |
| **Search and seizure warrant** | (1) Search premises where production order not complied with; or (2) Search premises where production order likely to be ineffective and seize material | (1) Director of the Agency (2) Any constable (3) Any customs officer (4) AFI with relevant accreditation | (1) Any constable (2) Any customs officer (3) AFI with relevant accreditation | Director of the Agency |
| **Disclosure order** | Require any person to produce documents, provide information or answer questions relating to investigation | Director of the Agency | Not available in a money laundering investigation | Director of the Agency |
| **Customer information order** | Trawl financial institutions for accounts in the name of a particular person or organisation | (1) Director of the Agency (2) Any constable with superintendent authorisation (3) Any customs officer with officer at Pay Band 9 authorisation (4) AFI with relevant accreditation and authorisation | (1) Any constable with superintendent authorisation (2) Any customs officer with officer at Pay Band 9 authorisation (3) AFI with relevant accreditation and authorisation | Director of the Agency |
| **Account monitoring order** | Monitor future transactions through a known account for up to 90 days | (1) Director of the Agency (2) Any constable (3) Any customs officer (4) AFI with relevant accreditation | (1) Any constable (2) Any customs officer (3) AFI with relevant accreditation | Director of the Agency |

1   Accredited financial investigator (a civilian investigator accredited by the Director of the Agency to have access to some or all of the powers of investigation) who falls within a description given in an order issued by the Home Secretary.

## APPLICATION FOR PRODUCTION ORDER
## (SECTION 345 PROCEEDS OF CRIME ACT 2002)

---

**The application of** {**appropriate officer**} an appropriate officer as defined by section 378 Proceeds of Crime Act 2002 of the {**name of force/agency**} who upon {**oath/affirmation**} states:

{**name of person**} is subject to a {**confiscation investigation/money laundering investigation**} and

(i)   There are reasonable grounds for suspecting that {**name of person**} has {**benefited from criminal conduct**} {**committed a money laundering offence**}

(ii)  There are reasonable grounds for believing that material which may be provided in compliance with the order is likely to be of substantial value (whether or not by itself) to the investigation for the purposes of which the order is sought

(iii) There are reasonable grounds for believing it is in the public interest for the material to be provided or for access to be given to it having regard to the benefit likely to accrue to the investigation if the information is obtained and the circumstances in which the material is held

An order is sought against {**specify the person who appears to be in possession or control of material**} who appears to be in possession or control of material, specifically {**specify the material sought, including where applicable account numbers and the period required**} which does not include material or information that is or consists of items subject to legal privilege or excluded material to {**produce it to** {**name of appropriate officer**} **or another appropriate officer**} {**give** {**name of appropriate officer**} **or another appropriate officer access to it**} within {**seven days/other as appropriate**}

The order is sought for the purposes of the investigation on the grounds outlined in the {**written**} {**oral**} information.

Signature                                    Date

## PRODUCTION ORDER
### (SECTION 345 PROCEEDS OF CRIME ACT 2002)

*IN THE CROWN COURT AT . . .*                        *DATE . . .*

---

### Penal Notice
**A failure to comply with the terms of this order may constitute a contempt of court for which you may be imprisoned or fined.**

To: {**person/organisation**}

An application having been made in pursuance of Section 345 {**(4)(a)**} {**(4)(b)**} Proceeds of Crime Act 2002

By: {**appropriate officer**}                      Of the {**name force/agency**}

I am satisfied, having heard the application, that the requirements for making a production order under section 346 Proceeds of Crime Act 2002 are fulfilled.

You are ordered to {**produce to {name of appropriate officer} or another appropriate officer**} {**give {name of appropriate officer} or another appropriate officer access to**} material, specifically {**insert details of material to be provided or given access to**} which does not consist of items subject to legal privilege for a period {**state dates between**} within {**7 days/other period as appropriate**} from the date of this order.

Where the material consists of information contained on a computer, it must be {**produced/ access given to it**} in a form which is visible and legible {and can be taken away}.

1. It is an offence to prejudice a confiscation or money laundering investigation or prospective investigation by making a disclosure about it or by tampering with documents relevant to the investigation. You should not therefore falsify, conceal, destroy or otherwise dispose of, or cause or permit the falsification, destruction or disposal of, relevant documents, nor disclose to any other person information or any other matter which is likely to prejudice any investigation into confiscation or money laundering investigation. The penalty for this offence on summary conviction is imprisonment for six months or a fine or both and on conviction on indictment of 5 years imprisonment or a fine or both.

2. Anyone served with, notified or affected by this order may apply to the court at any time to vary or discharge this order (or so much of it as affects that person), but they must first inform the applicant {**giving 2 clear days notice**}.

3. If you have any doubts or concerns about this order you should seek legal advice and/or contact {**contact details of appropriate officer**}

Court Stamp                                        Signature of Judge

                                                   Date

## APPLICATION FOR
## SEARCH AND SEIZURE WARRANT
## (SECTION 352 PROCEEDS OF CRIME ACT 2002)

---

The application of {**appropriate officer**} an appropriate officer as defined by section 378 Proceeds of Crime Act 2002 of the {**name of force/agency**} who upon {**oath/affirmation**} states:

{**name of person**} is subject to a {**confiscation investigation/money laundering investigation**} and a search warrant is sought in relation to material which does not consist of or include privileged or excluded material held on premises situated at {**specify premises**} and:

{On {**date**} a production order under section 345 Proceeds of Crime Act 2002 was made at {**name of Court**} Crown Court by {**His/Her**} Honour {**name of Judge**} which has not been complied with and there are reasonable grounds for believing that the material is on the premises.}

*Alternatively*

There are reasonable grounds for suspecting that {**name of person**} has {**benefited from criminal conduct**} {**committed a money laundering offence**}, and the {**first/ second**} set of conditions are satisfied; that

*[first]*

   (i)   {**There are reasonable grounds for believing that material on the specified premises is likely to be of substantial value (whether or not by itself) to the investigation for the purposes of which the warrant is sought,**

  (ii)  **There are reasonable grounds for believing it is in the public interest for the material to be obtained, having regard to the benefit likely to accrue to the investigation if the information is obtained, and**

 (iii)  **It would not be appropriate to make a production order for the following** {**reason/s**};}

*[second]*

   (i)  {**there are reasonable grounds for believing that there is material on the premises specified in the application for the warrant and that the material;**

     {**In relation to a confiscation investigation cannot be identified at the time of the application but it –**

     a) **relates to the person specified in the application, the question whether he has benefited from his criminal conduct or any question as to the extent or whereabouts of his benefit from his criminal conduct, and**

     b) **is likely to be of substantial value (whether or not by itself) to the investigation for the purposes of which the warrant is sought.**}

{**In relation to a money laundering investigation it cannot be identified at the time of the application but it –**

     a) **relates to the person specified in the application or the question whether he has committed a money laundering offence, and**

     b) **is likely to be of substantial value (whether or not by itself) to the investigation for the purposes of which the warrant is sought.**}

  (ii)  **It is in the public interest for the material to be obtained, having regard to the benefit likely to accrue to the investigation if the material is to be obtained, and**}

*[applies to first and second]*

i.     {that it is not practicable to communicate with any person against whom the production order could be made;}

ii.    {that it is not practicable to communicate with any person who would be required to comply with an order to grant entry to the premises;}

iii.   {that the investigation might be seriously prejudiced unless an appropriate person is able to secure immediate access to the material.}

The warrant is sought for the purposes of the investigation on the grounds outlined in the written information.

Signature

Applicant Name

Date

## SEARCH AND SEIZURE WARRANT
### (SECTION 352 PROCEEDS OF CRIME ACT 2002)

**IN THE CROWN COURT AT ...**                                          **DATE ...**

---

### Penal Notice
**A failure to comply with the terms of this order may constitute a contempt of court for which you may be imprisoned or fined.**

To: {person/organisation}

An application having been made in pursuance of Section 352 Proceeds of Crime Act 2002

By: {appropriate officer}                          Of the {name force/agency}

I am satisfied, having heard the application, that the requirements for issuing a search and seizure warrant under section 352 Proceeds of Crime Act 2002 are fulfilled.


I hereby authorise {name of appropriate person} to enter and search premises situated at {specify premises} and seize and retain material which does not consist of items subject to legal privilege or excluded material.


Court Stamp                                          Signature of Judge

                                                     Date

**APPLICATION FOR**
**CUSTOMER INFORMATION ORDER**
**(SECTION 363 PROCEEDS OF CRIME ACT 2002)**

The application of {**appropriate officer**} an appropriate officer as defined by section 378 Proceeds of Crime Act 2002 of the {**name of force/agency**} who upon {**oath/affirmation**} states:

{**name of person**} is subject to a {**confiscation investigation/money laundering investigation**} and

(j) There are reasonable grounds for suspecting that {**name of person**} has {**benefited from criminal conduct**} {**committed a money laundering offence**}

(iv) There are reasonable grounds for believing that customer information which may be provided in compliance with the order is likely to be of substantial value (whether or not by itself) to the investigation for the purposes of which the order is sought

(v) There are reasonable grounds for believing it is in the public interest for the customer information to be provided or for access to be given to it having regard to the benefit likely to accrue to the investigation if the information is obtained

An order is sought against {**specify all financial institutions, particular description/s of institutions or a particular institution/s** }in relation to customer information as defined by section 364 Proceeds of Crime Act to provide the information to {**name of appropriate officer**} or another appropriate officer in such manner, and at or by such time or times specified in the written notice.

The order is sought for the purposes of the investigation on the grounds outlined in the {**written**} {**oral**} information.

Signature                                            Date

Authorised by {**name of Senior Authorising Officer**}
                    {**rank/position**}

## CUSTOMER INFORMATION ORDER
## (SECTION 363 PROCEEDS OF CRIME ACT 2002)

IN THE CROWN COURT AT ...                                    DATE...

---

### Penal Notice
A failure to comply with the terms of this order may constitute a contempt of
court for which you may be imprisoned or fined.

To: {specify all financial institutions, particular description/s of institutions or a
particular institution/s}

An application having been made in pursuance of section 363 Proceeds of Crime Act 2002

By: {appropriate officer}                         of the {name force/agency}

I am satisfied, having heard the application, that the requirements for making a customer
information order under section 365 Proceeds of Crime Act 2002 are fulfilled.


You are ordered, on receipt of written notice from an appropriate officer, to provide any
customer information, as defined by section 364 Proceeds of Crime Act 2002, held by you in
relation to {name of person and any other information that could assist in
identification} to {name of appropriate officer} or another appropriate officer in such a
manner, and at such a time, as an appropriate officer requires.

Court Stamp                                          Signature of Judge

                                                                Date

CUSTOMER INFORMATION ORDER

NOTICE IN WRITING

To {**details of institution**}

**This is a notice in writing in pursuance of the terms of a customer information order granted on** {date of order} **at** {details of Crown Court} **by** {His/Her} **Honour** {name of judge}

Penal Notice

By virtue of section 366 of the Proceeds Crime Act 2002, you are required, on receipt of this written notice, to provide any customer information, as defined by section 364 Proceeds of Crime Act 2002, held by you in relation to {**name of person and any other information that could assist in identification**} to {**name of appropriate officer**} or another appropriate officer by {**insert details of the manner in which the information is to be provided**} {**at or by**} {**insert the time or times at or by the information is to be provided**}

"Customer information" is information whether a person holds, or has held, an account or accounts (whether solely or jointly with another) and where that person is an individual

a.  the account number or numbers;
b.  the person's full name;
c.  date of birth;
d.  most recent and any previous address;
e.  date or dates on which he or she began to hold the account or accounts, and if he or she has ceased to hold the account or any accounts, the date or dates on which he or she did so;
f.  such evidence of his or her identity obtained by you under or for the purposes of any legislation relating to money;
g.  the full name, date of birth and most recent address, and any previous addresses, of any person who holds, or has held, an account at your institution jointly with him or her;
h.  the account number or numbers of any other account or accounts held at your institution to which he or she is a signatory and details of the person holding the other account or accounts;

and where the specified person is a company, limited liability partnership or similar body incorporated or established outside the UK,

i.  the account number or numbers;
j.  the person's full name;
k.  a description of any business which the person carries on;
l.  the country or territory in which it is incorporated or otherwise established and any number allocated to it under the Companies Act 1985 (c.6) or the Companies (Northern Ireland) Order 1986 (S.I.1986/1032 (N.I. 6)) or corresponding legislation of any country or territory outside the United Kingdom;
m.  any number assigned to it for the purposes of value added tax in the United Kingdom;
n.  its registered office, and previous registered offices, under the Companies Act 1985 (c.6) or the Companies (Northern Ireland) Order 1986 (S.I.1986/1032 (N.I. 6)) or anything similar under corresponding legislation of any country or territory outside the United Kingdom under the Companies Act 1985 or corresponding legislation of any country or territory outside the United Kingdom;
o.  its registered office, and previous registered offices, under the Limited Liability Partnerships Act 2000 (c.12) or corresponding legislation of any country or territory outside Great Britain;

p. the date or dates on which it began to hold the account or accounts and, if it has ceased to hold the account or any of the accounts, the date on which it did so;

q. such evidence of its identity as was obtained by you for the purposes of any legislation relating to money laundering;

r. the full name, date of birth and most recent address and any previous addresses of any person who is signatory to the account or any of the accounts.

A financial institution has a right to refuse to comply with any requirement under the terms of a customer information order unless the appropriate officer has, if required to do so, produced evidence of authority to issue notice.

A financial institution commits an offence if, without reasonable excuse, it fails to comply with a requirement imposed on it under a customer information order and is liable on summary conviction to a fine.

A financial institution commits an offence if, in purported compliance with a customer information order, it makes a statement it knows to be false or misleading in a material particular, or recklessly makes a statement which is false or misleading in a material particular and is liable on summary conviction or on conviction on indictment to a fine.

A statement made by a financial institution in response to a customer information order may not be used in evidence against it in criminal proceedings except on a prosecution for an offence outlined above, on a prosecution for another offence where, in giving evidence, the financial institution makes a statement inconsistent with the statement made in response, or in confiscation proceedings in England and Wales or Northern Ireland

It is an offence to prejudice a confiscation or money laundering investigation or prospective investigation by making a disclosure about it or by tampering with documents relevant to the investigation. You should not therefore falsify, conceal, destroy or otherwise dispose of, or cause or permit the falsification, destruction or disposal of, relevant documents, nor disclose to any other person information or any other matter which is likely to prejudice any investigation into confiscation or money laundering investigation. The penalty for this offence on summary conviction is imprisonment for six months or a fine or both and on conviction on indictment of 5 years imprisonment or a fine or both.

Anyone served with, notified or affected by this order may apply to the court at any time to vary or discharge this order (or so much of it as affects that person), but they must first inform the applicant {giving 2 clear days notice}. If any evidence is to be relied upon in support of the application, the substance of it must be communicated in writing to the applicant in advance.

If you have any doubts or concerns about this order you should seek legal advice and/or contact {**contact details of appropriate officer**}

Signature

Name

Date

## APPLICATION FOR
## ACCOUNT MONITORING ORDER
## (SECTION 370 PROCEEDS OF CRIME ACT 2002)

---

The application of {appropriate officer} an appropriate officer as defined by section 378 Proceeds of Crime Act 2002 of the {name of force/agency} who upon {oath/affirmation} states:

{name of person} is subject to a {confiscation investigation/money laundering investigation} and

(k) There are reasonable grounds for suspecting that {name of person} has {benefited from criminal conduct} {committed a money laundering offence}

(vi) There are reasonable grounds for believing that account information which may be provided in compliance with the order is likely to be of substantial value (whether or not by itself) to the investigation for the purposes of which the order is sought

(vii) There are reasonable grounds for believing it is in the public interest for the material to be provided or for access to be given to it having regard to the benefit likely to accrue to the investigation if the information is obtained

An order is sought against {name/details of financial institution} in relation to account information, specifically {description of account information} to provide the information to {name of appropriate officer} or another appropriate officer in such manner, and at or by such time or times specified in the order.

The order is sought for the purposes of the investigation on the grounds outlined in the {written} {oral} information.

Signature                                          Date

## ACCOUNT MONITORING ORDER
## (SECTION 370 PROCEEDS OF CRIME ACT 2002)

IN THE CROWN COURT AT ...                     DATE ...

---

### Penal Notice

**A failure to comply with the terms of this order may constitute a contempt of court for which you may be imprisoned or fined.**

To: {**person/organisation**}

An application having been made in pursuance of Section 370 Proceeds of Crime Act 2002

By: {**appropriate officer**}                     Of the {**name force/agency**}

I am satisfied, having heard the application, that the requirements for making an account monitoring order under section 371 Proceeds of Crime Act 2002 are fulfilled.

You are ordered to provide account information, specifically {**insert details of information to be provided including the description of the material**} for a period {**enter amount of days** }not exceeding 90 days from the date of this order, to {**name of appropriate officer**} or another appropriate officer by {**insert details of the manner in which the information is to be provided**} {**at or by**} {**insert the time or times at or by the information is to be provided**}

1. It is an offence to prejudice a confiscation or money laundering investigation or prospective investigation by making a disclosure about it or by tampering with documents relevant to the investigation. You should not therefore falsify, conceal, destroy or otherwise dispose of, or cause or permit the falsification, destruction or disposal of, relevant documents, nor disclose to any other person information or any other matter which is likely to prejudice any investigation into confiscation or money laundering investigation. The penalty for this offence on summary conviction is imprisonment for six months or a fine or both and on conviction on indictment of 5 years imprisonment or a fine or both.
2. Anyone served with, notified or affected by this order may apply to the court at any time to vary or discharge this order (or so much of it as affects that person), but they must first inform the applicant {**giving 2 clear days notice**}.
3. If you have any doubts or concerns about this order you should seek legal advice and / or contact {**contact details of appropriate officer**}

Court Stamp                                     Signature of Judge

                                                Date

# INDEX

References are to paragraph number. References in *italic* are to
Appendix page numbers.